Coping with Alcohol and Drug Problems: The Experiences of Family Members in Three Contrasting Cultures

Coping with Alcohol and Drug Problems: The Experiences of Family Members in Three Contrasting Cultures aims to deepen and extend understanding of the experiences of family members trying to cope with the excessive drinking or drug taking of a relative.

Comprehensive and thoroughly up to date, this book draws on the results of a cross-cultural study of alcohol and drug problems in the family, and places these results within the broader context of the international literature on the subject. By investigating the similarities and differences in the experiences of family members in three parts of the world, the authors reveal results which have far-reaching implications for professional intervention and prevention. Subjects covered include:

- Models of understanding: how families continue to be pathologised and misunderstood.
- How family members cope.
- An integrated view of alcohol and drug problems in the family.
- Ways of empowering family members.

This book aims to demonstrate the possibility of a constructive alliance between professionals, substance-misusing relatives, and the affected family members by thoroughly investigating the dilemmas that face family members and the lack of support they experience.

This fascinating insight into the impact of alcohol and drug problems on family members will be a valuable resource for all those who are interested in substance misuse in family and cultural contexts, and particularly those who are interested in the treatment of alcohol and other drug problems.

The authors are an international collaborating group from the following three centres: the Epidemiological and Psychosocial Research Directorate at the National Institute of Psychiatry, Ramón de la Fuente, Mexico City; members of the Alcohol, Drugs and the Family Research Group in England, based at the Universities of Birmingham and Bath and their associated National Health Service Mental Health Trusts; the Aboriginal Living with Alcohol Program of Territory Health Services, Northern Territory, Australia.

Coping with Alcohol and Drug Problems: The Experiences of Family Members in Three Contrasting Cultures

Jim Orford

Guillermina Natera   Alex Copello   Carol Atkinson

Jazmín Mora   Richard Velleman   Ian Crundall

Marcela Tiburcio   Lorna Templeton   Gwen Walley

 Routledge
Taylor & Francis Group

LONDON AND NEW YORK

First published 2005
by Routledge
27 Church Road, Hove, East Sussex BN3 2FA

Simultaneously published in the USA and Canada
by Routledge
270 Madison Avenue, New York, NY 10016

Routledge is an imprint of the Taylor & Francis Group

Typeset in Garamond by RefineCatch Limited, Bungay, Suffolk
Printed and bound in Great Britain by TJ International Ltd, Padstow,
Cornwall
Cover design by Hybert Design

This publication has been produced with paper manufactured to
strict environmental standards and with pulp derived from
sustainable forests.

British Library Cataloguing in Publication Data
A catalogue record for this book is available from the British Library

Library of Congress Cataloging-in-Publication Data
Coping with alcohol and drug problems : the experiences of family
   members in three contrasting cultures / Jim Orford, co-ordinating
   author, and Guillermina Natera . . . [et al.].
        p. cm.
     "August 2004."
     Includes bibliographical references and indexes.
     ISBN 0–415–37146–5 (hbk)
     1. Alcoholism – Cross-cultural studies. 2. Alcoholics – Family
relationships – Cross-cultural studies. 3. Drug abuse – Cross-
cultural studies. 4. Drug addicts – Family relationships – Cross-
cultural studies. I. Orford, Jim.
     [DNLM: 1. Substance-Related Disorders – ethnology – Mexico.
2. Substance-Related Disorders – ethnology – England. 3.
Substance-Related Disorders – ethnology – Northern Territory.
4. Family Health – ethnology – Mexico. 5. Family Health –
ethnology – England. 6. Family Health – ethnology – Northern
Territory. 7. Family – psychology – Mexico. 8. Family – psychology
– England. 9. Family – psychology – Northern Territory. 10. Cross-
Cultural Comparison – Mexico. 11. Cross-Cultural Comparison –
England. 12. Cross-Cultural Comparison – Northern Territory.
13. Models, Psychological – Mexico. 14. Models, Psychological –
England. 15. Models, Psychological – Northern Territory. WM 270
C7834 2005]   HV5035. C647 2005
362.292'097253 – dc22   2005015962

ISBN 0-415-37146-5 hbk

Contents

List of tables and figures

Tables

Figures

Foreword

The role of alcohol and other psychoactive substances in mortality, morbidity and the overall public health and welfare of people around the world has been an important area of research interest for many years. Recent evidence has shown that harmful and hazardous use of alcohol and dependence on tobacco are major risk factors for the global burden of disease and disability (WHO, 2002). In the year 2000, tobacco and alcohol were associated with 4.1% and 4%, respectively, of the disability adjusted life years (DALY), a summary measure of health burden.

Though the association between alcohol and disease/disability has long been established in many Western countries, recent data are beginning to show a rising prevalence in alcohol-related problems in less developed countries. For example, in some developing countries with low adult and child mortality (i.e. those countries that are showing improvements in development indices), alcohol is the leading risk factor for disease and disability mainly because of the high-risk pattern of alcohol consumption.

Dependence on illicit drugs (e.g. cocaine, heroin and amphetamines) is associated with a variety of social and health problems, affecting the individual, his or her family, and society at large. For example, injecting drug use is a recognised cause of HIV infection and a driving force in the HIV/AIDS epidemic in many countries (WHO, 2004b).

Much of the professional interest in alcohol and other drugs has been driven by the observable (and hence measurable) health and economic consequences of use and dependence. What is often neglected is the impact of these psychoactive substances on the families of those who use and are dependent on them. This is probably due to the difficulty in measuring such impact but also to how the role of the family has often been conceptualised by researchers and professionals.

The publication of *Coping with Alcohol and Drug Problems: The Experiences of Family Members in Three Contrasting Cultures* is a commendable effort to address this issue. The book is an impressive collaboration by researchers in three countries to present a model of how people who have experienced alcohol and drug misuse in their families react to and cope with the situation.

It is a book about the experiences of family members who have to deal with alcohol and/or drug use problems in their spouses, parents, children, uncles and other close family members. Though the book is based on interviews from three countries in three very different parts of the world (Mexico, the UK and Australia), the experiences recorded in this book are shared by millions of people around the world.

As correctly stated in the book, it is difficult to estimate the number of people in the world who are touched by the substance use behaviour of a family member. Estimates of those who use one type of drug or another are staggering. The annual prevalence of illicit drug use in 2001–3 was 4.7% or 185 million people 15 years old or above (UNODC, 2004), while 2 billion people consume alcohol (WHO, 2004a). There are 15.3 million people with drug use disorders globally and 76 million with alcohol use disorders, including dependence. In more than 100 countries, the HIV epidemic is associated with injecting drugs (WHO, 2004b), complicating further an already complex situation in the families of people with alcohol and drug problems. These estimates suggest that very large numbers of children and adult relatives live in homes where someone has a substance use problem. In the USA, for example, 1 in 4 children under the age of 18 years lives with a parent with alcohol abuse or dependence (Grant, 2000), many of whom are affected in negative ways (Obot and Anthony, 2004).

One of the central tenets of the 'stress-strain-coping-support model' with which this book proposes to explain the behaviour of relatives in these adverse situations is that, while the impact of living with a relative is often stressful, there is also the capacity to cope and render the situation less traumatic. It is an empowering message, a sensible message, and one that we should heed. This is a book with profound implications for how professionals, researchers and policy makers should view the relationships within families with substance use problems.

One positive outcome of this message could be the emergence of a mindset that sees the relatives of people with alcohol and drug use disorders not as victims or villains but as individuals with major roles to play in reducing the overall impact of these disorders (Obot, 2001). It is, therefore, my hope that this book will find its way into the hands of all those who seek greater understanding of the role of the family in alcohol and drug problems, especially those involved in research, prevention and delivery of care.

Isidore S. Obot, Ph.D., M.P.H.
Department of Mental Health and Substance Abuse
World Health Organisation

Preface

This book is about an experience that is shared by tens of millions of people around the world. It is the experience of living in a family in which one of the members is consuming alcohol or taking illicit drugs to an extent that is seriously harmful to the family. The chief protagonists in this story are the wives, husbands or partners, mothers or fathers, sisters or brothers, adult daughters or sons, aunts or uncles, and other close kin who are affected by the excessive drinking or drug taking[1]. This group is referred to throughout the book simply as *family members*. The problem drinkers or drug takers about whom they are concerned we refer to as their *relatives*.

There is no way of gauging accurately how many such affected family members there might be worldwide. As we shall see, this is a group whose voices have been little heard and whose experiences have been little understood and not infrequently distorted and misrepresented. It is therefore not surprising that no figures exist about the numbers of family members affected by drinking or drug problems. The best we can do is to base an estimate on the known prevalence of alcohol and other drug dependence and misuse in those countries where epidemiological surveys have been carried out. In Chapter 3, figures are presented for the three countries in which the research to be reported later in the book was carried out. These three countries are among those where concern about substance problems and their effects on the family is sufficiently great for research to have been sponsored. It is very likely that there are large numbers of affected family members throughout the rest of the world, but their numbers are unknown.

Even with the possession of such prevalent figures, arriving at an estimate of the number of affected family members involves making a number of assumptions and can be only very cautiously undertaken. For one thing, there is a degree of overlap between alcohol and other forms of drug problem. There are also degrees of dependence and misuse, and not all is as severe in its effects on the family as that described by the family members who took part in the present research. Furthermore, a proportion of people with alcohol or drug problems live alone, and no family members are directly affected. A crude minimum estimate of the number of affected family members worldwide might be based on the assumption that one in three of persons thought to have alcohol or drug dependence has problems sufficiently severe to affect the family negatively, and that on average one adult family member is adversely affected in each case. If we assume also that Mexico, England and the indigenous population of Australia are between them representative of the rest of the world, our minimum estimate would be that around 80 million adults worldwide are affected by the excessive drinking or drug use of close relatives to an extent similar to that described in this book. Both the proportion of dependent people whose problem substance use is thought to affect the family and the number of family members affected in each family might easily be doubled, producing a much higher estimate. Clearly, such estimates can be only very rough approximations. Quite apart from the assumptions that go into arriving at those figures, there is no absolute definition of what constitutes serious harm to the family on account of a drinking or drug problem. Whatever the true figure, there can be little doubt that the experience of living with the harmful effects of a relative's problem drinking or drug taking is one that exists on a huge scale.

The aim of the work reported in this book was to deepen and extend understanding of the experiences of family members trying to cope with the excessive drinking or drug taking of a relative. Specifically, we aimed to do that by carrying out in-depth interviews with a diverse sample of family members in three contrasting parts of the world: in some of the poorest parts of Mexico City, in towns and villages in South-West England, and among the indigenous population of Australia's Northern Territory. We aimed to explore similarities and differences in the ways different family members found to cope with their circumstances, depending on a family member's socio-cultural group. A specific objective was to develop a detailed picture of the experiences of family members which should include not only commonalities across groups, but also important variations.

Details of the design and methods of that research are to be found in Chapter 4. The results are to be found in Chapters 5, 6 and 7, which deal, respectively, with the impact of problem drinking or drug use on family members (stressors and strain), the ways family members respond (coping), and the support they receive from others (social support). Those chapters concentrate on what is similar in the experiences of family members in the three socio-cultural groups. Chapter 8 focuses on the ways in which experiences in the three groups contrast one with another. Chapters 9 and 10 conclude by drawing together what we believe to be the implications of the present findings and those of other research. Chapter 9 looks at implications for our ways of understanding family members' experiences, and Chapter 10 the implications for professional intervention and prevention.

The first three chapters are of crucial importance as a description of the context in which that research was carried out and of the terms in which its interpretation must be framed. Chapter 1 sets out the main ways in which family members affected by relatives' drinking or drug problems have been understood in the professional and academic writings on the subject – what we call 'models of understanding'. Appreciating how family members have been viewed by the helping professions and supporting academics is necessary in order to comprehend the state of neglect that surrounds the experiences and needs of such family members. Despite the large numbers of people thought to be affected, health and social care professionals have largely failed to address the risks that are faced by family members in this position or to provide them with any of the help or support that they need. One of the principal arguments of the book is that this state of neglect is largely due to a failure to appreciate the experiences of family members or to conceptualise that experience in a way that promotes understanding and adequate responding. Professionals are often simply unaware of the existence of such problems. When they are noticed at all, the way in which professionals are taught to think about family members is crucial. As will become clear in Chapter 1, family members have in fact often been viewed by professionals in negative and stereotyped ways, which, far from promoting understanding, may have impeded a helpful response.

Chapter 2 reviews other research which, like the research reported here, tried to gain a greater understanding of what it is like to be a family member concerned about and affected by a close relative's problem drinking or drug taking, using qualitative methods of investigation. Although no other research has been conducted in parallel in three contrasting socio-cultural groups, and at the same time has considered the impact of both alcohol and other forms of drug problem, the findings of other research contribute knowledge of the experiences of family members in other parts of the world and add important insights that help us fashion what we hope is the more complete understanding presented in the concluding chapters. Chapter 3 provides another, and most important, part of the context for the present research, namely, a brief description of the three socio-cultural groups involved in the research, plus information about what is known about the consumption of alcohol and other drugs by those groups.

Acknowledgements

A large number of people have contributed to the work reported in this book. The authors are those who have made major contributions to the work as principal investigators, main contributors to the analysis and interpretation of research results, and/or as contributors to the final version of this book. Others who have made important contributions include Margarita Casco, Adriana Nava, Elizabeth Ollinger, Olga Rodriguez, Verónica Suárez, Rosalba Tenorio and Marie-Elena Hope in Mexico; Simon Bird, Colin Bradbury, Kate Wilde, Jenny Maslin, David Foxcroft, Leah Armistead, Patrick Veasy, Liz Howells, Jackie Withers, Susan Dalton, Lizzie Hartney, Charlotte Merriman and Paul Micallef in England; and Bridie O'Reilly, Anne Mosey, Steven Swartz, Janice Jesson, Helen Burgess, Blair McFarland, Maggie Brady, Robert Assan, Chris Brogan, Pamela Turner, Shirley Hendy and Alasdair McLay in Australia.

We would also like to acknowledge the support of the World Health Organisation, Division of Mental Health; the Consejo Nacional de Ciencia y Tecnología (CONACyT); the Mental Health Foundation; the British Council; the Mexican Instituto Nacional de Psiquiatría Ramón de la Fuente; the Living with Alcohol Program of Territory Health Services, Northern Territory, Australia; Departments/Schools of Psychology at Exeter, Bath and Birmingham Universities; the Avon and Wiltshire Mental Health Partnership NHS Trust; and the Birmingham and Solihull Mental Health NHS Trust.

Various extracts have been reproduced from *Women and Alcohol in a Highland Maya Town: Water of Hope, Water of Sorrow* by Christine Eber, copyright © 1995. Courtesy of the University of Texas Press. Material has been reproduced from *Coping with a Nightmare: Family Feelings about Long-Term Drug Use* by N. Dorn, J. Ribbens and N. South, reproduced with permission from DrugScope, 2005 (www.drugscope.org.uk; contact: info@drugscope.org.uk).

Our grateful thanks also go to Pat Evans in Birmingham, UK, for preparing draft and final versions of the manuscript for this book.

Our greatest thanks, however, must go to the family members who were interviewed. Our earnest hope is that, by being so willing to tell their stories, they will have contributed to a greater understanding of their circumstances and thence to the development of appropriate and sensitive ways of supporting and empowering those in similar circumstances who face the problem of excessive drinking or drug taking in their families.

Chapter 1

Models of understanding

How family members continue to be pathologised and misunderstood

How professionals and academics have described and conceptualised the experiences of the wives, mothers, fathers, husbands, sisters, brothers and other family members who experience at first hand a relative's excessive drinking or drug use is the subject of this chapter. In many respects it is a sorry tale, but one that helps us understand one of the reasons why family members might have been marginalised in the past. It helps us understand why the research to be reported in later chapters was necessary and provides a vital part of the context for the interpretation of its results.

A number of different models or perspectives on the subject are presented in the chapter, starting with the form of stress-coping model which informed the present work. That model is therefore the one which the authors of this book support and the one that we recommend as a basis for improving professional responses to family members. It is the way of seeing the subject with which the research to be reported later began, and in modified form the way of seeing the subject with which the book concludes. The present chapter then proceeds by presenting a number of rival perspectives, namely, the pathology, codependency and systems models. Lacking from all pre-existing perspectives, including the stress-coping model with which we started, is due attention to social and cultural context, and the present chapter concludes with a consideration of some possible elements of a social contextual perspective.

The stress-strain-coping-support model

The stress-coping model, or to give it its full name, the stress-strain-coping-support model (Orford, 1994, 1998), owes its origins and much of its terminology to a line of research in health psychology and related disciplines that expanded greatly in the later decades of the twentieth century. Early seminal writings included those by Lazarus and Folkman (1984) and Holmes and Rahe (1967). It conceived of certain sets of circumstances that people face in their everyday lives as constituting long-standing, stressful circumstances or conditions of chronic adversity. Such conditions embraced war or chronic unemployment, but they also included chronic personal illness or living with a close relative with such illness. Different people might respond to stressful conditions in different ways, and some of those ways might be better for their health than others. The mechanical analogy of stress and strain was thought to be useful: if stress was not satisfactorily coped with, strain would be evident in the form of some departure from a state of health and well-being. The idea that people differ in the amount or adequacy of social support that they receive from other people (Cobb, 1976; Tolsdorf, 1976) and that social support might for some people be effective in buffering the effects of stress on strain (Cohen and Wills, 1985) was an important addition to the basic model. But the central idea is that people facing such conditions have the capacity to 'cope' with them much as one would attempt to cope with any difficult and complex 'task' in life. It incorporates the idea of being active in the face of adversity, of effective problem solving, of being an agent in one's own destiny, of *not* being powerless. In one form or another, the stress-coping model has been applied to a very wide range of conditions and circumstances (Orford, 1987; Zeidner and Endler, 1996) including coping with cancer and caring for a close relative with dementia (Gallagher et al., 1994).

The main components of the stress-coping model, when applied to families where a member of the family has a drinking or drug problem, are shown in Figure 1.1. Like all perspectives or models of human experience, the coping perspective makes certain assumptions and draws certain analogies. Like all assumptions and analogies, those made from the coping viewpoint are simplifications. They are not total truths, but rather working tools. The first assumption behind the stress-coping viewpoint on alcohol and drug problems in the family is that a serious drinking or drug problem can be highly stressful both for the person whose drinking or drug taking constitutes a problem (the 'relative') and for anyone who is a close family member (the 'family member'). This is because serious drinking or drug problems are, by their very nature, associated with a number of characteristics which are very damaging to intimate relationships and can be extremely unpleasant to live with. Such problems frequently continue unabated, often intensifying, over a period of years and are appropriately construed as long-standing stressful conditions for family members. This model views family members as being at risk of strain, in the form of symptoms of physical and/or mental ill health, as a direct consequence of the chronic stress occasioned by living with a relative with a drinking or drug problem.

A central assumption is that family members are then faced with the large and difficult life task, involving mental struggle and many dilemmas, of how to understand what is going wrong in the family and what to do about it. In particular, this task includes the core dilemma of how to respond to the relative whose drinking or drug-taking behaviour is seen as a problem. The ways of understanding reached by the family member at a particular point in time, and her (or his) ways of responding, are what are referred to collectively

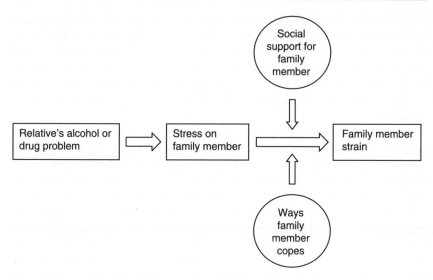

Figure 1.1 The stress-strain-coping-support model.

as 'coping' ('responding', 'reacting' and 'managing' are synonyms). The word is certainly not limited to well-thought-out and articulated strategies. It includes ways of understanding or responding that the family member believes to be effective as well as those judged to be ineffective. It includes feelings (for example, anger or hope), tactics tried once or twice and quickly abandoned (such as trying to shame the relative by getting drunk oneself), philosophical positions reached (e.g. 'I've got to stand by him because nobody else will'), and 'stands' taken (e.g. 'I'm not coming back until . . .').

A further assumption about coping with a relative's excessive drinking or drug taking is that some ways of coping are found by family members to be more effective than others. The word 'effective' is being used in two senses here. First, family members may find some ways of responding to be more productive than others in buffering the effects of stress and hence preventing or reducing the strain they themselves experience (or which other members of the family, children for example, experience). Second, family members may find some ways of managing the problem to be relatively effective and others relatively counter-productive in having a desired effect upon the relative's drinking or drug taking. It should be emphasised here that it is an assumption of the stress-coping model that family members *can* have an impact on their relatives' substance use in both desired and undesired directions. In other words, family members do have some potential for influencing their relatives; they are not totally powerless. That is an important assumption and one which distinguishes the stress-coping model from some other perspectives on the subject.

The model is completed with the assumption that social support is a powerful factor with potential to mitigate the effects of stress on health. By the same token, unsupportive behaviour can further exacerbate the stresses and strains that the family member experiences. Support, it is assumed, can come from many directions, and certainly includes both kin and non-kin informal sources as well as more formal sources offering professional services or self-help.

Note should be taken that the stress-coping viewpoint makes the assumption that there are such things as 'drinking problems' or 'drug problems' and that it is individuals (the people we refer to as the 'relatives') who have such problems. Although in this book we generally avoid terms such as 'alcoholism' or 'drug addiction' (although family members often use such terms), preferring the more general 'problem' or 'excessive' drinking or drug taking, the stress-strain-coping-support model is one that takes such problems very seriously indeed. It assumes that such problems generally represent disasters for families and represent serious hazards to the health and happiness of family members as well as their relatives. Family members, like the relatives they are concerned about, are victims of an uninvited and unwanted hazard. As we shall see, not all perspectives take that line.

Family pathology models

Much of the professional and academic literature on alcohol and drug problems and the family has adopted a very different position. Starting with writings about wives of 'alcoholics' in the 1940s, 1950s and 1960s, family members of relatives with drinking or drug problems have very often been viewed as individuals who were part of the problem themselves. They have been seen as suffering themselves from forms of 'psychopathology', and as people who have their own needs that are satisfied by living with someone who drinks or takes drugs excessively. The family pathology perspective has been quite influential in the past, and, as we shall see, it continues in various guises to be very influential still. It is important therefore that we be aware of it and examine it closely.

The psychopathology of alcoholics' wives was described by a number of early authors (e.g. Price, 1945; Bullock and Mudd, 1959) but Whalen's (1953) single contribution was one of the most outspoken and most quoted in the years that followed. The following extract makes the contrast with the stress-coping view abundantly clear:

> The woman who marries an alcoholic . . . is usually viewed by the community as a helpless victim of circumstance. She sees herself and other people see her as someone who, through no fault of her own and in spite of consistent effort on her part, is defeated over and over again by her husband's irresponsible behaviour. This is certainly not true. It merely

appears to be true. The wife of an alcoholic is not simply the object of mistreatment in a situation which she had no part in creating. Her personality was just as responsible for the making of this marriage as her husband's was; and in the sordid sequence of marital misery which follows, she is not an innocent bystander. She is an active participant in the creation of the problems which ensue.

(p. 634)

Whalen proceeded to outline four personality types which she considered were frequently found among wives of alcoholics, although she stressed that other types existed also. The first, Suffering Susan, displayed a need to punish herself as a dominating characteristic: 'she chose a marriage partner who was obviously so troublesome that her need to be miserable would always be gratified' (p. 634). The second, Controlling Catherine, dominated every aspect of the marital relationship. She had no doubt that she was the more capable of the two at making decisions and she controlled the family purse strings. Marriage was a vehicle for expressing her distrustful and resentful attitudes toward men in general. The third, Wavering Winifred, might separate from her husband for a few weeks but always returned when he pleaded. Her behaviour changed as much as his did; when he was drunk, she was furious and despairing, but when he was sober, she regained her good spirits and forgave the past. She had chosen a husband who 'needs her' (p. 638). Finally, Punitive Polly behaved toward her husband like a scolding but indulgent mother. She was often a career woman and might well earn most of the family living or else be responsible for getting the husband his job or obtaining contracts for him. Her relationships with other people, especially men, were characterised by rivalry, aggression and envy, and she had chosen a husband who was often several years her junior or who was limited in his masculinity in some way.

Those who wrote in that way in that era stressed the variation to be found among the personalities of wives married to men with drinking problems. Pattison et al. (1965) also described a range of 'character pathology' among wives of alcoholics, including the 'masochist' type, 'the hostile hysteric', 'the symbiotic dependant' and 'the maternal'. Some writers (e.g. Rae and Forbes, 1966) did acknowledge that most wives of men with alcohol problems showed elevated anxiety and depression which might be attributable to stress, but they believed that a definite minority displayed some form of 'character disorder'.

The view that wives actively contributed to their husbands' drinking problem was said to be supported by a number of observations. One was that many women married in the knowledge that their husbands drank excessively (e.g. Lemert, 1960; Rae and Forbes, 1966). Another was that wives had negative perceptions of their husbands whether or not the latter were sober or drinking, and even when they gave up drinking altogether. For example,

Macdonald (1956) stated, 'Many . . . women . . . are able to tolerate a marital relationship only with a non-threatening type of partner who they can subtly depreciate in a variety of ways, and an alcoholic may frequently meet those requirements.' Yet another observation, frequently backed up by anecdotal accounts of wives encouraging their husbands to return to drinking after an attempt at treatment (e.g. Rae and Forbes, 1966), was that wives discouraged their husbands' sobriety even to the point of attempting to undo the latter's attempts at change. For example, Ballard (1959) stated that, 'in spite of her protestations to the contrary the wife has an appreciable stake in maintaining the status quo'. Bailey (1961) in her review remarked that clinical observations of wives sometimes fighting their husbands' attempts to obtain help and appearing to have a vested interest in keeping their husbands actively alcoholic had evolved into one of the most frequently cited descriptions of 'the alcoholic's wife'. A related observation, much cited in writings of the wives' psychopathology school at that time, was the tendency of wives to become more distressed (or to 'decompensate') if and when their husbands became dry (e.g. Futterman, 1953; Igersheimer, 1959).

Many such observations were difficult to prove or disprove, and were often a matter of interpretation: for example, how much a prospective wife might know about her husband's drinking at the time of marriage, to what extent it fitted social conventions, and how at that time she might view his future drinking. Very little convincing research was carried out on these questions. Evidence has largely been against the decompensation hypothesis, suggesting rather that family members are *less* distressed when relatives give up drinking excessively (Moos et al., 1990). Although some of these 'pathology' notions are now of historical interest, the underlying idea that family members contribute to the problem has not gone away.

One observation which remains particularly pertinent half a century later was that wives were reluctant to become engaged in treatment. It was of course expected by those who supported the family pathology model that wives ought to engage in treatment aimed at their own personal change rather than simply counselling on account of stress experienced as a result of living with someone with a drinking problem. The resistance of wives to these treatment efforts was a frequently occurring theme, and much discussion revolved around the question of the wife's responsibility. For example, Price (1945) considered that only three of 20 wives of alcoholics studied were ready to see that they themselves bore any responsibility in the situation. Macdonald (1958) also referred to the difficulties encountered in running an analytic group therapy programme for wives. A high drop-out rate and the wives' criticism of the unstructured nature of the groups were referred to, as well as the wives' general lack of interest in gaining insight. This was interpreted as reflecting resistance to change. It was Igersheimer's (1959) opinion that 'only occasionally does a non-alcoholic wife wish to search within herself for attitudes and feelings which might contribute to her husband's drinking.

Generally speaking these wives are relatively refractory to intensive individual insight therapy.' But again Whalen's (1953) contribution was outstandingly frank on the matter:

> when we get an application from one of these women, we listen carefully to her complaints . . . [which] come to a focus on her basic concern . . . her anxiety about herself. . . . at this point . . . the counsellor says something like . . . 'Yes, it is clear to me that your husband's drinking creates many difficulties for you. But I can also see that you yourself have a problem which also contributes to your difficulties. It is this problem of yours which we can offer you help with if you want to work on it.' This is a challenging statement and one to which they respond variously in terms of their individual personalities.
>
> (p. 633)

In the past it has mostly been wives of men with drinking problems who have been the focus of family pathology models (as we shall see in Chapter 2, there has been much less focus on husbands of women with drinking problems, and there has been none on gay and lesbian partners). As attention has turned in the last few decades to drug misuse by adolescents and young adults, it turns out that the dominant perspective on the family within the academic and professional literature has also been one of family deficiency and pathology, but this time it is parents who have been the focus. Reviews of research and expert opinion on the subject typically take the form of a catalogue of failures and dysfunctions on the part of parents that, it is assumed, have contributed to a young person's drug misuse. Many examples could be cited but two will suffice. One is the extensive background section to a paper by Jurich et al. (1985) comparing the perceptions of their families held by 'drug abusers' and infrequent or occasional drug users. The second is from a monograph on a therapeutic community for drug addicts in the Netherlands, which, to its credit, took great steps to involve families in its work (Kooyman, 1993).

The long list of family deficiencies given by Jurich et al. included the following: a broken home, father absence, lack of closeness, parental immaturity and inability to adapt to changing situations, poor communication and mutual misunderstanding, lack of family coping skills, laissez-faire discipline, authoritarian discipline, parental 'alcoholism', and parental drug use. Kooyman's list included over-involved, overprotective parenting; detached, neglectful parenting; paternal drinking problem; traumatic family experiences, including violence, child molesting, incest, suicide, psychiatric admission, sudden death, and separation; parents rarely rewarding acceptable behaviour; anger or criticism rarely being expressed directly; unclear boundaries between the generations; and a strong mother–child and weak father–child relationship. One family pattern, described as 'neurosis', involved, according to Kooyman, an intense conflict in the family around the drug addict, weakness of boundaries in the family hierarchy, a polarity between the addict as a 'bad' child and another 'good' child, contradictory communications in the family, and explosive and violent conflicts. Clark et al. (1998) acknowledged the possibility that deficits in family functioning might be, at least in part, a consequence of the substance misuse, but it is comparatively unusual to find such acknowledgement in these types of depictions of the family.

The concept of codependency

A relatively recent variant of the pathology model is 'codependency', which since the 1980s has been a serious contender for dominant model in the alcohol and drug problems and the family field. Family members are said to be 'codependent'. Its origins are popular, with a number of best-selling books (e.g. Norwood (1986) and Beattie (1987), cited by Cutland (1998)) and a large number of codependency self-help groups in the USA (Troise, 1995). Despite these origins and its comparative lack of empirical study, it has had great influence on professional service providers in the USA, and attempts have been made to export services based on that model to other countries such as Australia and the UK.

The concept of codependency has been analysed and criticised by a number of writers. One of the foremost criticisms has been that the idea is all-embracing and difficult to pin down (Harper and Capdevila, 1990). Some definitions of codependency, such as those of Beattie (1987) and Subby (1987), make no direct reference to living with a drinking or drug problem, indicating that what is being talked of is a form of personality or a general way of relating in close relationships. Others, such as that of Gorski and Miller (1984), come close to acknowledging that a family member's behaviour is caused by the stress of living with a substance problem, but even then there is the implication, common to nearly all definitions of codependency, that the family member's behaviour has become in some way pathological or abnormal. These definitions and other writings on codependency are full of terms such as 'co-alcoholism', 'self-defeating', 'condition', 'disease', 'dysfunctional' and 'obsessed'. Indeed, a number of writers are clear in locating the ancestry of the codependency model in the pathological or disturbed personality hypothesis of earlier times (e.g. Lisansky Gomberg, 1989). Harper and Capdevila (1990) described a similar ancestry for codependency, going as far back as Gaether's (1939) supposed finding that wives of late-stage alcoholics are 'anxious, angry, abnormally dominant and masochistic . . . sexually repressed' (Harper and Capdevila, p. 286), and to Whalen's (1953) typology of wives.

The codependency concept has been roundly criticised on the grounds that no two definitions are the same, that so many characteristics have been listed as relevant that it could easily be applied to anyone, that it lacks empirical support, that it fails to recognise the stress-related nature of family members' responses, and that it is negative, blaming and stigmatizing (e.g. Lisansky Gomberg, 1989; Harper and Capdevila, 1990; Miller, 1994). Particularly trenchant criticisms are those of Krestan and Bepko (1991) and Troise (1995). The former authors interpret the behaviour of family members, mostly female, as overresponsible behaviour in the face of a relative's underresponsible behaviour associated with a drinking or drug taking problem:

> definitions [of codependency] are irresponsible and so vague as to be meaningless. If we view all behavior as adaptive, they demonstrate how adaptive responses to stressful and traumatic situations can be patholo- gised in ways that are of little benefit to those needing relief from them. They are definitions that suggest that one is 'bad' for having a problem with the difficult dilemma of being in relationship with an addicted person.
>
> (p. 53)

Troise's (1995) criticism is particularly pertinent because it came from someone who was familiar with psychoanalytic theory, and who recognised the appropriate and inappropriate use within that framework of a diagnosis of personality disorder. He agreed with Kokin and Walker (1989) that the concept of codependency was firmly rooted in some antiquated, long- abandoned Freudian concepts or in their misapplication. For example, Troise interpreted family members' apparent 'denial' of an alcoholic's illness, not as evidence of a defensive personality structure, but rather as a normal, often quite healthy response to the trauma associated with living with alcoholism. Similarly, the idea that a woman who remained in an abusive relationship without seeking help must be suffering from unconscious 'masochism' was a misuse of the definition of personality disorder:

> I find this notion to be seriously flawed, narrow and derogatory towards many women and the alcoholics they marry. The alcoholic is not *only* an alcoholic. He may be a father, genuinely loved for his basic personality, a sole provider, loving and caring when sober, creative, intelligent, etc. The wife, and children, may be totally financially dependent on the alcoholic spouse.
>
> (p. 9)

Krestan and Bepko (1991) also argued that codependency makes a disorder out of behaviour that is normal for women. Men, they stated, may also behave in codependent ways, but it is women who are usually referred to as 'codependent'. Since drinking and drug problems are more common among men, calling women who live with such problems codependent helps to restore the balance. Codependency had thus become a further tool in the cultural oppression of women. Living with an alcohol problem may exacerbate family sex roles, but

> What is going on is business as usual. It is, in general, a woman's pre-scribed role to tend to relationships, to focus on relationships, to make sure all relationships work, to put the needs and feelings of the other ahead of their own. . . . Why call this socialised behaviour codependency? Why use the language of sickness for behavior that has been celebrated as normal all along?
>
> (pp. 57–58)

Why, then, has the concept of codependency become so popular? Does it serve, as Krestan and Bepko suggested, to maintain the subordination of women? Or, as they further suggested, is it more to do with the economics of payment for treatment? Or might it be that the codependency concept, despite all its very evident shortcomings, does capture something of the otherwise neglected experience of family members? Lisansky Gomberg (1989, p. 124) cited Miller (1987):

> But what's wrong with calling a co-dependent just that? For many, the term has become a guiding light in the dark despair that has shrouded their lives for years. It is a word that connotes a sense of belonging so often lacking in their lives.

Although much of what has been written about codependency departs from the stress-coping view on which the present book is based, as we shall see it does touch upon a number of themes that we find to be central to the experi-ences of family members, both female and male, who live with relatives with drinking or drug problems. Among those themes are the way in which worry for a relative becomes a dominating feature of family life, the struggle that family members experience in finding effective ways of coping, and the many barriers to standing up to and challenging excessive drinking or drug taking.

A family systems perspective

The family systems view is an important one for us to consider because it represents a sophisticated, modern attempt to understand the relationship between family members and their drinking or drug-taking relatives. But its assumptions are totally different from those of the stress-coping perspective, and in a number of guises and particulars it resembles the family pathology model. In its application to alcohol and drug problems in the family, it rose to prominence in the 1970s and 1980s, with contributions from a number of European countries, including Yugoslavia (e.g. Lazic, 1977; Gacic, 1978) and Germany (Hemmer, 1979). It is particularly associated with the work of Steinglass and his colleagues on alcohol and the family (e.g. Steinglass, 1982; Steinglass et al., 1988), and of Kaufman (1981) and Stanton, Todd and their associates on drug misuse and the family (e.g. Stanton and Todd, 1992), all writing from the USA. In Britain, Vetere has more recently considered the application of the systems perspective to alcohol problems and the family (e.g. Vetere, 1998; Vetere and Henley, 2001).

Family systems theory and the various schools of family therapy associated with it are broadly based upon general systems theory, which sees the family as an example of a complex system of interdependent parts, each of which affects all the others. As such, the family illustrates 'organised complexity'. Causality is always circular rather than simply linear. Such a system develops patterns of interaction which often serve as mechanisms for regulating the system, for keeping stability and order. Systems such as families also show processes that serve adaptation, change and evolution, as across the stages of the family life cycle (Steinglass et al., 1988; Vetere, 1998).

In the context of problem drinking or drug taking, writers taking a systems view therefore talk not in terms of stress created by the behaviour of one family member, and about the coping efforts of others, but rather in terms of couple or whole-family patterns and processes. For example, Stanton and Todd (1992) wrote of the increasingly stereotypic behaviour of drug users, their family members and others, with the adoption of rigid roles and engagement of all in a family 'dance'. Drug users typically would adopt an 'underfunctioning' or 'underresponsible' role, while family members would adopt the opposite 'overfunctioning' or 'overresponsible' role. Vetere (1998) similarly wrote of family members adopting circular interaction patterns that would be repeated day in and day out, as in a wife spending less time with her drinking husband and more time with the children, making it more likely that he would be jealous and spend time drinking, which in turn made it more likely that she would distance herself from him emotionally. The biographies of wives that she was commenting on illustrated, she observed, a preponderance of complementary interactions, with drinking male partners exercising their power over their wives in a dominance–submission relationship. Other family theorists have concerned themselves with family belief systems or with intergenerational patterns of relating.

In his studies of families containing a member with an alcohol problem, sometimes observed in a specially designed hospital laboratory environment and sometimes at home, Steinglass concluded that family members often accommodate, over a long period of time, to heavy drinking on the part of one or more members of the family, and that the effects of the latter's drinking on family interactions can be positive and adaptive in a way that is frequently not consciously appreciated by family members and relatives. From this perspective, the excessive use of alcohol or other drugs, although it may in certain ways be dysfunctional for the family, is seen as being adaptive and functional in other ways. Steinglass (1982) wrote of the drinking of 'alcoholics' as functioning homeostatically, maintaining family stability, and Stanton and Todd (1992) similarly wrote of the drug use by young adults serving to maintain the family system, to the extent that removal of the 'symptom' would probably provoke a family crisis.

There has been much debate in the systems literature about the precise ways in which a symptom such as excessive drinking or drug taking might serve to maintain family stability (Vetere, 1998). According to Steinglass (1982), drinking behaviour in the family system might serve two possible functions: (1) it may appear as a sign or signal of stress within the system, and may be functional as a tension releaser or a way of recruiting help for the family; (2) it may function as an integral part of the system, maintaining, in homeostatic fashion, rigidly established, repetitive patterns of behaviour involving closeness or distance, dominance or submission. The relative whose drinking or drug taking is giving cause for concern might, according to that view, be seen as having been 'selected' to bear the weight of a more systemic family problem, or, as it is sometimes put, to be a 'scapegoat'. The symptom is viewed more as a stabilising than a disruptive force in the family. Vetere (1998) wrote of two theories, according to one of which the symptom helps the family to stabilise, for example, by uniting other family members in mutual concern and distracting members from other problems which might threaten the family. The other theory views symptoms as 'ironic consequences', as proposed solutions to family difficulties, which in turn themselves become problematic and require further family accommodation and adaptation. The latter type of theory is of course much closer to a stress-coping way of thinking.

There is in fact recognition on the part of systems thinkers that some families may fit better than others the model of excessive drinking or drug taking as adaptive or functional for the family. Steinglass (1982), for example, referred to some families in which drinking and its associated interactional patterns had become an 'organising principle' for the family, while other families corresponded more closely to a picture of family members having to cope with a deviant relative. His own home-based observations of families, and the interaction studies of Jacob and colleagues (e.g. Jacob and Seilhamer, 1987), suggested to Steinglass et al. (1988) that some patterns of excessive drinking (particularly the steady/in-home pattern) fitted the adaptive-for-the-system model, while others (typically the binge/out-of-home pattern) were more in keeping with a coping-with-dysfunction model.

Although writers in the systems tradition have claimed that they were not taking sides, and that both family members and the relatives they were concerned about are seen as being together in being oppressed by the problem, there are times when the systems view is difficult to distinguish from the old and long-standing view of family members as pathological. An example from the era of the 1970s and 1980s is a paper by Kaufman (1981) about family group treatment in New York, which contains a very clear statement of one kind of family pathology model based on systems thinking. Most of the family members involved were parents, more often mothers.

Kaufman used the categorisation of family systems, popularised by Minuchin (1975), into 'enmeshed', 'clear' and 'disengaged'. The most commonly observed pattern was that of a male addict enmeshed with his mother: 'Enmeshed mothers tend to think, act, and feel for their addict child' (p. 277). The large majority of mother–addict son relationships were categorised in this way. On the other hand, of those fathers who attended family groups, roughly equal numbers were judged to have enmeshed and disengaged relationships with the rest of the family, including their addict offspring (the average age of addict patients in the sample was 25 years). No relationship between an addict and a parent was designated as having the ideal, 'clear' boundaries. In families where both parents were judged to be enmeshed with their addict offspring, parents frequently 'collaborated with the addict to keep him or her infantilised under the guise of protecting them from arrest or other dangers' (p. 277). Those examples, which would be interpreted as signs of strain and efforts at coping, within the stress-coping model, were cited by Kaufman as illustrations of enmeshed family systems. The family pathology orientation of Kaufman's paper is made very explicit when he considered the possibility that the reactions of family members might be responses to the stress of addiction in the family:

> Narcotic addiction in a family member is such a strong stress on the family that secondary enmeshment or disengagement can be expected. However, the author's impressions are that these patterns, particularly mother–child enmeshment, antedated and indeed helped precipitate the abuse of and dependence on narcotics. . . . All joy has disappeared in these families, as lives are totally taken up with the sufferings and entanglements of having an addict child. However, in many cases the joylessness preceded the addiction.
>
> (pp. 276–277, 279)

Citing figures produced by Stanton (1971) and by Vaillant (1966) suggesting that large proportions of addicts still lived with their families of origin in their twenties and even into their thirties, but that abstinent addicts mostly lived independently of their parents, Kaufman stated confidently, 'This may be evidence of how strong an enemy the family is if it is not made an ally through treatment. . . . As addicts return to their families, they will be "sucked" back into patterns which inevitably lead to readdiction unless structural and behavioral changes occur' (pp. 280, 281). The idea that the family is pathological and to be seen as an enemy of change unless treated is in direct contradiction to the assumptions of the stress-coping model.

Adherents to the systems model continue to occupy a position that is at best ambiguous regarding family members' pathology. Vetere and Henley

(2001), describing the integration of family therapy into mainstream alcohol treatment programmes, gave an example that illustrates a pathology assumption when they wrote of 'understanding and untangling relatives' [i.e. 'family members' in our terms] intense involvement in the misuse of alcohol' (p. 93). The specific example they gave was of family members using a strategy such as 'keeping the drinker short of money' (p. 93), which in stress-coping terms would be seen as a very understandable response to being repeatedly hassled for money and seeing family finances diverted into purchasing drink or drugs. As a case vignette to illustrate their systems approach to treatment, Vetere and Henley (2001) described the case of a woman presenting with a drinking problem and her partner. In the course of treatment the latter 'came to realise' that he needed to change, 'recognised' his own insecurity, increasingly 'took responsibility' and 'held himself accountable' for his own past misdemeanours (pp. 98–99).

The systems perspective, for all its insights, can therefore sometimes be remarkably similar to the older family pathology position, and is at times markedly at odds with a stress-coping view. Not surprisingly, therefore, the systems model has been criticised by those with a feminist perspective and others for appearing to defuse responsibility for, for example, violent or abusive behaviour (Vetere, 1998), and for failing to acknowledge the social and economic realities of family members' lives.

Social contextual models

As a counterweight to the failure of pathology, codependency and systems models to acknowledge the broader contexts of family members' lives, especially those of women, others have written of the family in a way that tries to give context some weight. There is no widely accepted contextual model of substance misuse in the family. Anthropologists, from whom we might have expected such a model, have rarely made alcohol consumption a major focus, although the work of MacAndrew and Edgerton (1970) is an exception, as is the later work of Brady (Brady and Palmer, 1984; Brady, 1988), and the same is true of illicit drug use. A direct focus on both substances *and* the family has been virtually absent, although numerous other social scientists have touched on the subject of alcohol and the family while writing generally about the subject of alcohol use or in the course of a general account of a particular social group, community or culture. Despite the absence of a direct focus on the issue of alcohol and the family, the close entanglement of alcohol use and family life around the world is described again and again (e.g. Figueroa-Rosales, 1971; Wolcott, 1974; Ablon, 1979; Sansom, 1980; de Silva, 1983).

One theme that recurs throughout the social and cultural literature on alcohol and the family is that of sex roles and sex differences. For example, in the small group of people in northern Ghana whom she studied, Hagaman (1980) concluded that beer production formed an important basis of power among women, who controlled both its brewing and its distribution. Wolcott (1974), writing specifically about urban, largely male, beer drinking among the Ndebele in the former Rhodesia, suggested that traditional male and female roles were very separate, and the urban beer gardens served the function of enabling men to get together away from home, something they could not otherwise easily do.

Dorschner (1983) had much to say about sex roles and drinking in his report of the drinking of *daru* and other alcoholic beverages by the Rajputs of northern India. In that cultural group with its distinct sex roles, facing violence, fighting and fear were part of the masculine identity, while the woman's life was cloistered, centring on the performance of routine daily tasks. Within this context, alcohol was part of the man's world only, and men would drink in all-male groups out of sight of the female members of their families. The purity and innocence attributed to women and children precluded them from drinking, and part of the woman's role was to lecture their husbands about the evils of drink and the frivolity of wasting scarce money on it. It was reported to Dorschner that many Rajputs beat their wives on returning home after drinking.

Not that it is necessary, of course, to look outside Europe or North America to find traditional sex role structures described in the context of alcohol and the family (e.g. Bevia, 1976; Kozakiewicz, 1982). Ablon and Cunnningham (1981) stressed the role of male models of often-absent-at-work or silent Irish-American husbands and fathers, and female models of competent, 'dominant', wives and mothers who keep the family going. Nor should it be thought that traditional divisions in the drinking habits of the sexes are a thing of the past, confined to traditional, rural, or 'underdeveloped' communities or parts of the world. A participant observation study of 'public houses' (pubs) in one English village in the 1980s (Hunt and Satterlee, 1985) suggested that stigma still attached to the unaccompanied woman drinker, and Holmila (1988), who studied newly-wed Finnish couples, concluded that one of a wife's tasks was to control her husband's drinking.

Another recurring theme in many of these contributions on the social and cultural context of alcohol use within the family, and on sex roles, has been that of social change and the way this has affected the relationship between the family and drinking. The dramatic increase in exposure to the risks of excessive drinking in nearly all 'developing' parts of the world in the later years of the twentieth century has been attributed by many to modernity in the form of the growth of cash economies, the commercialisation of alcohol beverage production and globalisation of the drinks trade (e.g. Curry, 1993). Hedland and Lundahl (1984) described the traditional role of women in producing beer among the Ngoni in Zambia, and the changes that had come about as a result of increased migration, mainly of men, to work in urban areas. The new social order made it possible for women to utilise their old roles as beer brewers in an increasingly entrepreneurial fashion. Acuda (1983) also described the effects of rapid social change in Kenya, including large-scale migration from rural areas to towns and cities, the consequent separation of family members when husbands were forced to leave families in order to work, and a move from extended family life to nuclear families. Like many other authors, Acuda believed that these changes had reduced family and other controls on drinking and had hence contributed to an increased risk of excessive drinking.

Many other writers have commented on such socio-cultural changes, nearly always operating in the direction of a loss of traditional family and community regulations, a loss that was often presumed to put families at increased risk of drinking and other substance problems. Such changes are often thought to have the greatest effect on women, as a group formerly protected from such risks, or on students or migrant workers, who are exposed to greater risks. Social changes of these kinds have been noted in many countries and groups, including indigenous[1] Australia (Alexander, 1990; Bolger, 1990), India (Mohan et al., 1978), Italy (Rizzola and Rosadini, 1974), middle-class London Jews (Glatt, 1973), Irish immigrants to England (O'Connor, 1978) and Mexican immigrants to the USA (Corbett et al., 1991).

There is also to be considered the special position of families in socio-cultural groups dominated by others as a result of colonialism, which is of great relevance to indigenous Australians who took part in the research to be reported later in this book (Chapter 3). Probably most has been written about North American Indians and their drinking (e.g. Foulkes, 1987; Whittaker and Whittaker, 1992). For example, Jilek (1981) wrote from his experience of practising psychiatry in British Columbia, Canada, linking high rates of native 'alcoholism' with a state he referred to as 'anomic depression'. The latter he believed was a reaction to alienation from aboriginal culture under Westernising influences. Alienation involved both 'relative deprivation, the negative discrepancy between a minority group's legitimate expectations and its actual situation in a larger society, and . . . cultural confusion, the weakening of norms in members of a cultural group, unable to integrate the contrasting values of their own with those of a different culture with which they have been brought into close contact' (p. 161).

Eber (2001) has written of indigenous Mexican women in Chiapas (Southern Mexico) increasingly finding a public voice to speak up about the role of alcohol, which they saw as 'a tool of their oppression in the context of growing class stratification' (p. 256). Keenly aware of their households' material needs, women viewed drinking as a waste of the little cash their families had. The political dimension, totally neglected in all the leading models of alcohol and the family, was illustrated by the influence of the Zapatista groups' commitment to abstaining from drinking as part of a revitalisation movement in which indigenous Mexicans aimed to rid themselves of the vestiges of colonisation and domination by the formerly unchallenged main political party in Mexico. Staples (1990) wrote in similar terms about what he saw as the crisis facing urban Black families in the USA as a result of excessive drinking and illicit drug use. That crisis, involving, for example, children taking over as heads of families because of their incomes from selling crack cocaine and grandmothers taking on childcare in place of their addicted daughters, could not, in his view, be attributed solely to greater use of mind-altering substances by Blacks than Whites (surveys suggested, if anything, the opposite), but was also due to the vulnerability of urban Blacks as a subjugated group.

Although it is often assumed in these contextual views of substance use and culture that it is the family that bears the brunt of, or acts as the conduit for, such influences and changes, family functioning and the experience of family members are rarely considered in any detail. A number of writers, however, have contributed parts of what could be a contextual model of excessive substance use in the family. Harwin (1982) suggested an ecological perspective as a necessary corrective to the preoccupation of much of the literature with the microsocial psychology of personalities and personal relationships in the family. She wished to emphasise the current economic and social context, including such important 'reality' matters as housing, employment, finances and childcare. Fryer (1998) applied a community psychology perspective to an understanding of the biographical accounts given by six English women who had lived with men with serious drinking problems (in a book edited by Velleman et al., 1998), and Ussher (1998) applied a feminist perspective to the same six accounts. Fryer's position was that a family member's subjective experience has to be considered alongside socio-structural forces, and, in particular, the way in which personal agency may be restricted, undermined, disabled and frustrated by powerful formal and informal forces at all levels, and by inadequate social support of formal and informal kinds. He was struck by the way the women who gave their accounts

> had been undermined and disempowered as persons within their families and communities. Their capacity for self-determination – for making sense of, influencing and coping with the events they experienced – had been restricted and undermined . . . by being positioned as the parties responsible for the plight in which they found themselves . . . by the medicalisation of their partners' behaviour as 'illness', by their experience of chronic helplessness, by collusive secrecy and by absent or deficient social support from family, partners, friends, professionals and the labour market.
>
> (p. 167)

Ussher's standpoint was that account needed to be taken of three sets of factors to understand women's experiences: material, discursive and intrapsychic factors. By material factors, Ussher understood factors that institutionalise inequalities in heterosexual relationships, legitimating masculine power and control. This would encapsulate economic factors which make women dependent on men; presence or absence of accommodation which allows women in destructive relationships to leave; support for women of a legal, emotional and structural kind, which allows protection from further harassment or abuse. . . . The fact of whether children are present in the relationship (or are withheld in custody battles), and the material consequences of being married (or not) are also part of this level of analysis.

(pp. 152–153)

'Discursive factors' referred to prevailing 'discourses' about the role of women:

Within a heterosexual matrix, the traditional script of femininity tells us that women live their lives through a man. . . . In the late twentieth century, 'getting' [her man] still means monogamy, and usually marriage or motherhood; this is the script for the 'respectable' woman. . . . We are taught that a good woman can always tame or transform the monstrous brute or beast; through her ministrations or example the frog will turn into the prince, the violent man into the charming thoughtful lover. The woman who *can't* enact this transformation is positioned as being to blame; she must try harder, be more self-sacrificing, or attempt with greater vigour to be the 'perfect woman'.

(pp. 151, 152)

Intrapsychic factors were those that

operate at the level of the individual and the psychological: factors which are traditionally the central focus of any psychological analysis of women's lives. This would include analyses of the way in which women blame themselves for problems in relationships, and psychological explanations for why this is so, incorporating factors such as low self-esteem, depression, the impact of previous neglect or abuse, guilt, shame, fear of loss or separation, and the idealisation of both heterosexuality and of men.

(p. 153)

Conclusion

How best to think of the family members of relatives with drinking or drug problems remains surprisingly controversial. The modern history of professional thinking has been dominated by models that view family members in a negative, pathological light. The evidence for that statement is clearest in what has been written professionally about wives of men with drinking problems, but the same is probably true regarding other family members as well as family members of relatives with drug problems. A perspective that views family members as people faced with the task of trying to cope with stressful circumstances offers the clearest alternative to pathology models, but, like the latter, it has done little to view family members and the ways they cope within a broader social and cultural context.

Because of the weight of unsympathetic past theorising about wives of men with drinking problems, and about other family members in similar circumstances, the main aim of the present work is to extend and deepen our understanding. Thereby we hope to contribute to building a better model of the experiences of family members that will help to free them from the stigma associated with negative stereotypic representations. In terms of the perspectives presented in this chapter, we aim to elaborate the stress-strain-coping-support model with which we started, and, in particular, to incorporate more adequately the socio-cultural context. As will be described in Chapters 3 and 4, we attempted to achieve those aims by interviewing family members in three contrasting socio-cultural groups, using qualitative research methods. In Chapter 2, we review previous research that has also used qualitative methods in an attempt to understand the reality of family members' lives.

Chapter 2

Coping with alcohol and drug problems in the family

A review of previous qualitative research

Because family members have been so badly served by 'expert' theories and assumptions, the present book puts a premium on qualitative research because of its focus on hearing directly from family members about their experiences. The research project to be described in later chapters used qualitative methods. Although its scope was wider than earlier studies, it was not the first to use qualitative methods, and in this chapter we review previous research in the field that has been broadly qualitative in its methods. We have included work wherever the methods used allowed the voices of family members themselves to be heard, either in the form of direct quotations from family members or in the form of conclusions based on in-depth interviewing or observation.

Compared to that small literature which is of direct relevance to the work to be reported in later chapters, there exists a much more voluminous research literature consisting of studies that have employed quantitative methods. That literature includes psychometric and correlational studies (e.g. Crisp and Barber, 1995); prevalence studies among attenders at marriage guidance (e.g. Halford and Osgarby, 1993); studies of sexual functioning (e.g. O'Farrell et al., 1997); studies of the timing of, and attributions about, drinking problems and marital problems (e.g. Noel et al., 1991); laboratory observational studies of family interaction (e.g. Jacob et al., 2001); drinking among newly-wed couples (e.g. Leonard and Roberts, 1998); congruent and incongruent drug use patterns in couples (e.g. Fals-Stewart et al., 1999); studies of the overlap between drug or alcohol misuse and domestic violence (e.g. Brown et al., 1999); studies of interpersonal perceptions in couples where one partner has a drinking problem (e.g. Drewery and Rae, 1969); studies of symptoms among family members (e.g. Bailey, 1967); studies of family members during their relatives' treatment (e.g. Moos et al., 1990); and many other kinds of quantitative research besides. It would not be possible, nor, mostly, would it be relevant, to attempt to review that vast literature here. Some of that literature becomes relevant, however, when attempting to integrate our findings in Chapter 9.

Wives of men with drinking problems

In a paper published over 50 years ago, highly influential then and still quoted to this day, Jackson (1954) drew conclusions from attending meetings of Al-Anon (for spouses and other relatives of 'alcoholics', a group closely allied to Alcoholics Anonymous (AA)) over a 3-year period, and from interviews with other wives of 'alcoholics' contacted through hospitals, social work, probation service and other channels. On the basis of all her accumulated observations, Jackson suggested seven stages in the adjustment of the family. Only a very brief description of the proposed stages will be given here. At the first stage, incidents of excessive or inappropriate drinking might be only occasional but they placed strains upon marital interaction. Wives responded in a trial-and-error fashion but an illusion of an ideal marriage might be preserved most of the time. At the second stage, incidents of excessive drinking multiplied and the family's increased social isolation magnified the importance of the family events. Tension rose. The wife lost her self-confidence as her attempts to stabilise her husband's drinking failed. These attempts became more desperate, different remedies being tried in quick succession. Stage three found the family in chaos. The wife had given up attempts to control or understand her husband's drinking and began to behave in a manner geared to relieve tension rather than achieve long-term ends. She might begin to worry about her own sanity and about her inability to make decisions or to change the situation. At the fourth stage, the alcoholic's increasing 'illness' was recognised, and despite his resentment and his repeated promises to mend his ways, the wife took over much of the control of the family, which became more stable and organised in a manner that minimised the disruptive behaviour of the alcoholic husband. Stage four was followed either by stage five and then stage six, or by stage seven. At stage five, the wife separated from her husband after near-catastrophic events, such as an attempt at homicide in the family, or after an accumulation of less catastrophic happenings. Stage six concerned the reorganisation of the family without the husband. Stage seven involved the husband's achievement of sobriety and the difficulties encountered in reinstating the husband and father in his former role.

Jackson's work was a rich, early source of ideas, although her specific suggestions about stages were probably too precise. Lemert (1960) attempted a direct test of this idea of stages of family reactions by interviewing 112 close family members (mostly wives) of 'alcoholics' and asking about the sequence of the first occurrences of 11 events relating to the family's perception of, and reaction to, the drinking problem. The major conclusion was that the sequence of events showed a great deal of inconsistency and unevenness, and that it was premature to try to demonstrate a number of discrete stages occurring generally in families complicated by drinking problems. At best, Lemert's data suggested two broad and fairly distinct stages: recognition of the problem, first attempts to control drinking, social isolation of the family and transfer of part of the husband's family role to the wife were generally reported to occur earlier than fearful reactions, feelings of hopelessness about coping with the problem, sexual intercourse declining in frequency or ceasing, and the seeking of outside assistance.

The most thorough, previous study of an in-depth qualitative kind was that conducted by Wiseman and reported in her book, *The Other Half: Wives of Alcoholics and Their Social-Psychological Situation*, published in 1991. Her study was confined, as many studies of family members have been, to wives of men whose excessive substance-using problem was to do with drinking alcoholic beverages – 'wives of alcoholics', as she termed them. Her study shared a number of features with the one to be reported in the present book: the use of quite lengthy personal interviews, carried out with family members in more than one country, analysed and reported in detail, with the aim of developing theory about family members' circumstances and how they deal with them.

Wiseman's study was not initially planned as a cross-cultural comparison. She began by personally interviewing 50 Finnish wives, with the aid of a simultaneous translator, in her role as an invited US researcher at the Finnish Foundation for Alcohol Studies. Later, with the help of other, 'trained, mature, women interviewers' (p. 252), she interviewed 76 wives in the USA. More than three-quarters of the US wives were getting some form of counselling, seven out of every ten of those having been to Al-Anon. One in three of the Finnish wives had some Al-Anon contact. The sample excluded any wives of men who were reported to have recovered from their drinking problems. The Finnish study was carried out in the 1970s, and the parallel research in the USA was completed in 1980.

The two countries provided a contrast in a number of ways. Drinking in Finland was more polarised between the sexes, with men doing most of the drinking and women traditionally being in the role of the 'moral guardians' of the family, it being accepted that part of a wife's task was to help keep her husband's drinking under control. Male drinking patterns were also thought to be different in the two countries: most male drinking in Finland was reported to take place outside the home, with a much higher proportion of US male drinking taking place at home. Finland also had a much more systematic, state-run organisation of treatment services, involving a greater degree of coercion upon the problem drinker. Despite those differences, Wiseman was most impressed with how 'the phenomenon of the alcoholic husband eradicates the variations between the two countries and is overwhelming in its consequences for wives and marriages' (1991, p. 15).

Wiseman was interested in a number of the same topics that were a focus for the present research. For example, she devoted part of her book to the forms of distress that wives experienced. As she put it, 'wives report a veritable roller coaster of emotions, alternately hating their husband and, at the same time, worrying that he may be in serious trouble and/or hurt':

In the evenings, I would sit and brood about how he left me alone so much, and I was angry and hurt. Then, as time wore on, I would start worrying that he had been in a car accident.

(USA) (p. 166)

In the evenings, I used to imagine I would kill him, or whatever bad I could do to him. Then, at 2.00 a.m. I would ask God to get him home. Then if God did, I was ready to kill him again.

(Finland) (p. 166)

A large part of what we refer to as 'coping', Wiseman referred to as 'the home treatment'. The latter she divided into two parts: the direct and indirect approaches. The direct approach involved some combination of pointing out to husbands the negative consequences of their drinking; complaining, nagging or pleading; attempting to curtail the husband's supply of drink in some way; or threatening to leave him. Wiseman detected differences between Finnish and US wives, traceable to the less egalitarian nature of husband/wife relationships in Finland at that time. Wives in the USA mostly thought they had a right to tackle their husbands about their drinking. In Finland, where men were more dominant, wives felt their husbands would not admit the right to question men's drinking. Among indirect approaches, Wiseman listed acting 'normal' or 'natural', taking over, money manipulation, and drinking along with him. Finally, Wiseman referred to a small minority of US wives who from the outset used neither direct nor indirect approaches in trying to modify their husband's drinking but rather suffered in silence, usually through fear of confronting the problem openly or making their husbands angry.

Divorce or separation was problematic for wives, although most had thought about it, and in fact over half the US wives and four out of ten Finnish wives had been separated from their husbands at some time, some more than once. The barriers to separation were considerable and understandable, and included fear of poverty (especially in Finland, where alimony was not available), the difficulty of getting a job, often after a long period of not working outside the home, the difficulty of obtaining accommodation, and anxiety about legal costs. To those could be added informal social pressure and feelings of guilt at the prospect of deserting her husband, who might be ill and in need, the husband's resistance to separation, continued feelings of love for the husband, and particularly feelings that it might be wrong for the children's sake to break up the family (mothers were often begged by their children not to leave their fathers).

Wives were distressed at the deterioration they saw in their husbands' appearance, their husbands' physical degeneration and illnesses, and signs of their mental deterioration. Added to their husbands' irresponsibility around the home, disappearances for indefinite periods and worry over finances, the home lives of wives amounted to

a world of almost constant stress, anger, worry, and fear, which escalates
as the years go by. Furthermore, it is an existence in which new problems
are continually compounding the older ones – his health, his job, his
irresponsibility, his brutality, his deteriorating mind.

(p. 171)

Wiseman devoted a large part of one chapter to the issue of gaining help from
other family members. She referred to informal helping networks for these
wives being 'fragile', stating 'When the problem of a family member is a
long-term behavioural one with moral or character implications, the helping
patterns of the kin network are far more complicated than previous studies
would indicate. The offer of aid cannot be taken for granted, and even when
extended, the outcome is by no means certain' (pp. 186–187). Combined
with hesitancy and conflict about telling anyone about the problem, wives
asked themselves whether a particular family member was the right person
she should be asking for help. Nearly half of the wives in both countries said
that they had no relations close enough to ask for help. Finnish wives were
more dubious than US wives about getting help from any member of the
family: they were more reticent to tell anyone and subscribed more strongly
to a view of privacy, and their husbands were very strongly against anyone
else being involved.

   There is an assumption throughout Wiseman's book that the husbands'
problems were best construed as 'alcoholism' and that achieving that correct
'diagnosis' was an important step for wives and their husbands. The first
question in her interview topic guide was, 'When did you first suspect your
husband was an alcoholic?', and the first chapter of results is entitled,
'Diagnosing Alcoholism'. Much the same set of assumptions was made by
Asher (1992) in her book, *Women with Alcoholic Husbands*, based on in-depth
interviews with 52 women, all of whose husbands were being treated for
'alcoholism' and all of whom were themselves taking part in a family
programme in the USA.

   What is distinctive about Asher's work is that her conclusions were based
on the core theme of what she called 'definitional ambivalence', which placed
main emphasis, not on coping actions, but on the struggle for understanding,
meaning and the image of husband and self:

   A key struggle and challenge in the moral career of becoming the wife of
   an alcoholic is to sort out, sift through, and arrive at views of selves and
   situations among competing and changing definitions. . . . These women
   face circumstances of dramatically changing interactions that require
   ongoing reformulation of their views of self, husband, marriage, and 'the
   problem'. . . . The generic questions involved in the ambivalence of definition and meaning with regard to self are, Am I an okay person? wife?
   mother? What's wrong with me? Why is he treating me like this? Why

is my life like this? What can I do? What do I want? What have I
become? And what is to become of me?

(pp. 5, 7, 10, 11)

Like Jackson's (1954) much earlier account, Asher's was written around
stages, but in this case the stages are couched in terms of how ambivalence is
managed: beginning with *recognising* the ambivalence, *sorting* it, *limiting* or
depersonalising the ambivalence, and finally *transforming* it. At the first stage,
there were early signs, which were disregarded, that assumptions about
husband and marriage might not be able to be taken for granted (e.g. 'I
mentioned something to him [about] what the bottles were doing behind the
furnace. He just gave me some answer. I thought, Okay, fine, I'll let it go with
that' (p. 22)). Sorting involved *acknowledging* (e.g. 'I started probably a typical
behaviour of looking, getting a few clues, looking and finding hidden bottles.
I was trying to determine, too, a definition of what is "heavy drinking", and so
I would monitor the quantity' (pp. 36–37)); *valuating* (e.g. 'I think it's taken a
more subtle form of abuse. That's abuse in staying out all night and not
knowing where he is. That's abuse in my eyes' (p. 64)), and *personalising* (e.g. 'I
took it very personally . . . that he didn't care enough about me; he would
rather be out drinking than be home with me' (p. 86); 'I really believed at that
time the things that I was feeling, that I was mentally not all right' (p. 107)).
Asher did refer to what from a stress-coping perspective would be called
coping actions, referring to them as 'personalising stances' or 'overt stands', of
which she identified two that contrasted one with another: placating and
confrontational. She also identified two interactional contingencies that
appeared to maintain definitional ambivalence: 'bargaining' by the husbands
and 'hoping' by the wives. Two major changes were associated with limiting
definitional ambivalence: first, setting limits on what was acceptable; second,
refocusing on the self, depersonalizing the ambivalence and focusing on one's
own rights, obligations and needs. Recognising the husband's 'alcoholism'
was accepted by Asher as an important element in this transforming of the
ambivalence.

Apart from Jackson's (1954), Wiseman's (1991) and Asher's (1992) work,
there have been few thorough studies of a qualitative nature. The six biographical accounts included in the book edited by Velleman et al. (1998), and
referred to in Chapter 1, are a rich, additional source of insight into the
experiences of women married to men with drinking problems. Two other
studies are worth mentioning. Banister and Peavy (1994) identified three
main strands in the experiences of five Canadian women, married to 'alcoholics' for between 9 and 32 years and interviewed at some length: 'constantly
being on guard', 'living in a pit' and 'push and pull'.

One wife, for example, described the stress of being on guard:

It's extremely stressful . . . you just don't really know from one minute to the next just how things are going to be. There's never any consistency. There's constant up and downs . . . like a roller coaster . . . you're constantly in a state of tension. There's always tension or anxiety floating around you.

(p. 213)

As a result, wives described lack of trust in their relationship with their husbands, communication deteriorating to the level of shallow, meaningless monologues, and a feeling of living an inauthentic, superficial or artificial life with their husbands.

The second strand involved an erosion or weakening of the sense of self and the adoption of a victim mentality in which messages of unworthiness and disdain were accepted and self-blame adopted. The third strand, 'push and pull', concerned conflicts around independence, separation and individuation. Banister and Peavy suggested that their findings should be interpreted within the context of disparity of power in marriage, for these were wives who had entered traditional marriages at a time when inequality in marriage was expected. They were all from a generation, Banister and Peavy suggested, that lived in compliance with cultural norms relegating wives to domestic concerns and nurturance of their families.

Casey et al. (1993) pointed out that research on the experiences of wives of men with drinking problems had focused almost exclusively within the domain of the home and had not considered wives' outside employment. To correct that bias, they asked 60 wives of men being treated for drinking problems in the USA to answer a number of questions, including a job satisfaction scale. Casey et al. were impressed that the majority of women reported little or no impact of their husbands' drinking on their work, and that work acted for them as a 'haven':

One woman commented, 'My job performance was not at all affected. I threw myself into my work. I loved work and being there.' Another working wife stated, 'My work performance was not at all affected. I turned off . . . my home life was separate. I didn't think a lot about the drinking. It didn't really bother me that much.'

(p. 124)

On the other hand, sizeable minorities reported beginning or quitting a job due to a husband's drinking, and their ability to perform at the workplace being significantly negatively affected:

Comments included, 'I'm not there. I'm worrying about everything else.' Or as another woman said, 'When things were bad at home, my head was at home even though my body was at work.' Also, 'I would get upset at work and find myself concentrating on him instead of on the job.' One woman noted, 'I would jump on others at work for no reason. I had no patience.'

(p. 125)

The majority indicated that their work environment was supportive, and many reported that at least one person at work knew about their husbands' drinking (mainly coworkers, immediate bosses, distant bosses and friends at work). Others at work had come to know about the problem in a variety of ways: the wives had told someone themselves; or they had demonstrated behaviour indicating that home life was affecting their work; or they had fallen apart at work, and had been asked what was wrong; or a supervisor had noticed a change in job performance. Those who had not disclosed the problem to others at work had not done so because it was thought to be a private or a family matter, because of personal embarrassment, or because of concern that it would affect her job.

We conclude this review of qualitative work with wives of men with drinking problems by introducing two important studies from outside Europe or North America. The first is a study carried out by Yang (1997). The study involved interviews with 53 family members (31 wives on whom Yang concentrated) of 'alcoholics' in treatment (nearly all men) from 40 South Korean families. Although Yang referred to the rapid cultural change taking place in South Korea and the conflicts between traditional and Western values that many family members were experiencing, the majority of participating families were described by Yang as remaining traditional in their outlook. Family honour was important, as was respect for elders, particularly a wife's in-laws.

Early in her London University Ph.D. thesis, Yang quoted at length from the interview with a Mrs Lim, married for 15 years to a husband said to have been drinking heavily for many years, having been admitted on several occasions to a medical hospital and latterly to a psychiatric hospital. She had two children, and she worked in a public bathhouse during the day and delivered milk early each morning. Yang wrote, 'This is not just Mrs Lim's story, but the story of most wives of alcoholics in Korea' (p. 58). The following is part of the quotation that appears in the thesis:

> When I was 23, a match-maker told my mother about my husband-to-be. . . . After meeting him only once, my mother and brother told me I should marry him. I just followed their decision. . . . When I got married I noticed he drank a lot. . . . After a few years, he started to beat me, and life became very difficult. I contacted my mother-in-law for help but she said it was not serious. . . . My children were afraid of him. . . . He constantly hurled abuse at them. . . . I told my children never to challenge his behaviour, no matter how bad, as he was still their father and they should respect him. . . . I endured it and just cried by myself. I had never

thought of divorcing him, but life became unbearable and one day I left him. I took the children but we had nowhere to live. I asked my sister-in-law to put us up for a few days, but when I was coming from work I discovered my sister-in-law had locked the door and my children were wandering in the street. I was very upset and I had no option but to return home. . . . I asked my mother-in-law to give me permission to send him to a psychiatric hospital. She abused me on the phone and accused me of being the cause of his drinking. . . . I rang my brother-in-law for help but he said it was not his responsibility to send him to hospital. . . . My in-laws were furious when they discovered that I had had him admitted to a psychiatric hospital. . . . Whenever I visited him, he abused me and threatened to divorce me. I felt very sad and hopeless. I wanted to be loved by my husband and was hoping we might still have a chance of being happy again. . . . I was influenced by my mother not to break up my family and, 'to put my children before myself'. She had seven of us and we lived in a hut but she never divorced but endured the hardship. If my family knew my troubles they would be very upset. I often felt like shooting him but in fact I would prefer to be beaten by him.

(pp. 35–38)

By the end of her fieldwork, Yang stated that Mrs Lim had not killed herself, as she had thought of doing, nor left her husband but was still struggling with her difficulties: 'Her attitude towards alcoholism and her feelings towards her husband had changed very little because she received inadequate support and education during the course of her husband's treatment' (p. 58).

A number of themes, overlapping with those identified by the earlier qualitative researchers, are amply described and illustrated in Yang's work. They include the sense of hurt wives felt and the loss of any positive feelings that they may have felt for their husbands; being vigilant about the husband's drinking; responding emotionally and the escalation of violence in the relationship; shame, fear of criticism and keeping the problem secret; criticism and lack of support from family and neighbours; and concern for and protection of the children.

Yang described the pressures wives felt to endure the hardship caused by, and to be patient in the face of, their husbands' 'alcoholism'. She wrote also of the shame attached to such a problem, a tendency to blame wives, the potential loss of family honour, and the resultant keeping of the problem a secret within the family. These pressures Yang attributed to the legacy of the Confucian philosophy and traditional family organisation, with its emphasis on hierarchical parent–child relationships, patrilineal descent and dominance of male family members, and the premium placed upon preserving family honour and not 'losing face'. Yang's hypothesis, which she believed she had found support for, was that the more traditional the gender and family roles a family adhered to, the more likely it was that a wife would accept unwanted and problematic drinking, and the less likely it was that such behaviour would be challenged and resolved.

All but five of the wives interviewed by Yang appeared to her to have married for reasons connected with traditional gender roles. Several reported that they had been raped by a man known to the family and as a result had been forced into marriage against their wishes. Another group had felt pressure to marry because they were pregnant. The largest group had had arranged marriages and had been forced to submit to their parents' wishes despite not wanting to marry. By the time they were interviewed, nearly all were expressing unhappiness with their marriages, but over half had no plans to separate or divorce (a number were already separated). The most frequently cited reasons for not considering separation corresponded to the traditional pressures that Yang had outlined. A smaller number reported that the reason for staying in an unhappy marriage was the fear of leaving their husbands and living alone. Yang also noted that although most wives were working outside the home, often suffering from the pressure of unsociable, long working hours and a poor working environment, they had little or no control over financial arrangements, and lack of financial independence was also a stated reason for not considering separation in some cases.

Like all those who have researched and written at any length about the experiences of wives married to men with drinking problems, Yang devoted considerable space in her thesis to the subject of alcohol and domestic violence. All but three of the wives in her sample had experienced domestic violence. More than a third had suffered 'severe violence, much of which was life-threatening' (p. 191). Yang reported that in nearly all cases violence occurred after the husband had been drinking, and in only two families was violence not related to drinking. The majority of women told Yang that they allowed their husbands to beat them because of the anticipated consequences if they attempted to stand up to their husbands, since they feared they would be accused of being the cause of the problem. They thought their situation was due to their ill fortune or fate, or simply to the fact that they were unable to find a solution to the problem. A small group of women who appeared to Yang to be more assertive and less entrenched in traditional gender roles reported that they had tried to fight back or had left home with the children.

The relationship between daughter-in-law and mother-in-law was picked out by Yang as being one that was likely to experience particular tension in the face of a man's excessive drinking. She cited other work that has pointed to the sensitivity of that relationship in traditional Korean society, due to the hierarchical, patrilineal family arrangements: 'When a woman marries she enters into a position with status first as a daughter-in-law, second as mother and housewife, then as mother-in-law' (p. 144).

From a very different part of the world and cultural group was Eber's

(1995) anthropological work in a highland Mayan town in the Chiapas region in the south of Mexico. Although most anthropological studies have only touched on drinking or drug use, her intensive work, which involved interviews, participant observation and archival study over a period of several years, had women's relationship to alcohol and how they were handling their own and others' drinking problems as the central theme. Although women's descriptions of alcohol characterised it as a powerful healing agent and as having an important role to play in ritual, it was often seen as a principal cause of suffering and sorrow, as the following quotation from a mother illustrates:

> My son drinks too much. He drinks in the market, at the plantation, visiting, in the house. He drinks up about five to six thousand pesos of rum three times a week. He doesn't buy my clothes or my medicine. I tell him I don't want him spending his money on rum. But all he wants to do is drink. He doesn't eat. He just drinks rum. He gets crazy when he's drunk. He scolds me and tells me, 'Get out of here. I don't want you here.' Some times he says he's going to hit me. My daughter and I run to my married daughter's house. After he's asleep we come back quietly.
>
> (p. 52)

Of particular interest to us is what Eber had to say about the ability of native, indigenous women (Pedranas) naturally to stand back from their menfolk's excessive drinking without getting too much engaged in trying to control it or allowing their lives to be dominated by it. They did not, according to Eber, show 'enabling' behaviours, become 'codependent' or require self-help groups to enable them to 'detach' or 'let go', as would have been the case for Eber's compatriots in the USA. This Eber ascribed to the Pedranas' philosophy that not everything can be controlled; that one can never know how another person feels, nor how he or she will act, so it is useless to be preoccupied with others; and that the best way to live is to take care of one's own work and self and let others take care of theirs.

> Pedranas' approach to problems seems to militate against blaming themselves when things go wrong and being absorbed in their own pain or suffering. Unlike American [sic, meaning pertaining to the USA] women and Ladinas [i.e. non-indigenous, mestiza Mexicans], who often try to fix things, Pedranas generally accept what others do as the way things are, God's will, and often reserve judgment, waiting for the consequences of the person's actions. . . . The subsistence economy and relatively strict sexual division of labor in Pedrano households creates clear boundaries which seem to militate against enabling and co-dependency. . . . No Pedrana with whom I talked tried to protect a loved one's drinking. Even

if they tried, I doubt that family members could keep drunken behaviour secret.

(p. 136)

Eber recognised that women sometimes scolded problem drinking relatives, prayed to the saints to make relatives stop drinking or took on *cargos* (i.e. community responsibilities such as that of fiesta leader, shaman or midwife) to gain some independence and control, or might progressively take on family responsibilities which should be their husbands'. Even so, it was Eber's contention that women's lives were much less likely to become dominated by a relative's drinking than would be the case in the USA. With the added help of Catholic Action and, more recently, the indigenous Zapatista movement (Eber, 2001), women were able to externalise blame and to see the social and political origins of their sorrows.

> As one Catechist put it . . . 'The Padre [who had recommended acceptance of drinking] can't know how we think. He doesn't have a wife or children. He doesn't work the land. He can't know how campesinos like us live. He can't know how a woman suffers when her husband drinks too much and hits her and yells at her. The issue for us when we criticise rum is exploitation and injustice toward women. Everyone knows women and children who suffer from hunger, lack of clothing, or medicine because their husbands or fathers drink too much and don't handle their money right. Just down the road there's a woman who doesn't have any clothes and other things she needs because her husband drinks too much . . .'. Unlike American women who are often confused about their duties and responsibilities and are ready to blame themselves when things fall apart, Pedranas know who is to blame when they have problems – heavy drinkers (usually husbands, fathers, and stepfathers) and rum sellers.
>
> (Eber, 1995, pp. 227–235)

Men as partners of women with drinking problems

Just as the experiences of women whose partners drink excessively have been ignored in the past, and often continue to be so, the experiences of male partners have been, too. Indeed, even those who have used qualitative methods sensitive to the views of family members have sometimes not felt able to extend that sensitivity to male partners. For example, in Yang's (1997) South Korean research five of the 40 'alcoholics' were women, and Yang was able to interview a small handful of husbands. A small section of her thesis described their reaction, which Yang characterised negatively as one of anger, a cynical attitude and the use of physical force to control their wives.

The work of Ablon et al. (1982) is of special interest here because, unlike Yang and others, they focused specifically on families in which it was the wife-mother who was identified as having a drinking problem. What marks out Ablon et al.'s work, however, is the anthropological or ethnographic approach which they took, drawing inspiration not only from the systemic approach to alcohol problems and the family (e.g. Steinglass, 1982, and Chapter 1) but also classic studies including those by Lewis (e.g. 1961), who made intensive studies of a small number of Mexican families, carrying out long conversational interviews and life histories in order to capture the perspectives of different family members. Ablon et al. themselves studied eight families, making periodic visits lasting from 2 hours to whole days over a period of 6–22 months. Their research methods consisted of a mixture of naturalistic and participant observation and in-depth semi-directive and non-directive interviews.

In their 1982 chapter, they provided at some length their observations and conclusions regarding a single family, consisting of mother, father and three older teenage children, which was studied over a 22-month period. The mother's drinking was carried out totally at home, secretly and alone, often in her bedroom while the rest of the family got on with their own things elsewhere in the house. So secret had her drinking been in fact that it was not 'discovered' by the rest of the family for some time. When it did come out, her husband's father told him that he had known about the problem for 3 years and a neighbour said she had also known about it. So solitary was her drinking that each of the other members of the family stated that since the onset of her drinking problem not one of them had actually ever seen, or had any desire to see, her drinking. Because family mealtimes had often disintegrated into fighting and shouting, they had largely been abandoned, and the rest of the family mostly found things to do away from home in the evenings and at weekends. The husband had on several occasions slept outside in the caravan and once he spent the night at a friend's home.

One aspect of their description which struck us on reading their chapter is the difficulty that they had in maintaining a sympathetic understanding of the experiences and actions of the husband and children in that family. They say, for example, that the children 'never once in the 2-year research period referred to their mother as an "alcoholic", or to the condition as "alcoholism". It was referred to as her "deal" or "problem" or "screw-up"; it was not viewed as a health problem' (p. 219). Moreover, 'Carl and the children were still preoccupied more with the stigma-related aspects of alcoholism than with Molly's health. They never viewed her "problem" as an illness or disease' (p. 220). Later they say, 'In the span of one year, however, the family gradually made certain adaptive adjustments to the drinking – and for their own best interests, not Molly's' (p. 224).

Much more sympathetic to the position of husbands was a relatively small-scale study, by Estes and Baker (1982), from the USA. All 10 participants were men – 'spouses of alcoholic women'. These were mainly long-lasting marriages, the median duration of the marriage being more than 30 years.

A table listed the husbands' major overall concerns. These primarily revolved around their inability to stop their wives' drinking, and they made comments such as 'I hated to see someone I loved so much destroying herself'; 'I tried to correct her drinking and found I couldn't'; and 'I don't know whether to keep trying or to tell her to pack her bags and get!'

Husbands had found their roles in the family changing (e.g. they had to 'hold everything together by playing mother and provider at the same time'), they found their work affected (e.g. 'I'm not being a productive person on the job because my mind wanders and I'm not working at my absolute best. Right now my career is on temporary hold'), and they were worrying about the emotional and/or physical neglect to which they thought their children had been exposed as a result. Sex lives had been affected and communication between husband and wife had diminished. Because of poor communication, husbands had done such things as make unilateral decisions, delay discussions until the wife was sober, or establish alternative modes of communication such as writing notes or communicating via other people. All reported periods when they deliberately stopped talking to their wives. The most prevalent feeling identified by husbands was anger, followed by hopelessness, sadness, fear or pity. Eight of the husbands had resorted to avoiding their wives by escaping to activities such as hobbies or simply ignoring their wives' behaviour. The other two had become involved in taking care of their wives by trying to get them to sleep it off after drinking or to go to AA. Factors that had maintained the marriage despite the many problems included:

> the belief in the concept of marriage, professed love for the wife, concern for the wife's welfare, hope that things would improve, the financial burden of separate maintenance, the children, and inability to reach a satisfactory decision regarding separation or divorce.
>
> (p. 235)

Another more sympathetic portrayal of husbands was that of Corrigan (1980), who reported interviews with 20 husbands of women entering hospitals, clinics or AA. All of the husbands said that once they recognised their wives' drinking to be the problem they found it difficult to accept, with 15 saying that they disapproved and were openly critical of their wives. Three-quarters acknowledged that they considered separating. Much as others have asked why wives of men with drinking problems remain in their marriages, Corrigan asked why these husbands remained. Apart from the husbands never citing financial dependency as a reason, Corrigan found husbands most often referring to the needs of their children, 'willpower', or their continuing love for their wives. Corrigan suggested, 'Perhaps the reasons for persisting are similar, if not the same, for a man as for a women who is married to an alcoholic' (p. 102).

Family members of problem drug users

Although it is not formally presented as the results of a piece of research, the British booklet *Coping with a Nightmare: Family Feelings About Long-Term Drug Use*, by Dorn et al. (1987), is an important item to include in this review for a number of reasons. First, it is about the effects on family members of the problematic use of drugs other than alcohol: so much more has been written from a family perspective about excessive drinking. Second, it is a rare example of an extended presentation of the views of family members, making much use of the latter's own words. The tone of the work, in striking contrast to that of writings from the pathology perspective, is understanding of and sympathetic to the position of family members. Indeed, the following telling statement appears early on:

> This book is based on the experiences of ordinary people and allows them to speak for themselves. . . . The book was shown to a wide range of professional people before it was finalised, and some professionals were critical of what the family members in this book have to say . . . we have therefore allowed the parents' stories and points of view to stand without challenge from the professionals.
>
> (p. 31)

Interviews were carried out with family members, mostly, but not all, parents, and more often women than men, recruited through parents' groups and mainstream health, welfare, advice and drug agencies throughout England. The book describes the strong emotions that are aroused when a person first realises that a son, daughter or other relative has a drug problem, the feelings of guilt, loss, and sometimes of betrayal, and worries about such things as stealing, sex, drink and the possibility of death:

> Anger, angry that you can't do anything. My first response was anger that he was so weak to do it – horror, horror.
>
> (p. 9)

> What happens is this. A terrifying feeling of fear and a sort of desperate disappointment, you know, how can this happen – he was so lovely, my child, how can it have happened to my child?
>
> (p. 9)

There is acknowledgement, also, of the effects on a family member's mental health, and of the intense and mixed feelings that can be aroused:

> It doesn't matter what the relationship is, the people around somebody who really has a serious drug problem get terribly badly affected. You

know in my own experience I really think I am almost as ill as my daughter. You get dragged down with it, and it's such a baffling and bewildering thing to deal with.

(p. 18)

A number of quotations illustrated family members' search for an understanding of why the problem had arisen, and a chapter was devoted to ways that family members described having tried to cope and the dilemmas they found themselves in:

I had a timetable set up in their flat [daughter's and boyfriend's], and a duplicate timetable set up in my place – when they had to go to the doctor's, when they had to sign on for bail conditions with the police, when they had to go to the chemist to collect prescriptions etc, etc. I would be there, saying 'Come on and get your things, get in the car and I'll take you.' I was the one who carried all the emotional burden. I was doing all that for them.

(p. 37)

Family members testified to the difficulty of getting social support, but also sometimes to the very positive support they received:

You just haven't got anyone to talk to. You can't tell your friends, your family. I mean even now, there are none of our personal friends who know about Ann. You find they're just not sympathetic. . . . I know most of them would bend over backwards if they thought they could do something to help, but they don't know what to do, you know, no more than we know really. . . . I suddenly had to start having time off because we had to go to court, and I couldn't stay off and tell lies. So I went and told my boss, and he was absolutely marvellous, he was excellent.

(p. 23)

Finally, one family member well expressed the continuing uncertainty that family members can feel:

It'll be five years in November and I'm still wondering. I can't honestly say I know one hundred per cent she's off drugs because I don't, I really don't.

(p. 45)

Dorn et al. were struck by the fact that it was easier to recruit mothers and other female family partners to take part in interviews, and that men were apparently less interested or less willing, although in a few cases men were very much involved. One point of view about this, expressed by both mothers and fathers themselves, was that fathers simply found it even more difficult to express their feelings on the matter. Another view was that men found a sense of lack of control over the situation particularly difficult, as the following extract from a discussion among three fathers illustrates:

> See, as a man, when it comes to the crunch in the house, the man makes the decisions most of the time. Alright, he may be manipulated by the women in the home, but I mean the man is looked towards when it comes to the crunch. The man has to make the decisions ... now we come to a situation where a little bit of grey comes in, because you cannot deal with the problem you have in your own house because the very person that is creating the problem isn't listening because of his drug problem. . . . You're so right, Fred. The difficult thing for the man, to me, is really the fact that he is not able to cope with the problem but will not admit it to himself or anybody else.
>
> (pp. 10–11)

From the USA came a study of parents contacted through a private, community-based, adolescent, drug abuse[1] treatment centre (Barton, 1991). They were observed attending a weekly 'parents' survival group' over a period of several months, and a subsample of 10 parents recorded their experiences in a journal. Although some prescriptive, quasi-professional language creeps into Barton's report – for example, parents are said to pass through a stage of 'denial' before developing 'new and effective parenting behaviors' – there is much here that supports Dorn et al.'s (1987) picture. It includes the problems parents witnessed, including 'lying, truancy, failing grades, a complete breakdown of rules concerned with work around home and curfew, stealing from family members, running away, and verbal or physical abuse of the parents' (p. 41). There was evidence of coping dilemmas. For example, parents had to weigh up their desire to enforce rules for appropriate behaviour in and out of the home against a fear of the adolescent running away and being exposed to dangers such as street violence. In terms of their styles of adaptation to the new role of being the parent of a drug-abusing son or daughter, much the most common style among the parents in Barton's sample was one that she referred to as 'committed', perceiving that they had a responsibility for their child's drug use, and that they should be able to bring the problem under control. A minority position was the opposite one, termed 'letting go' by Barton. Whichever form of adaptation parents found, they often expressed finding a new meaning in life, learning more about life and having gained from the experience.

A particular interest of Barton's report was what parents had to say about the support they had received, or had not received, from a variety of quarters. Family, friends, coworkers and employers had for the most part been supportive, often to parents' surprise:

At first when we found out about our son [that he had a drug problem], I felt embarrassed, as if we had somehow failed and I didn't want to admit it. But when we did start to talk to people about it, we found out there are a lot more parents with the same problems. It made it a lot easier to discuss it and be more open about it.

(p. 42)

My boss was very understanding and never said too much. If I needed time off for going to court or whatever, he just wanted me to let him know.

(p. 42)

Neighbours and acquaintances had offered less sympathy and support:

Some individuals, I sense, quickly put a label on me as a 'bad' parent. The couple my daughter baby-sits for have adopted a distancing, as if it were a disease their children would catch.

(pp. 42–43)

It was from schools, police and the legal system, however, that parents met their greatest 'discrediting'. Schools were often seen as treating the parents as abusive or completely ignoring the parents' role in preventing further drug abuse, and parents found the law surprisingly reluctant to work with them in trying to gain control of their adolescent offspring's behaviour:

She had been skipping school, her grades were falling, and finally I was informed by the high school – the last week of the first quarter – that she was failing every subject.

(p. 43)

I found my daughter [who had run away from home for 6 weeks] without the help of the police. I tried to file runaway charges with two different police departments. They would not file charges and in fact threatened to file neglect charges on me. This upset me very much.

(p. 43)

Prior to the research to be reported in later chapters of the present book, one of the few pieces of relevant research was that reported by some of the present authors and colleagues, and which served as a preliminary study to the English arm of the research to be reported later (Orford et al., 1992; Velleman et al., 1993). It involved 50 family members, 40 concerned about a relative's illicit drug use (opiates, amphetamines or polydrug misuse) and 10 about a relative's dependence on tranquillisers. Twenty-eight were their relatives' partners (19 female, nine male), and 17 were parents (nine mothers, six fathers, and in two cases both mother and father were interviewed), with a sprinkling of sisters, brothers and a daughter.

Three themes predominated in family members' accounts. One, termed 'neglect and disruption', subsumed three subthemes: the unreliability of the drug-using relative as far as other members of the family were concerned (frequently missing from home when expected, being away for hours or days at a time without planning or warning, and disrupting family rituals such as birthdays or Christmas by being unreliably absent or intoxicated); the perceived failure of the relative to make what the family member considered to be an appropriate contribution to family functioning; and the negative and disruptive atmosphere caused by lying, deceit and stealing. A second theme was termed 'suspicions, worries and uncertainties'. Family members were worried about where the relative was, whether he or she was getting into further trouble, how other members of the family were being affected, and, among other things, what the family member had done wrong in the past and what he or she could now do to put things right. The third theme was referred to as 'altered feelings' toward the drug-using relative, those feelings almost invariably taking a highly ambivalent form. They included both negative characteristics attributed to the relative (e.g. jealousy, aggression, 'couldn't care less' attitude, stubbornness, demandingness, deviousness) and negative feelings toward the relative (e.g. a sense of hurt, reduction in affection, embarrassment, bitterness, being let down) and, on the other hand, the ascription of positive characteristics to the relative (e.g. gentleness, consideration, caring, sensitivity) and a feeling of having learnt things in the process, or feeling more meaning in life (Velleman et al., 1993).

The ways these 50 family members had attempted to cope were described in detail. They included ways of coping that were angry or withdrawing (covering emotional, inactive and avoiding ways), kind, non-confrontational (including being tolerant and supportive of the relative), being firm toward the relative (including controlling and confrontational ways) and self-protective (including being independent). The complex dilemmas family members faced emerged in a number of ways. One such was the recounting of ways of coping that could not easily be characterised and about which family members themselves felt very uncertain. Just one illustration was that of a woman who described following her drug-using partner even if he disappeared in the middle of the night to look for drugs. She would phone him from work and even take time off work when she was worried, believing that if she spent all day with him he might not go out to obtain drugs. Family members were often aware that there were thin dividing lines between being overtolerant, too controlling and providing support for the relative. The problematic nature of how to respond to a relative's excessive drug use was also brought out by the contrasts that family members often drew between present and former ways of coping. Like the family members included in Dorn et al.'s (1987) report, members of this sample of 50 family members often referred to having learnt how to cope in a different way by, for example, learning to be less emotional, more independent or firmer (Orford et al., 1992).

The issue of social support for family members was also touched on in that piece of research. Most described having had some form of support available to them, some informal, some formal, and a minority in the form of self-help groups. Many, however, were dissatisfied with the support they received, especially with that received from formal agencies such as general practitioners (GPs), social workers, community psychiatric nurses or a community drugs team (Velleman et al., 1993).

A comparatively small-scale study by Raine (1994), from England, will also be included here because it is the only study that we have found, other than the research reported in this book, which included in the same study family members of relatives with alcohol problems and those with problems relating to their use of illicit drugs. It involved eight interviews with women, all concerned about the drinking or drug use of a male relative – partner, father or son (two of the mothers were joined by their husbands for the interviews). The main theme that Raine focused on was the problem of social stigma experienced by family members, the difficulty of discussing the problem with outsiders, leaving family members with a pressing need to have someone to talk to about the problem and to be provided with good information. Not all families were cut off from support. Raine referred to some having a group of supportive friends, and one family who reported that their neighbours were 'smashing' in dealing with their son's solvent abuse. That was in a neighbourhood where glue-sniffing was common and there was a feeling among residents that they were united against it.

Because so little has been written about the experience of family members when a relative has a problem with illicit drugs, and because what has been written is so often unsympathetic to family members, even a short, single-case description is valuable. One such was written by Blank (1987), a project worker/charge nurse in a drug misuse service in England, regarding his contact with 'Hannah's' father and mother. They were described as 'shocked, upset and ashamed of Hannah's addiction . . . astounded that their daughter . . . could have sunk to the "depraved depths" of heroin use'. Her parents, 'as so many understandably do', resorted to efforts to control Hannah; for example, they escorted her outside the home and strictly timetabled her day. Hannah found this unbearable and perceived her parents as being accusatory and of wreaking vengeance on her for disappointing and shaming them. In meetings with Hannah and her parents, both Hannah's feelings of being constrained by the watchfulness of her parents, and her parents' desperate worry that, if given more space, Hannah would return to drugs, were discussed and a compromise reached. The sympathetic understanding shown toward the parents' feelings, as well as those of Hannah, comes through strongly in Blank's (1987) short article:

we should not forget that her parents must have felt utterly devastated as their worse, most lurid media-induced nightmares were realised . . . Hannah's family were not 'sick', or dysfunctional. They were confronting a situation beyond their wildest imaginings, a situation which all their previous experience could not have equipped them to deal with. Our work with them merely gave them the chance to begin to cope with, and explore, the problems exposed by Hannah's addiction in a 'safe' environment. . . . Hannah's family are not atypical. What has changed for them and for so many other families is the increasing complexity of our society and the problems it produces. Most families muddle through. . . . We did not 'cure' or 'treat' Hannah's family; all we did was give them the opportunity and the information with which to help themselves.

(pp. 61–62)

Concluding comment

Put against the number of family members who are faced with having to cope with problem drinking or drug use in a close relative, believed to be in the tens of millions worldwide, the amount of research that we have been able to draw upon in this chapter is regrettably small. Some studies offer great insights into the experience of family members and suggest exciting leads for research. Jackson's (1954) pioneering research on adjustments made by 'wives of alcoholics', and Wiseman's (1991) focus on, among other things, wives' 'home treatment' methods and their difficulties in getting social support, are classics in the field. Their studies are complemented by Asher's (1992) greater focus on the need for mental adjustment, particularly in coping with ambivalence.

Nearly all of that work focused on wives in the USA concerned about their husbands' excessive drinking. There has been very little work focusing on husbands concerned about their wives' excessive drinking, although there are some suggestions from what little research there has been that the experiences of husbands may be quite similar (Corrigan, 1980; Estes and Baker, 1982). There has been comparatively little research on the experiences of family members in coping with forms of excessive drug use other than excessive drinking. What research there has been again suggests similarities, and extends this line of work to parents, including fathers (e.g. Dorn et al., 1987; Barton, 1991; Velleman et al., 1993). Particularly exciting, and relevant to the present work, is work from cultures distinct from that of the USA (e.g. Eber, 1995; Yang, 1997) or, as in the rare case of Wiseman's (1991) work, studies that have taken a comparative cultural approach. Those studies suggest that, while there may be many similarities across cultures in the experiences of family members and the ways they cope, there may also be striking differences. That work will help us later when we come to develop a more detailed view incorporating the socio-cultural setting (Chapter 9).

Chapter 3

The three study locations

Mexico City, South-West England
and indigenous Northern
Territory, Australia

The programme of research which will be reported in later chapters was originally conceived of in 1989 in conjunction with the Substance Abuse Programme in the Mental Health Division of the World Health Organisation (WHO), during a sabbatical leave spent by the first author at WHO, Geneva (Orford, 1990; Grant, 1992). It was based on earlier work carried out in England with the stress-coping model, studying the ways of coping used by wives of men with drinking problems (Orford et al., 1976). That work had been quantitative, based on the results of questionnaires, whereas the new programme of research was designed to combine qualitative and quantitative methods.

The new work was carried out during the 1990s and involved three separate socio-cultural groups, each from a different country. Mexico City was chosen as one of the first locations for the research because of the presence there of a WHO collaborating centre, the National Institute of Psychiatry, with a record of research in the area of alcohol and drug problems. It was also selected because of its contrast with the UK. The requirements, in order to provide that contrast, were simply that the location be outside Europe, not be in one of the rich, 'Western' countries, and should be non-English speaking. Mexico fulfilled those requirements. The Institute of Psychiatry had a track record of relevant research that had led to a body of knowledge about population alcohol and drug consumption (e.g. Medina-Mora, 1988). The Social and Epidemiological Research Division of the Institute had been one of the groups that had taken part in the WHO-sponsored Community Responses to Alcohol Problems Project (WHO, 1984). Its work included research specifically on alcohol problems and the family (Natera and Holmila, 1990).

A feasibility study was carried out in Mexico City in 1989 involving 10 family members from 10 separate families (Orford et al., 1990). In each case, the family member was concerned about the problem drinking or drug taking of a household relative. Family members were recruited via specialist alcohol and drug problem treatment agencies or primary care settings, in one or other of two geographical areas: an area of multiple-occupancy, traditional housing in the very centre of the city, much of which had been destroyed in the major earthquake of 1985, and two semi-rural communities in an area on the edge of the city. As a result of the feasibility study, there existed equivalent research materials in Spanish and English and a plan for the main study in Mexico City, which was carried out by the Institute of Psychiatry with the support of the Consejo Nacional de Cicencia y Tecnología (CONACyT) and the British Council.

The second location for the study was South-West England. Because the earlier English work had used questionnaires and had been confined to a study of wives of men with drinking problems, the preliminary qualitative study already referred to in Chapter 2 was conducted. It was carried out by a collaborating group (the Alcohol, Drugs and the Family (ADF) Group) based in a number of universities and National Health Service alcohol and drug treatment agencies in a number of towns in South-West England, particularly Exeter, Bath and Bournemouth. A total of 50 family members of relatives with drug problems were interviewed, using the English version of the interview guide used in Mexico City. Three reports based on the findings from that study have been published (Orford et al., 1992; Velleman et al., 1993; Miller et al., 1997). One outcome of that study was a successful application to the Mental Health Foundation (UK), which made a grant to the University of Exeter to carry out the main study.

The larger component of the main studies in Mexico City and South-West England was a long, open-ended interview, which resulted in data that were analysed qualitatively. The present book focuses exclusively on that kind of analysis, and the methods are described in more detail in Chapter 4. Also included in the main studies in those two locations was a set of three standard questionnaires for the assessment of perceived family environment (the Family Environment Scale (FES): Moos and Moos, 1981), ways of coping with a relative's drinking or drug problem (the Coping Questionnaire (CQ): Orford et al., 1975), and physical and psychological symptoms (the Symptom Rating Test (SRT): Kellner and Sheffield, 1973). Those quantitative data have been analysed and results reported elsewhere (Orford et al., 1998a,b,c; Orford et al., 2001; Copello, 2002).

The third study location was the Northern Territory (NT), Australia, where the participants were indigenous (or Aboriginal) Australians. In December 1991, one of us (JO) gave an invited presentation at the Window of Opportunity: The First National Congress – An Intersectoral Approach to Drug Related Problems in our Society, which was held in Adelaide, South Australia. The presentation outlined the stress-strain-coping-support approach to alcohol, drugs and the family that was being adopted in the programme of research being conducted in England and Mexico. The then Director of the Alcohol Policy Unit of the Northern Territory of Australia was present and suggested a collaboration. After a visit to the Northern Territory in 1995 by another member of the English research team (RV), the

Living with Alcohol (LWA)[1] Program agreed to an interview study of indigenous people living in the Northern Territory who were affected by the excessive drinking of family members. This fitted both with the aims of the Aboriginal Living with Alcohol Program, an important component of the total programme, and with our overall interest in understanding how families coped with alcohol problems worldwide. It was hoped that the study would obtain important information that could be used to good effect in the treatment and prevention of alcohol problems among indigenous people in the Northern Territory, and contribute to a global understanding of excessive drinking in the family by providing data from an indigenous group that would complement the information from people living in one of the largest cities in the new world (Mexico City) and in small towns and villages in a Western European region (South-West England).

Before we describe the details of the research methods in Chapter 4, the remainder of this chapter sets the broader scene by providing a description and some basic background information about the three study areas. The three areas will be considered in the order in which they joined the project, starting with Mexico City.

Mexico City

Mexico covers two million sq. km. in surface area, making it the third largest of the 22 countries that make up Latin America. Like the majority of those countries, Mexico at the time of the research was experiencing profound economic changes in its search for a form of development that would enable the country to overcome the inequalities experienced by its population of over 90 million, of whom 70% were estimated to be living in poverty, and nearly half of those in extreme poverty. It was estimated that in the early 1990s social security reached only 53% of the population (INEGI, 1996). Mexico is a country categorised as being at an intermediate level of human development, occupying the 51st position among the 162 countries that belong to the United Nations. That should be seen in the context of a continual process of changes in most aspects of Mexican society, including all aspects of health, the labour market, politics, increased migration from the country to the city and continual journeys of emigration to the USA (some remaining there, and others coming and going). In demographic terms, a decline in infant mortality plus a continuing high rate of childbirth were having a marked effect on the population age structure. Mexico is a country of young people. A third of the population were aged less than 15 years, 60% were in the active work years of 16–64, and only 6% were aged 65 years or over (INEGI, 1995).

Change was also in the wind politically during the period of the research. The country was still governed by the same political party (*Partido Revolucionario Institucional* (PRI)) that had been in power for more than 70 years since the Mexican Revolution. Although it would be another few years before the presidency would be occupied by a candidate of another party, a desire on the part of Mexican citizens was already apparent for greater democracy and an end to what was seen as government corruption.

Mexico is a heterogeneous country. Three-quarters of the population by the 1990s lived in urban areas, the remaining rural and indigenous population being widely spread throughout the length and breadth of the republic. The large majority of the country's population are mestizo, of mixed indigenous and Spanish ancestry, and Mexican Spanish (differing from Castilian or peninsula Spanish only in certain lexical and grammatical details) is the principal language. In 1995, there were about five and a half million people who spoke an indigenous language. Although that figure is high, the indigenous population has remained marginal in modern Mexican society.

The predominant religion is Roman Catholicism (over 80% of the population, although Protestant groups are continuing to increase in numbers), and religion and the Church play important roles in situations of conflict, such as periods of unemployment, times of crisis, or when relatives are in prison or families need to cope with the excessive consumption of alcohol or drugs. Under such circumstances, the Church is approached as an institution that can provide moral support and also resources that may provide a route to solving or improving the problem. On the other hand, Catholic festivals, which generally represent a syncretism of pre-Hispanic, colonial and modern customs, are always linked to the consumption of alcohol.

The population of Mexico lives in approximately 20 million households (INEGI, 1996). It has a strong cultural tradition of the family home as the place where Mexicans obtain their main sense of identity, expressed in the phrase, the family is 'the soul of Mexico'. For Alfonso Reyes, who coined the phrase, this soul was 'formed out of devotion, tolerance and vocation' (Fuentes, 2000). The family in Mexico, according to Fuentes, has become a socially understood 'great idea' or vision; it is a niche that allows its members to protect themselves against the violence and indifference that have become omnipresent. The family provides solidarity. The psychologist Díaz Guerrero (1994) has stated that the individual in Mexico is nobody if he or she has no family. By the late twentieth century, however, globalisation and the free market were contributing to a loss of traditions. A good example is the tradition of different generations of an extended family coming together regularly to eat, a custom which, among other things, served the function of pooling resources and assisting mutual survival, but which is no longer the rule.

Mexico City is the second most populated metropolitan area in the world, with all the urban problems that brings with it. It is a 'megacity'. Its population growth since the 1950s has been dramatic, rising from around nine million inhabitants in 1970 to around 20 million in 1990. The lack of strict regulation of the city's growth has encouraged a huge quantity of land settlements (*asentamientos*) on the edge of the city, often referred to as the 'urban sprawl' (*mancha urbana*), literally the urban blot or stain, responsible for socio-spatial disparities within the city.

The creation of 'popular', marginalised neighbourhoods (*colonias populares*[2]) on common land has promoted the creation of belts of poverty around the city, which have brought with them problems of land usage, accommodation, nutrition, reproductive and general health, distribution of services and forms of organisation. There has been an increase in unemployment and poverty and a number of socio-cultural consequences, including a weakening of a sense of common identity, a loss of expectations of the likelihood of social progress or mobility, uncertainty about the future, and a large increase in the informal economy and in rates of violence and delinquency (García Canclini, 1996). All of this has meant a change in family rituals and practices, including increased signs of vigilance in the face of insecurity, such as the putting up of barriers that protect both physically and symbolically. Small or collective households among the 'popular' or marginal classes have meant that children and young people make their lives of play and socialising outside the home in the street. All these factors constitute risks that favour a greater consumption of drugs and alcohol.

The country's capital, the federal district of Mexico City (Mexico DF (*el Distrito Federal*)), contained in the mid-1990s a total of just over two million households, a number that had tripled since 1970. Of those households, 68% consisted of nuclear families comprising a head of the family, a partner and children, and approximately a quarter were considered to be extended family households including other relatives (INEGI, 1996). In a quarter of all families in Mexico DF, the headship of the family fell upon the woman, although women's salaries continued to be inferior to those of men, even in domestic service.

Many households in the capital city are estimated to be overcrowded by the criterion of an average of more than two occupants per bedroom. Nearly 60% of families owned their own homes, although not all could count on receiving all basic services. For example, 2% of households were without either running water or drainage. Twenty-three per cent of homes had asbestos, board or metal roofs. In the 'popular' neighbourhoods, the percentage of private homes with separate bedrooms was only 43%, and 9% shared a kitchen. It was common for several families to live in one *terreno* with private bedroom but shared kitchen and bathroom. It was possible to find apartments measuring as little as 60 m^2 in which might be living 10 people from three different families. That way of living obviously constrains the possibilities that can exist within a family for reciprocity, solidarity and resolving family problems. On the one hand, it allows tasks of cooking and childcare to be delegated to a particular member of the family, generally a mother, a grandmother or a non-working sister. But, on the other hand, it encourages family conflict. The woman in these conditions fulfils the role of the family head, with responsibility for maintaining family cohesion, allowing her to exercise control while at the same time displaying apparent submission. The father is seen as the feared authority figure since, unlike the mother, he would view the family as his property. It is thought by some that the description *macho* has become so attached to the Mexican man for the very reason that the latter's honour is centred in this sense of ancestral proprietorship.

Much has been written about the machismo of the Mexican man. Its main characteristics have been said to be authoritarianism, domination, aggression, jealousy, irresponsibility, promiscuity, violence and excessive drinking. On the other hand, 'positive characteristics of machismo' have been described, including forcefulness of personality, strength of will and self-assertiveness, as well as more emotional aspects such as affection, caring and protectiveness toward women and children, providing for the family, and strength in situations of adversity (De la Cancela, 1991; Mayo, 1993; Torres, 1998). Others have written of a 'neo-machismo' which fosters respect for women in accordance with current conceptions of human rights, but which continues to support many traditional gender role patterns in the family (Leñero, 1992).

Although there is much heterogeneity in the position of women in Mexico, and rapid social change was and is occurring in many social groups, much has also been written about gender inequality and the subordinate role of women in Mexico. Even when engaged in the job market, the role of the woman in the family continued to be that of principal carer, a role carrying high social prestige in Mexico, supported by official statements from the government health department. One observer of the role of women in Mexico put it thus: 'They are not only mothers of their children, but also mothers to their husbands, fathers, bosses, colleagues, patients' (Lara and Salgado, 1994). It has been said that a mother's role in Mexico encourages unreachable expectations, and is associated with an excessive degree of abnegation, devotion, self-denial, generosity and altruism. Women wear themselves out trying to fulfil everyone's desires. Although women make most of the family decisions, they describe themselves as dependent, insecure and passive. That position encourages the uncomplaining endurance of hardship, including putting up with men's excessive drinking, and even the cultural acceptance of alcohol-related domestic violence (Medina-Mora, 1994).

The mother is the one who knows about undesirable situations, such as a son's use of drugs or an unmarried daughter's pregnancy, and keeps them secret, albeit at the cost of increased stress to herself. This role of concealer and protector often extends to keeping secrets from daughters-in-law and sons-in-law, and it is very common that a divorced son or daughter returns to live with the family of origin. A wish to be free of the parental home despite being unmarried is a tradition principally of the middle classes. The ever increasing involvement of women in salaried employment, however, has permitted many women to negotiate their roles in the family, not only as a protector, and this has brought about new forms of family relations that remain to be properly studied.

Some 10–20% of the Mexican population do not have access to public health services. One source of support for that group has been the existence of traditional medicine, the practice of which combines ritual, myth and magic with strong elements of pre-Hispanic colonial and modern medicine, traditional midwifery and elements of the Roman Catholic religion. The main therapeutic specialities include midwives, herbalists, bone therapists, folk healers and shamans. Currently, no one has official permission to exercise traditional medicine, with the exception of homeopathic medicine, but traditional forms of medicine have been well accepted by the population, and there is a growth in the incorporation of traditional medicine into the formal system of health care. Traditional medicine is very widespread in both rural and urban areas, and is particularly oriented toward illnesses 'that the doctors can't treat', which are often thought to include addictions, particularly addiction to alcohol. The same explanation could be applied to the Catholic Church's institution of the 'jura', which involves making a written pledge to the Virgin or another saint, particularly in the presence of a priest, not to drink or to consume some drug for a particular period of time. Another remedy is to drink water that has been blessed. Generally, it is a wife or mother who goes to the church in search of such a remedy, and the water is given to the alcohol or drug user without the latter being aware of what is being consumed. Long queues form to obtain these 'waters', especially on the day of the particular saint worshipped by the family in question (Natera et al., 2002).

Drinking and drug taking

The treatment and prevention of addictions is a priority area for the Mexican government. Through the Department of Health standards are being laid down in this area, and the National Council against the Addictions (*Consejo Nacional contra las Adiciones*) has the task of directing the coordination of those plans throughout the country. Prevention is an integral part of these plans, particularly prevention through the schools, from early primary level onwards.

The social response also includes the creation of treatment agencies. By the mid-1990s there were 75 Youth Integration Centres (Centros de Integración Juvenil) offering drug rehabilitation services nationwide. The Treatment Centre for Alcoholics and their Relatives (Centro de Ayuda al Alcohólico y sus Familiares, CAAF), located in the heart of Mexico City, assists members of the low-income population with drinking problems. Private clinics and Alcoholics Anonymous groups (up to 13 500 groups spread all over the country[3]) are also important resources.

The principal problem in Mexico in the field of the addictions is the consumption of alcohol, which is ingrained in the culture as part of the lifestyle of the male Mexican. From pre-Hispanic times, continuing during the colonial period and in the modern era, alcohol consumption habits have continued to be reinforced throughout all sections of society.

One of the most traditional drinks is pulque, fermented from the maguey cactus, and produced in the region for thousands of years. Pulque has a close link with religious ritual. During drinking sprees in pre-Hispanic Mexico, everyone drank pulque – men, women, children, older people and youths – following strict regulations. After the Spanish conquest, those regulations disappeared and pulque lost its ritual importance. In recent times, pulque, like other regional drinks (often referred to as *aguardientes*), was mainly consumed by the rural population lacking a basic supply of safe drinking water, principally in the centre of the country. Distilled beverages and wine were introduced by the Spanish and constituted one of the most prosperous sectors of the economy of New Spain (Mexico). Since the beginning of the twentieth century, beer has become a national drink; by the end of the century, it was the alcoholic drink of highest consumption.

In 1993, the prevalence of alcohol dependence was estimated to be as high as 9.4% (Secretaría de Salud (SSA), 1994) and the harmful consequences are considerable, particularly illnesses, such as cirrhosis, and accidents and violence, each of which is among the top 10 causes of death nationally (SSA, 1997). Misuse of alcohol contributes 9% of the total burden of illness in Mexico, with mortality from liver cirrhosis, associated with alcohol consumption, making the largest single contribution to loss of healthy years of adult life (FUNSALUD, 1994).

Annual per capita consumption of alcohol – the equivalent of approximately 5.5 litres of absolute alcohol for adults of 16 years of age or older (Rosovsky, 2001) – is considerably lower than in countries such as the USA and Canada. On the other hand, it has been estimated that the amount of alcohol produced illegally, including home-produced beverages, and which is therefore uncounted in official figures, is the equivalent of more than 60% of officially recorded production (Consultores Internacionales, 1999). The very serious consequences of alcohol consumption may in part be due to the way in which consumption is distributed in the population. Many Mexicans report to surveys that they are abstainers. That has been particularly the case for women and youth, although it is now believed that they are rapidly becoming alcohol consumers in larger numbers (Medina-Mora, 2001).

Among traditional cultural norms surrounding the consumption of alcohol is the expectation that a man will generally not drink with his wife, even though he might drink at home, and his wife might be expected to serve the drink, attend to his friends, and put up with the consequences. The norm has been that a woman should not drink, while a man is expected to do so. Surveys have suggested that the Mexican way of drinking is of an 'explosive' form, drinking usually being for the purpose of getting drunk. Generally, such drinking is done at the weekends, one frequent consequence being a loss of work on Mondays, the latter being popularly referred to as *san lunes* (Saint

Monday). Qualitative studies have served to support that picture, with replies such as, *'beber bien, si no, no sabe'*, which means, 'when you drink, you should drink enough to get drunk' (literally, 'drink up; otherwise you won't get the taste'). Among the 29% of urban dwelling women nationally whom it has been estimated have been subject to physical violence by their partners, alcohol is thought to have been a factor for 60% (SSA, 1999). For women, having a husband who regularly gets drunk is something quite undesirable but also something that has to be tolerated (Natera and Orozco, 1981), although it might be said that the situation is changing, principally under the influence of feminist movements.

The consumption of drugs also dates from pre-Hispanic times, when it had ritual significance and had the twin purposes, as in indigenous communities to this day, of placating the gods in the context of a cosmology that was very particular to the culture, and of achieving an altered state of consciousness.

In the middle years of the twentieth century, drugs were consumed only in certain, mainly artistic and military, circles. By the end of the century, illicit drug taking had become a greater public health issue, although, compared to the USA, it has been estimated that for every nine US citizens there was only one Mexican who had consumed some illicit drug in the last 12 months (SSA, 1994). In the 1993 national urban survey (SSA, 1994), the prevalence of illegal drug use at least once in a lifetime by persons aged 12–65 years was 3.9%. Male prevalence exceeded female by 13 to one. Changes had been observed over the previous 10 years. There had been a slight increase in the consumption of marijuana, the most commonly consumed drug (5.5% among the urban population of 16 years or older). Solvents, previously the second placed drug in terms of prevalence of use, had been overtaken by cocaine, the use of which had increased rapidly, particularly in lower socio-economic status groups. Heroin had not yet become a popular drug in Mexico, although there were signs of an epidemic outbreak of heroin use in the north of the republic, and the beginnings of greater consumption of heroin elsewhere in Mexico. There were also signs of the beginnings of use of crack and other 'designer' substances such as the metamphetamines. New medications, such as Refractyl and Rohypnol[4], as well as tranquillisers and sedatives, were being used for their psychoactive effects. The prevalence of heroin use in Mexico was found to be less than 0.1%, equivalent to 30 000 persons (SSA, 1994).

The low rates of drug consumption in comparison with some other countries may be partly attributed to the control Mexican parents exercise over their offspring until a comparatively advanced age. Increases in drug consumption can be anticipated, however, as those family patterns change under the influence of both globalisation and the free market, which are diluting traditional values, and movement back and forth between Mexico and the USA, resulting in exposure to cultural models other than traditional ones. It has already been noted that the age of initiation into drug use has been falling (ENA, 1998). A further factor is the increasing availability of drugs in Mexico, which is probably partly due to the dispersal of drugs within the country that were en route to the USA but were stopped by strict frontier controls.

South-West England

Despite its appearance as a settled, unchanging society, the UK had also been experiencing change at the time the research took place there. The changes that took place in the social and economic lives of Britons in the second half of the twentieth century have been documented in many government and other reports (e.g. *Health Inequalities*, published by the Office for National Statistics in 1997, which relates to England and Wales). For a start, a number of demographic changes occurred between the 1950s and 1990s, including increased longevity, delayed pregnancy and falling fertility, and the resulting ageing of the population. There was an overall rise in the population, an increase in divorce and in one-person households, and an increased diversity in the ethnic composition of the population. Of particular relevance to the work reported here was the change in household composition. In 1961, households consisting of a married couple with children constituted 48% of all households, a figure that had declined to 33% by 1991. At the same time, households consisting of a lone parent with children had risen from 6% to 10%, and one-person households had more than doubled from 11% to 27%. In a purely demographic sense, with more people living alone or in smaller units, the country might therefore be said to have become more individualistic.

Although the UK is not the richest country in the world, it was already comfortably off in the years immediately after the Second World War, and by the 1990s had become by any standards a rich country. Between 1951 and 1995, the gross domestic product (GDP) grew at an average of 2.4% a year, and average real household disposable income (removing taxes and the effects of inflation) rose by 72% between 1961 and 1994. There can be no doubting the enormous social change and increase in general prosperity that were evident in the 1990s compared to 50 years earlier: 'England is changed utterly from the place it was . . . austerity is a distant memory' (Adonis and Pollard, 1998). The overall trend of increasing British prosperity masks, however, a picture of changing employment patterns and increasing inequality. For one thing, there has been a shift in the economy of the country away from manufacturing toward service industries. By the early 1990s, only 26% of employed men were in manufacturing, although that sector remained the largest for men. It was no longer so for women, of whom 36% were now employed in the public administration, education and health sectors. The years immediately after the Second World War were ones of virtually full employment, but unemployment rose markedly from around the mid-1970s, reaching a peak of around 12% in the early 1980s, and falling somewhat and fluctuating since then. The experience of unemployment, almost unknown two or three decades earlier, had become a common experience for families and individuals by the 1980s and 1990s. At the same time, the participation of women in the labour force had increased, including by the mid-1990s just over half of those whose youngest child was not yet at school. Part-time working had become more common for both sexes, but was much more likely for women (45% compared to 8% for men). On the other hand, many people were working very long hours, 30% of men working 49 or more hours a week, for example.

While average disposable household income had increased considerably, the gap between those with high and low incomes had also increased. A threefold difference between the 10th and 90th decile points in 1961 had increased to over fourfold in 1990. In 1961, around one in 10 households was living on incomes of half the average national income or less, a proportion that had risen to one in five by 1990. In real terms, the gap between the earnings of the highest- and lowest-earning men had more than doubled between 1971 and 1995, and the same was true for women's earnings.

Between the 1950s and 1990s, there continued to be major improvements in housing standards in Britain. For example, in 1951, 38% of households lacked a fixed bath or shower, and 8% had neither an internal nor external flush toilet. By 1991, both proportions had fallen to well below 0.5%. On the basis of number of bedrooms in a household compared to a calculation of bedroom requirement, the proportion of households judged to be over-crowded fell from 7% in 1972 to 3% in 1994. Nevertheless, there were still reckoned to be 7% of dwellings below standard in 1991, and there had also been a marked change in the pattern of new house building. The building of affordable housing by local authorities, which constituted the largest sector in the 1950s, had almost ceased by the early 1990s. Private sector building, by then much the largest sector, had not compensated for that loss. It has been of concern in Britain that homelessness should continue to exist in the midst of general affluence. Between 1980 and 1990, for example, the number of households accepted as homeless more than doubled, from 60 000 to over 150 000. By the 1990s, street begging, rarely seen in Britain in the 1950s or 1960s had become an expected feature of town and city life.

Much has been written about the supposed national character of the British. More accurately, we should refer to the character of the English, since the Scots, Welsh and Irish have their own distinctive cultures. Jeremy Paxman, a prominent British television journalist, wrote a semi-serious but very pertinent account, *The English: A Portrait of a People* (1998). He discussed a number of characteristics that the English are famous for, or which the English like to ascribe to themselves. One is a bullish individualism, a cherishing of freedom, and a love of independence and liberty. The English are proud of that part of their history that involved standing up to the authority of Church and monarchy, and are sceptical of authority in any form, including that of the state. They prefer a head of state that is symbolic but powerless, on the whole preferring their Queen to other countries' presidents. Being situated in a smallish group of islands physically separated from other countries by sea (the defence of which figures large in British history) is often thought to have a lot to do with the English love of independence. The English are not averse to having a good fight to protect their rights, either in war, after a sporting event, or after a few drinks in the pub.

Perhaps reflecting their love of privacy, the English have always been suspicious of flats, aspiring nearly always to own a proper house with a garden. From the boom of the 1870s and 1880s onwards, there have been waves of house building, with the result that much of the population of England lives in a rather anonymous ('inelegant' and 'hideous' are words Paxman uses) suburban sprawl around cities and towns and on the edge of villages, such that the majority of people live in places that cannot really be described as either urban or rural. Loss of rural village facilities such as schools and post offices has caused much concern, while edge-of-town facilities, such as supermarket and cinema complexes, have flourished in recent years.

When it comes to relations between the sexes, it is true to say that twentieth-century England inherited a legacy of 'patriarchalism' left over from the Victorian period. For example, it had not been until the first Married Women's Property Act of 1870 that Parliament recognised the right of married women to control their own finances. But Paxman may be right when he stated that in the England of the late twentieth century, altered by two World Wars and the loss of empire, women had gone a long way in achieving parity with men in private and public life. At the same time, he acknowledged that there was still a long way to go. Dobash and Dobash (1987), for example, writing about domestic violence against wives in Britain toward the end of the twentieth century, attributed the existence of such violence on a large scale to the persistence of patriarchy:

> We cannot over-stress the importance of the position and status of wives in the patterning of violence, and the importance of the man's sense of domination that accompanies marriage, as the most significant factors in wife-beating. . . . An important aspect of the patriarchal form of author-ity is a moral order emphasising obedience and loyalty of inferiors. Women are bound to the home not merely by domestic labour and child care, but also by a strong sense of moral responsibility for such tasks.
>
> (p. 178)

Modern Britain also inherited a notorious class system and a reputation for snobbery. It has been said of the English class system, however, that it has always allowed the opportunity for people to move between classes. Some are of the opinion that British society now provides so much such opportunity that Britain is now 'classless'. Adonis and Pollard (1998) certainly believed the idea of a classless modern Britain to be a myth. They pointed to the way in which income inequality grew faster in the UK in the decade of the 1980s than in any other developed country apart from New Zealand, and to the perpetuation of wealth, with the richest tenth still holding nearly half of all individual wealth in the early 1990s. Class distinction was, they believed, being perpetuated and even exaggerated in modern Britain as a result of two tendencies: the creation of a 'super class' of highly paid private professionals and managers at the top end of the class hierarchy, and, at the bottom, the creation of a socially excluded 'underclass' of citizens who were effectively cut off from opportunities for advancement. They pointed particularly at the education system – 'the most class-segregated education system in the western world' (p. 33). Despite full-time education to the age of 16 having been compulsory in Britain since 1972, and despite greatly increased proportions of young people remaining in education at 16–19 years of age and during the university years, there has been public concern about continuing large numbers of 16-year-olds leaving school without any formal qualifications, among whom the subsequent unemployment rate is particularly high.

Although the health and social welfare systems were under great financial pressures by the 1990s, residents in Britain in the second half of the twentieth century have been fortunate to have a socialised National Health Service (NHS) that provides free primary care medical services (all are registered with their own local general medical practitioner) and free hospital and other specialist care. In addition, although entitlements were being somewhat eroded by the 1980s and 1990s, residents also enjoyed the benefits of a comprehensive social welfare system, including an allowance for mothers with children, unemployment benefit, housing, school meal and other benefits for those on low incomes, disability benefits and a state pension. It might also be said that Britons, compared to residents of many other countries, enjoy a trustworthy police force. Many young people have experience of being stopped by the police in a way that is considered harsh and unnecessary, and that particularly goes for young Black Britons. Nevertheless, the popular image of a British policeman as a friendly 'bobby on the beat' dies hard, and Paxman was of the opinion, rightly or wrongly, that still 'most of English society is not frightened by the police' (p. 254).

The English arm of the present research was carried out in South-West England, which is a large, tapering peninsula jutting into the Atlantic Ocean. Unlike the heavily populated South-East of England, it has a number of upland areas, a long, often rugged coastline and many sandy beaches and coves. Warmed by the Gulf Stream, it enjoys comparatively mild winters. It has been a popular destination for tourists since Victorian times. People brought up in many parts of the South-West speak with a country accent, which is sometimes the butt of jokes by the English from other areas.

But nowhere in England is very far from anywhere else, and road and rail connections are good. Of the three centres for the research, Bournemouth and Bath are one to two hours' distance from London by car or train, and Exeter is less than three hours. Apart from those three centres, each a medium-sized university town, the region includes two larger cities (Bristol, population 500 000; Plymouth, population 300 000), many other small to medium-sized towns, and numerous small villages. Local cultures vary from the highly urban to the very rural.

Much of the South-West can be described as being made up of mixed urban-rural areas, a number of resort and retirement areas, some remoter, largely rural areas, and a small number of cities. Unlike the formerly more industrial north of England, the South-West contains fewer districts listed as the most deprived in the country. At the same time, it is less affluent than the South-East of the country, and its social class profile in the early 1990s was very similar to the national average (Champion et al., 1996). During the period of the study to be reported in this book, many parts of the region experienced quite high rates of unemployment, and there were many pockets of both urban and rural poverty.

In the first half of the twentieth century, the population of England had been ethnically very homogeneous, but, largely due to immigration from former colonies, it had become more diverse by the mid-1990s with an estimated 6.3% of the population made up of Black and minority ethnic groups. The largest ethnic minority group was Indian, followed by Pakistani and Black Caribbean. This growing diversity was not equal across the country, with minority groups tending to be concentrated in urban, and often poorer areas such as parts of London, the West Midlands and the old industrial North. This was one respect in which the South-West, with few large conurbations, experienced rather less of a change than was occurring in some other parts of the country.

But, like the rest of Britain, all parts of the South-West are part of a country that is otherwise fairly culturally uniform. It has been suggested that Britain has been a homogeneous, centralised country since the transformation to 'modernism', which occurred in the late nineteenth and early twentieth centuries (Harris, 1994). Children in the late twentieth century, when the present research was carried out, were following more or less the same school curriculum throughout the country, and adolescents were wanting the same clothes, listening to the same music and being exposed to the same drugs. The British, wherever they were, were shopping in much the same shops, had the same choice of newspapers, and were drinking the same drinks, and paying more or less the same prices for them. The South-West, although it has its own character, was in all important respects typical of White Britain at the time, and certainly of England.

Drinking and drug taking

Britain is famous for its public houses, or 'pubs'. Throughout most of the twentieth century, British pubs were governed by a strict system of local licensing established in the second half of the nineteenth century. Further strict rules about opening hours (opening for a few hours in the middle of the day and again from early evening to 'closing time' at 10.30 or 11.00 p.m.) and the prohibiting of entry for children or the serving of alcoholic drinks to those under 18 years of age date from the First World War, when restrictions were introduced in order to combat the drunkenness and absenteeism which were felt to be adversely affecting the war effort (Greenaway, 1998). Up until that time, the Temperance Movement of late nineteenth- and early twentieth-century Britain had been very strong (Shiman, 1988), but from then on its influence declined rapidly, and Britain became for the most part a nation of moderate drinkers restrained both by restrictive licensing laws and lack of spare money to spend on drink. Unlike some other European countries such as France and Italy, England was largely a beer-drinking country. Men preferred their beer 'flat' (i.e. uncarbonated) and served at room temperature. According to Mass Observation (1943), who carried out their classic and most detailed ever study of English pubs in the late 1930s, the most popular drink was 'mild ale', mostly drunk in half-pints. Women, who were much more likely to be occasional or very light drinkers, drank a wider range of beverages, including bottled 'light ale', sherry, vermouth, gin or whisky.

In the last decades of the twentieth century, with increasing prosperity, greater experience of travel in other European countries, increasing globalisation of the drinks industry, and, most recently, a preference on the part of government for deregulating previously tightly regulated industries, such as the hospitality and drinks industries, drinking in Britain changed. The most evident changes have been improvement and diversification in the décor and services offered by pubs (in the 1930s, the less comfortable rooms in pubs were literally 'spit and sawdust', and the more comfortable rooms not a great deal better by present standards, whereas by the 1990s the insides of most pubs had been transformed, and many were serving both full meals and bar snacks); the gradual removal of restrictions, such as those on opening hours; a great diversification of types of alcoholic drink (for example, large increases in the consumption of wine and lager); and an increase in the prevalence of heavy drinking, especially among women and young people (Office for National Statistics, 1998; Parker et al., 1998).

According to the 1994 General Household Survey (Office for National Statistics, 1998), 20% of adults in Britain were drinking at least fairly heavily or 'more than recommended sensible levels' (more than 21 units[5] a week for men and more than 14 units for women), and 4% were drinking very heavily (men more than 50 units and women more than 35 units). Rates were higher for men (27% at least fairly heavily and 6% very heavily) than for women (13% at least fairly heavily and 2% very heavily). Rates of heavy drinking were highest in the youngest age group (ages 18–24 years), among whom 27% were drinking at least fairly heavily and 7% very heavily.

When it comes to estimating the prevalence of drinking problems, one of the most comprehensive general population surveys carried out in Britain was that conducted by the Office of Population Censuses and Surveys (OPCS) in 1993 (Meltzer et al., 1994, 1995). The sample consisted of 10 000 adults aged 16–64 years living in private households. The proportions considered to have been 'dependent' on alcohol in the year prior to the survey were 75 per 1000 men and 21 per 1000 women (equivalent to a total of around two million people). The highest prevalence was among young men aged 20–24 years, where the estimated rate was 176 per thousand.

The history of illicit drug taking in Britain is of course very different, with the development since the 1960s of a drug 'scene' with little or no continuity with the past. Although opium was widely available in the nineteenth century and came to be recognised as capable of causing addiction (Berridge, 1979), and drugs such as opium and cocaine were used by small minorities in the early twentieth century, it was not until the 'epidemics' of heroin taking among young people in certain parts of Britain in the 1960s and early to mid-1980s that the modern picture started to emerge. Cannabis use, already becoming popular among university students and others in the 1960s and 1970s, became much more prevalent. Amphetamines, inexpensive compared to heroin, became quite widely used, with patterns of use varying from occasional 'pill popping', through 'bingeing', to regular daily use, sometimes involving injecting (Klee, 1992). A new category of drugs, generally referred to as 'dance drugs', associated with the nightclub scene, came into fashion, most notably Ecstasy, thought by some to have comparatively low addiction potential, but believed by others to act as a 'gateway drug', leading to experimentation with or regular use of other drugs (McDermott, 1993). Ecstasy captured high media attention because of a small number of fatalities associated with its use. Among other drugs complicating the picture still further are cocaine (Ditton and Hammersley, 1996) and, more recently, crack cocaine, as well as hallucinogens such as LSD, and forms of drug taking appealing to special groups, such as the sniffing of inhalants by children and adolescents (Gossop, 1993), and anabolic steroid use, particularly among bodybuilders (Korkia and Stimson, 1993). In the rapidly changing picture of youthful drug use in Britain, the general trend has been toward polydrug use.

According to Egginton and Parker (2002), the 1990s saw not only an increase in regular heavy drinking among British adolescents, and a far greater diversity in what they drank, but also 'highly statistically and practically significant increases in illicit drug use. Young Britons became identified as the most drug involved in Europe . . . and especially in respect of the dance drugs' (p. 98). They cited a UK-wide survey in 1995 that found, among 15–16-year-olds, that 40% of girls and 45% of boys had tried an illicit drug. Other survey results (e.g. Measham et al., 2000) found different drugs being used in combination, favoured combinations including alcohol, tobacco and cannabis, and alcohol, amphetamine and Ecstasy. The majority of young people who had tried drugs, however, were either 'triers and experimenters' (who had not taken a drug in the previous year and did not intend to do so again) or 'light users' (who had taken a drug fewer than 10 times in the previous year). In their longitudinal study of school students in the North of England, Egginton and Parker (2002) found that by the age of 16–17 years 6.6% were moderate drug users (having taken a drug between 10 and 49 times in the past year) and a further 6.8% were regular/heavy users (50 or more times in the past year). The most frequently used drug was cannabis (tried by 44.4% of 16–17-year-olds, of whom 13.3% were now regular/heavy users), followed by nitrites (16.5% tried, of whom 1.1% now regular/heavy), amphetamines (15.9% tried, of whom 1.1% now regular/heavy), Ecstasy (9.0% tried, of whom 5.2% now regular/heavy) and LSD (7.2% tried, of whom 1.3% now regular/heavy).

Estimating the prevalence of drug problems or drug dependence is difficult since the task is fraught with definitional problems and the dangers of under-estimation due to the 'hidden' nature of the problem. Drawing on a number of methods, including British and Scottish crimes surveys, and the use of multiplier techniques (e.g. multiplying the number of drug users in treatment by the inverse of the proportion of the population of drug users thought to be in treatment), Frischer et al. (2001) estimated there to be 161 000–169 000 Britons who had ever injected drugs, 162 000–244 000 problem opiate users, and around 268 000 problem drug users of all types. The national UK household survey referred to earlier (Meltzer et al., 1994) estimated 2.2% of 16–64-year-olds (2.5% of men, 1.5% of women) to have been dependent on drugs other than alcohol or tobacco within the last year, a figure that equates to almost one million people.

Indigenous Northern Territory, Australia

As previously explained, indigenous Australians from the Northern Territory were the focus for the Australian arm of the study. In order to understand the context of their lives, it is necessary to consider the position of indigenous people in Australia more generally and the historical basis from which this position has been determined.

The name 'Aboriginal or Torres Strait Islander' refers to the two groups of indigenous Australians whose ancestors lived in the area prior to the British invasion and subsequent colonisation of 1788. Until recently, Australia was wrongfully viewed as being uninhabited at the time of the British arrival, and that view formed the basis of the legal principle of *terra nullius*. This principle held that the land of Australia and the Torres Strait islands belonged to no one because it had been unoccupied (Bourke and Cox, 1998). This clearly ignored the history of 40 000 years or more of indigenous people living in the country and failed to recognise their complex socio-cultural systems and practices, including dimensions of spirituality, linguistics, land tenure and usage, relationships and economic structures. Put simply, the diverse and complex range of cultural practices of the indigenous people were alien to the invaders and led them to regard the indigenous occupants simply as primitive savages.

The concept of *terra nullius* combined with the portrayal of indigenous people as 'savages' coloured the way the first settlers dealt with indigenous people and influenced the way that government policies and practices were fashioned. It comes as little surprise, then, that the legacy today is a situation in which:

> The first Australians are now the most disadvantaged Australians. In every available measure of social and economic disadvantage, Aboriginal and Torres Strait Islander people record worse outcomes, face greater prob- lems and enjoy fewer opportunities than the rest of the Australian population. The poverty and relative powerlessness of Australia's indig- enous people is reflected in inferior education, employment, income and housing.
>
> (Ministry of Aboriginal Affairs, 1992; cited by Roberts, 1998, p. 266)

There is no agreed estimate of the size of the indigenous population at the time of the invasion, but it may have been anywhere between a third of a million and one million people. In the early decades of the twentieth century, this population had suffered a dramatic decline in numbers, to a low point of fewer than 100 000. Numbers increased from around the 1930s onwards (Bourke, 1998; Saggers and Gray, 1998; Reid and Trompf, 1991), with the 1996 census identifying Aboriginal and Torres Strait Islanders as numbering just over one third of a million people, or around 2% of the total Australian population (Australian Bureau of Statistics, 2000).

The same census showed that the Northern Territory had the largest pro- portion of indigenous people in the population when compared to all other Australian States and Territories. The total Northern Territory population of 189 000 people live in a vast but thinly populated area of central and northern Australia, stretching from desert south of Alice Springs in the heart of the continent through to the capital city of Darwin and the tropical northern coast. It covers a total area of 1.35 million sq. km.

In citing these figures, we may note that the identification of who is and who is not indigenous has been by no means straightforward, and in recent Australian history has often been highly problematic. One analysis of European law dealing with Aborigines found no fewer than 67 different definitions of Aboriginality (McCorquodale, 1987, cited by Bourke, 1998). Until quite recently, the government drew a distinction between 'full-blood' Aboriginal people and those who were 'part Aboriginal', only the former being recognised as really Aboriginal. These distinctions and different def- initions did not help people of Aboriginal descent to identify themselves as Aboriginal, and this was compounded by policies which resulted in the removal of many Aboriginal people from their cultural and geographical roots. Since 1973, indigenous people have had to fulfil three conditions to meet the official definition of Aboriginality: be of Aboriginal or Torres Strait Islander descent, be identified as such, and be recognised by the community as such. Over recent years, more people have been identifying themselves with pride as Aboriginal (Bourke, 1998; Bourke and Edwards, 1998; Keen, 1991).

Despite some growth in the Aboriginal and Torres Strait Islander population over recent decades, there is little disputing the picture of subjection of Aboriginal people from 1788 onwards. As Saggers and Gray (1998) put it, 'Following British colonisation, the indigenous populations of these land areas suffered the combined assaults of introduced disease, malnutrition and starvation consequent upon the denial of access to natural resources which had been theirs, violence, and policies of assimilation' (p. 5). The effects of introduced diseases began immediately when smallpox ravaged the Aboriginal population around Sydney Cove in 1789. Part of the Aboriginal population decline was also the result of murder by punitive expeditions of Europeans carrying out systematic killing (Burden, 1998; see also Riddett, 1990; Rose, 1991; Saggers and Gray, 1991).

Even in the twentieth century, policies were pursued in relation to Aboriginal people which met the United Nation's definition of genocide. What particularly brought this home to many people in Australia and beyond was the report in 1997 of the Human Rights and Equal Opportunity Commission, 'Bringing Them Home', The National Enquiry into the Separation of Aboriginal and Torres Strait Islander Children from Their Families. In the early years of the century, all mainland states and the Northern Territory introduced 'protectionist legislation' which gave them control over indigenous people. It is estimated that as many as one-sixth of all Aboriginal children were taken into 'care', and that there may be as many as 100 000 Australians of Aboriginal descent who now do not know their ancestors or the communities from whence they came (Bourke and Edwards, 1998; Groome, 1998; Hunter, 1993).

In the same vein, as land was appropriated to meet the needs of the new settlers, the freedom of Aboriginal people to pursue their own way of life and their right to self-determination was destroyed. Indigenous people were either forced off their traditional lands and into artificial settlements, missions or reserves, or ended up working on their land that had become the property of others (e.g. pastoralists). As Roberts (1998) put it, 'Their situation as a colonised people, small in population and widely dispersed across Australia, has forced them into working in and around a complex and foreign system of rules, structures, priorities and controls established by the dominant society' (p. 264). This was exacerbated further by simultaneously being restricted, either in part or in total, from carrying out customary laws and cultural practices.

For millennia, the knowledge of traditional law, often referred to as 'The

Law', which includes a detailed understanding of sacred sites and their appropriate use, was passed down orally from generation to generation of indigenous people. It is of great concern to many Aboriginal people that, as their close links with the land diminish, this knowledge is not being passed on to young people. Moreover, given the very different world-view and understanding of land held by non-indigenous settlers, Aboriginal rules about how the land should be treated were repeatedly violated. For example, traditional hunting grounds and sacred sites were used for sheep and cattle grazing (Bourke, 1998). Bell (1983) gives the example of the road from Alice Springs to Darwin being built through the very centre of a rocky area, known as the Marbles, containing important ritual sites for the Kaytej, so that certain important rituals could no longer be performed.

To some extent, Europeans continue to misunderstand the complex belief systems of Aboriginal people, their spiritual nature and the fundamental importance of the land to their beliefs. Although this is slowly changing, a full appreciation by Europeans continues to be made difficult by the complexity of those beliefs plus a lack of familiarity and the wide number of variations that occur across the continent. The following brief quotations touch on the complexity and the core role of the land.

> Ancestral activity in country provides a metaphor for relations between the living: the comings and goings of the dreaming animate the landscape, infuse it with significance, and provide paths along which links between living people may be traced. Each individual has a unique complex of relations to land, its sites and dreamings, but it is the corporate nature of interests in land which is emphasised.
>
> (Bell, 1983, p. 137)

> The whole of the landscape is conceived as having been formed through the activities of the Spirit Beings. The whole environment is viewed as the arena in which the dramatic events of The Dreaming were and are enacted. The continent is dotted with significant sites associated with the stories, for example places where the Spirit Beings first emerged, where they performed a ceremony or where they died and re-entered the earth. It is criss-crossed with the tracks of the Spirit Beings as they travelled from site to site.
>
> (Edwards, 1998, p. 81)

Given the fundamental connection with, and subsequent loss of, land, it is not surprising that the issue of land rights has become a major political and legal battleground. A series of events in recent Australian history have been crucial to this issue. One event was the Gurindji Walk-off from the Wave Hill cattle station in the Northern Territory in 1966, when Aboriginal station workers refused to work until their traditional lands, which had been appropriated by pastoralists years before, were given back and they were recognised as the landowners. In 1972, the Tent Embassy was set up on the lawns of Parliament House in Canberra to protest dispossession. In 1992, the Mabo case was heard by the High Court of Australia and is generally considered to have been a turning point in righting the wrongs in Australia's history. Eddie Mabo and others had sought legal recognition of their family's common law title to land on an island in the Torres Strait. The case was in the courts for 10 years, but the significance of the final court ruling was the rejection of the principle of *terra nullius* (Bourke and Cox, 1998; see also Rowse, 1993).

It is only within the last 40 years that indigenous Australians were also recognised to have voting and citizenship rights. Aboriginal people were able to vote in elections from 1962 onwards. In 1967, a referendum was successful in changing the Constitution to allow indigenous people to be counted as Australian citizens and enable Commonwealth laws to be made on their behalf. This resulted in policies and programmes aimed at raising the living standards of indigenous people and acknowledging that equality to other Australians had to come within a framework of a unique indigenous culture. It was also around this period that different State laws which had prohibited drinking by Aboriginal people for many decades were removed. For some, having access to alcohol became a symbol of new-found citizenship, and drinking became a demonstration of citizenship (Race Discrimination Commissioner, 1995).

Despite these developments, the culture of indigenous Australians continues to be under threat, but the threat is in the more subtle forms of lack of employment opportunities, social exclusion and dependency on welfare. While Australia had a high demand for unskilled and semi-skilled labour, especially in rural areas, opportunities for Aboriginal employment were good (although wages were low or non-existent). But with changes to the labour market, rates of Aboriginal unemployment have been high (estimated at about six times the rate of all other Australians by the Miller Report of 1985). Aboriginal income has increasingly been provided by the government in the form of pensions, unemployment benefits and family allowances (71% of Aboriginal income according to the same report), and most income has gone back into non-Aboriginal-controlled businesses (Bourke, 1998; Roberts, 1998).

This has been countered to a degree by significant increases in national funding to the Aboriginal sector and the development of Aboriginal initiatives, services and social and economic programmes, with a particular emphasis on building capacity within the indigenous community to support itself. There has also been a greater devolution of decision-making processes to recognise indigenous people: for example, the national Aboriginal and Torres Strait Islander Commission was established to oversee development and welfare of indigenous people and has a Board comprising indigenous leaders.

Land rights are now recognised, sacred sites are being observed and there has been growing support for cultural and social traditions (see O'Donoghue, 1997; Djerrkura, 1999).

Another aspect of indigenous Australia that is important to consider is the variety it encompasses. It often continues to be incorrectly assumed by non-Aboriginal people that Aboriginal Australia was and continues to be a homogeneous culture. Nothing could be further from the truth. The vast continent of Australia contained at the time of invasion, and continues to contain, a large number of different groups following varied customs. This is illustrated by the large number of diverse languages in use at the time of first contact with Europeans: 200–270 different languages were spoken, incorporating 500–600 dialects. One hundred and sixty of those languages are now extinct, 70 are under serious threat and only about 20 are considered strong enough to survive (in the short term at least). This loss of language has been attributed to government policies which actively reinforced the use of English (primarily through education and employment), the shame associated with using ancestral languages in public and the loss of intergenerational transmission of a language that relied on oral rather than written traditions (Walsh, 1993; Arthur, 1996; Amery and Bourke, 1998).

The living conditions of Aboriginal people also vary. As many as three-quarters of Australian Aboriginal people now live in capital cities or large towns, where they are generally in the small minority. The remainder live, broadly speaking, in three types of non-urban setting (Fleming et al., 1991). One non-urban setting consists of Aboriginal settlements or 'communities', usually in remote locations, where Aboriginal people are in a majority and non-Aboriginal people are present principally to provide support and infrastructure for the Aboriginal population. These settlements typically constitute small towns, with populations varying from several hundred up to one or two thousand and are very different from the much smaller, more mobile groups of precolonisation Australia.

Cattle stations and other rural settings where indigenous people work for non-indigenous pastoralists have also been significant in recent history, and an alternative rural setting consists of 'outstations', 'homelands' and other small groupings. The homelands movement, which grew rapidly in the 1970s and 1980s with encouragement and assistance from governments, provides settings in which indigenous people can live more in keeping with their cultural traditions and often on land with which they have historical associations (Bourke, 1998; Roberts, 1998). These settlements are usually defined by family groups.

Town camps, located on the outskirts of urban areas, constitute another common living situation for Aboriginal people. These camps have evolved over many years from places where town visitors stayed on a transient basis to become permanent urban communities with their own governing councils. These councils are funded by government to provide independent services to residents. There can be a number of camps around a particular town, and each tends to cater for people with shared languages.

One feature that has been constant in culture over time is the Australian Aboriginal concept of the family – a concept characteristically very different from the European one. For Aboriginal people, this concept invariably means an extended family that might include parents; children; numerous aunts, uncles and cousins; and grandparents. Moreover, family members can be both genetic, and non-genetic or 'classificatory'. As a person moves out from the immediate family to the local group and even the total linguistic group, it is possible to identify others by the same relationship terms applied to the more immediate family ('mother', 'father', 'sister', 'brother', etc.). Other people are usually referred to by a relationship name rather than a personal name, and the nature of the relationship determines mutual rights, responsibilities and interactional behaviour (e.g. defining the special roles some have in caring, discipline and education, as well as prescribing ways people deal with one another and what they can expect from each other). Even non-Aboriginal people who have a lot of contact with Aboriginal people may be given a classificatory or 'skin' name and instructed in the proper forms of social behaviour that follow from possessing that particular name (Bell, 1983; Bourke and Edwards, 1998; Keen, 1991).

The precise way in which classificatory kinship systems work varies around Australia, but one common principle is the *equivalence of same-sex siblings*. Thus, two brothers are considered equivalent, and if one has a child, that child views both the biological father and the father's brother as father. The brothers' children are brothers and sisters, rather than cousins. The same principle applies to two sisters and their offspring. A mother's brother, being on the same sibling line but of the opposite sex, is identified by the child as an uncle, and, similarly, a father's sister as an aunt. This is important because a classificatory title indicates the same responsibilities and level of obligation as the genetic equivalent. A child's classificatory mother or father, for example, holds the same status as the genetic parent. Further complications are introduced by the frequent division of a group into halves or moieties, and some groups divide into sections or subsections. These divisions are important in ritual and social interaction and have a profound influence on what a person can or cannot do.

Aboriginal culture continues to be described as being one in which cooperative contribution, obligations and responsibilities are more important than individuality, but, at the same time, as being a culture that is egalitarian with great respect for individual autonomy (Brady, 1992; Bourke and Edwards, 1998). In the context of an analysis of petrol sniffing by Aboriginal youth, for example, Brady (1992) described the great value placed upon generosity and sharing. The Western Desert people with whom she worked used the term 'hard' to describe someone who was not generous. Peterson (1993), on the other hand, describes 'demand sharing' in Australian Aboriginal society, where sharing was not so much a matter of unsolicited generosity as the norm for giving to another if the latter asked. Thus, giving can be synonymous with meeting cultural obligations as well as an expression of love, care and compassion for another. Due to the complex system of expected obligatory behaviour that is involved in the maintenance of relationships, subtlety is needed to deflect excessive demands of the former type if an individual is not to face accusations of not 'liking' the person refused. Autonomy is, however, also learned from an early age, and, according to Brady (1992), Aboriginal society is characterised by an unwillingness to impose one person's will on another. This acknowledges that while advice, instruction and other forms of influence can be brought to bear on an individual, it is ultimately the prerogative of the individual to decide what transpires.

Health and substance use and misuse

Although there have been improvements, the state of health of indigenous Australians continues to give great cause for concern, with unacceptably high rates of child malnutrition, high levels of acute and chronic illness in children and adults, and high mortality rates (Burden, 1998; Holmes et al., 2002). As a poor minority in a rich country, Aboriginal people have been said to carry a double health burden, suffering both the typical 'diseases of poverty' as in poorer Third World countries (e.g. acute infectious diseases, malnutrition and parasitic diseases) and the degenerative 'lifestyle' diseases more characteristic of developed countries (cardiovascular disease, chronic lung disease, hypertension, diabetes and cancer) (Reid and Trompf, 1991; Saggers and Gray, 1991; Burden, 1998). Infant mortality rates in the 1990s were two to four times greater than that for the total Australian population (Burden, 1998), and for the period 1991–6 life expectancy was about 57 years for males and 66 for females – much lower than for other Australians and comparable to those found in much poorer countries (Holmes et al., 2002). Mortality rates are particularly high for diseases of the circulatory system, diseases of the respiratory system (an Aboriginal death rate of seven to eight times that of the whole Australian population), diabetes (12 times higher for men and nearly 17 times higher for women in the early 1990s), and death resulting from external causes, including injury from motor vehicle and other accidents, poisoning, suicide, and homicide and other interpersonal violence (a rate for external causes four times that of the whole Australian population) (Burden, 1998). In all age groups, Aboriginal death rates exceed total Australian rates, but the greatest difference is for young to middle-aged adults.

Although there has been much stereotyping and prejudice regarding Aboriginal drinking, the evidence does suggest that many indigenous people drink in ways that are harmful to themselves, their families and communities. In their book, *Dealing with Alcohol: Indigenous Usage in Australia, New Zealand and Canada*, Saggers and Gray (1998) reviewed national and regional

Australian drinking surveys, finding that they revealed a broadly similar pattern: a larger proportion of indigenous than non-indigenous Australians, particularly women, never having drunk alcohol or having given up drinking; fewer current regular drinkers; and more of those who did drink doing so at harmful levels.

For example, Fleming et al. (1991) reported the results of a survey of 1764 Aboriginal people living in the Northern Territory, and Hall et al. (1993) the results of a random sample survey of 516 Aboriginal people living in the Kimberley area in the north of Western Australia. Both found high rates of abstention from drinking (59% in the Northern Territory and 48% in Western Australia) with a significantly higher rate among women. Both surveys found the majority of drinkers to be consuming amounts considered harmful (more than 60 g of alcohol per day for men and 40 g for women). In addition, Hall et al. (1993) asked about a number of alcohol-related problems. For example, of drinkers, 55% had thought that they should cut down on their drinking, 49% reported getting into fights, 41% reported an alcohol-related injury, and 79% and 30%, respectively, had been incarcerated in a police lock-up or a regional prison.

The social patterning of drinking was revealed in the Northern Territory finding that the percentage of the drinkers there varied systematically with the type of community in which people were living and the 'liquor status' of the community. The majority of those living in town camps in or close to urban centres were drinkers (74%), compared to a third or less living in more remote cattle stations or outstations. Since 1979, communities in the Northern Territory could opt to become 'dry', and 34% of Fleming et al.'s sample were living in communities that had done so. Only 28% of this group were drinkers, compared to 52% of those living in communities with no restrictions. Their results suggest a strong sex effect here, with men being much less constrained by the lesser availability of alcohol than were women.

Aboriginal people have increasingly spoken out about the damage they believe drinking has been doing to them and their communities. Saggers and Gray (1998, p. 12) cited the following:

> Couldn't sleep last night after listening yesterday. Thinking about how grog is killing people, family problems, culture dying, lost respect. Grog is a form of poison, can make a good man or woman go mad, kill, forget their kids. . . . Grog is tearing Aboriginal people apart. We don't know how to care for family now. In the old days we were family, need to look back. There are a lot of good things there. . . . Before Europeans our life was spot on.
> (brother of one of those who died in custody in South Australia, speaking at Central Australian Aboriginal Congress, cited in Langton, 1992, p. 3)

The damaging effect of excessive drinking on Aboriginal health and longevity has been well documented in various parts of Australia, including the Northern Territory. Saggers and Gray (1998) cited figures suggesting that 46% of all deaths of indigenous people living in town camps in Alice Springs were attributable at least in part to alcohol, and they cited others who have noted the horrendous death toll for individual families.

Of as much concern has been the effect of drinking on violence, including domestic violence, and on violent crime (Hunter, 1991; Brady, 1994; Saggers and Gray, 1998). Although he was critical of simplistic assumptions about the causal relationship between drinking and violence, Hunter (1991) stated, 'The association of alcohol and violence is glaringly apparent in remote Australia' (p. 89). Saggers and Gray (1998, p. 132) also stated, 'Among many indigenous people there is a clear view that alcohol causes violence.' It has been estimated, they reported, that 60–80% of violent crimes committed by indigenous Australians involved alcohol, and it was found that 57% of holdings of Aboriginal people in police cells in Australia in 1988 were for drunkenness-related offences. The proportion of young Aboriginal men who have been in prison is high: about half a randomly surveyed population of men under 50 years of age in the Kimberley area in one study.

Brady (1994) has written of the high risk for Aboriginal women of alcohol-related domestic violence. Saggers and Gray (1998) cited figures suggesting that indigenous women were nearly 40 times more likely than non-indigenous women to be victims of domestic violence, with an even higher relative risk in rural areas (Harding et al., 1995). Among other harms that have been attributed to excessive drinking are suicide (the 11-volume report of the Royal Commission to Aboriginal Death in Custody, published in 1991, featured alcohol prominently), harmful effects on children, financial effects on families, detrimental effects on community life, and threats to the maintenance of traditional culture (Saggers and Gray, 1998).

A number of factors have been proposed in explanation of the harmful nature of much Aboriginal drinking. Kahn et al. (1990) reported that the most often cited causal factors for Aboriginal heavy drinking were those taken to be the psychological consequences of exploitation, socio-economic conditions, prejudice, discrimination and disruption of indigenous culture. These factors included loss of identity, particularly for men; loss of traditional lands, bringing Aboriginal people to a state of being dependent fringe dwellers; loss of self-esteem; boredom; unemployment; lack of hope; and feelings of rejection and/or inferiority. A large number of other factors have also been suggested, however, including deliberate exploitation by Europeans using alcohol as a bribe for sex and entertainment, or for gain and manipulation, because it induced poor judgement and ineffectiveness, making Aborigines easy prey; economic exploitation via 'grog-running' and taxation; observation of the heavy binge drinking habits of white farmers and miners; drinking as a symbol of equality and 'citizenship', since Aboriginal people were denied unrestricted access to alcohol until quite recently; traditional Aboriginal obligations to share resources and accept gifts, in line with customs of sharing and consuming food as soon as it becomes available; lack of opportunity to develop social controls over alcohol use in the limited time that indigenous people have been exposed to it; the fact that much Aboriginal drinking takes place in public or in relatively unsafe or uncontrolled settings; and the expectation that drinking will be associated with uncontrolled and violent comportment. Many or all of these may be important factors, but, whatever the case, Kahn et al. concluded that 'The majority of attempted explanations implicate factors connected in some way with the subordinate position of Aborigines in Australian society' (p. 361). This clearly places Aboriginal alcohol use in a socio-historical framework (see Alexander, 1990; Saggers and Gray, 1998).

Since 1967, when Aboriginal people were granted full citizenship, and therefore had as much right to drink as others, there have been many attempts to control excessive drinking by Aboriginal people. In the Northern Territory, for example, legislation has enabled indigenous communities to declare themselves 'dry' or to apply for various restrictions on the availability of alcohol (e.g. the Northern Territory Liquor Act of 1979) and in Tennant Creek a trial was conducted in 1995 of 'grog-free days', which prohibited trading in hotel front bars and bottle shops on Thursday (pension and social security payment day) (Saggers and Gray, 1998). Brady (1994) discussed the role of Aboriginal women in speaking out for such controls – a public march by local women in Alice Springs was a major catalyst for the Northern Territory government to design its innovative Living with Alcohol programme (see Crundall, 1995; d'Abbs, 2001; Stockwell et al., 2001). Needless to say, all such attempts at control have been controversial. For example, there has been concern in rural communities that local prohibition simply results in more trips to town and an increase in alcohol-related motor vehicle accidents and fatalities when coming back.

Another form of attempted control consists of patrols, also known as night patrols or warden programmes. Saggers and Gray (1998) reported two dozen such schemes operating in different parts of Australia at the time they were writing. Usually run by local community volunteers, patrols seek to minimise alcohol-related harm by removing intoxicated people from situations that put them or others at risk. According to Saggers and Gray, they encourage drinkers to slow down their consumption, help settle drunken disputes and return intoxicated people to their communities or homes and move them away from roadsides where they would be particularly at risk.

Alcohol is without doubt the substance that has been of most concern. Indeed, the use by Aboriginal people of other drugs (apart from tobacco) pales into comparative insignificance (Saggers and Gray, 1998). That is not to say that use of other substances is not also of some concern. The 'sniffing' of inhalants is a significant problem (Gracey, 1998; Saggers and Gray, 1998), particularly the petrol sniffing among young people in remote and rural

Aboriginal communities which Brady (1992) documented in detail. Another substance of special interest in the Northern Territory context is kava, used for centuries in Polynesia and Melanesia for its anaesthetic, sedative and soporific qualities, and introduced into northern coastal Aboriginal communities in Australia in the 1980s in the hope that it might take the place of alcohol and reduce alcohol-related violence. There were soon reports that it was being used in much greater quantities than in the Pacific Islands, and was causing problems (Gracey, 1998). Marijuana is also used (Perkins et al., 1994) and there is increasing worry that other illicit drug use is on the increase among Aboriginal people, particularly young people with access to drugs in urban areas (Saggers and Gray, 1998).

Although a number of Aboriginal-based treatment services have adopted the 12-step model or refer to drinking problems as an illness (d'Abbs, 1990; Cook et al., 1994; Hazlehurst, 1994; Alati, 1996), a number of writers have noted the relative absence of an indigenous concept equivalent to the Western idea of 'alcoholism', or dependence or addiction as a disease-like condition suffered by individual people. Saggers and Gray (1998) referred to the absence of the concept of alcohol dependence among indigenous Australians, citing Heath (1987), who believed that a disease model of excessive substance use was inappropriate for indigenous societies. This apparently different conceptualisation of excessive substance use is no doubt linked to what has often been described as a radically different view of health and ill health among Aboriginal people compared with Western perspectives (Morgan et al., 1997; Burden, 1998) and should be considered in conjunction with the aforementioned socio-historical context of substance use. Indeed, this perspective is much closer to the Aboriginal view, which is much broader and holistic, encompassing 'the social, emotional, and cultural well-being of the whole community . . . a whole-of-life view' (National Aboriginal Health Strategy Working Party, 1989, cited by Burden, 1998, p. 204).

As an invaded people, Aboriginal and Torres Strait Islanders have suffered enormous loss. This is evident in their material and spiritual well-being and links to patterns of alcohol use that place them at significantly greater risk of ill health and social harms. On a more positive note, it is also evident that Australian indigenous people have a strong foundation from which to progress, particularly in view of their cultural resilience and holistic world-view. The priority now is to find new ways to help indigenous people manage change in a setting in which families and communities are put first.

Chapter 4

A description of the study in three socio-cultural groups

In the present chapter, the reader will find details of the method that was used in the research in Mexico City, South-West England and northern Australia: how family members were recruited to participate, how the interview was conducted and by whom, and how the results were analysed. Something of the social context of the lives of family members is also provided, including their material circumstances, which differed markedly from one socio-cultural group to another. This chapter concludes by noting some of the pitfalls of carrying out such cross-cultural research.

Recruitment of participating family members

The criteria for inclusion of a family member were as follows:

(1) The family member was not her/himself believed to use alcohol or any illicit substance currently in an excessive or problematic way. This criterion was relaxed slightly during the course of the project to include the occasional family member who her/himself had a drinking or drug problem, but only where that problem was judged to be significantly less serious than that of the relative whose substance use was of concern to the family member.

(2) The family member considered that the drinking or drug taking of another member of the household (the relative) had been a major source of distress for the family member.

(3) The relative had been drinking or consuming drugs at some time during the last 6 months.

(4) Family member and relative had been living under the same roof at some point in the last 6 months. This criterion was also relaxed slightly during the course of the project to include the occasional family member who, while not living under the same roof with the relative at any time in the previous 6 months, lived very close by and interacted with the relative on a daily or very regular basis.

In Mexico, participants were recruited from three areas of Mexico City, the centre, south and east of the city. All three areas were considered at high risk of alcohol- and drug-related problems. Recruitment focused on both treatment services and community agencies. Family members were recruited from three treatment centres, where they were approached when they attended to accompany their relatives. In other community agencies, written materials were given inviting family members to participate in the project and offering information and referral to specialist treatment if desired, in exchange for participation. These recruitment strategies were used in primary care agencies and government organisations running community health programmes. In addition, contact was made with private enterprises and with trade unions, and the project was advertised at a number of cultural events. The sample contained a range of people from different neighbourhoods and religious associations.

One difficulty that emerged during the recruitment in Mexico was that despite attempts to recruit people from middle and upper social classes into the project, their representativeness in the sample was low. Nearly 80% of the whole sample came from lower socio-economic status groups. A possible hypothesis in relation to the low representation of the middle and higher classes is that those groups had better access to sources of help and hence might have been less interested in taking part in projects such as the one described here. Poorer families were very interested in receiving support, and a number of families maintained contact with the researchers after the interviews took place.

A total of 107 families were involved in Mexico. The research protocol allowed the recruitment of more than one family member per family, and a total of 129 separate family member interviews were conducted. For 57 (53%) of the families, it was a relative's illicit drug use that was of principal concern, the most commonly reported drugs being inhalants and marijuana, usually in combination, and for 50 (47%) of the families it was excessive drinking that was of concern.

In England, the net was cast wide both geographically and in terms of sources of recruitment. Family members were recruited from a number of community agencies specialising in the treatment of alcohol and drug problems, as well as from other generic services, and via public advertising, throughout much of the South-West. Family members lived in cities or towns in the region or in the rural areas surrounding them and were of very varied socio-economic status. One hundred English families were represented, and the total number of separate interviews carried out with family members was 121. In 61 English families, it was a relative's alcohol problem that was of concern, and in 39 families an illicit drug problem, most commonly the use of amphetamines, opiates or a combination of drugs.

In Australia, unlike Mexico and England, interviewers, who had research expertise but were not otherwise employed as researchers, were paid for each interview successfully carried out. Because of the dynamics and time involved in developing relationships which would enable sensitive personal information to be divulged, the Australian interviewers were chosen on the basis of having existing associations with Aboriginal people and their communities. It was part of the interviewers' task to recruit suitable participants, which they were free to do in whatever way seemed effective and sensitive within their settings. In practice, many of the interviewees were already known to the interviewers, either via university contacts in the capital city or community contacts in the remote areas. Some of the interviewers had assigned ('skin') family relationships with some of the Aboriginal people whom they recruited for interview. Some of the interviewers had worked with some of the family members. Two of the interviewers who worked in the remote communities paid their participants. The women interviewers were more likely to recruit women participants while the men were more likely to recruit male family members. One of the women interviewers said, 'I just felt more comfortable about that . . . they felt more comfortable about it . . . [it was] far more culturally appropriate to talk to women.'

Several aspects of the basic design employed in Mexico and England were thought to be potentially problematic in the indigenous Australian context. Interviewers held the view that it might often be culturally inappropriate to focus an interview on the problem behaviour of a single, clearly identified relative. It was also thought likely that 'living under the same roof' would not always be so easily defined. As a result, some additional flexibility was built into the study design in Australia. In practice, focusing on the problems created by the drinking of one focal drinker proved less difficult than we had thought, although one interview lacked that focus, and nearly all referred, in addition, to excessive drinkers other than the focal person in their large extended family and kinship networks. The 'living under the same roof' criterion was more difficult to achieve, however, and a number of interviewees had not recently been living with the drinker about whom they were talking. We were impressed, however, with the fact that 'living with' was not as straightforward to define as it had been in Mexico and England (although it is not always straightforward in those countries either), on account of large extended family networks and the frequency with which kin toward whom a family member had obligations visited and stayed for periods of time or lived in close proximity. Hence, it was felt that it would have been unnecessarily restrictive to apply the criterion too strictly.

Family members were recruited from three rather different types of location: remote community, town and capital city. Participants were recruited and interviews held over a period of 2 years. Half-way through the first year, it became clear that most interviews were being conducted in remote communities or in one small town serving a large, remote part of the Northern Territory. To provide greater diversity, and to obtain representation of the large proportion of indigenous Australians who live in cities, it was decided to recruit additional family members in the Northern Territory's capital city, and two new interviewers based in the city joined the team for that purpose.

Since the Australian arm of the study was confined to alcohol, a smaller number of interviews was deemed sufficient. A total of 48 interviews were carried out with family members in the Northern Territory, although in one interview it was not possible to focus on concern about any one particular problem drinking relative. The resulting 47 family members were concerned about the drinking of a total of 44 relatives.

The interview and the interviewers

The team of interviewers in Mexico consisted of nine psychology graduates employed at the Institute of Psychiatry as researchers (or in one case as a clinical psychologist at a specialist agency for the treatment of alcohol and drug problems). The team in England was made up of eight psychology graduates employed as researchers by one of the participating universities or National Health Service clinical psychology departments, plus one under-graduate psychology student during his placement year. In the Northern Territory, Australia, interviewers were selected for their special knowledge of and relationships with indigenous communities, and as a result came from more varied disciplines and were further advanced in their careers than the Mexican and English interviewers. The team of five were graduates in applied linguistics, art, law and philosophy, psychology, and social work. They had worked in a variety of jobs including Bible translator, cross-cultural trainer, night patrol coordinator, anthropologist, parole officer, community social worker and public health policy analyst.

The method of data collection consisted of a lengthy, in-depth, semi-structured individual interview. Table 4.1 lists the seven topic areas, and the subtopics, that interviewers were instructed to cover. The emphasis, however, was upon obtaining detailed information about aspects of the family member's experience which were personally salient. Hence, although interviewers were asked to cover all topics and subtopics, the priority was on obtaining sufficient detail to answer the central questions (e.g. what have been the effects of the relative's consumption of alcohol or other drugs on the family member, other members of the family, and the family generally?). The interview guide, which ran to 20 pages, constantly reminded interviewers to do three things: (1) *follow leads* opened up by the family member; (2) *probe* thoroughly until meaning was full and clear; (3) *obtain concrete examples* of things that were said about family events and associated thoughts and feelings. When interviewers are experienced and this protocol is fully carried out, interviews can become very lengthy. Interviews lasted from 1 to 12 hours and often needed to be conducted over more than one session or in a single marathon session broken by rest periods and refreshments.

In all three socio-cultural groups, interviews were held at times and in

Table 4.1 In-depth interview for family members: main topics and subtopics

(1) The Family
Construct a family diagram
Description of household accommodation and neighbourhood
Description of the family's social and cultural background

(2) The history and nature of the relative's drinking or drug taking
Nature of the relative's present drinking or drug taking and how it developed
Type of drink or drug(s), method of administration, quantity, pattern, source, place
Family member's own drinking and drug taking

(3) Effects on the family member and the whole family
What life has been like at home for the family member, what problems the relative's
drinking or drug taking has created, or in what ways the family member is concerned
Have the lives of other members of the family been affected?
Has the relative's drinking or drug taking had any positive effects?
Have there been recent changes in effects on the family?

(4) How the family member has attempted to cope with the relative's drinking or drug
taking
Has the family member found her/himself reacting in certain ways?
Which ways of reacting or coping has the family member found most useful; which
least useful?
Have changes occurred in the way the family member copes?

(5) Support for the family member in coping with the relative's drinking or drug taking
Support the family member has, or has not received from each other member of the
household
Support from individual members of the wider family or from friends
Support from the local neighbourhood or community
Formal or informal support from expert sources of help including mutual help

(6) Health and well-being of the family member and other family members
Family member's recent state of health and well-being, and how this has been affected
by the relative's drinking or drug taking
Health and well-being of other members of the family, and how affected by the
relative's drinking or drug taking

(7) Overview and the future
Is the relative's drinking or drug taking the real problem?
What does the family member think are the causes of the relative's drinking or drug
taking?
Family member's hopes and realistic expectations, and what the family member feels
s/he now needs to help cope with the problem

locations convenient to family members. In England, interviews were held in
family members' homes, at a treatment unit where they had been recruited to
the study, or at the local university. In Mexico, family members were more
reluctant to be interviewed at home, and nearly all took place at a treatment
unit, primary health-care facility or the research institute. Interview locations
in Australia were even more diverse, including family members' own homes,

community buildings such as health centres or community centres, and, in a few cases, out-door locations, such as the edge of an informal gathering in a rural community or in a dry creek bed in town.

Although interviewers were free to tape-record interviews if they thought it appropriate and helpful for preparing reports, the method used to record interviews did not depend on such recordings. Instead interviewers were asked to take very detailed notes during the interview, and, as soon as possible afterwards, preferably within 24 hours, to word-process or dictate a detailed report. Such reports may themselves be quite substantial documents, from 2000 to 12 000 words in length, averaging about 4000–5000 words. There were two principal reasons for using such a method, one pragmatic, and the other conceptual.

In our experience, tape-recording can be awkward, is sometimes disliked, and is prone to technical faults. Interviews can be carried out anywhere including people's own homes, and tape-recording requires extra equipment (however small) and the need to make sure that it is working (almost everyone who has used recorders for interviews has at least one disaster story to tell). Furthermore, although interviewers often say that interviewees always rapidly get used to being tape-recorded and think nothing of it, that has not always been our experience. People may tell interviewers that they do not mind being recorded, but they sometimes complain about it if later given the opportunity to be debriefed by another person. One of the most important pragmatic reasons for not relying on tape-recording is the time, cost and difficulty of making transcripts, or even of listening to recordings of long interviews. In Australia, where some of the interviews were conducted at least in part in an indigenous language, and many terms were used which required explanation by the interviewer, tape-recordings and transcriptions would have been impossible for us to deal with.

More fundamental still is the intended purpose to which the results will be put. If the intention is to carry out some kind of discourse or conversational analysis (Willig, 2001), then *how* things are said is of the utmost importance and a full recording is necessary. If, on the other hand, the interest is in *what* is said, then the full recording is not necessary, provided the interviewer-reporter can capture the main bulk of an interviewee's meaning (and some exact quotations from the interviewee are usually helpful in doing that) in the report. Indeed, a full transcription, with all the *ums* and *ahs*, repetitions and irrelevant asides, is often frustrating and unhelpful. In any case, a transcription is already a condensed version of what took place: most of the non-verbal aspects of the exchange are omitted, and some degree of cleaning up of grammar, local accent, hesitations and repetitions, will have occurred. The kinds of reports we asked interviewers to provide were simply further condensed versions of what took place. In essence, they were the interviewer's answers to questions such as: what did X say on the subject of how she has coped with her daughter's drug use?

All interviewers received training that included reading and discussion of the interview guide and other documents relating to the project, as well as practice in the administration of the interview. An important element of the training was the provision of feedback on at least the first two interview reports produced by each interviewer. Such feedback helped interviewers write reports that were clear in all details (unless it had been impossible to clarify a point during the interview, in which case the report should provide a statement to that effect), that showed evidence of following leads introduced by the family member and evidence of probing in order to deepen understanding of a point being made, and that included examples to illustrate family events. Such detailed reports are not easy to produce, and interviewers accomplished the task in different ways. For example, one interviewer in Australia tape-recorded most of his interviews and prepared his reports after listening to the recordings. Another, in contrast, took detailed, almost verbatim notes during the interview. Others, including nearly all in England and Mexico, took sufficiently detailed notes, including some quotations verbatim, in order to construct the kind of report required.

The result of using this method is that the interviewer becomes a kind of informant, in his or her own right, summarising what the interviewee has said and recounting this in a lengthy report. In other words, the interviewer has already started the process of reducing a mass of unstructured data to a shorter (but still lengthy) and more manageable form. We believe that this method is a good one for obtaining in-depth material from people who have a lot to say about a complicated matter which is very personal and about which they feel keenly. It does rely, however, on the interviewer having been a fairly faithful sounding board for the interviewee, and providing a report which reflects what the participant said.

Analysis

Analysis of the interview reports from the three socio-cultural groups involved a number of steps and a large number of analysts, working in subgroups on parts of the data, over a period of several years. Interviews in Mexico and England were carried out earlier than those in Australia, and researchers in both England and Mexico were able to be involved in the analysis by virtue of the research commitment of the organisations for which they worked. Such resources did not exist in the Northern Territory in Australia, and the analysis of Australian data was carried out by the English researchers in England. Results of the latter analysis were fed back at interim and later stages at specially convened meetings in Darwin attended by both Aboriginal and non-Aboriginal alcohol workers as well as policy makers and the interviewers.

There are a number of well-established qualitative epistemologies and associated sets of techniques for analysis. They include the grounded theory approach (GTA), interpretative phenomenological analysis, and different types of discourse analysis (Willig, 2001). The approach used in the present research comes closest to GTA (Glaser and Strauss, 1967; Strauss and Corbin, 1990, 1998). Within the ambit of GTA are varieties of method. Glaser (1992) was at pains to defend what he saw as the original aims of GTA, which were to explore a phenomenon in depth and to produce a 'dense' descriptive model, as against the more analytic, hypothesis-generating and testing direction taken by Strauss and Corbin. Others, such as Henwood and Pigeon (1994), have distinguished 'realist' and 'constructivist' versions of GTA. The approach adopted in the present research contains elements of each of those varieties of GTA, although perhaps we lean toward Glaser's philosophy and a realist approach. On the latter point, while recognising the subjective element in all qualitative analysis, and hence the way in which the product is inevitably a joint construction of the participants, interviewers and analysts, what we have aimed to do is to give voice to family members by describing, in depth, important aspects of the reality of their lives as people affected by and concerned about a close relative's excessive drinking or drug taking.

All forms of GTA share a number of common features, including open coding, later focused coding, constant comparison, analytic 'seminars', memo writing, selection of core categories and model building. All those elements have been present in the methods used for analysing the present data. Prominent among the features of that analysis were the following:

- The analysis has taken full advantage of the opportunities for collaboration. At certain stages of the analysis (usually earlier stages), analysts worked on their own. At other stages, analysts worked in pairs, coming together at a later stage to share ideas in a four-person 'seminar'. At other stages (generally later), larger meetings of analysts were convened.
- Interview reports were examined line by line, and segments of text (ranging in size from part of one line to the whole of a paragraph or more) were coded as examples of recurring themes. At a certain stage of the analysis of Mexican and English data, that process was assisted by the use of a code-and-retrieve computer program (Text Based Alpha: Tesch, 1990).
- The work of detailed coding always began with small subsets of interview reports (e.g. six reports), building up in stages to an examination of larger subsets (e.g. 24 reports).
- That process of detailed coding and searching for themes that recurred across interviews was complemented by detailed examination of individual reports. Individual, single-page 'case' summaries were created.
- The emerging results were subject to a process of comparing, checking and challenging. Data from different interview reports, from different analysts or analyst groups, and from different socio-cultural groups were compared and contrasted. The use of codes by different groups of analysts was checked for consistency. Preliminary models were challenged by examining fresh subsets of reports.

- Core categories were chosen, preliminary models developed and challenged, and more complete or satisfactory models developed.
- Individual analysts or, more usually, groups of analysts wrote working papers summarising the analyses carried out and the models developed. Often these were models of a section of the total analysis (e.g. a model of social support for family members) and in some instances models that attempted to depict all the data from one socio-cultural group (e.g. from the indigenous Australian interviews).

Some characteristics of the family members and their relatives

Table 4.2 shows how the Mexican, English and Australian family members, and the relatives about whose drinking or drug taking they were concerned, were distributed according to a number of socio-demographic variables. It can be noted that there were more women than men family members, although the proportions were more equal in the Australian sample. Relatives, on the other hand, were much more likely to be male, but the sex difference was

Table 4.2 Socio-demographic characteristics of family members in Mexico City, South-West England and the Australian Northern Territory (NT)

	Mexico City % (n = 129)	SW England % (n = 121)	Australia NT % (n = 47)
Sex			
Male	30	32	45
Female	70	68	55
Age (years)			
20 or less	5	5	0
21–30	19	18	23
31–40	25	18	38
41–50	30	30	21
Over 50	21	29	17
Household size			
One (interviewee does not live with relative)	6	11	4
Two	2	28	11
Three	7	26	13
Four	16	19	17
Five or Six	34	15	30
Seven to 10	28	1	19
More than 10	7	0	6
Sex of relative			
Male	92	77	75
Female	8	23	25

most marked in Mexico. The contrast between the samples from the three socio-cultural groups in terms of household size is also evident from the table, with smaller household sizes in the English sample. It should be noted, however, that exact comparisons on such a variable are very difficult to make and should be treated as providing only a rough indication of the ways in which the three groups differed. The problems of defining the household and deciding who should be counted as falling within it (e.g. should a son or daughter who lives most of the time with friends, but who returns to the parental home periodically, be counted?) are heightened in the indigenous Australian context where the boundary around an individual household is even more difficult to define.

In a table such as Table 4.2, an entry might be expected for socio-economic status (SES), but there is no single, agreed scale that applies equally to three such contrasting socio-cultural groups. More will be said about socio-economic circumstances later in this chapter, in Chapters 8 and 9, and elsewhere in the book.

Table 4.3 shows how family members in the three groups were related to

Table 4.3 Relationship of interviewed family members to the relatives whose drinking or drug taking was of concern

	Mexico City % (n = 129)	SW England % (n = 121)	Australia NT % (n = 47)
Relationship (i.e. the interviewed family member is the —— of the relative whose drinking or drug taking was of concern)			
Wife (or female partner)	29	33	13
Husband (or male partner)	1	11	9
Male partner (gay)	0	2	0
Mother	33	31	11
Mother-in-law	0	0	2
Father	12	10	2
Father-in-law	0	0	2
Sister (or sister-in-law)	10	4	9
Brother	5	2	9
Daughter (or daughter-in-law)	2	5	4
Son (or son-in-law)	5	2	6
Aunt	2	0	11
Uncle	0	0	6
Female cousin	0	0	6
Male cousin	0	0	6
Nephew	1	0	2
Grandfather	0	0	2
Friend	1	0	0

the relatives whose excessive drinking or drug taking they focused on during the interviews. It can be seen that spouses or partners (including some ex-partners) and parents (including some parents-in-law) were the most represented family members, spouses or partners being the largest group in the English sample and parents the largest in Mexico City. Family members with other relationships to their relatives, including sisters and brothers, daughters and sons, aunts and uncles, and cousins, formed a larger proportion in the indigenous Australian group, and the smallest percentage in the group from South-West England. It should be noted here that terms used to describe family relationships in the Australian interviews were sometimes different from those that would be employed by a Western researcher. For example, a father's older brother would probably be referred to as 'father' rather than 'uncle', and a woman might refer to a (parallel) 'cousin' as her 'sister'. The Australian interview reports included different usages of such relationship terms. For comparative purposes, and to avoid confusion, the Western system of terms has been employed here.

Families' material and social environments

Mexico City

Mexican families who took part in the research mostly lived either in 'popular' (see Chapter 3), recently developed neighbourhoods on the eastern side of the city, or in semi-rural neighbourhoods to the south of the city. The majority owned their own homes, which they had usually built themselves. Some families lived in their houses prior to construction being completed, and in some cases building had never been finished. Although the majority had the benefit of basic services such as running water, drainage, electricity supply and paved streets, this was not always the case. Families complained, for example, about flooding caused by poor drainage, as well as irregular water supply. It was common for family members to buy water and keep it in containers in case it was needed. People also described an inconsistent electricity supply, as well as lack of proper pavements, poor refuse collection service, and the absence of public telephones in working order.

The street use of alcohol and drugs, and vandalism were part of the daily experience of family members in these areas. For example (in this and later chapters, indented material consists of direct citations from interviewers' post-interview reports, with the exact words of family members indicated by quotation marks):

> The *'colonia'* [neighbourhood] is described by the family member as 'unsafe' given that there are lots of gangs although there is constant monitoring/vigilance because there is a secondary school where people are

known to sell drugs to young people. It is also a common place to find young people using drugs in the street.

(sister of a problem drug user)

The main problem in this area is that since they built up the metro, delinquency has increased as the areas where they live are isolated, with 'night centres, gangs and a lot of drug and alcohol use'. The family member states that it has become a very risky neighbourhood.

(mother of a problem drinker)

Although family accommodation usually contained more than one bedroom, that was not always the case, and it was common for many relations to share the same plot of land. Hence, overcrowding was common, with sharing of bedrooms, and sharing of bathroom and toilet facilities between family units. That situation arose because one way of dealing with the housing need involves different groups of family members, who are related, building housing on land which belongs to one of the family members or has been passed on as part of an inheritance. Each group then builds the number of rooms that are necessary to live in or that they can afford:

The family member lives with the rest of the family and her mother within a piece of land owned by the mother. The family member's house has got two levels: on the higher level lives the mother in an apartment and on another part of the land there are two rooms that are being let. The relative and his wife are waiting for one of the apartments to be vacated so that they can move in and live together.

(father of a problem drinker)

The family member's room is both a bedroom and a dining area. The bathroom is outside the house and it is shared by those living in the two rooms (family member's room and her daughter's).

(mother of a problem drinker)

The house where they live has been built on a piece of land that is shared with other family members (aunts/uncles of the family member). The house has a dining room, a bedroom and a bathroom. The kitchen is separate. In the only bedroom, the family member, her mother and brother, sleep together. The relative lives in another room with another member of the family (on the same piece of land).

(sister of a drug user)

Another way of obtaining property was through government or other special schemes to assist workers in purchasing housing through loans. Although owning a home was a factor mitigating a poor financial situation, the value of the Mexican peso fluctuated greatly during the period of the research, and most families had just enough money to cover basic necessities. It should also be noted that in some families wives were contributing to the household finances by bringing in more money than their husbands, in some cases being the sole breadwinners.

As is apparent from Table 4.2, many Mexican households contained a large number of relations. Families could be thought of as situated on a continuum ranging from small nuclear families, such as the one depicted in the first family diagram (Figure 4.1), to complex family groups containing several generations and two or more family subgroups sharing physical space and amenities. The second family diagram (Figure 4.2) depicts an example of the latter kind of family: a family member living in the same house as her mother and several brothers and sisters, as well as a large number of children, grand-children, nephews and in-laws. The family house belonged to her mother and was inherited.

Social contacts for most families were confined to family members and it was rare to find family members reporting social contact with non-kin or attending sporting or cultural events or exhibitions. Religious activities, however, constituted an important exception. A minority of families were Protestant and actively practising their religion. A large majority described themselves as Catholic and many were active:

> The family member and her family are Catholic. She goes to church with her younger son every eight days. The rest of the week she engages in religious activities. 'We take the virgin from home to home and we pray.'
>
> (mother of a problem drug user)

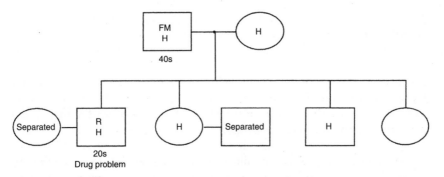

Figure 4.1 Example of the family of a Mexican father living in a smaller household with his wife and three of their children, including a son with a drug problem.

Key to Figures 4.1–4.6: FM = Family member who participated in the research; R = Relative whose drinking or drug taking was of concern; H = Living in the same household; Curved-sided symbols = Female family members; Straight-sided symbols = Male family members. (These figures are based on actual families but details have been changed.)

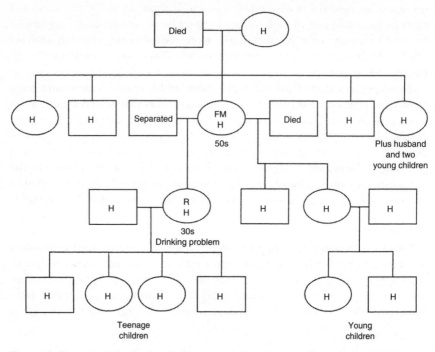

Figure 4.2 Example of the family of a Mexican mother living in a larger household consisting of four generations, including her mother, brothers and sisters, and three children, including a daughter with a drinking problem, and their families.

> The family member is a Catholic and goes to church frequently. She belongs to a group that gives talks on religion.
>
> (mother of a problem drinker)

Others described themselves as not being active, since they did not regularly engage in religious activities, but almost all maintained some occasional religious attendance and continued to hold religious beliefs that could provide an important source of support:

> The family member is Catholic although does not attend a church with any frequency. The family celebrates birthdays, Independence Day, the Day of the Dead, and the December festivities.
>
> (sister of a problem drug user)

They describe themselves as Catholic, but not active. During the interview, however, the family member came across as a person with a great deal of faith. She said that she stopped going to church . . . but she herself has a strong faith in God and believes that God can help her resolve her difficulties.

(mother of a problem drinker)

In terms of education and employment, many of the Mexican family members had not progressed in their education beyond the primary level, and their work had been semi-skilled or unskilled and insecure. Others had progressed to varying levels of secondary education, and occasionally beyond, and pursued careers:

Born in Mexico City, he studied up to secondary level and took some courses in clothing manufacture. He worked as a designer, and now is pensioned.

(father of a drug user)

Originally from the state of Hidalgo, she says she has no education but knows how to read and write. She looks after the home and sells *elotes* [corn on the cob] and costume jewellery.

(female partner of a drinker)

South-West England

Unlike many of the Mexican families, those living in South-West England nearly all enjoyed comfortable, well-serviced accommodation. The spaciousness and luxury of their accommodation varied widely, however, from detached, multiple-bedroomed houses to much more modest accommodation. Examples of those at the former end of the continuum included the following:

The family member and her husband (the relative) have lived in their present home for six years. Her husband is in the Army and they have travelled about a lot. . . . She expects their present home to be permanent now, at least until he comes out of the Army. . . . The house is detached and has five bedrooms and two reception rooms, and a large garden.

(wife of a problem drinker)

The family member lives with her son (the relative), her husband, her daughter and the latter's two children. She and her husband own their own five-bedroom house, in 'a nice area' situated on the outskirts of a small city . . . she reported that she and her husband were financially 'well off. We weren't when the children were small, but people have died and left us money.' When asked about savings, the family member said that they had 'plenty – we're very, very frugal.'

(mother of a male problem drug user)

Examples of more modest accommodation included the following:

> The family member and her husband and their two-year-old child live in
> a two-bedroom terrace house. She describes no problems with
> overcrowding.
>
> (wife of a problem drinker)

> The accommodation is a two-bedroomed maisonette with warden con-
> trol. The family member and her husband live in the home with their
> adopted son. The house is plenty big enough for the three people who
> live there. However, there is a certain resentment about living in this
> house since they had owned their own house. They rent their present
> home from the local council. She is fairly happy with it but says that her
> husband hates it, calling it a 'dump'.
>
> (wife of a problem drinker)

Although some English families reported neighbourhood problems, including easier access for their relatives to buy drink or drugs than they would have
wished, most neighbourhoods were described as agreeable and well supplied
with amenities:

> They have lived in the house for nine years, and the family member has
> always lived locally. She said that she likes the area, which has all the
> major amenities locally (library, large supermarket, doctor and dentist,
> swimming pool). She does not drive but there is a regular minibus link to
> the centre of town about a mile away. The area is quiet, being a cul-de-sac
> and 'nobody bothers you' – many of the residents are pensioners.
>
> (wife of a problem drinker)

> The neighbourhood they live in is a nice neighbourhood . . . with a very
> good bus service, shops close by and a couple of OAP [old age pensioner]
> groups.
>
> (wife of a problem drinker)

> The family member said that there were no problems with drug suppliers
> in the area and added that the only problem with crime was burglaries
> and car break-ins, as the neighbourhood is an affluent one.
>
> (mother of a male drug user)

Religious belief and activity varied widely, including many family members,
such as the following, who were inactive and for whom religious belief was
not stated to be important:

> They are both C of E [Church of England] but don't attend church
> regularly, only on occasions.
>
> (wife of a problem drinker)

About herself and her husband, she said 'we aren't anything . . . well, my husband certainly isn't. I'd like to take——[their child] to church on the odd occasion. I tend to think Christianity is more about the way you behave.'

(wife of a problem drinker)

And those for whom religion was more important:

She said religion was important for her and her husband. They are C of E [Church of England] and they go regularly to church, probably monthly.

(wife of a problem drinker)

The family member is a Christian, and attends an evangelical church with her two sons every Sunday. She was brought up as a Christian, but lapsed until finding religion again as the problem with her husband got worse. She says she went for support.

(female partner of a problem drinker)

In terms of education and occupation, English family members had all studied to secondary level and most had passed examinations at the end of their secondary schooling: the General Certificate of Education at 'ordinary' or 'O' level (at age 15–16) or at 'advanced' or 'A' level (at age 17–18). Occupations and careers varied greatly in status and security, however, so that some family members had occupations that were continuing or to which they could return, while others did not:

The family member is now retired, although she used to work part-time. However, she added that she'd 'never really had a career' . . . she left school with no qualifications. . . . Neither her nor her husband's mother had a career.

(mother of a drug-using son)

The family member is a nursery school assistant, and she is currently studying for a diploma in childcare at the local technical college. She attends the college two nights per week . . . within the next year, she wants to start up a nursery school in her home . . . she believes that this is a realistic aim as someone has done the same thing in the area already and she has the qualifications that she needs.

(female partner of a problem drinker)

He left school with five CSEs [Certificate of Secondary Education, higher grades equivalent to passes at 'O' level], and one 'O' level. He also completed a City and Guilds [vocational] catering course and a City and Guilds hygiene course. He has been working in local government for five

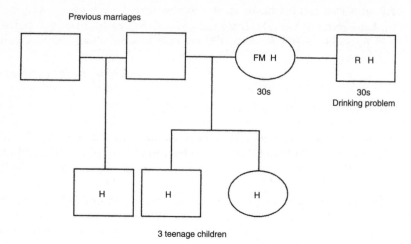

Figure 4.3 Example of the family of an English partner living with her problem drinking husband and three of her children by previous marriages.

years, and also works part-time in an off-licence [alcohol retail sales outlet] for two evenings a week.

(male partner of a problem drinker)

Family diagrams depicting two typical English families are shown in Figures 4.3 and 4.4; in the former figure, the interviewed family member was concerned about the partner's drinking, and in the latter the concern is about a daughter's drinking.

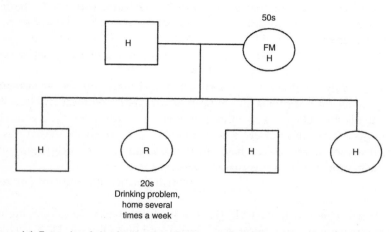

Figure 4.4 Example of the family of an English mother living with her husband and four children, one of whom has a drinking problem and currently lives only partly at home.

Indigenous Northern Territory, Australia

Indigenous Australian family members living in remote rural communities were described as living in very basic accommodation:

> The family member and her son's home is one of the older (15+ years old), stilt houses which lie in a row two streets from the airstrip and opposite the church and store. This house is a typical, three-bedroom, metal clad unit with cement floors and a minimum of interior furniture. There is a small yard surrounding the house. Typical of most homes in——security is minimal with the front door standing open most of the time, and access easily gained through broken or damaged windows. At most homes like this at——there might be one room inside the house where the door is padlocked and in which personal valuables, such as they might be, are stored.
>
> (aunt of a problem drinker)

> The family member lives on the south side of——because her family are from——community which ... is——km south ... she and her husband live on their own in a very small tin house, and are hoping to get one of the new concrete block houses in the next round of building. These tin houses are the size of about two small rooms, with a little verandah, and are unbelievably hot in summer (but very cheap to erect as they come in a flat kit). Their occupants usually eat, sleep and cook outside, either on the verandah or out in the open, if it's not too hot or raining. They are not fenced. Some houses have small tin or branch shelters nearby for some shade in summer.
>
> (wife of a problem drinker)

A family diagram showing a typical, rural community-dwelling family is shown in Figure 4.5.

The circumstances of those living in urban areas was much more varied (see Figure 4.6 for an example of a family diagram). Included were family members living in either very basic town camp or public/commission housing accommodation:

> The family member is currently living in a rented two-bedroom housing commission flat. . . . The unit itself is part of a rather large apartment complex inhabited mostly by Aboriginal or part-Aboriginal people. His unit is fairly barren with little in the way of interior furnishings and considerable amounts of rubbish littering the outside.
>
> (brother of a problem drinker)

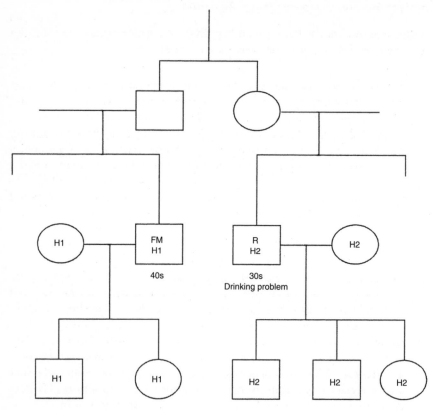

Figure 4.5 Example of the family of an Australian cousin living in a remote, rural community with his wife and two children (household 1: H1) next door to his problem drinking cousin and his family (household 2: H2). FM has family obligations of discipline and instruction to R, and the two households share daily activities.

The family member shares a cement block house with his natural mother and sometimes with an older brother . . . and his brother's wife. . . . Up until about a month ago his younger sister and her husband were living with them. . . . The two of them stay with him when they come back to——which is relatively often given their transient lifestyle. . . . He has lived for several years in different houses within the same camp. Years ago he used to live at——(a different camp) before he became blind. . . He is usually looked after during the day by his mother but also by various friends and relatives who happen to be visiting at the time. . . . Up until a few months ago, he would spend considerable time sitting outside the house, also at——Camp where his maternal cross-cousin lived or at another house in nearby . . . Camp——where the latter's sister lived.

(brother of a problem drinker)

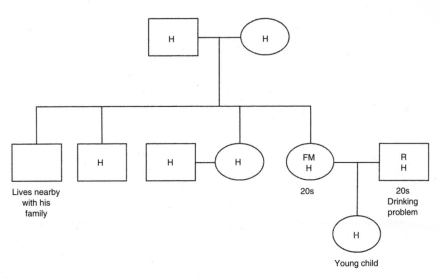

Figure 4.6 Example of the family of an Australian partner living in an urban area with her parents, brother, sister and brother-in-law; her problem drinking partner; and their young child.

Others were living modestly:

> The family member was interviewed in her home, which is rented accommodation, a very basic flat underneath a house (in the city). It was very homely.
>
> (wife of a problem drinker)

Exceptionally, family members were very comfortably off:

> Both interviewees [an indigenous woman and her non-indigenous husband] have a high status in —— [the town] and —— [rural Aboriginal community] due to their level of education, their employment level and their ownership of a house and two good cars. They own their four-bedroom brick bungalow . . . which is set in a pleasant middle-class area. The house has several security features – a large dog, a seven-foot mesh fence that is padlocked, and pressure-sensitive lights that come on when someone walks into the area.
>
> (aunt and uncle of a problem drinker)

The backgrounds of indigenous Australian family members reflect the family and cultural disruption that is part of Aboriginal history, the lack of educational and occupational opportunities, and continued dependence on opportunities provided by non-Aboriginal society. This particularly applied to those continuing to live in rural and remote indigenous communities:

> Regarding her personal history, the family member said, 'I was born at——[another rural indigenous community], and my mother and father brought me here to——This was back in the mid-50s when Welfare trucked us all up here . . . (she reminisces about the journey) . . . That's where they dropped us, when I was small. I've lived here ever since. I used to work as a cleaner at the school and also a little bit at the clinic. When I was a bit older, then I got married. He took me to——where we lived for a couple of years, and I worked a bit at the clinic there' . . . She is currently . . . attend[ing] classes five days a week. Neither she nor her mother hold any particular status within the community, less so now-adays in that they are both widows, but both are active members of the local——Church.
>
> (aunt of a problem drinker)

Urban-dwelling family members had mostly been brought up in rural areas and had vivid memories of their former lives. For example:

> The family member comes from the wheatbelt area of another Australian State. 'Dad would be away most of the time up in the bush fencing, so Mum was being the supporting mother. We lived in tents out in the bush when I was little. I can remember travelling on the back of a truck and camping here and camping there while Dad did fencing, and we ate kangaroo. Dad showed us how to hunt for emu eggs and we cooked them in the ashes. Cooking was always on an open fire outside, and of the bedding . . . he made when we didn't have a bed, he'd make a bed out of putting four forks up in a tree . . . and then chopping all the leaves so that – he then made a mattress out of that. I can always remember that, and all us girls slept on it' . . . When speaking of cultural ties and people speaking their own language she stated, 'It wasn't really heard of. It was something that I grew up feeling ashamed of it, and grew up ashamed of really who we were, and because we lived right out in the bush it was like if you heard a car Mum would tell us to run and hide. We'd run for our lives and hide from – hide behind anything we could find. It just put fear into us all.'
>
> (wife of a problem drinker)

> The family member grew up on a cattle station . . . her father was a stockman and her mother was a housewife and raised eight children. . . . She met her husband at——community [a small Aboriginal community] when she was 15 years old. She was working as a kitchen hand and he was a stockman. They married and she had their first child when

she was 17 years old and she had four children in about six years. Most of their married life was spent moving from one cattle station to the next and it wasn't until 1988 that the family moved to the city. According to her it was a hard life in the bush. . . . A few years ago she returned to study and has undertaken a general education course at the Northern Territory University. She has also undertaken alcohol awareness training through an Indigenous program.

(wife of a problem drinker)

Some of the pitfalls of cross-cultural research

A number of authors have considered the pitfalls of doing poor cross-cultural research. Gil and Bob (1999) provided an ethical perspective on doing 'culturally competent research'. They pointed out that ethnic minorities may often be a focus for research on psychological and social problems because of their visibility or availability, but researchers are more likely to be representatives of majority or Western groups, and procedures assumed to be etic[1] or culture general may really be emic to European or White American cultures (i.e. they are pseudo-etic). They suggest that research priorities should be fully discussed with members of the relevant community, and that members of the culture should be recruited as co-researchers since ethnic minority and White researchers who examine the same data usually come up with completely different conclusions. Inappropriate use of instruments puts minority groups in a position of being judged in comparison to Euro-American normative standards.

Kim et al. (2000) also referred to the way in which psychological theories and concepts, assumed to be universal, are in reality often deeply embedded in Euro-American values. Indigenous psychologies have evolved as a reaction against such unjustified claims. The approach they referred to as 'integrationist' has as its goal the integration of knowledge from cross-cultural study and local indigenous study. Following Enriquez (1993; cited by Kim et al., 2000), they contrast 'indigenization from within' with 'indigenization from without'. The latter transports theories, concepts and methods, modifying them to fit the local cultural context, adapting theory and retaining aspects that can be verified across cultures as possible cultural universals (or 'derived etics'). Although attention is paid to the local cultural context,

indigenization from without represents an external imposition. . . . Indigenous knowledge is treated as auxiliary and not as the primary source of knowledge. Indigenization from without represents an accommodative change in which new and different perspectives are simply added on to an existing paradigm.

(p. 65)

By contrast, indigenisation from within uses methods developed locally, and indigenous information is considered the primary source of knowledge.

Van de Vijver and Leung (2000) divided cross-cultural researchers into two groups, 'natives' and 'sojourners'. Whereas the work of the former is concentrated on cross-cultural topics, the latter have prior expertise in some other area and then attempt to extend their research to different cultural groups. They are either interested in psychological differences between different cultural groups, or are eager to show the generalisability and universality of their theoretical propositions. They tend not to work on theories that capture the patterning of cross-cultural similarities and differences, but more modestly aim to explore cross-cultural similarities and differences in a specific domain. It will become increasingly difficult, they stated, for sojourners to publish what they call the 'safari' type of research, in which a test is administered in two highly dissimilar groups and the average is compared, without concern for the suitability of the instrument or the equivalence of the scores. The dangers involved in using questionnaires in cultures other than the one for which they were originally developed have often been pointed out (e.g. Rogler, 1999; Van Hemert et al., 2001).

The need for researchers to be especially sensitive in carrying out research with indigenous Australian populations has often been noted. As well as the danger that researching and writing about indigenous problems may appear to be 'blaming the victim' (Saggers and Gray, 1998), there is also the need to be aware of the history of negative representations of indigenous people produced and controlled by colonists and other outsiders in a way that has been biased and culturally prescriptive (Bourke, 1998). Psychologists acquired a bad reputation early on as a result of mental ability testing which suggested the intellectual inferiority of indigenous people, and which contributed to holding back Aboriginal education for many years (Groome, 1998). Understandably, Aboriginal people have resented the way their culture has often been studied, which, among other things, has frequently contravened cultural norms about the appropriate sharing of information; such research has been seen as a cultural appropriation and the latest expression of colonial dispossession (Gostin and Chong, 1998).

Those issues have been discussed in the context of research and indigenous peoples worldwide by Tuhiwai-Smith (1999). She suggested four models of culturally appropriate research by non-indigenous researchers. The first is a mentoring model in which indigenous people guide and sponsor the research. The second is an adoption model in which researchers are incorporated into the daily life of people and sustain a lifelong relationship that extends beyond the research. The third is a power-sharing model in which researchers seek the assistance of the community meaningfully to support the development of research. The fourth is an empowering outcomes model that addresses the sorts of questions indigenous people ask and that has beneficial outcomes. She pointed out there is now a burgeoning international community of indigenous scholars and researchers who are seeing and doing it differently, positioning themselves clearly as indigenous researchers, informed academically by critical and often feminist approaches, and grounded politically in indigenous contexts and histories, struggles and ideals. Indigenous researchers are expected to have some form of historical and critical analysis of the role of research in the indigenous world. Key questions are 'Whose research is it? Who owns it? Whose interests does it serve? Who will benefit from it? Who has designed its questions and framed its scope? Who will carry it out? Who will write it up? How will its results be disseminated?' (p. 10).

From a Maori perspective, for example, according to Tuhiwai-Smith, non-indigenous research had not only often depicted indigenous people in a bad light, but also had failed to address the real social issues facing Maori people. It could often feel as if knowledge was being stolen and exported, like cultural artefacts, to the supposed centre of the academic world in Western Europe or North America. Texts might use words such as 'we', 'us' and 'our', which appeared to exclude indigenous people:

> When undertaking research, either across cultures or within a minority culture, it is critical that researchers recognise the power dynamic which is embedded in the relationship with their subjects. Researchers are in receipt of privileged information. They may interpret it within an overt theoretical framework, but also in terms of a covert ideological framework. They have the power to distort, to make invisible, to overlook, to exaggerate and to draw conclusions, based not on factual data, but on assumptions, hidden value judgements, and often downright misunderstandings.
>
> (p. 176)

Because the initiative for the research reported in this book was first taken by English researchers, much of the analysis of the data was carried out in England, including all the analysis of the Australian data, and because the lead in writing this book has been taken in England, there was a real danger that the current work could have fallen into many of the same pitfalls described by writers such as Gostin and Chong (1998) and Tuhiwai-Smith (1999). There is no doubt that the English research group are, in van de Vijver and Leung's (2000) terms, 'sojourners' when it comes to the present research: our interest is in the specific domain of excessive drinking, drug taking and the family, and we wanted to explore cross-cultural similarities and differences in that specific domain. In terms of the ideals of indigenous research outlined by Tuhiwai-Smith, there are some pluses and some minusus. In Mexico and England, interviews were carried out by people who were at least indigenous to the broad cultures in which the participants lived, although not necessarily to the participants' social classes. That was not the case in Australia, where interviewers were chosen because of their familiarity with indigenous culture. They were not themselves indigenous people, but most had worked and sometimes lived in indigenous communities, forming friendships and working relationships that were often very close. At a preliminary meeting in the Northern Territory, some of the likely difficulties of repeating exactly the Mexican and English work were highlighted. There was doubt expressed about whether the criteria for inclusion in the sample of family members, and the general method of interviewing adopted in the earlier studies, could be repeated in the Northern Territory indigenous context. The use of the set of standard questionnaires employed in Mexico and England, either in their English forms or after translation into indigenous Australian languages, was judged to be inappropriate, and the Australian arm of the study was therefore confined to its open-ended and qualitative aspects. In addition, because it was thought that it might often be culturally inappropriate to focus an interview on the problem behaviour of one other, identified relative, and also that the 'living together' inclusion criteria used in Mexico City and South-West England could not so easily be applied in the indigenous Australian context, some additional flexibility was built into the study design on those two counts (see above).

It is important to note, however, that the Australian arm of the research was carried out under the auspices of a Northern Territory-wide treatment and prevention programme that had the support of Aboriginal communities and that had on its staff indigenous people with whom the research was discussed at several stages. Indeed, the connection between the research and community concern about the effects of excessive drinking was far closer in Australia than in either of the other two socio-cultural groups. In all three areas, we believe the research addressed issues that were of vital concern to families and communities and that were otherwise being largely neglected.

Chapter 5

The impact of excessive drinking and drug taking on family members

In this chapter and the following two, we describe what we conclude is the common experience of family members around the world living with excessive drinking or drug use. The present chapter considers the ways in which family members find the drinking or drug taking to be a problem, how they try to make sense of it, and how it makes them feel. The following chapter examines how family members try to deal with these circumstances, and Chapter 7 considers the support they receive from others in their efforts to cope. We found many of the same experiences retold in places as different as poor communities on the edge of Mexico City, villages in semi-rural South-West England, and remote Aboriginal communities in Northern Australia. These experiences, we suggest, may be universal. Later, in Chapter 8, we offer a number of conclusions about the ways in which the experience of living in close proximity to a drinking or drug problem varied according to socio-cultural group.

But we begin with what we believe may be the universal impact of living with a close relative who has a drinking or drug problem. There are a number of different ways in which that experience might be conceptualised. One way of representing the experience is in terms of a number of interlocking facets. The total experience cannot be understood without appreciating each of those facets. One is the sheer *stress* that family members have been under as the result of the various difficulties encountered in living with someone with a drink or drug problem. Another is the *threat to the family and home* that the excessive substance use poses. It is important to appreciate that family members living with problems such as these are not only stressed or adversely affected by their experiences, but also *worried*. They worry about themselves on their own accounts, but also about the home, the household and the family in general. Children in the home become a particular focus for family members' concern. But the major focus for their worry is their excessively drinking or drug-taking relatives, and it is that focus of concern that confers on the experience much of its particular quality. The experience is one that combines witnessing one's closest (or one of the closest) relationship deteriorate and one's home life being spoilt, with worry and concern about the loved one whose very behaviour appears to be the source of the trouble. The fourth facet which completes the picture is the consequent *strain* which family members show in the form of personal upset, distress, and poor mental and sometimes physical health. Each of those elements of family members' experience will now be described in turn, with illustrations from reports of interviews carried out in each of the three socio-cultural groups.

Facet one: living with a relative who is drinking or taking drugs excessively is highly stressful

The experience of living with a problem drinking or drug-taking relative in the family was described to interviewers as a highly stressful one. These descriptions were greatly detailed, often rich in accounts of incidents, attend-ant emotions and attempts at understanding. Foremost were accounts of how the family member's relationship with the relative had deteriorated and become an unpleasant one. If any one aspect had to be chosen to explain why it is so stressful to live with someone who is drinking or using drugs exces-sively, it would be that a key relationship in which the family member had invested so much, or on which so many hopes had been pinned, has gone badly wrong. There are many aspects of that deteriorated relationship. For the sake of reasonable brevity, three will be described, each recurring regularly and each highly emphasised by participants in each of the socio-cultural groups. The examples that will be given to illustrate these three elements will, we hope, make clear the multifaceted nature of this key deteriorated relationship.

The relationship has become disagreeable, aggressive and sometimes physically violent

The unpleasantness of the relative's behaviour toward the family member, and often toward other members of the family as well, was described as taking a number of different forms, each representing a departure from the normally expected, mostly agreeable, form of family relationships. In some instances, the relative was described as isolating himself or herself, communicating little, and taking less part in family life than was expected. There were fre-quent references to sudden changes in mood on the part of the relative, which was found to be stressful by family members both because of the uncertainty of knowing how the relative would react at any given time, and the uncertainty for the family member of knowing what had caused the change of mood. Family members expressed difficulty in communicating with the relative so as not to provoke the latter's annoyance, feeling that they had to treat the relative with great care and sensitivity. The following quotations from interview reports illustrate family members' distress at the change that had occurred in what were formerly affectionate family relationships, and at the apparent rejection they were experiencing from their drug-using relatives:

She knew there was something wrong with him. He was, 'just not himself, totally different'. The way he reacted to things; you couldn't rationalise with him. If something happened and there was a discussion and she proved him wrong, he 'would move the goalposts and in the end I would think I'm the one that's going mad.' . . . She said that life was 'unnatural', like 'treading on eggshells'. She hated coming into the house. It was 'as though a black cloud was over it . . . a black cloud of doom; I literally got that feeling when I walked through the door.'

(England, wife of a drinker)

He has noted a change of attitude in her [his partner, the relative] since she got involved in taking drugs. 'Before she would make an effort, she was always happy and affectionate with me and my children, now she wants to separate and take my two small children. She wants to leave in order to be free but I don't want her to because she could fall into bad [sexual: 'libertinaje'] ways . . . I seem to be her worst enemy . . . [one day] she arrived at 3.00 in the morning, with her clothes torn, crying and saying, "hit me, kill me, look at what happens, I'm not worthy of you." She was very drunk and had been beaten up'. When she talks about separating and he tries to convince her not to go because things would be worse that way, she says to him, ' "My body is mine and I can do what I like with it." '

(Mexico, male partner of a drug user)

The relative's aggressiveness was described in the following ways: irritability, anger, verbal abuse, arguments, rudeness, shouting, insults, complaints, criticism, domineering behaviour, pushing, punching and hitting, breaking furniture or other household objects, threatening with weapons, such as a knife or a screwdriver, hitting with dangerous objects, and making death threats. To these forms of direct aggression were added deceitfulness and lying and sometimes the making of false accusations about the family member to other people. The following two extracts illustrate the seriousness of the violence that was sometimes described and the fear and sense of threat that can be experienced:

'Arguments start, then fighting, then violence and I'm usually the punching bag, and the verbal abuser bag, and the physical abuser bag. . . . Then the violence, he started to get really violent all the time. It didn't matter if I was pregnant or not, he would push me around, abuse me, call me names, racist names at times, chuck food on top of me, chuck anything, really abusive, verbally and physical.'

(Australia, female partner of a drinker)

She described her life with her son as 'difficult' because since he has been abusing alcohol she lives in a state of constant fear and tension. The scenes of violence in this family are very frequent when the relative is drinking, running from shouts, insults and complaints to hitting and actions that have put her life and that of her daughter at risk. She says that when he is drinking he gets infuriated, with the slightest provocation, or even without it. He starts getting violent, throwing furniture, breaking windows, doors and anything that gets in his way. . . . On another occasion she and her son were arguing, and he took a knife and threatened to kill her. 'I was very frightened but I didn't move. I said, "OK, if that's what you want to do." He was furious, threw the knife to one side and left the house. I really would have preferred him to kill me rather than to continue to live in that hell, although now I think it's better that he didn't do it because he couldn't have lived with the blame.'

(Mexico, mother of a drinker)

The next two extracts show how confusing it can be for family members; for example, a relative may not remember aggressive behaviour or may at other times be quite agreeable.

Because he is drunk when he is verbally abusive he forgets it; because she [the family member] is sober she doesn't. She feels, 'It makes you out to be a liar.' She thinks, 'Did I exaggerate it?'

(England, female partner of a drinker)

'You can tell on Sunday, Monday when everything wears off he has bad moods and he can be really vicious. On Friday, when he is going out you can tell [that he is going out to take drugs] because he is really nice to you and really happy.'

(England, female partner of a drug user)

In the latter example, it was clear to the family member that the relative was more aggressive when the effects of drugs were wearing off. Others were equally clear that aggression was more likely after drinking alcohol, or when the relative was unable to have access to substances, or whenever the family member or others challenged the relative about his or her consumption. For many family members, however, the exact nature of the relationship between the relative's drinking or drug use and mood was unclear, and that was itself a source of confusion.

Although the unpleasant and often abusive behaviour that was described in the interviews with family members was mostly that of the excessively drinking or drug-using relative, and was mostly (but not always) attributed to the relative's excessive use of alcohol or drugs, the deteriorated family circumstances had often provoked family members into aggressive feelings and sometimes actions. The following two extracts are illustrative:

> She felt there had been a complete breakdown of trust and their relation-ship had been affected. . . . 'I think if we didn't have children we wouldn't be together.' . . . When he used to come home drunk, if she let him come in . . . she felt like hitting him. . . . She is more likely than he to have broken things in frustration, e.g. she has thrown a teapot at him which he picked up and then smashed against the radiator. . . . At times she has hit him and he backed away, it has made him angry but he hasn't retaliated.
>
> (England, female partner of a drinker)

> 'I get visions of hitting him or stabbing him or destroying his possessions, something to make him feel what I've felt.'
>
> (England, female partner of a drinker)

In all three socio-cultural groups, whether or not there had been physical violence, the element of deterioration in a close family relationship that should be and had been a loving one, was regularly near the centre of family members' accounts of what life had been like.

'Humbug': conflict over money and possessions

One aspect of the deteriorated relationship about which family members regularly spoke, and which was a source of great discomfort, was conflict over money. The most often recounted scenario was one in which the family member felt pressured by the relative to give or lend the latter money. The request was often accompanied by a reproach, an accusation, a threat or actual violence, such that family members had often in the end acceded to such requests or demands. If they did not, they might become the victims of stealing and robbery on the part of relatives. In Australia, a term in Abo-riginal English is *to humbug*[1], which captures well the demanding nature of these requests for money and the uneasy dilemma in which such a demand places the family member.

More specifically, the kinds of events described included the following: buying things for the relative, such as cigarettes or bus or train fares, which the relative then sold; being asked for money for other things but suspecting that the money would be used to buy drugs; borrowing without asking; putting extra pressure on the family member by asking for money in the presence of another person, making it more difficult for the family member to refuse; taking objects from the home; taking things of sentimental as well as financial value such as a jacket, records or jewellery; breaking into meters in the home; failing to pay rent as expected or to contribute to family finances;

and the relative controlling finances and leaving the main homemaker short of money for necessities.

The following interview extracts illustrate 'humbugging', which is such a central part of the experience for many family members:

> He [the relative] has not been working for the last three months and his parents have taken charge of [financially] supporting her [his partner, the family member] and their children. Because he is aware of this situation he demands part of this money to buy drugs. 'The little that he earns goes on his drugs, and from what my mother-in-law gives me I had to put some aside for drugs, about 30 or 40 000 pesos. He says to me, "that money is from my parents, it's mine, you know that." Then he blames me and says if I don't give it to him he'll go out and steal the money. I'm always living with that blackmail.'
>
> (Mexico, female partner of a drug user)

> On many occasions she [the relative] asks her [her sister, the family member] or their mother to lend her money. She [the family member] always refuses, whilst the mother does lend the money. She [the family member] says she doesn't know what her sister actually uses the money for.
>
> (Mexico, sister of a drug user)

Both of the foregoing examples illustrate the fact that requests for money are often made in a family context that provides additional opportunities for relatives to put pressure on family members, making the dilemma faced by a family member a doubly difficult one. Humbugging is rarely a simple request which can be unemotionally considered and easily denied. The following extract adds a further dimension. Demands sometimes come, not solely from the relative who has been identified as having a drinking or drug problem, but from a group of excessive drinkers or drug users of whom the relative is a part.

> When asked if the drunks who continuously came around ever asked for things, he said that they always asked for food, money, everything, none of which was ever returned or reciprocated. He said, 'She [his wife] used to give things to them all the time. I'd go and buy the tucker [food], and she would just give it all away to them. She still does it. I try to stop them from taking because they never bloody work.'
>
> (Australia, non-Aboriginal husband of an Aboriginal wife with several drinking relatives)

The following extract refers to stealing, although, once again, the exact circumstances make for a complicated and confused set of events with much room for disagreement about rights and wrongs and for self-castigation and conflict among family members.

> 'She [the relative, the family member's daughter] took bank cards from the house in the middle of the night while we were asleep. She knew the numbers for the cards because we were trusting people. On a different occasion she took our cash-point card when she was going out on a Saturday night and put it back when she returned to the house having taken as much money as she could from the account.' On another occasion his [the family member's] partner had given their daughter the cash-point card which was for the joint account because she had no money and wanted to go to the fair. She gave her the account number and told her to take £10 to spend at the fair. She kept the card and took £40 a day over a period of four weeks.
>
> (England, father of a drug user)

The family member is unsure where the relative is or when the relative will arrive home

Much of the anxiety associated with being a family member when a close relative is drinking or taking drugs excessively has to do with the uncertainty and unpredictability of the relative's mood and behaviour. One regularly recurring form which that uncertainty takes concerns the reliability of the relative's presence in the home. It was very common for family members to express their anxiety about the following habits of the relative: coming home in the early hours of the morning under the influence of drink or drugs; spending time during the day on the streets, mixing with bad company and being in danger; going on drinking or drug-taking 'trips' or 'escapades', often in the company of other heavy drinkers or drug users, and perhaps involving journeys to a neighbouring town or city; and not appearing for family events that had been arranged. The following passages illustrate the anxiety on the part of family members that such uncertainty creates:

> On occasions he hasn't come home at night . . . and on occasion hasn't come home for a whole week. The first time this happened she was so worried that she went to his work where they told her that he hadn't been there. One of his colleagues told her 'that he had been in a hotel with some friends, some gambling, others drinking, some sleeping around. That made me very annoyed and we had a big argument. When he didn't come back to sleep, my son got up and saw how upset I was, and commented "this isn't right". Then I made excuses for him, such as he had stopped at work, but I don't think he [the son] believed me. I have a great deal of faith and I ask God to help us, that the situation be put right.'
>
> (Mexico, female partner of a drinker)

'I just wished she'd come home, she's got herself in such a mess, she's in a state she can't look after herself. I can't relax until she's upstairs.'

(England, father of a drug user)

She [the relative] moved to——about three years ago . . . and is drinking heavily whenever she can get some money. Her mother is doing the same. She has no fixed address and follows drinkers around.

(Australia, uncle [younger brother of father] of a drinker)

These frequent references to relatives 'coming and going', being absent when they were expected to be home, and arriving home at uncertain times and in uncertain states, were an integral part of the deteriorated relationship that existed between family members and relatives. Along with aggression and 'humbug', it is part of the abuse of the family that family members are subjected to when drinking or drug taking has become excessive. At the same time, uncertainty about the relative's movements and timekeeping contributes to a family member's general state of uncertainty about what has happened, what is currently occurring and how things are likely to develop in the future. Family members are often having to cope with very imperfect knowledge of exactly what is going on, why it has happened, who or what is to blame, and whether things will get better.

In Figure 5.1, we have attempted to summarise the content of the foregoing section. It depicts what are probably universal features of the stress

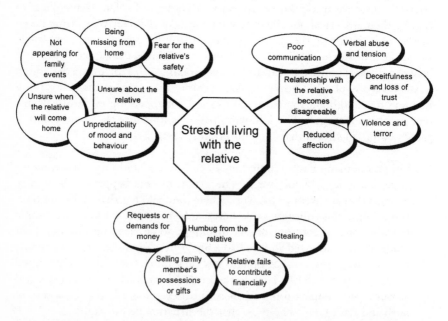

Figure 5.1 The stress of living with a close relative with an alcohol or drug problem.

experienced by family members, wherever they are, who live with close relatives with drink or drug problems. Of course, the exact picture varies from family to family, and some of the socio-cultural sources of variation will be considered in Chapter 8. But the conclusion is that what particularly characterises the stressful experience for family members is the growing discomfort of life with the problem drinking or drug-taking relative. We conclude that some combination of aggressiveness in the relationship, being on the receiving end of hassle or humbug from the relative, and experiencing the relative's behaviour as increasingly unreliable and uncertain is always present.

Facet two: the family member is worried about the relative

To view family members who live with problem drinking or drug use only as people who are seeing a close relationship deteriorate, and who are subject to personal stress or abuse as a result of the excessive drinking or drug taking, would be to neglect a central element of the core experience. Family members were not only personally affected in adverse ways, but they were also worried and concerned about their relatives whom they viewed as having become the victims of the drink or drugs. They saw a deterioration in their relatives, and generally attributed that in whole or in part to excessive drinking or taking of drugs. Their relatives were 'loved ones', although the love family members felt for their relatives might have worn thin or disappeared altogether in some cases. Relatives gave family members cause for concern on a number of counts. Family members were worried about relatives' physical health; their neglect of self-care or their appearance; their eating habits and gain or loss in weight; their mental health or general attitude to life and other people; their performance at work, in education or at favourite sports; the state of their finances and their future prospects; the company that they were keeping; or, in some cases, their social isolation. The excessive frequency or quantity of alcohol or drug consumption, the degree of intoxication, and particularly relatives' levels of preoccupation with or apparent dependence upon drink or drugs, were in themselves also causes for concern. Table 5.1 provides a list of some of the specific things that family members were worried about.

Although the word 'worried' (*preocupadoa* in Spanish) may have somewhat different connotations in different cultures, it is a word that well sums up much of the feelings and thoughts about their relatives that family members expressed in the interviews. The following two short quotations from Australian interview reports put it simply:

'When I know he is out drinking I just can't settle. I'm just worried about him the whole time.'

(Australia, daughter of a drinker)

Table 5.1 Sources of family members' worries about relatives drinking or taking drugs excessively

Worry about the relative's physical health

The relative's body can no longer stand it; stomach pains, parasites; unhealthy, affecting relative's body; neglecting self physically; pancreatitis; pneumonia, hospitalised, is this drug-related?; overdoses; looks physically ill; bad legs; high blood pressure; chest and kidney problems; diabetes, vomiting blood; lost weight, anorexic; didn't eat, too thin; weight loss dramatic when back on after a detox; came home fat.

Worry that the relative is neglecting himself or herself

Blotches on face, eyes bloodshot; bruises, puncture marks; arrives home dirty smelling of thinner and Cemento; dirty and dishevelled; period of neglecting appearance; smelt bad; sleeps late; doesn't sleep; had an abortion, has unprotected sex; for all the family member knows, the relative could have AIDS; wets the bed from time to time; the way she lives, if anything happened to her nobody would know; cut himself; damaging self; having accidents e.g. setting fire; neglecting self; not clean; taken advantage of by others; stab wound and effects of blows to the head; lack of care of personal possessions; being run over while drunk.

Worry about the relative's mental health

Blackouts, hallucinations; strange reactions, talking to himself, under the influence began not to know them; just to see her so down; mentally run down, preoccupied, apathetic; state of mind, desperation, helplessness, miserable; going out and coming back totally wasted, funny and weird; lost all former 'get up and go', withdrawal into self, can't be bothered; very preoccupied and withdrawn; talks of suicide; suicide attempts; demented from alcohol abuse; resigned himself to carry on drinking and dying; doesn't trust himself to have a relationship; sometimes couldn't even talk; 'slanted' look in eyes; as if lost, speaking incoherently; very anxious, strange behaviour.

Worry that the relative's education, work or sporting performance is failing

Lost job, temporary work only, irresponsible, neglectful of business; sacked from jobs; doesn't want to work; now too worried even to go for a job; thrown away education; dropped out of course; didn't study, spent all time with friends; used to be in the sports team and so keen; disciplinary action at work; lack of goal in life, he should be thinking about what he is going to do; instability, particularly abandoning good jobs.

Worry about the relative's financial affairs

Stealing from shops; family member deduces that the relative obtains money through prostitution; worried at one time that the relative was selling her body; the relative selling his things, cancelling bank account; the relative had a lot of money but has nothing now; the relative spends more than he earns, owes a lot.

Worry about the frequency, quantity or form of the relative's drinking or drug taking

Out at the wine bar, only interested in intoxication; paralytic drunk; constant drinking; daily drinking; using daily, inhaling whatever he could, shut himself in his room to inhale, spent hours in the bathroom taking drugs; can't predict if he will be drunk; buys drugs locally, takes them away from the home but frequently arrives home under the influence; falls through the door at 11.30 p.m. when on binges; drunk in bed when gets back from work; popping into the bedroom to have another vodka from under the bed; a friend told them he'd seen the relative inhaling Cemento; knows when the relative is injecting, you can see it in her eyes; comes home with shiny eyes, knows he's drugged; since recovery from drugs he has started drinking, coming home drunk every weekend; seeing him inject, frightened for his safety; seeing her hands covered in marks from injecting; stress of relative not wanting to 'do speed' but he's going to be doing it; worrying about vomiting and choking.

Worry about the company the relative is keeping

Mixes with younger people; rougher people and places, even brought tramps home; in with a bad crowd; for six months lived with a hardened drug addict twice the relative's age.

'I just worry about him when he gets sick and he's heavy on the grog.'
(Australia, cousin [father's brother's son] of a drinker; note that 'worry' in
the Aboriginal context is a much more active term than is generally
understood in non-Aboriginal English)

Mexican and English family members also expressed their concern about their relatives' states of health and well-being generally, as the following extracts illustrate:

She had more than once found her son drugged and lying on the floor . . . he did not eat, he was too thin and sometimes could not even talk. The look in his eyes was slanted and he 'smelled very bad.' . . . She is highly worried about her son's drug use, mainly because several youngsters in their neighbourhood have died as a result.

(Mexico, mother of a drug user)

He wouldn't come out of the room, not even to go downstairs. . . . He just sat in his room, invariably alone and drank. . . . Sometimes he will have finished the bottle of whisky by 7.00 p.m. If that is the case he'll have no reason to stay up and so he goes to bed 'to sleep it off.' Very often though he wakes up again at about 11.00 p.m. and goes downstairs and just sits staring out of the window for three or four hours. . . . He has neglected himself in the past . . . it was 'just as if he had no reason to live.'

(England, female partner of a drinker)

Family members in all three socio-cultural groups expressed their continuing worry and concern for the health and welfare of their relatives, while at the same time cataloguing the family harms that the relatives' behaviour was causing. It was that juxtaposition that lent to family members' accounts much of their special nature, and it is that combination of concerns that needs to be appreciated if the position of family members is to be understood.

Facet three: home and family life are threatened by the relative's behaviour

To think of the experience of family members living with drinking or drug problems in terms solely of a deteriorated relationship with the problem drinking or drug-using relative, and the family member's worry or concern about the relative, would be to miss a third vital component of that experience. It was not just an individual relationship that was affected, but the very life of the family itself as an entity and the home as a place that were threatened. There are a number of aspects of this threatened violation of the home and family, each regularly described by family members in each of the three socio-cultural groups.

One obvious way in which the life of the family may be adversely affected is the serious depletion of its financial resources by excessive expenditure on alcohol or other drugs. Accounts of the financially damaging effects on the family of a relative's excessive drinking or drug use include both the loss of considerable assets as well as already poor families made poorer by the relative's diversion of funds and failure to contribute to the family economically. Other family members, very often women, had to support the family economically to an extent that they had not expected or wished for.

> 'He started to fail to support the family, to limit my income, giving me no money to look after, and not buying shoes for the girls.' She had to maintain the family. Her children were against her working, but she didn't give up and since then spends her weekends selling *elotes* [corn on the cob]. She has never asked him for money to cope with household needs, nor received any amount from the sale of his *terreno* [plot of land on which a family can build its own home], and she has never tried to take part of that money. She says, 'Because it is a sin to waste money, one must behave as the law of God commands.'
>
> (Mexico, female partner of a drinker)

> There have been great changes in the family's financial situation. They owned five racehorses and had savings of £50,000 plus earnings and winnings from gambling. . . . The family now live on invalidity benefit.
>
> (England, female partner of a drinker)

Of just as much concern to the family members who participated in the interviews were the harmful effects on the whole atmosphere in the family, and particularly effects on the younger members of the family – the children of adult drinking or drug-using relatives, or the brothers and sisters of young adult relatives. Effects on the atmosphere of the whole household, often extending more widely still to other members of the family, were described in a number of different ways. For some, it was a case of it being difficult for the family to talk about how to deal with the problem, and even sometimes difficult for the family even to sit down together. In some instances, there were consequences for the whole family on account of disagreements about how to handle the relative (e.g. criticism of family members for rejecting the relative, or in other cases for *not* rejecting the relative). Disagreements arose about whether to give the relative money. The problem was often said to have created strain on marriages where the drinking or drug-using relative was a son or daughter. For one family member, the atmosphere in the home had been 'tense and strained, not happy'; for another, it had been 'a disaster all round'. The following extract is from an interview with a mother concerned, among other things, about the effects of her son's drug use on her husband.

> She said that when there's trouble or an emergency she deals with it and it is left to her to deal with it. Her husband makes himself scarce. He is 'a very gentle, sensitive soul', but she has noticed that things are getting difficult for him. . . . There have been occasions when she has had to stand between her husband and their son [the relative] because she was 'afraid they were going to kill each other, and that's unheard of for . . . [her husband], he's very gentle.'
>
> (England, mother of a drug user)

But the greatest weight of concern about the family as a whole was directed toward worry about effects on children. That worry involved a number of elements. There was worry about children being exposed to violence or neglect. There was also a more general worry about interference with the upbringing of children. Third, there was the idea of 'cycles': fear and worry about children repeating the cycle of excessive drinking or drug use. Specific worries ranged from concern that children were not getting enough to eat, that they became involved in family fights or were exposed to witnessing violence, that the relative might drive with the children aboard while intoxicated or in other ways could not be trusted to look after the children, that relatives were not passing on appropriate family and cultural traditions to the children, and that relatives were not setting a good example, both generally as adults and more specifically in terms of their consumption of alcohol or drugs. The following are two illustrations:

> The whole family has been affected but particularly their two small daughters. . . . [the elder] doesn't have a good relationship with her father [the relative] and she is indifferent to what happens to him. Her mother [the family member] says that she hates her father. . . . [the younger daughter] does love her father, but by contrast their father rejects them both. 'He says to them, "Get out of here!" and upsets . . .

[the younger daughter]. I say that I'm no longer going to put the girls through this trauma.'

(Mexico, female partner of a drinker)

'He knocked me down to the ground. I was bleeding badly from my nose and mouth. He gave me hard punch. And that's when my daughter was trying to stop him from hitting me. And he got really angry . . . so then he hit her [the daughter] on the knee with a big stick/club. That broke her knee and she couldn't move – we were all on the ground, bleeding.'

(Australia, mother-in-law of a drinker)

Nor is it just the psychological environment of the family that can be affected, but also its physical integrity and security on account of damage or neglect by the relative or by invasion of the home by excessive drug use or by other excessive drinkers or drug users. The boundaries between the family and the outside world may be altered in uncomfortable ways. For one thing, the home can be invaded in very concrete ways as a result of excessive drinking or drug use. In some families, substance use took place in the home itself with consequences that family members found objectionable: for example, drug-using paraphernalia being left around the home or drugs being used in front of children. In some cases, relatives would shut themselves in bedrooms or bathrooms in order to consume drink or drugs. Even when consumption took place elsewhere, effects on home life might be apparent in the form of noise late at night when the relative returned intoxicated, or when relatives kept hours that did not fit with the rest of the family, but wanted to talk or make a noise when others wanted to sleep, causing family members to be tired the next day. In other instances, there was damage to the home, or essentials such as food went missing. Experienced as particularly invasive was the unwanted presence of other excessive drinkers or drug users, and sometimes family members worried about unexplained calls to the home presumed to be connected with drug use. The following extracts illustrate the threatening nature of these events and circumstances:

'There'd be the big mobs coming in from——. Once they had a big party underneath my house, they were making a lot of noise. The next minute they were carrying on shouting and yelling and fighting, making a lot of noise, and I told them, "Hey, if you want to drink grog take it down to the creek. This isn't the place to drink. I didn't get this house for you, I'm the one paying the rent." They just trashed the place, beer cans, empty wine casks all over outside.'

(Australia, female cousin of the wife of a drinker)

At first she had stopped him smoking at home, saying, 'Here we respect the home.' He understood on that occasion and stopped doing it, but on another occasion he came home under the influence, hit her, and said, ' "Here we do as I say", so then I couldn't say anything.' He drinks in the house every day, even bringing his friends home where they take drugs. She says the principal problem is that 'There is a lot of idleness, dissolute behaviour, taking of substances, injecting, wine, vulgar talk. The gang, 15 or 20 of them, get together, and he gets them all in the kitchen taking drugs.'

(Mexico, female partner of a drug user)

At this point in the interview the phone rang and when answered the caller hung up. He said that this happens often and thinks that it is connected to her [the relative's] problem. His wife said that it is a pity that they cannot be ex-directory because she runs her own business. He explained that they have had to have a police . . . alarm fitted because they were petrol bombed.

(England, father of a drug user)

Many examples of distressing family contact with the police were described. Police may have been involved for a number of reasons and in various ways. Sometimes family members were notified that the relative had been picked up by the police, and sometimes this required the family member or other family members or even a neighbour to visit the police station and stand bail or pay for the relative's release. In other cases, the police had arrived uninvited at the family home, or even raided the home. In yet other instances, the police had been called by a member of the family to calm down or remove the relative for the safety of family members, or to bring charges against the relative.

Two days later, the drug squad came and took the door off. They found nothing. He and his partner gave the police all the information they had, e.g. the telephone numbers on the bill etc. [earlier he had explained how strange people had been staying in the house and made lots of phone calls]. They cooperated with the police although their son [the relative] didn't want them to. At the time, the police said they were grateful, but since then they have had nothing but hassle from the police.

(England, father of a drug user)

Normal social life, on the other hand, was often restricted. Hunting expeditions; trips out into the bush; going to parties, the cinema or the theatre; or even family walks in the locality; as well as occasions for entertaining others in the home, were often curtailed. From experience of previous such occasions, family members were often worried about how the relative would behave, and as a consequence did not relish the thought of such social occasions. Some were concerned that neighbours or other family or community members should not see the relative intoxicated, fearing shame and even criticism from others.

Figure 5.2 summarises the foregoing theme of threat to the household and family. Again, our conclusion is that this threat is probably an invariant feature of life for family members facing alcohol or other drug problems in their homes. The exact nature of that threat varies – whether to the family finances, the well-being of children, the family atmosphere or climate, the integrity of the home as a private space, or relations with outsiders – but the existence of those threats in some combination is a regular feature of family life when a member of the family drinks or takes drugs excessively.

Facet four: signs of strain for family members

The picture of what it is like to have a close relative with a drink or drugs problem is completed by the fourth facet: signs of strain experienced by the family member and others in the household. When asked how the experience of having a close relative who had been drinking or taking drugs excessively had affected them personally, family members regularly described the kinds of effects shown in Table 5.2. The links between these bad feelings and the experiences of living with problem drinking or drug use were very readily and easily made. Many such links were drawn immediately and directly and were displayed within the structure of a single sentence. For example, one family member was preoccupied with thinking *'about* the relative's drug

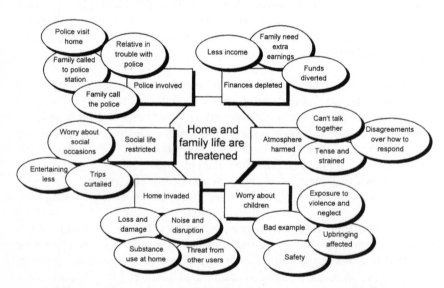

Figure 5.2 Threat to the home and family posed by a close relative's excessive drinking or drug taking.

Table 5.2 Bad feelings associated with being a close family member of a relative with a drinking or drug problem

Anxious, worried

Emotional, upset, e.g. worried; preoccupied; wrung out; emotional; can't compose self.

Worried, preoccupied, e.g. worried; preoccupied; can't enjoy a meal waiting for the relative to arrive; can't concentrate; can't get it off my mind; you think, where are they, what are they doing?; forget things because thinking about the relative; plays on your mind.

Tense, nervous, e.g. tense; anxious; anxiety attacks; nerves in pieces; nervous; suffer from nerves; panicky; trembling; on edge; on tenterhooks.

Irritable, quick-tempered, e.g. react to criticism; fly off the handle; ratty at work; quick-tempered with everyone; sensitive and irritable; annoyed over the smallest thing; always in a bad mood.

Helpless, despairing

Helpless, can't cope, e.g. hopeless, helpless, can't control the problem; frustrated, don't know what to do; impotent; can't cope; can't put up with it; can't stand it; desperate; hanging on by a thread; too much to handle.

Resigned, despairing, disillusioned e.g., don't care any more; no future; no hope; despair; apathy; resigned; putting no effort into things; don't expect things; don't make plans; stopped fighting; disillusioned.

Lost faith, trust or hope in the relative e.g., expecting to be let down, thinking the worst; fearful that the relative will use again; don't know whether what the relative says is genuine; lost faith in the relative; lost trust; frightened for the relative and the relative's future.

Low, depressed

Depressed, miserable, e.g. depressed; miserable, dragged down; low, down; sad, unhappy.

Low energy, enthusiasm, e.g. not light hearted; don't do pleasurable things; low enthusiasm, spirit, energy level and stamina low; not in the mood for going out socially.

Suicidal thoughts, e.g. wanted to kill self, meant to commit suicide; preoccupied with death; wished to die.

Guilty, devalued

Guilty, remorseful, e.g. have I abandoned him?; have we done the right thing?

Feel a failure, unconfident, e.g. ask 'what have I done wrong'?; feel a failure; wonder if I am to blame; inadequate; feel no good; unsure of self; am I that useless?

Devalued, used, e.g. feel you're just there to do the cooking and the cleaning; felt that I and the children came second place most of the time; feel I want to be in charge of my own life; devalued.

Angry, resentful, hatred

Angry, resentful, e.g. annoyed, cheated; let down; disappointed; damned if I'm going to do anything if the relative's not; offended; rejected, let down.

Hatred, dislike, e.g. hate the relative; feeling of rejection toward the relative; feel like hitting or shouting at the relative; jealous of the relative; want to lock the relative away; love and hate; glad to get rid of her; want him out of the way; you don't want them near you.

Table 5.2 (Contd.)

Frightened
  Frightened, dread; scared; shocked; alarmed.

Alone
  Alone, abandoned; feel we're the only family with problems.

use'. Another was despairing '*about* the relative's continued drinking'. A third was angry '*about* what the relative was doing to the family'. Other links between feelings and the experience of excessive substance use were slightly more elaborate and made at greater length; nevertheless, the links were almost always drawn clearly and unambiguously. The following are illustrations:

> He [the family member] attributes his state of health in part to his brother's [the relative's] drug use, saying that he feels nervous and that his hypertension possibly started when he discovered his brother's drug taking, because he was starting to get headaches at the same time. He stopped taking care of his own health, hardly finding time to eat. . . . Emotionally he feels depressed but not defeated.
>
> (Mexico, brother of a drug user)

> 'Physically I'm well but the emotional load is always there worrying me, it's a basic thing in my life, and is a dilemma for me. If I'm depressed when I feel tired I see no way out, no answer, everything seems very black, but on other days I can put up with it. It's difficult to know how different our relationship would be without him drinking this way, my torture comes from the way he drinks and the fact that I have no trust in him.' . . . On occasions she feels her heart is beating very rapidly. She has told the doctor about this and he says there's nothing wrong. She attributes it to stress. As far as her psychological health is concerned, as a result of her husband's drinking she has felt angry, deceived, worried, tense, unconfident, frightened, lonely, feelings of remorse and insecurity. . . . 'I've also felt to blame, I'm the type of person who blames myself for everything, although my meeting with the doctor helped me to overcome my feeling of blame to a large extent.'
>
> (England, wife of a drinker)

According to the family member, her husband was very jealous, did not trust her and would keep asking the children questions about what she was doing when he was away drinking. She said all these questions resulted in her becoming very stressed and she always felt there was a lot of pressure on her.

(Australia, wife of a drinker)

A family member's social and work life can also be affected. An English mother of a drug-using son said her social life had been restricted because she had 'felt so sick inside', and an English brother of a drug user explained how his college work had suffered because he had missed mornings trying to find help for his brother and also because he had fallen asleep in lessons after his brother had kept him awake all night.

One of the feelings commonly expressed by family members was that of anger. For example:

'See I tried to leave – tried to get away from it, let it go. You know what it's like. What they tell you to do, don't they, and not to get hooked into it, or argue, but to just let it go. Yes, I got angry and upset about it, but I had to cope with it.'

(Australia, wife of a drinker)

When she realised [that he was taking drugs] she felt very let down. . . . She still feels very angry towards him . . . the fact that he went out in the evening to drink leaving her and the children alone at home made her angry.

(Mexico, wife of a drinker)

Family members' self-image and self-confidence were often badly dented by their experiences. Sometimes this was attributed to self-blame for what had happened. In other instances, it was explained as the result of verbal attacks by the relative, or as a consequence of what neighbours or others say or might think about the family member. The following are illustrations.

She looked very tired and said she did not feel well. . . . 'There would be times that I would be trying to study and there would be heaps of people here and I just couldn't concentrate and because I couldn't get up and go because of the children my studies suffered. It is another sacrifice on my part.' This statement was very sad, not bitter, more resigned, an air of hopelessness.

(Australia, daughter-in-law of a drinker)

'You feel terribly responsible for bringing them into the world, you think what have I done? . . . You see them making mistakes and think what can

I do about it, you feel you must have made awful mistakes not getting through to them about the dangers.'

(England, mother of a drug user)

He certainly feels that he has lost a lot of confidence because of her problem. 'I don't find it easy to talk to people anymore.' He said that he has noticed a timidity in himself in asking for things, for example at work when he has to meet other people and get information. . . . Sometimes when she's been drinking she will lay into him, and she will tell him how useless he is. For example, she has commented on the way he speaks and his accent and about dropping his h's. She has told him that you don't get high up people with his accent, and has said no wonder he hasn't got promotion because of the way he speaks.

(England, husband of a drinker)

In the majority of interviews from all three socio-cultural groups, mention was made of symptoms of physical ill health. These included specific symptoms such as headaches, back pain, palpitations, or references to poor health in general terms, such as 'in decline', 'put years on me' and 'felt fragile'. Signs of strain for family members also included eating and sleep disturbances of a variety of kinds; increased or fluctuating (or, in a few instances, reduced) smoking, drinking or drug taking; and increased use of medication. Table 5.3 provides more detail of the different things that family members said.

Unlike their feelings of worry, despair, depression, anger, and feeling personally devalued, where the link with the relative's excessive drinking or drug taking was usually confidently made, in the case of physical ill health, eating, sleeping, smoking, drinking or drug use, the link was less obvious for family members. That was particularly the case where family members themselves had long-term illnesses or concurrent stresses of other kinds. Family members very often supposed, but could not be sure, that the relative's problem drinking or drug use had brought on or exacerbated their own health difficulties. In some instances, however, the link was more confidently drawn, as in the cases of the following three women:

'It's just a constant worry. I lost hair when he [the relative] was in prison. It's just as much a sentence for me as perhaps for him. You're hooked onto the addict, you also become an addict', always thinking about the problem. She will 'constantly feel upset, tired, sometimes sleep and sleep for a couple of days. . . . Sometimes I get headaches', normally in relation to specific stressful events such as 'something to do with the courts'.

(England, mother of a drug user)

Table 5.3 Signs and symptoms of family members' ill health

Poor sleep, tiredness

Sleep affected, up at night; sleep more; insomnia; spend more time in bed as an escape; lay awake the whole night; wake early; up at night talking with the relative; sometimes sleep for two days; tired; fatigued; weary with it all; difficulty sleeping; waking in a cold sweat.

Substance use

Smoking, drinking or drug taking or prescribed medication, going up, fluctuating more, or decreasing.

Eating, weight

Eat a lot when nervous; neglect eating; loss of appetite; weight change; have over-eaten under stress; some days eat a lot, others not at all; eat less because the relative doesn't eat; weight reduction.

Physical symptoms

Sickness; anaemia; headaches; neuralgia; back pain; 'pains'; hypertension; asthma; hair loss; change in pattern of bowel movements; gall bladder trouble; shortness of breath; palpitations; diarrhoea; migraines; 'minor ailments'; itching.

General poor health

Health poor; weak; in decline; felt ill; health 'went'; put years on me; in bad health; felt fragile; neglected self.

Miscellaneous

Sexual diseases transmitted by husband (the relative); danger of the recurrence of epilepsy; miscarriage; worsening of heart problems.

When she learnt about his drug consumption she felt ill. 'My body was paralysed and I had a bad feeling in my chest.' Sometimes when she has been desperate she has wished to die, 'because he doesn't get better'. About her general health she has noticed lately that she forgets things because she is thinking about him and sometimes she can't sleep.

(Mexico, mother of a drug user)

'Last time only I got really upset and angry with him, and I got really sick that time, I thought I was having problems with my kidneys, I thought my kidneys had had it. That's when I got really angry with him, and I said to him, "You're not leaving my side if it happens that I do get kidney problems, because you've done this to me, you've done this to me from all that drinking and arguing and stuff like that." He said, "I didn't make you sick." Sometimes I get those pains when I am worrying. I sit there sometimes thinking about what am I going to do about me.'

(Australia, partner of a drinker)

Effects on the health of other family members

Family members who were interviewed were very often worried, not just about the problem drinking or drug-taking relative, or their own mental or physical health, but also about the health and well-being of other family members. The latter included the problem drinkers' or drug takers' parents (when the interviewed family members were partners) and fathers or grand-parents (when the interviewed family members were mothers). But those who were regularly thought to be most affected by the problem, and to be most in danger, were the younger members of the families. They included brothers and sisters of the excessively drinking or drug-taking relatives, particularly when they had a good relationship with the latter and were upset, saddened and sometimes frightened in the face of their brother's or sister's excess. It was when the family included children of the problem drinking or drug-taking relative, however, that family members showed most concern. Children were thought to be particularly vulnerable to the effects of the problem in the family. They were said to experience, like the interviewed family members themselves, unease and tension, sadness and depression, apathy and lack of interest in things, and, in some cases, fear of the drinking or drug-using relative, and, in other instances, preoccupation with the latter's consumption and behaviour toward members of the family. School work was said to be affected, and sometimes the children were said to have gone hungry as a result of what was happening in the family.

A Mexican wife, for example, noted that her daughter was depressed because of her father's excessive drinking, and was suffering from headaches, sickness and dizziness, and another Mexican woman, whose partner was a drug user, described how her daughter 'doesn't eat, she sits in a corner and doesn't speak to anybody, she just stays there, not letting her sister approach her, not coming out of it, as if she is traumatised, lost in thought'. The following extract is particularly pertinent because it illustrates how a whole family can be affected. It illustrates a mother's concern both for the relative's (her daughter's) children (the interviewed family member's grandchildren) and for the interviewee's mother (the drinking relative's grandmother).

> Her [the relative's] children had also been much affected by her drinking. For example the older daughter isn't studying or working and finished secondary education at 16. She began to have problems of drug addiction, starting to smoke marijuana with some girlfriends. Now she is emotion-ally affected, apathetic, not studying, working or playing sports, she doesn't seem to enjoy doing anything, goes out to parties every weekend, has no boyfriend, having little trust in men. Her [the relative's] son has also been affected as far as his studies are concerned because he is 16 and hardly attended for the first part of his secondary education. He no longer lives at home, living for the last year in the home of one of his paternal

uncles. 'He got away from his parents' circle'. . . . Her [the family member's] mother has seen how she [the relative] drinks, has told her off, but finding there was nothing she could do for her has become depressed about it. At first she tried to talk quietly with her, but later scolded her more strongly and said to her, 'You're killing yourself, you're killing your children, can't you see that your daughters are in danger when you go out into the street? Think of them.' When [the relative] is calmer she says to [her grandmother], 'Yes, I promise you I'm going to give up, this is the last time', but other times she responds angrily, 'What does it matter to you? Don't interfere in my life.'

(Mexico, mother of a problem drinking daughter)

The extent and exact nature of family members' concerns about family health and well-being, and whether those concerns focus upon themselves or upon children or other members of the family, vary from one family to another. Whether family members' symptoms of physical ill health can be attributed to the relative's excessive substance use is often not at all clear to family members and that constitutes yet another source of uncertainty. What is universal, however, is an appreciation by family members that problem drinking or drug taking affects family health and well-being adversely in one way or another.

The impact on family members: the total picture

The four core facets described in this chapter are by no means all that was important to the experience of family members, in Mexico City, South-West England and indigenous communities in Northern Australia, but they do represent what we understand to be the core of that experience. Although in Chapter 9 we shall ask the question of whether the experiences these families were facing can be compared with any other kinds of family circumstances, we should already note here that the experience of living with a relative with a drinking or drug problem is a very particular experience. It brings together in some combination elements of stress, threat, and even abuse, often simultaneously affecting different family functions and different members of the family. Worry about the loved relative is a core characteristic. It is bad for the health of family members and for the health of the family as a whole. There is no simple name for that kind of experience, nor a simple label to describe the role of family members. Are they 'victims', 'worriers', or 'carers'? None of those alone fits the bill. The next chapter adds the dimension of 'coping', as we consider the difficulties family members face in deciding how to respond to their circumstances.

Chapter 6

How family members cope

In the face of the experiences described in the previous chapter – the stresses and strains of living with a deteriorating close relationship with a relative who is using alcohol or drugs excessively, and the accompanying uncertainty and worry for that relative, for oneself, for other members of the family and for the home itself – family members searched for ways of responding. There was a perceived need to act, to do something. This chapter is about that search for what to do. It is about finding ways of coping. Sometimes it is about family members feeling they had been successful and done the right thing. More often it is about dilemmas, compromises, frustrations and feeling helpless.

In Chapter 5, the idea of 'worrying' was introduced. The family members who are the principal protagonists throughout this book were worried and had good cause to be so. The verb 'to worry' has a number of connotations. It may imply a silent, private, inward-looking worrying, or *angst*. It may equally carry the connotation of concern shared with others – a worry shared is a worry halved. It may also carry the meaning, perhaps particularly so in some cultures, of active *doing* on behalf of the people whom family members are worried about. To be worried for someone combines having concerns for that person and being on the search for what can be done.

A feeling of responsibility, even obligation, to help the relative, and thereby to help themselves and their families, was often taken for granted and implied in the interviews with family members. Although it was not always explicitly stated, we believe it is a general characteristic of close family members of people with drinking and drug problems, and one that may particularly distinguish them from less close family members and from most outsiders to the family, that they are worried about what is happening to the relative and the family and at the same time feel responsible for trying to find ways to respond.

We turn now to an exploration of what family members said about the ways they had responded. This topic has been central throughout the research on which this book is based, and we have tended to use the generic English word 'coping' to define this domain. It is a moot point, however, whether that is the most appropriate term. The term has been widely used in psychology, sometimes with a wider focus than the one adopted here (Folkman et al., 1986; Moos et al., 1990). Our interest is in the actions and positions taken by family members toward their problem drinking or drug-taking relatives and the latter's problems. We have focused less on 'coping' in the sense of the behavioural and mental ways that family members as individuals deal privately with the stresses they are experiencing. Nor are we interested only in well-thought-out and articulated strategies, or ways of responding that a family member believes to be effective, as might be thought to be implied by the word 'coping' – although they are certainly included. The field of interest here includes feelings about the relative or directed at the relative, tactics tried once or twice and quickly abandoned, and 'stands' or positions taken. It is interesting to note that the Spanish translation of 'coping' preferred in Mexico is *enfrentar*, or the reflexive *enfrentarse*, which is somewhat closer to our usage, and which, literally translated, means 'to face' or 'to face up to'.

Feeling powerless

There are no rules about how to act if a close relative is consuming alcohol or taking drugs excessively. There is no guidance generally available for family members about how to fulfil the obligation they feel to do something to help the relatives they are concerned about and whose behaviour is so affecting the family. How family members should cope under these difficult circumstances is not part of the cultural heritage of any of the three socio-cultural groups included in this research. By and large, family members had to work it out for themselves. It is hardly surprising that many expressed feeling impotent:

> She just wants some normality in the family. She just wants for his [the relative's] sickness to go away; feeling that she is powerless to change anything: 'I don't want him to die. I'd like to see him old and grey. I'd like to see that we'd spend another Christmas together. I just guess I want it all to go away, to share – you know, to have that sort of sharing in the family. I wish there was a way that I could help him . . . but he's chosen not to have it'.
>
> (Australia, sister of a drinker)

> 'I don't know how to deal with it. I ask myself if it's worth carrying on, but the truth is I have faith and hope. I always convince myself that he is going to give up his consumption. Now I view it with indifference, I just withdraw from wherever it is that he is.'
>
> (Mexico, female partner of a drinker)

But that sense of impotence was not by any means universal, and those who did express such a sense of resignation had usually arrived at such a position after engaging in much more active attempts to deal with the problem. Finding out how family members in different socio-cultural groups cope in the face of such problems was a central aim of the research, and those interviewed were very forthcoming on the subject. It was something they knew a lot about. In this section we attempt to illustrate the wide range of ways in which family members responded, pointing out similarities, contrasts and distinctions, and suggesting a possible typology of coping actions. As in Chapter 5, we shall describe a picture which appears to be common in all socio-cultural groups, suggesting later, in Chapter 8, how we believe that picture varies from group to group.

The following extract provides a suitable place to begin describing the variety of ways that family members act, because this one single passage contains a number of very typical elements. It illustrates a number of important distinctions between possible ways of acting, and a number of recurring dilemmas that family members face in all cultures:

> 'I show him I'm not happy if I think he's been smoking it but I do what I can to help him.' If he asked for money she would not give him any. She would fill up his car with petrol and would get him shoes, but she wouldn't trust him with money. She said he never gives them any of his unemployment pay. She had told him not to get the car because he could not afford it. He had said, 'You get the road tax, I'll get the insurance.' She said, 'You feel blackmailed into doing what they want.'
>
> (England, mother of a drug user)

The first sentence in that passage illustrates one of the main dilemmas that family members faced: how to stand up to the excess while at the same time trying to support the relative. In the face of requests for money or provisions or goods that cost money – referred to as 'humbugging' in the previous chapter – family members can give in, take a very firm stand, or compromise, as that mother had done. One can imagine her concern that her son was without good shoes and why she might decide to buy them for him despite the money that he would have been spending on his drug use. She had advised against his buying a car, but helped him with petrol. In fact she was doing a lot that it is difficult for a mother to do in the face of requests from her son about whom she was concerned: she was being assertive by making clear her unhappiness with his drug use and by not trusting him with money. Even so, she felt unhappy that she was giving in to demands – being 'blackmailed', as she put it.

Putting up with it

Reports of interviews from all three socio-cultural groups were full of examples of ways in which family members gave in to their relatives, put up with the latter's problematic consumption, became resigned, or did nothing to confront the problem. This is a large category of family members' actions, and it has a number of distinguishable facets. Some statements of this position refer simply to *inaction* in the face of the problem, while others have a flavour of *accepting* things as they are, others of *sacrifice* by restricting oneself or putting oneself out in some way to accommodate the relative drinking or taking drugs, and still others express *support* for the relative. Some of the phrases that family members used are listed in Table 6.1.

The following are examples of putting up with a relative's behaviour, each containing an element of inaction:

> She was 'almost afraid to phone [the alcohol advisory centre] and ask.' . . . She likes to feel that he [the relative] isn't drinking and doesn't want to know that he might be. . . . she was afraid that he was going to start drinking again and was 'resigned that he will'. She added, 'I'll be pleasantly surprised then if he doesn't, won't I?' . . . She had not told him about the [research] project because she feels it would be saying to him, 'I don't trust you', and at the moment she 'won't rock the boat', she will wait until he slips again.
>
> (England, sister of a drinker)

> She knew he [the relative] 'dabbled' in drugs but she didn't know 'the extent of the drugs he was taking'. She thinks perhaps she didn't want to know.
>
> (England, mother of a drug user)

> At first he [the family member] had wanted to know nothing about his [the relative's] drug taking, and he had continued that way up to now because the matter had never been dealt with openly in the family, because he'd [family member] never surprised him [the relative] consuming at home – 'I've never caught him in the act.' He [the family member] thinks that if that were to happen then he would speak openly about it with him [the relative].
>
> (Mexico, father of a drug user)

> He says he doesn't talk much, 'so she [his wife] gets upset with me because I don't talk about things, I just keep it to myself. That's what I used to do all the time.'
>
> (Australia, stepson-in-law of a drinker)

Although we shall later see examples of religion referred to in the context of more active ways of coping, there were also references to religion in the context of a resigned position. For example, a Mexican family member said, 'I

Table 6.1 Phrases family members used that indicated putting up with a relative's excessive drinking or drug taking

Unsure how to react	Pacify	Wouldn't go on a girls' night out
Don't know what to say	Keep him calm	Wouldn't leave her son alone with the relative
You drift on in a daze	Talk her down	Play a tape she likes
Get more resigned than angry	Just talk	Give her a bath
Don't care any more	Pretended	Cook for him
How can you stop him?	Denied	Sometimes sleep with him
There's nothing you can do	Covered up	Buy him half a carton of beer
Pray to God to do something	Excused	Sometimes take him beers
Don't expect anything	Gave in to the relative	Ration out drinking
Don't make plans any more	Overprotected	Give her money
Felt hopeless and depressed	Being too soft with the relative	Give food and tobacco
No longer believe in her	Drank more when living with the relative	Provide food and a bed
Feel hopeless about her	Went and got another bottle	Buy food and clothing from own money
Block it off	Would use dope and 'speed' together	Get him to eat
Want to put it under the carpet	Accepted the relative in this condition	Bail him out
None of my business	Never demanded anything of the relative	Don't fight back
Don't want to get involved	Let the relative get away with so much	Put up with
Things you don't want to remember	Tried not to rub the relative up the wrong way	Accept
Feel angry but can't say anything	Let things ride to keep the peace	Love and understand
Wrote abusive letters but didn't send them	Tried to make sure everything ran smoothly	Show compassion
Let him get on with it	Plod on and get through today	Be more loving
Has opted for indifference	Tried to keep things normal in the family	Forgive
Take no notice	Fetched relative from the pub when he phoned	Give him a chance
Don't antagonise	Tried to get him to bed	Just hope
Say 'poor thing'	Maintained the relative's flat	Went to clean the house up

Go along with his story	Helped financially	Replaced windows relative had broken
Play along	Paid some of the debts	Never asked for any of relative's earnings
Keep him happy	Didn't go to weddings	Paid the odd bill that relative couldn't afford to pay
Drove 200 miles to see him when he rang	Put relative to bed when drunk	Paid for a holiday for the relative
Made relative a meal even when he didn't turn up	Doesn't work now so has to look after relative	

pray to God, I beg for him [the relative]. You, God, can be a good doctor and cure him. I've lost all hope.'

These more passive or inactive forms of putting up with excessive drinking or drug taking also included the following: never demanding anything of the relative in the way of money or doing anything in the house; just allowing the relative to walk in after going off on binges; trying not to rub the relative up the wrong way, letting things ride to keep the peace; trying to make sure everything runs smoothly, plodding on and getting through today, trying to keep things normal in the family, to keep the family together; getting more resigned than angry; the family member changing her attitude, expecting anything and not making plans any longer; feeling hopeless and depressed; and no longer believing in the relative. One family member put it well when she said: 'You don't care anymore, how can you stop him going to the offy [off-licence], there's really nothing you can do, you can't force them to do what they don't want to do.'

Of those forms of putting up with drinking or drug taking that appeared to involve the family member making some personal sacrifice, many involved sacrifice of a financial kind, as in providing food, paying bills, giving money or other things that the relative could not afford because of the money spent on drink or drugs, paying for a holiday for the relative, or maintaining and refurnishing or redecorating accommodation for the relative. The following is a clear example:

'If I had the money every day from Monday to Friday and if he came to my work Monday to Friday I'd give him the money. So I mean sometimes I am just as much to blame for the amount of alcohol he drinks half the time, most of the time. Every now and then he will come and say that he wants it for food. I say to him you go home and I will bring some food around, then he just smiles at me, and I know that smile. Sometimes I feel like saying no when he asks for money.'

(Australia, daughter of a drinker)

Other examples involved making social sacrifices, such as not going to family occasions such as weddings, parties or nights out. Other examples were fetching the relative from the pub; trying to get the relative to bed when the latter was incapable; replacing windows every time the relative broke them; continuing to make meals for the relative even if the latter didn't turn up for them, didn't want to eat, or even threw them in the rubbish; giving up work to look after the relative; and having sex with the relative even though it was disgusting:

> She said that until recently she had never done anything because she had felt so frightened. She had always done what he wanted, including letting him insult her, and even having sexual relations with him when she didn't want to. This had made her particularly disgusted, 'being with him when he came home having been drinking since he was often very dirty and smelling very bad.'
>
> (Mexico, female partner of a drinker)

Other references to forms of action that imply putting up with problem drinking or drug taking included an element of support, or attempted support, for the relative:

> 'He came back drunk, drunk, not [drunk enough to] make trouble, he ask me to make bed, then go to sleep. I'm saying, "Poor thing poor thing, you've got to have a shower, have a bath, clean yourself", and I have him clean shirt and trousers.'
>
> (Australia, female partner of a drinker)

> 'At least we are going to make sure he's fed, is clean and gets to work clean, we're going to look after him well so that he leaves us a little in peace.'
>
> (Mexico, female partner of a drinker)

> She thinks her attitude now is different; that although she has hope for him she doesn't expect him to get better. . . . She feels it is 'very possible and possibly probable that he will never get over it', so she feels she will give him the best time that she can and listen to him when he needs it, and 'that's the best I can do'. If he needed her she would get someone to do her work for her that day. . . . There have only been a few occasions when she has sat up through the night with him. There was a time when she got up in the night because that was the only time possible to talk to him, and there was a time when that was what he wanted to do.
>
> (England, mother of a drug user)

Why do family members put up with excessive drinking or drug taking?

It is often asked by onlookers why family members put up with the inconvenience, hassle, stress and often abuse to which they are subject. In fact, as we shall see in Chapter 7 when considering the social support that family members receive or lack, other family or friends are often critical of family members for putting up with problem drinking or drug-taking relatives, and as we saw in Chapter 1, professional people often label family members as 'codependent' or resistant to change. The reports of interviews carried out with these family members in Mexico City, South-West England and Northern Australia put a very different complexion on this question. A number of the quotations given above to illustrate the theme of putting up with drinking or drug taking in the family already give hints of the reasons why family members might act in these ways – not wanting to know the worst, not wanting to provoke further drinking or drug use, or feelings of fear, hopelessness or sympathy for the relative. In addition, there were other clear statements by family members about the reasons for responding in inactive, accepting, sacrificing or supportive ways. These reasons for putting up with problem drinking or drug taking are summarised in Figure 6.1.

In the context of talking about such ways of acting, family members described the following: feelings of caring and concern about the user (e.g. 'I couldn't envisage saying I'm leaving and never seeing him again. . . . When I see him on the way down he cries and he's confused and he's thin, you feel sorry'); the need to look after children and to keep the family going (e.g. 'When everything is going on smoothly . . . I want everything to be normal and back how it was'); to avoid trouble (e.g. the relative becomes very irritable, rebellious and angry if the family member does pressure her); to avoid embarrassment or being let down; reduced self-confidence or accumulation of stress (e.g. 'You get to the point where you don't care any more, you've been dragged down for months, you lose confidence in yourself'); the family member's own positive attitude to drinking or drug-taking (e.g. the family member could see the attractions of 'speed' and has used drugs together with the relative as part of the social scene); and the family member's philosophy about change (e.g. 'They've got to do it for themselves, there's really nothing you can do').

These coping actions of the 'putting up with' kind are powerfully underpinned by the sense of responsibility that family members feel toward their relatives and the obligation they feel to help and support them. The following quotations make that clear:

> 'I think he worked hard all his life, he put food on the table for us, clothing, so he spent all his life looking after us and I feel that it is my turn to look after him. I feel really guilty if when he comes to work

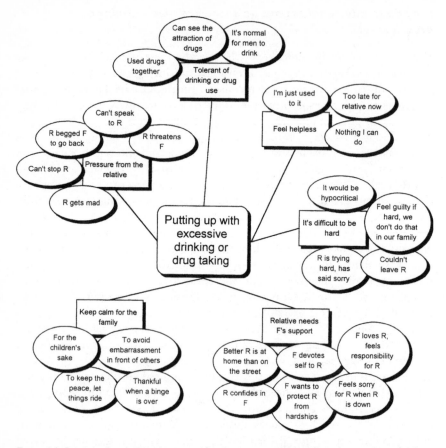

Figure 6.1 Reasons family members give for putting up with a relative's excessive drinking or drug taking (F – family member; R – relative).

and I have no money to give him, I feel really bad. I just think about it all day.'

(Australia, daughter of a drinker)

'Life with him has involved a lot of patience, a lot of sacrifice, perhaps it's because of love or because of the way I was brought up. My grandmother said that marriage is for always and one should always be faithful to your husband. I am not going to leave my home and I shall put up with it all, but the situation is very hard. I would only separate if he asked me to do so.'

(Mexico, female partner of a drinker)

The first overall conclusion to be drawn from what family members told interviewers about ways they had tried to respond is, therefore, that family members everywhere, much of the time, and in different ways, put up with their relatives' excessive drinking or drug taking. They may not always have responded that way, and these ways of coping are fully understandable when the circumstances are appreciated. A casual observer might be critical of family members who appear to have accepted relatives' substance misuse, but when family members are given the opportunity more fully to explain their circumstances, their actions are easily understood.

Trying to regain control

Family members often drew contrasts between responding to their relatives' drinking or drug taking with acceptance, self-sacrifice or resignation on the one hand and, on the other hand, trying to regain some of the control over family and home life that had been lost. The latter involved standing up to the relative's excessive drinking or drug taking by one means or another. Family members described a wide range of ways of trying to stand up to the problem, but they are presented here as a single group. There are two reasons for grouping together these diverse ways of coping. First, we believe they serve the same basic function for family members: that of trying to restore control in that place which is central to most people's lives and where people expect to be able to exert control, namely, the family and home. Excessive drinking or drug taking by a close relative threatened that most fundamental sense of control.

The second reason for grouping together these varied ways of responding is, simply, that they are in practice very difficult to separate. Theoretically, we may wish to distinguish between being assertive and being controlling, between getting angry and calmly stating the facts, or between protecting one's own interests and supporting a relative. But the data from the interviews did not easily allow such separations. Family members mostly spoke about ways of responding that either mixed forms of coping that we had thought might be distinct, or described actions that could not easily be categorised as one thing or another. Another way of thinking about this is to conceive of subtle distinctions between ways of acting as *dilemmas* for family members. They may have come to the conclusion that getting angry with their relatives is counter-productive, or that they should take a firm stand and refuse to be humbugged. But those are very difficult things to do, and what family members actually spoke of was trying to talk to their relatives in ways that were more or less calm or unemotional, or of responding to requests for money or the equivalent with some degree of compromise. To be calm or to be angry, to refuse or to accede to requests, were just two of the many dilemmas that family members faced.

In the paragraphs that follow we try to provide some idea of the variety of ways in which family members in all three socio-cultural groups engaged in trying to exercise control over their family and home life in the face of relatives' problem drinking or drug taking. Those ways of coping include being *aggressive, confrontational, talking and telling, refusing and resisting, compromising, setting limits,* and *protecting oneself and the family.* They combine elements of being emotional, assertive, controlling and supportive toward the relative.

Talking and telling

A general class of action repeatedly described by family members was, naturally enough, that of talking to the relative about the latter's behaviour. But talking to a close relative whose substance use has become a threat to the family was no straightforward matter, and this class of coping action nicely illustrates in itself the difficulties that family members face in choosing how to respond. When it comes to responding to their relatives, family members are not non-directive counsellors, disinterested and therefore able to respond with unconditional warmth and empathy. On the other hand, they had often learned the hard way that to respond naturally with anger and even violence was counter-productive and possibly dangerous. Family members had had to find some middle ground between those two extremes. Some of the words and phrases they used when describing the ways in which they had talked to their relatives are shown in Table 6.2. The range was wide, covering ways of talking and telling which were more confrontational, and some of which were more critical. Others involved reasoning with the relative, offering support, or trying to understand the relative's point of view. Family members themselves often drew distinctions between appropriate and inappropriate ways of talking to their relatives. Distinctions were drawn by Australian interviewees between 'soft' or 'sweet' talking on the one hand, and 'rough' or 'smart' talking on the other hand. A Mexican mother said that she needed to tell her son off in a 'strong' way in order to make him stop using drugs at least temporarily. A Mexican wife, on the other hand, said that she had tried to speak quietly with her husband about his drug use, saying to him, 'Don't smoke any more, it's bad for you. Do it for the children's sake, don't you realise that they are a reflection of us?' Australian family members had tried to point out to their relatives the physical damage that drinking was causing, the violence and cruelty to others, and the harmful consequences that were likely to ensue if drinking continued, including the inability to pass on traditions to the next generation.

In all three groups, talking and telling had sometimes taken the form of critical challenges or emotional threats. These included telling relatives that they could choose between killing themselves or getting on with their lives, pointing out that their behaviour was making other family members ill, or charging the relative with not loving the family member. Threats included telling relatives that they would be beaten, run out of the house or locked up

Table 6.2 Ways of talking and telling that family members used with their relatives

Talk good way	Everyone says what they feel; there's no shouting	Gave relative an ultimatum to stop drinking or family member would leave
Talk really soft and gently, not cheeky or hard words	Not get irritable, tell him what she disagrees with	Threaten the relative with calling the family member's brother
Listened to what relative had to say	Need to be strong	If you do that to her again you'll have me to deal with
Told her the family are always there to turn to	Listened to what he has to say, be very strong, and stick to your own values and beliefs	Threatened that she would bring a man to hit him
Talk things through and listen to what she has to say	She knows I won't take any bullshit	Either behave or I'll throw you out
Tried to find out what was causing him to feel depressed	Confront	I haven't hit you yet, but the day I do, be careful
Acted as a pseudo-counsellor	Reason with	Threatened to have him locked up
Asked him about his reasons for taking drugs	Challenge	Threatened to run him out of the house
Chatted with her to understand the reasons for her addiction	Explaining	Threatened to beat him if he didn't give up
Told her she shouldn't worry since she is loved and accepted	Advise	You can choose to slowly kill yourself or get on with your life
Telling	Trying to talk him into doing something	Don't your realise you are making Mum and Dad ill?
Pointing out	Suggest	Can't you see how you've provoked me?
Sit down, talk and get through to him	Tell off	You wouldn't do this to me if you loved me
Talk with a few reasoned words	Lecture	Made a cutting remark about the relative intended for the relative and family to hear
Be very open and frank	Question	Cried
Give the kinds of advice anyone would get with the advantage of age	Told relative not to bring it into the house	Cried and got angry at the same time
Tried to convince him to go to AA	You know my views and you've got to respect them	Pleaded
Try to get him to see the damage alcohol and drugs are doing to him	Told him to bring the bottle out; he could see I was determined	Begged

Table 6.2 (Contd.)

Tried to get him to see the dangers he runs in the street when he's drunk or drugged	Told him not to come up here if he doesn't go through with treatment	Growling
Make him see that if he loves his girlfriend he must value what she does for him	If this is how it's going to be, I think we should go for a legal separation	Nags
Moans	If there is another incident like that, her junk will have to go	Moans
How dare you speak to me like that?	Starting on	Shouts
Brings it up all the time	Getting angry	Rants and raves
Harps on about the past	Swearing	Argues
Losing temper	Hard talk	Hit
Going berserk	Arguing	Thrash out at
Lost his temper and pinned her against the wall shouting at her face-to-face	Yelling	Scream at
Finished up at each other's throats	Jumping on (verbally)	
Talking angrily	Confronting and challenging	

in an institution. The more emotional ways of talking to relatives shade off into, and are difficult to distinguish from, physical struggles and confrontations such as trying to snatch from relatives the latter's drugs or paraphernalia (e.g. a bottle containing an alcoholic beverage, toilet paper soaked in inhalant, or a marijuana cigarette), and outright physical fights, rows and arguments.

Resisting, refusing and limiting

Other ways of standing up to the problem involved family members in doing more than just talking, telling and sometimes fighting with their relatives. Many of the actions described by family members were attempts to change the rules of engagement which governed their lives with their relatives. These were, by one means or another, much more explicit attempts to exercise control. Some of these ways of coping involved refusing relatives' requests. The things that were commonly refused were money, items that could be exchanged for money, food or the preparation of food, and access to the home. The following is a particularly clear example:

He [the family member] said, 'You've just got to be cruel to be hard on some of the family, strict with them.' . . . [his wife] interjected, 'You've got to be cruel to be kind.' He continued, 'You know, when some family come here drunk you just can't say to them, "Come on in", you just have to tell them that you've got kids here and other people that you're looking after and so they can't stay.' . . . [his wife] said, 'We've got to look after our own food, we'd run out if we gave it to everyone who came and asked.' He added, 'Yeah, you've just gotta be strict with them, gotta be hard, they might hate you for it. . . . They take it badly, they take it the wrong way. They always do. Aw, some they understand what we're trying to do, but the most of them take it all the wrong way.'

(Australia, a couple with a number of drinking relatives)

Other responses involved attempting to limit the relative's drinking or drug taking. Some of these ways are shown in Table 6.3. One way in which family members often felt that they had authority was in forbidding altogether, or limiting in some way, drinking or drug use taking place in the home itself. This sometimes extended, even among adults, to trying to set rules about coming and going to and from the home:

She has also established rules about the time when he should arrive home. She told him that he should be back by ten o'clock at night, but for a while he tricked her. However, on one occasion when he arrived home at midnight she didn't open the door to him and left him outside in his car all night. She said that she felt very frightened about how he would react the next day but she had confronted him saying, 'I have shown you. I am in the right, although you won't admit it because of your machismo.' From then on he has arrived home by nine in the evening or by ten at the latest.

(Mexico, wife of a drinker)

In their efforts to regain control and to do something about the problem, family members often found themselves adopting tactics that are in the nature of compromises. The example of the English mother was given at the beginning of the chapter. Other examples include a son who bought his father a few cans of beer when the latter had no money, but otherwise got his father to earn his beers by cleaning up the family yard, and an uncle who gave his niece five dollars for food when she humbugged him, provided she was sober, but gave her nothing when she was drunk. Other ways of trying to take control involved family members in maintaining a high level of vigilance, noticing and searching for signs or evidence of drinking or drug taking, even throwing away or destroying drink, drugs or paraphernalia, and otherwise carefully watching over and even following their relatives, as in the following example:

He [the family member] watches him [the relative] closely, goes out

Table 6.3 Ways of trying to limit a relative's excessive drinking or drug taking, as described by family members

Pour away the drink	Looked for places where the relative could be looked after
Throw away all the bottles in the house that he's been given after the fiestas	Moved with the relative to another house
Got rid of bottles of inhalants several times and marijuana another time	Managed to get the relative to go the doctor
If find syringes throw them away	Careful to give him his medicines
Keep out of the relative's way but keep an eye on her	Sees that he goes to his therapy sessions
Careful to keep him under watch	Accompanies relative to outpatients
Stay at home and make her better	Put a leaflet about the dangers of Ecstasy with the relative's things
Go through her handbag and credit cards	Won't allow needles in the house
Take small bottles of inhalant off him or hide them	Tried to find out more for him to do or looked for jobs so he'd be more occupied
Won't leave her because she thinks that way she can look after her and control her	Found her a beautiful studio flat in a residential area
Phoned the relative's friends to check up on the relative's story	Try to encourage him in his interests
Made a mutual decision to have no alcohol in the house	Help the relative find work
Phoned the police to tell them that the relative would be drinking and driving	Got him a job as a chauffeur in the same factory where she works
Told the police about dealers	Tried to find a detox place for the relative
Tried to get the police to follow and search her	Phoned AA
Made a rule that he couldn't come in after 10.30 p.m.	Passed on leaflets to the relative
More than ever careful not to have drink in the house	Called the doctor
Arranged to have a cold beer in the fridge as alternative to drugs	Set about the task of finding somewhere professional that would take the relative
Didn't pass on messages to the relative	Gave him a month to start getting treatment
Told a friend not to buy them the usual bottle of drink at Christmas	Gave up dabbling in drugs herself
Tried to put his friends off, telling them not to come round so often	Stopped drinking for 6 months
Sent her to France to stay with her grandmother	Hasn't had a drink since the relative stopped
Took him to an AA refuge and later a hospital	

and looks for him in the street, sometimes following him to see where he goes. On one occasion he found a beer bottle top in the house, and he went to his work to look for him. He didn't find him and that night he [the relative] came home drunk. . . . The parents [family member and his wife] have come to an agreement to give him [the relative] medicine, to prohibit him from drinking, and not have alcoholic drinks at home. He has been threatened with being turned out of the home.

(Mexico, father of a drinker in his early twenties)

Controlling and supporting

Other ways of trying to do something positive about the problem combined attempts at control with efforts to be supportive of the relative. Although that is a hard act to pull off, family members often expressed recognition of the need to be both firm and kind. For example:

Now instead of reproaching him, she tries to get close to him like friends. They both like rock music and they talk together about different groups. At such times she takes advantage of the moment and tries to convince him to give up his drug use.

(Mexico, wife of a drug user)

The father of a Mexican drug-using teenage son explained that finding out about the drug use had not been a bad thing for anyone in the family since there had followed a big coming together of his three sons. The elder brother had tried to speak with him [the relative] and to ask why his brother had been taking drugs, and a younger brother had said to him [the relative], 'No, brother [using the affectionate form *manito*], don't do that.'
The following is an extract from an English interview:

She has reacted to his [the relative's] drinking by 'confronting him with it and not ignoring it'. As an example, she said that after the first time he was in hospital . . . she thought about it over the weekend and finally wrote to her brother, saying that he sounded as if he had been drinking and that he should get in touch and come and talk to her. She said it was a supportive letter. . . . She has told him, 'You have got to do it for yourself; if you come in drunk I'm not going to throw you out.' . . . She said she has never made any threats to him.

(England, sister of a drinker)

A mother expressed well the dilemma of combining standing up to excessive drug use in the family with supporting the drug using relative, when she said:

'You need to be very strong, to be there and talk to him but still stick to your own values and beliefs in life.'

(England, mother of a drug user)

Other examples of statements implying a mix of control and support involved trying to encourage the relative's interests or finding more for the relative to do; helping the relative look for a job, sometimes in the same place of work as the family member, in order that the relative would be better occupied; or helping the relative find suitable accommodation. A commonly reported action took the form of a family member encouraging or assisting the relative's involvement in treatment. Such actions included putting a leaflet about the dangers of Ecstasy with the relative's things, managing to get the relative to go to the doctor, a grandmother and sister being placed in charge of giving the relative his medicine, a sister carefully watching her relative take the antialcohol drug Antabuse, and family members encouraging their relatives to continue with treatment by accompanying them to treatment sessions.

Protecting self, family and home

Finally, in this lengthy catalogue of ways family members found to stand up to their relatives' problem drinking or drug taking, are a number of ways of coping which had the aim not so much of controlling the excessive drinking or drug use itself as of protecting the family member, the home and particularly the children from the harmful effects of the problem. Examples are shown in Table 6.4.

Such protective actions were sometimes accompanied by pessimism about relatives ameliorating their drinking or drug taking. Separating from the relative was a recurring idea for many family members and might be thought of as the ultimate form of protection against continued excessive substance use and its harmful effects on the family. Separation was only one way, however, of withdrawing from drinking or drug-using relatives or achieving greater independence. It is to that large class of coping actions that this chapter now turns.

Withdrawing and gaining independence

The third large class of ways of responding to the stressful family circumstances described in the previous chapter consisted of actions which had in common the element of gaining more independence from the relative and the latter's problems, or of moving away from the relative, or putting distance, physical, emotional or both, between the relative and the family member. Such action took many forms. Some of the words and phrases used by family members are shown in Table 6.5. They varied from small-scale and time-limited actions, such as hiding in a bedroom or locking oneself in the shower

Table 6.4 Protecting self, family and home: examples of family members' actions

No one would fight at my grandmother's place; people have a lot of respect for Grandmother, you don't argue and fight there	Approaching the housing authority, who might help by arranging a transfer to alternative accommodation
Keeping one's eyes open for signs of trouble	Asking the housing authority to fit the home with security measures such as window screens and fences
Defending oneself or others, or fighting back	Runs [controls] the money
Separating drinkers from fighting	Both do weekly shopping because family member goes to pay for it
Running away from an aggressive drinker	Don't use a joint account
Refusing drinkers access to one's home or controlling number or type who enter	Tries not to give him money
Stopping going out with a drinker	Gives her money for her needs but not to buy drugs
Not letting children go to stay with their father	Won't leave her son in the house on his own with his father when the latter is drinking
Told the relative you don't steal when you're with me	Told relative to leave the flat which they owned and which the relative had misused
Playing along with the drinker for the sake of the children's safety	Calling the night patrol
Calling the police	Seeking protection from a court that might issue a restraining order

or another room, to those that were on a larger scale and represented potentially longer-term solutions, such as living apart in the same home, leaving home or asking the relative to do so. In between was a multitude of other options. A related dimension, which family members often thought was of the greatest importance, contrasts those withdrawing actions in which the emphasis was on avoiding the problem drinking or drug-using relative with those actions that place a greater emphasis upon the family member's own quality of life. The former focused on the family member protecting herself or himself from the harmful effects of too close a contact with the relative, while the latter shifted the focus onto the family member and the latter's independence.

The greater the focus on family members' own quality of life, the more coping actions involved personal enjoyment, distraction, maintaining an undisrupted life, thinking of themselves, distancing themselves from the drinking or drug problem, and not actively engaging in trying to control it. That stance can be contrasted with one in which family members were pre-occupied with relatives and their problems, and were leading a disrupted and

Table 6.5 Phrases family members used that indicate putting distance between themselves and their problem drinking or drug-taking relatives

Moving away	Get out and enjoy yourself
Getting away	Escape, get away
Escaping	Distract yourself, switch off
Taking off	Don't let it disrupt life
Walking out	Get on with things regardless
Running away	Put your own needs first
Getting away from the drunks	Put it out of your mind
Getting away from drinkers	Step back, distance yourself
I sat away, in the shade	Learn to live with it
Escaping drinkers	Give up trying to control
Telling the drinker to leave or stay out bush	Accept things as they are
Getting the drinker away from his drinking mates	Sort yourself out
Avoiding drinkers while they're drinking	Friends
Avoiding the grog	Holiday
Spending time working away from home, out of town, or travelling extensively	Meals out
Removing oneself from the family or from the drinking scene	Running
Finally settled in——[capital city]	Aerobics
Flew away to——[capital city]	Swimming
Moving out bush	Theatre
Moving back to the homeland	Football match
Returning to a traditional lifestyle on a remote community	Voluntary work
Setting up one's own camp	Music lessons
Retreating to our outstation	Reading
Better because I was away from my family	Prepare meals as usual
Becoming strong in herself, feeling hope and that she could just get up and leave	Go ahead with social events
I wash my hands of him	Don't wait for him
Let him get on with it	Keep life as normal as possible
I won't give up my whole life to him	Put it out of your mind
There must be boundaries; you can go only so far	Ride above it
If I can't help her, I'm sorry	Step back from it
I can't run his life for him	Control maternal feelings
Life goes on	Keep a diary
We do what we want to do	Look hard at myself
I can't put a full stop to my life	Study philosophy
Do your own thing	Take counselling
Put yourself first	Make a 'personal inventory'
You've got to think of yourself	Won't be abused

Not to be trodden on	Get out
Kick him out	Leave
Cut, push away	
Strong enough to get out of the cycle, strong enough to leave	A new life/re-established life
Nice things in the house	Study
Desire to better self, prove self	White education for the children
Self-taught	Going to work
Have control	They respect me now, respect earned
Doing something good about myself	Be a person, just me, look after me
Accepted as a man	

unenjoyable life, often feeling guilty, worried and frightened, and allowing their own needs to be submerged. The former focus, or 'gaining independence' as we have chosen to call it, includes varying degrees of the following elements: *not worrying, doing what the family member wants to do, getting involved in other activities, escaping or getting away, sorting oneself out, and getting a new and better life* for oneself and other members of the family.

The following interview extract illustrates this independent form of coping:

> He had experienced a series of changes in his way of coping with his father's drinking problem, reflected in the following statement: 'In my way of being with the family, in the whole way I see things, I've changed. Before I believed in God and wanted to sort out everyone's problems – I'm surrounded by people who drink too much and I was so caught up in the problem that I was quite depressed and it was affecting my activities. Now I am worried about them and about my father, but only up to a point. Although I haven't become totally indifferent, my attitude is that I'll help them if I can, but if I can't, I'm sorry.'
>
> (Mexico, son of a drinker)

The degree of distance or independence that many family members spoke of was not gained without a struggle, as the following extract illustrates:

> The psychologist at the Drug Advisory Centre whom he [the family member] and his wife have seen has told them that life has to go on. Recently he has almost got to the situation of thinking this himself, 'to minimise the effects of what has happened'. He has thought, 'I can't allow him to do this to us.' Financially he [the family member] must work so he has tried to put thoughts of his son aside for a few hours each day. Recently he and his wife have made a decision. 'The tactic we have decided to adopt is that our life has to carry on for ourselves and the two children who are living here and we mustn't allow him to disrupt that.' They had already

adopted this idea and the psychologist confirmed that it was an acceptable and reasonable way to behave. They had felt guilty about adopting this sort of attitude but it was 'a relief' to have outside corroboration.

(England, father of a drug user)

For family members who were partners, the issue of separation was clearly fraught with difficulties. One example was a Mexican wife who said she longed to be able to live as far away from her husband as possible, but thought it unjust that she should leave the home which she had inherited from her mother. She had difficulty in selling the property since it was on a plot [*terreno*] without the necessary documentation:

'I have fought with him and we swear at each other. I've come to hate him. I once said to his step-father that we should get him into Alcoholics Anonymous, and they came but he didn't want to go. I've chucked him out but where would he go? He says that he is "the king". I've thrown him out thousands and thousands of times but he says to me, "OK I'll go, I'm not going to have you messing me about, keep your bloody house".'

(Mexico, wife of a drinker)

The following extract is from the report of an interview with a man, living on a different continent, but also facing a struggle about separation:

He has demanded that she not live with him and the daughters, as her drinking is too disruptive to their lives. She lives in a town camp on the other side of——[the town] with relations. . . . Because of the kids, he can't leave the area and get away from her, though he is considering moving to——[the city]. He would like to separate from her but this is not possible in the Aboriginal context. They will always be related, and he will always believe he is obligated to her for bearing the kids. . . . He sees no way out, other than to move back out bush. He is unwilling to do this because he wants his daughters to have the opportunities of a white education. He knows that out bush the three girls would get married young, have lots of kids and almost certainly end up raising them with little help from their husbands, who would be away drinking and probably getting other wives.

(Australia, husband of a drinker)

Other partners spoke of the measure of independence that they had been able to gain without separating from their problem drinking or drug-taking relatives:

'I've become more and more convinced that I cannot do anything about his way of drinking, so I've sought my own interests, I knit, I sell jewelry,

I visit my friends, and I don't tell him about it. This has been very effective because now he invites me out to go to the movies, to have a cup of coffee. Maybe he wants to compensate for his behaviour.'

(Mexico, wife of a drinker)

'When I began to take over the responsibility of supporting the family, I stopped feeling submissive to him and started making my own decisions. Before that, I would only sit down and cry. Now, even though I don't know how to read, I feel I can do many things with the help of friends and neighbours. Sometimes I feel I hate him, but now I know I can make my own decisions and, yes, he is my husband and I owe him respect, but only to a certain point.'

(Mexico, wife of a drinker)

Finding out what works by trial and error

It is clear from the foregoing that family members of relatives with drinking or drug problems have a wide range of coping options. It is already apparent from some of the extracts from interview reports cited in this chapter that family members have often found by trial and error that certain actions do not serve their cause, and have tried to change their ways of responding. Can it be concluded, therefore, that there are ways of coping that are universally favoured and others that are always found wanting and are sooner or later abandoned? If the question is posed starkly like that, the answer is almost certainly no. Even within any one of the socio-cultural groups, the relationships between family members and the relatives they worried about were highly diverse, and family members' circumstances differed widely in other ways as well. In the data it was possible to find statements both for and against each of the forms of responding that were described earlier. Table 6.6 provides examples.

While it can be concluded that all options for action have something that can be said for them, and each may be advantageous in certain circumstances, certain ways of responding accumulated many more pro than con statements, while others were associated with a preponderance of statements against. The clearest example of the latter was ways of confronting the relative that were perceived by the relative to be hostile or aggressive. Family members would commonly describe responding in such ways at an early stage of the process of facing up to the drinking or drug problem. Although it might allow a family member to vent her or his feelings, the general view was that this yielded poor results, since angry feelings would escalate, sometimes leading to fights. Women family members sometimes thought that even their lives were at risk. Male family members also explained that emotional or violent ways of responding did not work:

Table 6.6 Family members' opinions for and against different ways of managing a relative's excessive drinking or drug taking

	For	*Against*
Resigned, accepting	May be more realistic than some other ways of coping	FM may continue to feel very unhappy with circumstances
	May help FM become more independent	FM may feel nothing is being done to change the situation
Sacrificing, compromising	Arguments are avoided and life at home may seem less stressful	FM may feel R is taking advantage
	It may help create a trouble-free atmosphere for the rest of the family	FM may feel the problem is simply being kept going and not confronted
Supporting the relative	Makes FM feel that R is not being rejected	If R does not respond, FM may feel it is a waste of time
	May be more effective in helping R change than direct attempts at controlling drinking or drug taking	FM finds its difficult to know when being supportive becomes overprotective or overtolerant
Confronting, talking rough	FM is acting naturally and expressing real feelings	May annoy R and contribute to escalating arguments and fights
	It may at least temporarily relieve FM's feelings of tension and anger	May upset other members of the family, particularly children
		R doesn't listen to FM's arguments, and it leaves FM feeling guilty
Refusing, resisting and being assertive	Gives FM the feeling that the situation is not simply being accepted and FM is not being pushed around	R may not respond favourably
	May be more effective in helping R change than trying to control drinking or drug taking directly	Runs the risk of alienating R or of losing R altogether
Controlling, protecting the family	Helps FM feel something positive is being done	May make R feel resentful and may not be effective in controlling R's drinking or drug taking
	May help FM feel there is some hope for change	It may be very stressful trying to control R's behaviour, and very frustrating when attempts to control drinking or drug taking don't work

| Avoiding, escaping | May help FM feel less stressed
May help FM feel more in control | May make R feel rejected and isolated
Instead of helping R, it could make matters worse
It can contribute to a feeling of lack of family cohesion |
| Not worrying, getting a new life | May be helpful to FM in dealing with stress
May prevent FM from becoming overinvolved in worrying about or trying to change R's drinking or drug taking | FM may feel that R is being excluded or rejected
FM may feel that not all is being done to try to help R change |

FM – family member; R – problem alcohol or drug-using relative.

At first he [the family member] battered him [the relative] because, 'I wanted to force him to straighten up.' As this strategy did not work, he adopted tolerant and controlling attitudes. 'I know where he meets his friends to drink, but I'd rather stay away because at least I know where he is and who else is there.' He has also tried to talk to him: 'I have cried, but he just doesn't care.' The father [who himself attends Alcoholics Anonymous (AA)] has tried to convince his son to attend AA, he has brought AA literature home.

(Mexico, father of a drinker)

In Australia, family members described having done a lot of 'rough talking' to drinkers, but on the whole that way of interacting with relatives was not approved of, and was associated with being angry and with violence both to and from relatives. The Australian interviews were full of references to drinkers 'listening', or 'not listening', as the case might be. The impression given was that family members believed that, provided an appropriate person talked to the drinker, and provided they talked in an appropriate, non-aggressive way, drinkers should listen. What was said to them should not 'go in one ear and out the other' – a phrase used more than once – and drinkers should change their ways as a result. In practice, however, this apparent faith in the process of talking and listening had often turned out to be misplaced. Occasionally, drinkers were said to listen. For example:

'We [the family member and his wife] told him off so many times, we don't want to see him when he's drunk . . . usually I face him head-on and tell him what I think. I talk to him. . . . [he says] "Hit me, you can growl at me. . . . You're a hard man, but I really respect you, I've learnt a lot from you." '

(Australia, uncle of a drinker)

In a number of reports, drinkers were said to listen for a while or even to reduce their drinking for a short time, or to be compelled at least to listen (e.g. because it was a brother who was talking to him). The majority view, however, was that drinkers didn't listen, were not interested or just laughed, and that you couldn't tell them anything, or that talking to them did no good.

But, in practice, the line is difficult to draw between 'rough' and 'soft' talk, or between coercive confrontation and calm assertion, as the following example makes clear:

> When she has thought she smelt alcohol on him she has also confronted him. One evening he arrived home . . . [and] offered to go out and get some take-away food for supper. She said to him, 'You are not going to the off-licence are you because I can smell you've been drinking?' She feels she said this in a fairly straightforward way but she was upset. He 'coloured up' and explained that they had stopped at a pub and he was really thirsty, and said, 'I know I'm stupid.'
>
> (England, sister of a drinker)

Also disfavoured, more often than not, were ways of attempting to exercise control by such tactics as closely watching the relative's movements, and searching for or destroying the means of drinking or taking drugs. Sometimes family members expressed the fear that their relatives would be angered by such methods, and it was common for family members to acknowledge that they did not produce positive results. One Mexican wife summed it up by saying, 'It's absurd because if they want to continue drinking they find the way to do it anyway.'

Here again, it is not easy to distinguish between attempts at control that were subsequently thought to be excessive, provocative and ineffective and those that were found to work. It appeared that family members were more positive about setting clear limits or rules in domains where it was accepted that they had authority. Mexican wives, for example, had sometimes been able to establish rules about the limits on drinking or drug taking in the home. Trying to restore control was never easy for family members, but in general their attempts to do so appeared to have met with greater success when their actions had more of the characteristics of clear and calm assertion of limits and rules, and of positive support for the relative, and less of the characteristics of hostile exchange and interfering efforts at controlling the relative's substance use.

It was not easy to recognise these fine distinctions, and to acknowledge that certain ways of trying to regain control were less productive than others. It was probably even more difficult to recognise that the adjustments, sacrifices and compromises that family members make may also be counter-productive. It was not uncommon, however, for family members to question whether they were doing the right thing by, for example, purchasing small quantities of alcohol for a relative, paying for some things that a relative could not afford, or putting themselves out to clear up after the relative, or rescue the relative from arrest or homelessness. The clearest negative statements about putting up with a relative's excessive drinking or drug use were made by those family members who were able to give accounts of how their ways of responding had changed markedly in the direction of greater assertion and independence. The following are parts of two such accounts from Mexico:

> 'Now my children are less afraid of him. I see them less anguished and calmer. . . . Now I don't want to live with him any more because I don't want to feel humiliated.' This woman lets her husband know that she loves him, but she won't allow him to mistreat her any more. When he begs her to stay, she answers that the only way she will accept is if he goes for treatment because she wants to be 'his wife and not his mother'. She admits that she threw him out of the house and did not feel guilt about it, but it did hurt her to do so. He begged for forgiveness. Now she saves all the money she earns and does not give any of it to support the family. If she has to buy something for her children, she tells him that he has to give her that money back. If he doesn't do so, she threatens to go to his workplace and ask for money for essentials. She has also set rules regarding sexual relations. She won't accept him unless he is clean and sober.
>
> (Mexico, wife of a drinker)

> 'At first, I didn't do anything because I didn't know what to do. I avoided talking about the problem. I was very depressed to see how she [the relative] was destroying herself and that I couldn't do anything about it. I wanted to die. I was afraid to find her drunk. I would scold her and we would get into a fight. It was a terrible situation with a total lack of respect. I was the only one who defended her from the talk of others. I would throw away or hide her bottles. I had to take over her children and take care of her whenever she arrived drunk. Three or four times I even drank along with her. I borrowed money in order to buy amulets, medicine and anything I could think of. I made a vow to go to church every day if the miracle was performed. They told me she was bewitched and that she needed a purge. They charged me 2000 pesos for that treatment. I prohibited her from drinking in the house, but her husband didn't support me. He would beat her up constantly. Once I began getting treatment and attending Al-Anon meetings I began to have other activities, reading and going to gatherings. Now I respect my daughter . . . I do not interfere any more. One day she called me, completely drunk, and said she didn't want to come home any more and that she wanted me to take care of her children. I refused and told her

that I had other things to do and besides she was old enough to decide for herself. I said, "I am not going to interfere at all, not even to take care of your children." . . . It is not good to pamper the drinker. It is better to let them hit the ground first. It's sad and painful, but it is the only way for them to understand. If they go to jail, let them know it's their own fault. Men feel comfortable with this situation, but women worry because of their children.'

(Mexico, mother of a drinker)

What was most impressive on reading the reports of what family members in three contrasting parts of the world said about their coping efforts was the struggle that partners, parents, siblings, uncles and others had gone through in reaching the positions that they had attained by the time they were interviewed. Some felt they had progressed while others felt stuck. It had not been easy for any. For most, like the Mexican mother just quoted, trying to work out how to respond to a relative's problem drinking or drug taking had been a sad and painful experience. We shall return to consider ways of coping again in Chapter 9, where we attempt to integrate the present findings and those of other research. First, we have a further important piece of the picture to fill in: Chapter 7 deals with the support that family members received, or failed to receive, from other people.

Chapter 7

The support family members get from other people

What support do family members get from other people when faced with the task of responding effectively to the problem of excessive drinking or drug taking in the family? This was a planned area of discussion in the interviews carried out in Mexico, England and Australia. The results were disconcerting in a number of respects. They reinforced our belief that social support should play an important role in an understanding of the experiences of family members. At the same time, the results deepened our appreciation of what constitutes good and poor social support under the circumstances that these family members were facing.

We begin by describing ways in which family members did receive support from others that was found to be helpful and was appreciated – a set of positive findings and perhaps the least surprising. The chapter continues by presenting findings which emphasise the significance of the triangular relationship between the family member, the relative whose drinking or drug taking is of concern, and another person or persons who may or may not be perceived as supportive by the family member. The importance of this triangular relationship is one of the central points to be made in the present chapter. There then follows a discussion of the several ways in which family members are cut off from effective social support, or, to put it another way, the barriers to receiving good support. At first, we were surprised and disappointed to discover how common was the experience of being unsupported by other people from whom family members might have expected support. Wiseman's (1991) work had alerted us that positive social support might often be lacking in England as she had found it to be in Finland and the USA, but we had naively expected support to be much stronger in other cultures such as those in Mexico City and indigenous Australia. As we became more familiar with our material, however, and as we considered its significance in the context of the findings on family members' circumstances and ways of responding in all three groups (see Chapters 5 and 6), these negative results made greater sense. As a result, the more complete picture of the experiences of family members that will be described in Chapter 9 started to emerge.

Family members' experiences of positive social support from others

The main categories of positive social support mentioned by family members are shown in Table 7.1, and the main sources of such support are listed in

Table 7.1 Categories of positive social support received by family members

Emotional support	Talks to, listens to FM
	Accepts FM
	Available to FM
	Helps FM realise there are others in a similar situation
	Prays with or for FM
	The church as a refuge
	Does things with FM that FM likes
	Cheers FM up, looks on bright side
Backs up FM's coping	Defends FM
	Backs FM
	United, helpful with coping
	Shares work of worry about R
	Aware of the problem
	Understands what it's like
	Tells off others who criticise FM
	Warns, tells off R
	Keeps R safe
	Stops R making trouble
	Helps FM change behaviour
	Gives FM a philosophy, helps FM change mentally
	Suggests to FM a method of healing
	Gives FM therapy
Provision of accurate information	Advises FM, lends useful material
	Keeps FM informed
	Provides information, education
Practical or material help	Offers FM accommodation
	Offers R accommodation
	Takes care of R while FM is away
	Gives or lends FM money
	Provides cleaning, childcare or other help
	Patches up R's injuries
	Prescribes medication for R or FM
Positive toward R	Relates positively to R
	Worries for R
	Offers R help
	Tries to talk to R
	Meets with FM and R together

FM – family member; R – problem drinking or drug-taking relative.

Table 7.2. *Emotional support* in one form or another was the type of support mentioned most often. Simply having someone to talk to and who listened to the family member was the most common form. Family members consistently said that they appreciated other people making themselves available in a way that allowed the family member to talk openly about the problem in an atmosphere of acceptance and support. Sometimes the source was the family unit that found cohesion in the face of the family problem, as in the case of a Mexican father who described how his family had instituted regular family discussion sessions, which he termed 'the hour of truth'.

Often support was said to have come from outside the family, as in the following example:

Table 7.2 Sources of positive social support for family members

Family relations

Husband	Mother
Wife	Parents
Partner	Wife's parents
Daughter(s)	Relative on husband's side
Son(s)	Grandmother
Sister(s)	Grandfather
Brother(s)	Uncle(s)
Aunt(s)	The whole family
The family	

FM's friends and neighbours

Friend(s)	Work colleagues
Close friend(s)	Others who have been through it
Neighbour(s)	
People in the church	
God	

R's friends and associates

Several of R's friends
A good friend of R, and that friend's parents
Others who have experience from R's perspective

Professionals

FM's GP	Drug advisory centre
The relatives' group	Receptionist at the addiction service
Centre for group therapy	Citizens Advice Bureau
Psychologist at the drug and alcohol centre	Christian voluntary organisation
R's doctor	Priest
R's social worker	Night patrol
R's treatment centre	
Police	

FM – family member; R – problem drinking or drug-taking relative.

'I feel I can share a lot with . . . [friend who was present at the interview] because she knows my dad and it is only four years I've known her, but I feel I can talk to her a lot more and a lot more open than I can do to my own family. . . . I feel as long as I have . . . [friend] to winge and bitch to I will be able to cope. We just sit there and talk, sometimes it doesn't make sense.'

(Australia, daughter of a drinker)

Support can come from work colleagues and, as in the following example, other people can sometimes be appreciated simply because they are liked companions who distract a family member from the latter's problems, looking on the bright side and cheering the family member up:

He said that he talks a lot about the problem at work and this might provide him with support which in turn helps him support . . . [his wife]. He described how colleagues will get a laugh out of him about the problem at work. For example, they had a case when a man had jumped into the sea . . . to try and end his problems, and he said to his colleague, 'the problem is I don't like the sea.' To this the colleague light-heartedly suggested that he gas himself instead.

(England, father of a drug-using daughter)

A special category of supportive other people were those who had 'been through it themselves'. One English sister of a drinker referred to other family members in similar circumstances as being 'on the same wavelength', and another talked of others with similar problems in their families helping him to

'come down off that high perch and relax. . . . You don't feel you're on your own so much. It doesn't feel so much of an uphill struggle. There are other people in a similar and worse situation than myself.'

(England, male partner of a female drinker)

There were examples, although fewer in number, of positive support of an emotional kind from professional sources. For example, one English mother spoke positively of her general medical practitioner, who had spent a whole hour with her, and another mother had appreciated the receptionist at the addiction treatment service who had 'such a supportive voice'. It had been helpful, the mother said, 'knowing you are not alone'. A Mexican wife communicated with the research interviewer a month after the latter had put her in touch with a treatment centre. She was grateful because, 'In the clinic they listen to me and they are interested in my problem, and treated me in a helpful way.' A Mexican father commented, 'It would be good if the people who help us were like you [referring to the interviewer]. In that case we would go to get treatment.'

A different type of support, considered to be of great value to family members, was the *provision of accurate information*. Information was supportive in enabling family members to become better informed or to remain informed about what was going on. Such support came in a number of forms. One was helping the family member understand the nature of the relative's drinking or drug problem, and how family troubles or the relative's ill health, for example, were a consequence of excessive drinking or drug taking. As one English father put it, it was valuable to him to be able to understand his daughter's behaviour in more depth, 'to know when she is being a naughty girl and when she's ill'. Others had found it helpful to receive a clear statement from the doctor that a relative's present illness was caused by excessive drinking.

Talking to an informed person about ways of responding was also valued:

'You need somebody who you can go to and discuss overall strategies – how to handle it in the long term, how you handle the umpteen crises which invariably crop up . . . someone who'd have at their fingertips all the information.'

(England, father of a female drinker)

Although treatment professionals were prominent among the sources of informational support, such help could come from a number of sources. Other family members or friends gave family members books or other reading material on the subject of drink or drug problems. Other people who themselves had direct experience of excessive substance use might be valued for the information they could provide. For example, an English brother had found the other members of his music band supportive because one had been a heroin addict and another was familiar with the drug culture. He found it helpful to 'talk to people who realised what the situation is and understand it'. An English mother also said that she found it especially helpful to talk to people who themselves had had alcohol problems, as she felt it gave her insight into what her son [the relative] was feeling.

In the Mexican interviews, neighbours were mentioned as sources of information for family members about what their relatives were up to in the street, and in Australian Aboriginal communities the police and the night patrol (see Chapter 3) sometimes served a similar function.

It was also important for family members to be able to access information about where help for the relative could be obtained. A good example of networking among organisations which a family member had found very helpful was provided by the male partner of a woman drinker in England, who first went to the Citizens Advice Bureau. Information they provided led to contact with a clinic and thence to a health visitor at his general medical practice surgery, and from there to specialist sources of help, including the local drug and alcohol advisory service and a Christian volunteer organisation.

In addition to emotional and informational support, family members in all three socio-cultural groups made mention of the importance of *practical or material support* from others. Such help might be in the form of economic aid, either to help the relative when, for example, the latter was in trouble with the police or was being threatened by drug suppliers, or to help pay for expensive treatment. Another form of economic aid consisted in putting work the family member's way, as in the case of a Mexican wife who had been given sewing work by a woman friend to help her financially. One of the most common examples of practical assistance from others was the offer of respite or temporary accommodation for the family member, in the case of the relative's violence, a decision to leave home, or simply because the family member wanted to get out of the home for a while. In other instances, it was an offer of temporary accommodation for the relative that was appreciated by the family member. This was particularly the case when relatives were sons or daughters, and parents considered that a change of environment would be beneficial for them.

Other family members or friends were of practical help in ways that family members valued, if and when the relative attended treatment. Friends or relations accompanied relatives to treatment, offered family members or relatives lifts, or stayed in the family home while the family member accompanied the relative to treatment or when the family member took time away. In other instances, family members appreciated offers of help with childcare or cleaning. Help from medical specialists was often seen as very supportive in a practical sense, as by patching up a relative's injuries or prescribing medication for the relative or for the family member.

It is not surprising to find that family members facing the stressful circumstances described in Chapter 5 appreciate support from others of emotional, informational and material kinds. These are just the kinds of support that have often been described as valued by people in all manner of stressful and threatening circumstances. The point to emphasise here, however, is that the actions of other people that are found supportive by family members trying to cope with problem drinking or drug taking in the family have special significance when one understands the particular nature of the stressors they are typically under and the coping dilemmas that they typically face. Hence, being listened to is of importance because family members in these circumstances are often not listened to, and being given information is valued because family members are often cut off from accurate information about what is going on. They appreciate the offer of an occasional place to escape to, since their circumstances sometimes become intolerably stressful or dangerous.

Back-up from others in responding to the relative and the relative's problem

We move now into territory less well charted in the general literature on social support. Besides forms of help that can be categorised under the familiar headings of emotional, informational and material support, family members were found to be particularly appreciative of other people who supported their own coping efforts rather than criticising or opposing them, as had often been their experience. This could be thought of simply as a variety of emotional support, but it is separated out as a category here because we believe it plays a key role in the full, complicated picture of social support, or its absence, that surrounds family members trying to cope with relatives' excessive drinking or drug taking. This category we term *coping support* or *feeling backed up*. Others might offer unity or collaboration with family members by making the latter feel that they are aware of the problem or understood what it is like for the family member, or, for example, agreeing to a common tactic such as not bringing alcoholic drinks to a party. Family members drew strength from the back-up they received from partners, other family members, a church group or elsewhere. For example:

> 'I thank God that we're [family member and his wife] in tune . . . if we weren't together I think I'd bugger off, I don't think you'd cope with it on your own.' . . . He said that [his wife] is 'very supportive – marvellous'. He feels that they share the problem and largely agree on approaches to the problem.
>
> (England, father of female drug user)

> Her 'aunts' and 'uncles' are part of the most powerful family group in—— [rural community], so she relies on support from them in dealing with her elderly husband [the relative]. They tell off other people who might disapprove of her for 'allowing' him to keep drinking, and they feel sorry for her staying with such a cranky old man.
>
> (Australia, wife of a drinker)

> She has received support from his work for a long time, including last time . . . he attended AA because his firm intervened, since it was a condition that they made in order to let him remain in his job. They had said, 'He's a better worker when he doesn't drink.' His attendance at AA was supervised by someone from work for two months.
>
> (Mexico, wife of a drinker)

Family members often sensed disapproval from others about the ways they were coping, or received direct criticism about the ways they were responding, hence being backed up in the position they were taking was valued. Another good example of what we mean by being backed up is provided by a woman interviewed in Australia who had been involved in coping with the problems of several members of her family, including her mother and a son, and had come in for some criticism for moving from a rural community to the city. It was in this context that she said:

> 'But the people in the church, they've been wonderful, they've been sup-
> portive of me. They said, "———[family member] has given so much to
> her family over the years, now it's her time." Which is really good. I don't
> feel any guilt.'

Family member, relative and other; supportive and unsupportive triangles

One of the most striking aspects of the material on support was the large number of remarks made about other people's attitudes and actions toward the problem alcohol or drug-using relatives, and the consistent direction of those comments. Consistently positive things were said about relations, friends, neighbours or professionals who interacted positively with the rela-tive or who expressed positive sentiments about the relative. Negative actions toward the relative were found to be unsupportive. Family members were appreciative, it appeared, of other people who listened in an accepting way to their accounts of how stressful it was to live with someone with a substance misuse problem, but who at the same time maintained a view of the drinking or drug-using relative as someone who should also be helped and supported, and who potentially could change.

On the positive side, some supportive other people were simply said to have a good relationship with the relative. Sometimes, another person was said to be someone that the relative listened to. Others were found supportive because they had interacted sympathetically and positively with the relative; for example, they went out of their way to speak to relatives or to advise them, calmed an intoxicated drinker, or remained with and looked after the relative while the latter was drinking or taking drugs, and looked out for difficulties on his or her behalf. In other instances, another relation or friend had taken the relative to a treatment setting or had talked to the relative about doing so. The following describes a rather special example of positive support for the family member and her relative jointly:

> She [the family member] said of her mother's brother-in-law's sister and
> her husband . . . 'Yeah they come and talk to us, both of us, they don't
> come and tell him [the relative] off, they talk to us both. They ask us,
> "What do you two want to do, do you still want to drink or keep living
> this bad way, or are you going to change?" They talk to us together, the

four of us sit together, and they talk quietly to us really nicely, explaining things to us.'

(Australia, wife of a drinker)

On the negative side, other people were generally found to be unsupportive if their actions toward the relative were negative or unsympathetic. These ranged from beating the relative up, or spreading unpleasant rumours about the relative around the neighbourhood, to stating that the relative was not liked. Or the person made it clear that he or she did not want to know the relative or have anything more to do with the relative. Apart from a small number of family members who referred to others supporting them by defending them in the face of the relative's aggression or helping them to control the relative, there was no other mention of other people being thought supportive because they took a position *against* the relative.

There was, however, one substantial category of remarks about other people who were found to be unhelpful to family members despite the positive relationships which those other people had with the relatives. These were remarks about other people, mostly relatives' friends and associates, who were thought to have a *bad influence* on relatives principally because of their own excessive use or dealings in drugs or drink. A prominent feature of the networks of other people surrounding family members were those others who were seen as encouraging the drinking or drug use that had caused family members so much stress. They might be suppliers of drink or drugs, but were more likely to be fellow drinkers or drug takers who were seen as having led the relative astray or encouraged the relative to continue using. Hence, the complicated picture of support received or lacking from potential allies was regularly made more difficult by the presence of those who appeared to be working directly against family members' best efforts.

This picture of social support makes sense in the light of the material presented in the previous two chapters. The family members who constitute the subject of this book were experiencing highly stressful circumstances attributable to the behaviour of an adult member of the family. They searched for effective ways of responding and especially ways of standing up to the behaviour in question. These are very particular circumstances, sharing features with many other forms of stressful and challenging situations, but possessing special features all their own. In these special circumstances, in order to understand how adequate is the support provided by a particular other person, it is necessary to know not only something about the relationship of the family member (F) and the other potentially supportive person (O), but also something about the relationship between O and the problem drinking or drug-using relative (R). Fs, Rs and Os form triangles of the kind shown in Figure 7.1. Although the relationship between the family member and the relative may be deeply troubled, the supportive relationship between

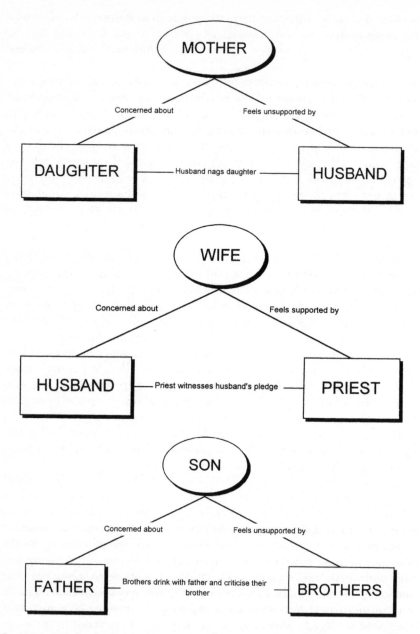

Figure 7.1 Examples of family member, relative, and potential supportive other triangles (according to an English mother, a Mexican wife and an Australian son).

O and F is likely to work best if F perceives the relationship between O and R also to be positive. It must, however, be positive in what the family member perceives to be a helpful fashion. From the family member's perspective, even worse than someone who is critical and hostile toward the relative is someone who is supportive of the relative's continued problem use or undermines change toward reduced use.

Why support for family members so often fails

One of the biggest surprises, striking in the reports of interviews from all three socio-cultural groups, was hearing how often in all three locations the networks of people surrounding the family members failed to provide the social support that was needed. It was not that the family members were totally isolated and lacking in potential sources of support; far from it. Family members were generally surrounded by large numbers of people who were in a position to provide the concerned and affected family member with some kind of help and support, whether that be emotional or material, or in the form of information or back-up for the family member in the position that the latter was taking in the face of the excessive drinking or drug use. It was all the more surprising, therefore, to find that this potential support was very often not forthcoming or was found to be wanting in some important respect. As we studied the interview material, the many reasons for support failure became clear. In the end, the problematic nature of support for family members of relatives who drink or take drugs excessively was so evident to us that we started to be surprised, not at the failure of support, but rather at the fact that support was ever satisfactorily received.

The hindrances or barriers in the way of family members receiving good support, or, to put it another way, the 'sources of support failure', are various. In the following pages, we try to convey the nature of these barriers to good support, and to provide extracts from the interview reports that illustrate them.

Reluctance to seek support: myths, fears, shame and secrets

Family members themselves often expressed reluctance to open the problem up to people other than those living in the immediate household. A variety of reasons for that reluctance were mentioned. Sometimes this was because family members considered privacy to be more important than active support from others, and expressed a preference 'just to get on with it' (England, sister of a male drug user) and not have anyone know. In other instances, reluctance was linked with views about family cohesion and the responsibilities of families to solve their own problems. Closely associated with such views were strongly held feelings about what it meant to be a good parent or a good wife, and the shame that the family member might feel if it was known outside the family that the partner, son, daughter or other close relative was drinking or taking drugs excessively. For example:

'We've never sought help, because these are family problems and I don't want others to know. I prefer things to carry on as they are.'

(Mexico, brother of a drug user)

'I didn't go to his family so as not to upset them. What I sought (by getting married) only I can sort out.'

(Mexico, wife of a drinker)

Family members were sometimes explicit about the negative reactions that they had received, or anticipated they might receive, from others. Some found that talking to family members outside the household had led to the need to reciprocate support and in the end had led to a greater burden being placed on the family member, as with the male partner of a female drinker in England who had talked a lot to his father but found himself supporting his father more than the other way around, and the English mother of a drug-using son who had found the same when trying to talk to her ex-husband about the problem. A Mexican wife related her experience of being accused by neighbours of being responsible for her husband's 'alcoholism', because 'I didn't know how to look after my husband.' A Mexican mother explained it in the following way:

'I haven't even told the family because they wouldn't support me, they'd just criticise me, they are so self-centred. . . . I told my sister, and she gave me encouraging words and tried to help me, but it's so difficult because she has a problem with her husband. . . . I don't like to mention the problems to anyone. . . . I don't have women friends, they are a bunch of old gossips who go round checking up on everything. . . . My sister is a bit of a gossip, so if there are problems at home everyone gets to know about it. There is no one who helps me. If I was really stuck no one would help and then everything would come out.'

(Mexico, mother of a drug-using son)

Nor was it uncommon for family members to express fear of the reactions from the rest of the family that were anticipated to follow if outside help was sought. One Mexican mother, for example, was frightened of the reaction she would get from her own parents if she were to seek help. But it was the reaction of the problem drinking or drug-taking relatives that was most commonly anticipated with fear. Sometimes relatives had convinced family members not to seek outside support because, for example, it was normal for a man to drink, the drug use was not so problematic, or the relative didn't need anyone else to help stop drinking. A daughter [the relative] had been angry with her mother [the family member] because the latter had told the relative's brothers about the drug use, and they had in their turn responded critically to their sister. Another mother had been told by her problem drinking daughter, 'If you go to other people it's just because you want to put me in the wrong.' Some family members had been threatened by relatives, as in the following example:

> Her [the family member's] principal concern is to get her husband into hospital, but she is frightened of his reaction because he once said to her, 'If you do that I shall kill you.' She feels that in part he is right that the problem should be resolved at home.
>
> (Mexico, wife of a drinker)

The reactions of others may be found to be unhelpful

When family members had overcome their understandable reluctance to talk to others about their problems, other people were frequently found to be unavailable, unsympathetic to the drinking or drug-using relatives, or simply unhelpful in the things they said or the advice they gave. Sometimes, someone to whom a family member would have liked to turn to for support had died, moved away or now had little contact. Some potential supporters were thought to have too many problems or responsibilities of their own, or were simply unavailable because they were too busy. Others were said not to want to get involved, or not to appreciate the problem. Neighbours were a category of others who were mentioned as often not wishing to get involved, or to whom a family member did not want to turn for support, even though neighbours might witness and be upset about the effects of excessive drinking or drug taking. Even friends were found not always to want to listen when family members tried to talk about their problems, as in the case of the English male partner of a female drinker, who said that he and his partner had lost most of their friends: they didn't want to see her and they didn't want to see him because he talked about her all the time.

Other members of the wider family figured large as potential sources of support, but they were often found to be unsympathetic to the relative whom the family member was concerned about, or else it was anticipated that they would be unsympathetic. For example, one English female partner of a male drug user said of her son, 'His attitude is very much "put up or shut up or kick him out." ' The following extract displays a mix of reasons for keeping a drug problem secret:

> He said that none of his family know about her drug problem and he said if they did know it would alienate her in the future 'if things come right' for her . . . his parents would make it worse if they did know about her problem . . . they would worry. . . . He said that he hasn't told his friends about her . . . if he told them it would alienate her . . . he wouldn't dream of telling them. . . . He . . . has only been out with them once since he has been with her . . . his friend's reaction would be, 'My God, what are you doing with her?'
>
> (England, male partner of a female drug user)

In Mexico, it was common to hear that other relations had viewed it as their responsibility to get involved, but often in a heavy-handed way about which family members were uncertain. On the one hand, family members sometimes found it useful that other members of the family spoke severely to the relatives, gave them ultimatums, made threats or suggested punishments. Women family members often looked to men in the family for that sort of support. On the other hand, other relations' reactions might involve insults, rejection or physical violence toward drinking or drug-using relatives, and family members expressed uncertainty over whether this was good or bad for relatives. It often created heightened tension in the family.

The police were a special category of other authority figures who were seen in this uncertain light. Family members, particularly male family members, were sometimes inclined to use the police, or to threaten to turn to them, as a last resort. For example:

> At times he [the family member] threatens him [his son, the relative] with going to the police as the last resort because he's desperate. He says, 'I wish the patrol would pick him up so that he'd learn.'
>
> (Mexico, father of a drinker)

Another Mexican father who regularly paid off his son's debts in order to keep the latter at liberty, had nevertheless on one occasion asked the police officers to give his son a beating, 'to see if that would stop him'.

In other ways, too, the reactions of other people might be found unhelpful, often because their understanding of the family member's circumstances was limited, and their knowledge of alcohol or drug problems incomplete, or because they offered advice which was too limited or simple, or did not back up the family member's position. For example, other members of the family who themselves had put up with much suffering might advise greater tolerance of the relative. Mexican family members were sometimes advised to see a pharmacist, who generally prescribed Antabuse for excessive drinking, and one wife was advised by her mother-in-law 'that I should serve my husband tea to stop him drinking, like she did with her husband'. Others gave unsympathetic and unhelpful advice such as, 'I would have left him', or 'You should have got rid of him.'

An Australian wife concerned about her husband's drinking perceived her family as alternating between support for her, and support for her husband against her. An Australian mother-in-law, worried about her son-in-law's drinking, made much mention of her son-in-law's father whom she had found to be very unhelpful because he had denied his son's drinking problem. Another Australian family member, when asked what other family relations thought, stated that they told the relative to

'Piss off! . . . They tell me to kick him out. But I said it's easier said than done and if mum or someone were staying with me, I'd do the same (for her).'

(Australia, stepson-in-law of a drinker)

Nor were professional people always as helpful as might have been hoped. For example, the inability or unwillingness of professionals to talk through strategies for dealing with problems left some English family members feeling that they had received inadequate information or support. In some instances, family members wanted more advice and direction. As the English father of a male drug user put it, 'an ABC plan which you try to follow . . . no one seems to be able to advise you, although there appears to be a lot of experts'. It was felt by several English participants that they were not being given full information about the problems of drug or alcohol use. For example:

He said that her social worker won't tell him all the effects that heroin has on people. 'He won't tell me everything . . . he'll give me enough to give me hope . . . he's cagey . . . he knows more than he lets on.'

(England, male partner of a female drug user)

The feeling of being cut off from information that would have been helpful was exacerbated when family members felt they needed information about the relative and the relative's problem, but professional people were unable to give that information out of respect for the relative's confidentiality. Family members were also confused sometimes by conflicting advice or information from professionals regarding a relative's needs for treatment.

Mexican family members were sometimes unimpressed with the quality of available treatment:

When she took him to the Drug Addicts Anonymous house where he received group therapy, she formed a negative impression of the centre because he was allowed to go around dirty and dishevelled and there was no respect for his things, in fact he was robbed while he was there.

(Mexico, mother of a drug user)

In remote Australian communities, where the police and the night patrol had a large presence in the lives of families dealing with drinking problems, and where their positive help was often much appreciated, family members were nevertheless conscious of the limited role of those agencies in effecting any real change in drinkers. For example, they could not do much if they arrived after the damage had been done; some had been disappointed because their role was limited to dealing with acute problems and they provided no lasting relief; if they had been rung several times, they might say don't ring us again, you've got to help yourself; no legal charges might be brought after a relative was detained overnight; apart from settling a drinker down and locking him up, there was nothing they could do; the drinker might simply run away; or have no respect for the police; the police had taken one family member to hospital after a violent incident, but had left without asking her questions and had never caught the drinker; the police had been reluctant to get involved because the family member phoned frequently and was often drunk himself; in one very remote community, there simply were no police; some night patrol workers were thought to be relatively unskilled at dealing with aggressive drunks; there were frequent staff changes, and often no women on the team, so that a woman would be reluctant to get into the patrol vehicle.

Family members often feel undermined in their efforts to stand up to excessive drinking or drug taking

One of the greatest hindrances to receiving good support lay in the difficulty that so many family members expressed of obtaining a united view from others that would back up their attempts to cope. This failure to obtain concerted support in their handling of the problem took a number of forms, but it often included criticism by others of the family member's actions in the face of the drinking or drug taking. One family member in Mexico, for example, was criticised by other members of her family for contributing to the problem by giving in to the relative and not being strict enough. Another explained that she couldn't express her feelings of depression, sadness and blame about her sister's substance use because she didn't want to worry the rest of the family. She felt she had to put up with things for the sake of her mother and brother, and needed to be a support for them.

There were many examples of undermining in the Australian interviews. For example, there were instances of members of one family blaming a member of another family, related by marriage, for not doing more to control a drinker's behaviour or for encouraging a relative to drink. One family member received conflicting advice from other members of the family about whether to deal with a drinker in the family by 'growling' [angrily admonishing] him or by leaving him alone. A family member whose son-in-law (the drinking relative) had been violent toward his wife (the family member's daughter) felt unsupported by the son-in-law's parents, who thought that he had done nothing wrong. Another family member, living in an urban area, felt under pressure from other family members to drop everything and help the relative whenever the latter was in town. In another instance, family members found it difficult to confront a drinker who seemed to be protected by a powerful older man in the community. In yet another example, family members were reluctant to talk to a drinker about the latter's drinking because of the danger of giving offence to the drinker's family.

The relationship between a mother and father concerned about their son's or daughter's excessive drinking or drug use was one that appeared particularly susceptible to these family tensions and failures of support. One English mother of a drug-using son described how she and her husband disagreed about how to manage their son. She was critical of her husband for not being sufficiently affectionate and not giving more of himself, and for criticising their son for having let him down. She said, 'These are horrible, stupid things to fight about.' She had sometimes felt that she would be a better mother if she were single.

Another English mother, in this case with a drug-using daughter, had found it difficult to talk to her husband about the problem, and they disagreed about the approach to take. She felt that he nagged and had a wrong idea of what was normal for young people. Furthermore, he never challenged his mother, whom she felt also had an old-fashioned domineering attitude, and who had been unkind to their daughter (although she didn't know about the drug problem).

The relationship between family members of different generations, and particularly between daughters and their mothers-in-law, is another that seems prone to experiencing these conflicts and hence to difficulties in providing family members with the support they need. For example, an Australian Aboriginal wife, now separated from her non-Aboriginal husband, said of her mother-in-law:

> 'She thinks the sun shines from him. She thinks there is nothing wrong with him. She doesn't focus on that he's got kids and he should have that responsibility. She just lets it roll on and, "Yeah, he's fine and he's wonderful" and "Yes, he can look after the kids too. He's not a drug addict, or he doesn't drink. It's OK."'

A Mexican mother, concerned about her son's problem drug use, was highly critical of her daughter-in-law:

> 'his wife talks to him when it suits her, and when it doesn't she says nothing, she's so hypocritical, she humiliates him in front of other people, she shouts at him about all sorts of things, she says, "you are a poor fool", her way with him is with shouts, anger, criticism and recriminations. She should be boosting his morale more so he can get out of this, she's just an uptight person who's not going to help him.'

An English wife, trying to cope with her husband's excessive drinking, talked of the lack of support from her own mother, who blamed her for everything:

> 'She doesn't say it but she makes it understood. I think it's because my mother knows nothing about alcoholism and thinks that it's a family problem, and she hasn't seen how we have been living. . . . To her I'm a

daughter that can do nothing right. Even in this situation he [the relative] is always in the right and I'm always wrong, and that doesn't help me at all.'

Daughters and sons can also be critical of a parent who is a family member trying to cope with the drinking or drug use of the other parent. For example, one Mexican daughter reproached her mother, saying, 'Why did you marry this man?', although she also said to her father, the relative, 'You don't love us. You always go around drunk like this. Leave my mother alone.'

In Mexico, there were several examples of other relations acting as protector of the drinking or drug-taking relative in the face of tough or aggressive actions toward the relative by the family member. For example, while a mother (the family member) hit her son (the relative), an aunt 'spoilt and protected him'. In another case, it was a grandmother who defended her grandson (the relative) from his mother's (the family member's) aggression, and when the latter ran the son out of the house, it was the grandmother who brought him back. Another example was that of a wife (the family member) who confronted and put limits on her husband, an excessive drinker, while her actions were obstructed by her husband's mother, who supported his drinking and protected him from his wife's aggression.

The role of others in restraining family members' independence

One of the most prominent features of the data was the way in which the intervention of other members of the family acted as a restraint on a family member's search for some distance or independence. There were some clear examples from Australia. Sometimes, family members who had found some independence had been thought by others not to be fulfilling their obligations to 'talk' to drinkers. Sometimes, family members described how they had been criticised for trying to get a new and better life for themselves, as by moving away or studying. Others felt they had been criticised for refusing drinkers money or accommodation, since this was seen as breaking an obligation to share with others, particularly with those to whom one had responsibilities. Family members had been described by others as 'cold', 'hard' or 'cruel', or 'getting too big for yourself'. Some feared rebukes from others if they responded to drinking relatives in any way that seemed to break with traditional responsibilities; for example, a wife refusing to continue to cook for her husband. Indigenous wives were sometimes blamed by members of their own or their husbands' families for causing more trouble by arguing with their drinking husbands rather than being more compassionate and accepting. One woman, whose husband had a long-standing drinking problem, described the very influential part that her older sister had played in persuading her to take a more loving, compassionate, passive stance toward her husband's upsetting behaviour:

'Yes [we were] both fighting. . . . And after that my sister told me, "You don't want to be fighting all the time, better you stop . . . he's brother-in-law for me, leave him [alone], you don't want to be in the fight all the time, leave him, you had better stop." I don't do that, fighting like that, I don't fight, I love the people, I don't want to be seeing with my sister growling to me.'

(Australia, wife of a drinker)

The same point was often to be seen in the reports of Mexican interviews, where advice from mothers, mothers-in-law or other family members was often strongly influenced by traditional customs and values associated with marriage and religion. One mother, for example, advised her daughter [the family member], in relation to the latter's husband [the relative], that she should try to save her marriage, and get more involved in the church. Another example was that of a mother-in-law who tried to console her daughter-in-law [family member], trying to get her to stop worrying about her husband [the relative], saying to her, 'What are you worried for, in the end it's his stomach that is getting sick and not yours?' A further example was an aunt who had said to her niece, the wife of a problem drinker, 'Let him drink, and get on with looking after the home, you should respect your husband.' The daughter of a father with a drinking problem, in her 20s, said, 'For my own mental health it's better that I go', but this sentiment had provoked considerable family tension because of 'what people are going to say'.

Nor is it only women family members who experience lack of support in their attempts to achieve some independence from a relative's drinking or drug problem. The account given by one indigenous Australian man illustrates this point. He was now living in an urban area, and was proud of having a strong foot in both Aboriginal and non-Aboriginal cultures. His concern was about his problem drinking father who continued to live on a remote outstation, regularly visiting his son in town. He prided himself on not being tolerant of his father's drinking, adopting a kind of assertive independence and withdrawal from his father's problem, asserting that it was his father's problem and not his, and certainly refusing to go drinking with his father. A dominant feature of his interview was the contrast that he drew between his own position and that of his brothers. The latter were heavy drinkers themselves, drank with their father, felt sorry for their father, and, according to the interviewee, were not bringing their children up correctly, and generally not following his own good example of the way in which an indigenous person could achieve things in life. Although he received some praise for the position he was adopting, particularly from his sisters, he also came in for criticism, especially from his brothers, not only because of the way he was coping with his father but also because of his administrative and political activities, which were sometimes seen as being unsupportive of indigenous ways.

A composite picture of social support for family members

Thus, a composite picture of a person whom a family member finds supportive emerges: someone who knows enough about the problem and is sufficiently available to provide the family member with a listening ear; who is non-judgemental and accepting of the family member and her or his position, and does not condemn the relative or take sides; who is sensitive enough to know when bits of information or advice might be helpful and acceptable to the family member; and who, within the limits of his or her role, supports the family member in standing up to excessive drinking or drug taking, perhaps by offering material help in getting access to treatment for the relative, perhaps by direct intervention with the relative to help the latter modify drinking or drug taking, and sometimes, if that is what the family member wants, by support for the family member in achieving a measure of independence.

What family members told us they had often found in practice, however, was that that kind of support was a rare and precious commodity. Table 7.3

Table 7.3 Barriers in the way of family members receiving positive social support

Others don't get involved

    Others live too far away
    Others have moved (or FM has moved away)
    Others have died
    Others are too busy
    Others don't want to listen
    Others won't recognise R's problems
    Others don't know what it's like
    Others know what R is like, so keep away
    Neighbours don't get involved

Family members don't involve others

    FM and others never talk about it
    FM doesn't get on with others
    Relationships with others are tense
    FM thinks others would not understand
    Don't talk about it to others out of loyalty to R
    It could lead to extra burden on FM to give support to others in return
    FM prefers privacy
    Feel it is FM's responsibility to solve her/his own problems
    Would feel shame if others knew about R's problems
    Would experience the shame of not being a good wife or parent
    Fear of others' reactions, especially R's family
    Danger of giving offence if others thought FM's involvement inappropriate
    Others thought to have too many problems of their own
    Not wanting to worry the rest of the family
    Don't turn to neighbours

Lack of faith in doctors' knowledge, abilities or understanding
Bad reputation of rehabilitation institutions and the police for maltreating Rs
Believe there is a limited amount police or night patrol can do

Family members find others to be unhelpful

Others encourage R to drink or take drugs
Others protect R
Others give R money
Others are too heavy-handed with R
Others give unhelpful or unsympathetic advice
    Suggest FM separate, withdraw support from R
    Doctors say can do nothing unless R goes to see them
    Give conflicting advice about treatment
    Doctors prescribe R or FM medication which FM is ambivalent about
Professionals won't give FM full information
Professionals won't talk through strategies for dealing with the problem

Others are critical of family members

FM and others have differences of opinion
    To be soft or strict
    To stay or leave
    How compassionate to be toward R
    To gain independence or to stay involved
    Whether R is being encouraged to drink or take drugs
Others undermine FM in the latter's efforts to stand up to problem drinking or drug taking
    Criticise FM for trying to be more independent
    Criticise FM for not sufficiently supporting R
    Criticise FM for not performing traditional family duties

FM – family member; R – problem drinking or drug-taking relative.

summarises what has been said in this chapter about the barriers to receiving good support. As the three examples of family members shown in Figures 7.2–7.4, one from each socio-cultural group, demonstrate, support is often very mixed. Family members often have many people in their networks who fall short of the ideal supportive person in one or more ways. That is particularly true of the relative's friends and associates, who are often seen as unsupportive because of the bad influence they exert upon a relative. But this is often true also of other family relations, who are frequently seen as uninvolved, uninformed, condemning of the relative, out of sympathy with the family member's position, or restraining rather than supporting the family member's struggle for independence. It is also frequently true of helping agencies, who are sometimes seen as inaccessible, overly harsh in attitude toward the relative, or unhelpful in the advice that they offer to the family member. The difficulties family members experience in finding social support in their task of worrying about the close relative with a drinking or other drug problem is an important part of the whole experience for such family members.

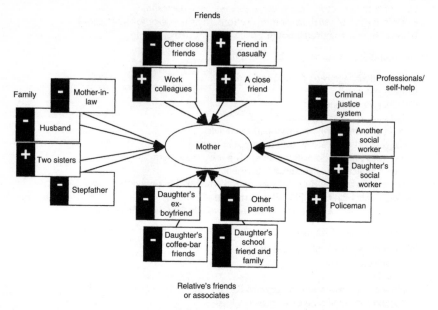

Figure 7.2 The network of supportive (+) and unsupportive (-) others surrounding a family member coping with a relative's excessive drinking or drug taking: an English mother.

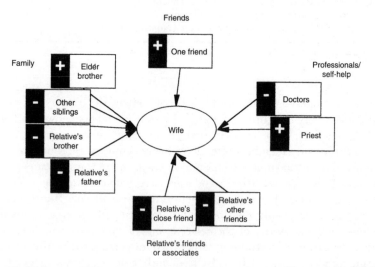

Figure 7.3 The network of supportive (+) and unsupportive (-) others surrounding a family member coping with a relative's excessive drinking or drug taking: a Mexican wife.

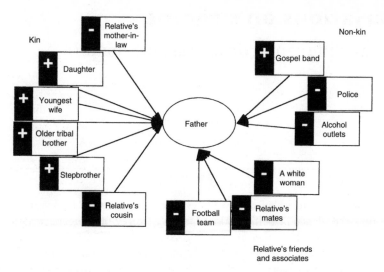

Figure 7.4 The network of supportive (+) and unsupportive (-) others surrounding a family member coping with a relative's excessive drinking or drug taking: an Australian father.

Chapter 8

Variations on a theme
What difference does culture make?

In the previous three chapters, we have described what we believe to be the common experience of being a close family member of someone whose consumption of alcohol or other drugs is excessive and problematic for the family. The experiences described, we conclude, are likely to be universal under those circumstances, irrespective of the socio-cultural group to which the family belongs. The second overall aim of the research summarised here was to explore the other side of the same coin, or the ways in which the experiences of family members in the face of drinking or drug problems might vary by socio-cultural group. Meeting that aim turned out to be more difficult than anticipated. Over and over again, while analysing the reports of interviews carried out in Mexico, England and Australia, we were impressed by the similarities. The frustration and despair of a father's brother in the face of continued excessive drinking and being 'humbugged' for money by his brother's daughter in remote indigenous Australia, for example, struck us as being essentially the same social phenomenon as described by a mother of a drug-using son in England or the wife of an excessively drinking husband in Mexico City, both hassled by their relatives for money to maintain their habits.

At the outset, it had been imagined that it might be possible to express ideas about variation in terms of straightforward hypotheses. For example, Mexican family members might experience shame while English family members might talk more about guilt. Or indigenous Australian family members, unlike those in England and Mexico, might be reluctant to talk about the excessive drinking of individual family members because of cultural constraints on referring to others critically in conversation. Or English family members might be more inclined to withdraw from their relatives. Each of these ideas had previously been suggested or was suggested to us during the planning stages of the research. To state such simple hypotheses, we have concluded, would not be in the interests of advancing our understanding in this field. There are a number of reasons for that conclusion. The first is, very simply, that we kept finding exceptions to any such hypothesis. There were indigenous Australians who were just as ready to identify and talk about the problem drinking of a particular relative of concern as were family members in England and Mexico, and there were Mexicans who displayed guilt over what was happening and English family members who found it as difficult to withdraw as others.

A still more persuasive argument for rejecting an approach based on the statement of simple hypotheses is that sources of variation co-vary. For example, it is not simply a matter of there being a culture in Mexico City that can be contrasted with that to be found in South-West England; and in addition, there being different ways that men and women experience drinking and drug problems in the family; and, furthermore, there being differences in the ways excessive drinking and excessive drug use are experienced. Those three factors co-vary. Men's drinking is not the same in those socio-cultural groups, nor is the role of women (see Chapter 3), and cultural patterns of drinking, gender roles and ways of coping co-vary and interact. There are in fact numerous sources of variation interacting in complex ways.

Third, and more fundamentally still, the value of a purely hypothetico-deductive approach to advancing knowledge in a field such as this can be questioned. The kind of qualitative research reported here cannot in any case test hypotheses of the simple kind envisaged at the outset. It can, on the other hand, suggest such hypotheses, but that would probably be fruitless. We might hypothesise, for example, that English family members are more concerned than those in the other two groups on account of the threat that excessive drinking or drug taking in the family poses to the family members' self-identity and independence. We might link that hypothesis theoretically to the concept of cultural individualism versus collectivism. But, even though some of our data could be adduced in support of such a hypothesis, we would immediately be dissatisfied with it. We would question whether indigenous communities in Australia are collectivist or individualist. In many ways, they correspond to the former, but it has been suggested that Aboriginal culture is a very individualistic one in some ways. If we were to suggest that Mexican culture was collectivist, we would be challenged, as indeed we were when presenting preliminary results in Mexico, to explain which of the various strands of 'collectivism' we were talking about, and to which of the many Mexican subcultures we thought our results were most applicable. We would worry, also, about interaction with gender: surely, women in some of our socio-cultural groups, perhaps in all three, in practice bear more responsibility for worrying about relatives and have less realistic expectations of independence? Even if we could satisfy ourselves on all those counts and come up with some hypotheses that were felt to be sufficiently complex to do justice to our material, we would still have to face the fact that all three cultures were changing, some faster than others, and even now are different from what they were when the research was carried out. None of our hypotheses would serve for longer than a few years.

The solution to this problem that has been adopted here is as follows. We try to describe some of the variations that we believe we detected in the data, without suggesting any fixed relationship between culture and experience. Our suggestions should be understood as indications of the ways in which family experiences in the face of drinking and drug problems can vary according to the cultural, social, economic and personal circumstances of the family and its members. Taken together with the description in the previous three chapters of what we believe may be a universal core experience, our suggestions in the present chapter about variations may be taken as a fuller mapping of the territory of interest. Although it is now our view that family members facing drug or alcohol problems share much of the same experience irrespective of the drug, the relationship with the relative (with a parent, partner or other) and the part of the world in which they live, each family member is situated differently, even uniquely, in demographic, social, cultural, economic and other terms. The aim of the present chapter is to fill out the picture by suggesting some of the ways in which the general experience is moulded by the particularities of family members' socio-cultural groups. In the remainder of the present chapter are suggested a number of themes in terms of which may be understood the particular experiences of family members coping with drink or drug problems on the outskirts of Mexico City, in towns and villages in South-West England, and in urban and remote, rural indigenous communities in northern Australia.

The difficulties of standing up to excessive drinking and drug taking in Mexico City

Three themes stood out in reports of the Mexican interviews. One was the financially precarious position that many Mexican family members found themselves in. The second is one that has long interested local and foreign observers of Mexican culture, namely, the respective roles of men and women in the family, related to the concept of male machismo (see Chapter 3). The third was the particular difficulty of finding support, either informal or professional, outside the Mexican family circle.

The threat to family financial stability in Mexico

Of the three socio-cultural groups involved in the research, those living in Mexico City were the only family members not covered by a comprehensive social security system, and this was reflected in the effects of their relatives' excessive drinking or drug taking about which the Mexican family members spoke in the interviews. Although the majority of Mexicans in theory had access to health care, coverage was very thin in large areas of the country, including many urban areas, such as those in Mexico City where most of the research participants were recruited. Many of the participating family members were living in conditions of poverty, and living conditions had often been made much worse by the economic crisis that had affected the country in recent years. A high rate of unemployment had had a profound effect, for example, requiring many women to work outside the home, often in the informal economic sector, in many cases becoming their families' principal economic providers.

The financial harm to the family was mentioned by participants in all three socio-cultural groups but appeared particularly prominent in the reports of Mexican interviews. Family members there spoke of material deprivation, including the need for food, clothing or housing. There was reference also to feelings of fatigue and generally being worn out as a result of having to take more than one job or having to travel a long distance to get to work. Poverty, caused or made worse by the relative's drinking or drug taking, was associated with chronic worry and anxiety, and often self-blame and remorse on account of not being able to provide adequately for the family.

The conclusion to be drawn from the above observation is not that economic hardship is a core feature of the family effects of excessive drinking or drug taking in one of the socio-cultural groups, and not in the others. The conclusion, rather, is that, while we believe there to be a relatively invariant core to family members' experience in the face of such problems, the totality of the experience varies with economic circumstances. The whole experience cannot be understood without appreciating that the effects on a family of problem substance use are coloured by the household's economic circumstances. Those already in poverty or who are near the poverty line are threatened by the diversion of resources toward supporting a large drinking or drug-taking habit in a way that families with greater resources are not.

Gender inequality and the position of women in Mexico

Gender role issues were to be seen in the data from all three socio-cultural groups involved in this research, but it was in the Mexican interview reports that such issues were most prominent. The burden of responsibility for caring for members of the family, looking after family members' health, and even, in many cases, sustaining the household economically was reflected in what many Mexican women participants said about their experiences. Their accounts were full of statements about being worn out by the burden of care and responsibility. Remarkably often, they also contained statements attributing blame to themselves, either for the family's conditions or even for the relative's excessive drinking or drug taking, especially in the case of mothers. Once again, however, it would be quite wrong to conclude that these features were in some way essential and unchanging characteristics of Mexico, or of a particular socio-cultural group within Mexico, and not of groups elsewhere in the world. Although gender and inequality may have been a particularly notable topic in Mexico, it has of course been described almost everywhere. Women in the other two socio-cultural groups were also often burdened by care and responsibility, and sometimes blamed themselves. That way of describing the experience of living with a drinking or drug problem, which occurs around the world, was particularly impressive in the interviews with some of the Mexican women. Once again, what we should properly conclude is that the core experience of being a family member, worried about and affected by the drinking or drug taking of a relative, is modified by one's sex and the gender norms and expectations associated with that sex within the wider socio-cultural group. The core experience remains the same, but the experience in its fullness cannot be comprehended without taking sex and gender into account.

One characteristic of the Mexican sample, unlike those from England and Australia, was the absence of any men who took part because they were concerned about the excessive drinking of their wives or partners. That may have been a reflection of the gender-polarised nature of heavy drinking in Mexico (see Chapter 3), and possibly the unacceptability of admitting and talking about family troubles in which the wife was the excessive drinker and the husband a concerned and affected other family member. Whatever the explanation, men figured as family members in the Mexican sample largely in the role of fathers, in a few cases as brothers, and in one instance as the male partner of a female problem drug user.

The responses of parents in the face of problematic drinking or drug taking by young adult offspring was therefore one of the arenas in which gender roles were played out. The powerful identity of the Mexican mother as a carer and the one responsible for the well-being of members of her family no doubt had a major influence on the ways mothers coped. Actions of self-sacrifice were very frequent, mothers giving up their own activities, stopping meeting with friends or relatives because the problem of excessive alcohol or drug consumption in the family represented a matter of great shame that should be resolved within the family without external involvement. Some mothers struggled to respond with a measure of independence; for example, they tried to place some limits on the son's or daughter's substance use, attempted to get the offspring to take responsibility for their own clothes and self-care, withheld money or declined to make purchases for the son or daughter, tried to engage the latter in other activities, and generally made an effort to ensure that the mother's own life was not too much affected.

Mexican mothers, if concerned about a son's or daughter's problem drinking or drug use, were very inclined to attribute the cause to their own shortcomings as mothers. For example: 'If I didn't know how to look after him, then this is what you'd expect'; 'It's a way of showing her non-conformity because I didn't give her all that was necessary'; 'I have come to the conclusion that I abandoned him; probably it was me being such an egotist, just looking after myself.'

In their struggle to stand up to sons' or daughters' drinking or drug use, Mexican mothers often felt that they lacked as much support from their husbands as they would have liked. For example:

'My husband sees the problems at home and retreats into his shell, doesn't get involved. . . . He [her husband] tells him [her son, the relative] off, and wants to make him understand things as if he was a little boy. He doesn't know how to speak to him or help him. My husband is very domineering, and always thinks he is in the right, but he simply doesn't have a good relationship with my son. . . . I have plenty of defects myself but the one virtue I do have is a great love for my children, although perhaps that's also a defect because I am inclined to give to others without receiving anything in exchange, and then other people expect a lot of me. . . . I feel so alone.'

(Mexico, mother of a drug user)

Mothers often reported not being able to rely on their husbands, sometimes because the latter were excessive users of alcohol or drugs themselves, sometimes because they feared the father's reaction would simply be an angry one, and sometimes because of an attitude of indifference on the father's part. It was also found, however, that fathers might be left without information about important events occurring in the family, sometimes because mothers, perhaps realistically, feared that the problem would be worsened by telling their husbands. More commonly, mothers' reluctance to involve their husbands appeared related to a collective idea among Mexican women that men are not to be disturbed with domestic or family problems. The following is an extract from an interview with a father:

The family reproaches the father that he has never done anything to help his son [the relative]. He immediately wants to answer, 'You should have told me about it if you knew about it.' . . . His wife knew their son was taking drugs but did not tell him. 'Maybe she thought I was going to make a big deal of it and harm him. . . . I have not been a loving parent, but when I detect a problem I do try to solve it right away. I work during weekdays and only spend the weekends with my family.' When he knew about the problem he started to look for someone to treat his son.

(Mexico, father of a drug user)

Nevertheless, a number of Mexican fathers took part in the research, and a number of them had been active in seeking and encouraging treatment for their offspring. There were a number of circumstances that fathers described as being responsible for this level of involvement. One was when fathers had themselves had alcohol problems, in some cases having attended Alcoholics Anonymous. One of these fathers wanted to be a model, to 'change my own attitudes in order to make them see me as I want them to be'. Another felt guilty since his wife had been very supportive when he had a drinking problem, and it was he who had given their son his first drink. In other instances, fathers were motivated by the seriousness of the consequences, as, for example, when offspring had stolen large amounts of money from their parents. In other Mexican families, fathers had taken more responsibility either because a working wife had the more strict job schedule while the fathers could be more flexible because they owned small businesses or were unemployed, or because it was recognised that the mother had borne the brunt of the problem and had been most affected emotionally or physically. As one father said, 'My wife got worn out during the last three years.'

The difficulty of finding social support outside the family in Mexico

Advice that family members receive from others in Mexico has a strong content oriented to strengthening important aspects of Mexican culture, in particular the family unit. For participants in the present study, advice was often in line with the view that it was the family unit that should and could support the relative, and that the problem should not go outside the ambit of the family. At the same time, the typically large size of the Mexican family, compared to that in England, did not necessarily mean that family members received more and better help. Indeed, in many instances, it was difficult for families to reach consensus in order to provide such support. In a number of interviews, it was observed that the responsibility for handling the relative fell on the shoulders of a single family member, sometimes because that person had a feeling of personal responsibility, but often because others could not see what help they could give, or could not reach agreement among themselves about the help that should be given.

Barriers to obtaining support outside the family included shared cultural beliefs and values, as in, for example, that family problems shouldn't go outside the family because that would be to violate the intimacy and loyalty of the family, or that a wife should not complain about her husband because if he drinks it's because she doesn't know how to look after him, or that men drink and their wives must put up with it. Another cultural aspect in Mexico was the high level of tolerance of men's consumption of alcohol and drunkenness (see Chapter 3). The same level of tolerance did not apply to the consumption of 'drugs' nor to drinking by women.

Other kinds of obstacles to family members receiving support in Mexico City derived from feelings, much influenced by shared 'social representations', such as the following: the feeling of shame, the expectation that others would criticise one for not having fulfilled the role of mother or wife, the feeling that while their young adult sons were single it was the responsibility of Mexican mothers to look after them until the responsibility could be passed on to another woman when the son married or remarried, fear of the husband because of his threats about what he would do if problems were spoken about outside the family, fear of what others would say and the fear that there was no help to be had or that no one else could provide support.

Such beliefs were sometimes found to be compounded by attributions that put the blame for problems on family members themselves. All these elements combined to give Mexican family members strong feelings of fatalism and lack of hope that anyone could help them. Such feelings were often compounded by family members' neighbourhoods, which represented an uncontrollable external force that made it impossible for relatives or family members to escape an environment of heavy drinking or drug use.

Thus, it is understandable that the majority of Mexican families who took part in the research had not sought any treatment for themselves despite the severe problems they were experiencing on account of relatives' excessive drinking or drug use. Family members had often had bad experiences of health institutions, were badly informed about types of treatment that might be available for their relatives or themselves, and in some instances had experience of, or had heard about, inhumane treatment in some residential institutions (e.g. *granjas*). Poverty in Mexico, which was generally worsening rather than improving at the time this research was carried out, made it more difficult for families to find the resources to attend treatment or obtain medicines, which at times were very expensive.

Reliance on religious faith and prayer were frequently mentioned by Mexican family members. In some cases, as referred to in Chapter 5, such mention of religion was in the context of having become resigned to accepting a relative's excessive drinking or drug use. In other instances, religious observance was mentioned in a more active sense. One often-mentioned active involvement of religion in Mexico, portrayed by family members as a positive and often effective way of re-establishing control, was the encouragement of the problem drinking or drug-taking relative to take an oath (*jurar*). When family members take such an oath (*una jura*), they promise the Virgin Mary (*la Virgin de Guadalupe*) to stop drinking or taking drugs for a certain period of time (perhaps 6 months or 1 year) and a priest receives the oath before a witness or witnesses. This is something not to be undertaken lightly, and that often gave family members the feeling that something positive had been achieved and hope that family life would improve as a consequence.

Uncertainty and threat to individual autonomy in England

English family members, by comparison, were able to draw on more diverse networks of support. Whereas in Mexico, poverty forced family members back on to community sources of support, particularly the extended family, English family members were just as likely to mention non-kin and professional sources of support. Support networks for Mexican family members were more dominated by kin and, to a lesser extent, neighbours, while the English family members frequently mentioned the support they obtained through confiding in friends. Furthermore, English family members could count on the safety net of a comprehensive social security system and the services of a general medical practitioner, who might refer patients to appropriate specialist services. Even the poorest English families were therefore better off in those respects than the majority of those in Mexico City.

What was particularly noticeable in the reports of English interviews were mentions of the impact for family members in terms of their own health, their own feelings of well-being, and their recreational activities and social lives outside the family. Common were expressions of feelings of resentment and anger at the way the drinking or drug problem had restricted family members' lives. References to the family member's or the whole family's social life being adversely affected included statements about invitations to private parties, inviting friends home, and other references implying the existence of a non-kin friendship network and freedom to socialise that was being interfered with as a result of the relative's drinking or drug problem. As one English wife put it:

> 'I decided that I needed to look after my own health, that I'd go and do something in my life that would make me feel happy. My children were leaving, after being dependent on me for so many years, so I started to write (she edits a magazine), which is an excellent medicine. I feel I'm achieving something.'
>
> (England, wife of a drinker)

Although a measure of independence was never achieved by English family members without a struggle (see Chapter 6), even mothers could recognise that a prescribed gender role and their own individual autonomy might be in conflict, and that they could decide to limit the former in the interests of the latter:

> She said she copes because she sees her son [the relative] as an individual rather than as her son. If she gives way to those maternal feelings she wouldn't be able to cope. Occasionally, however, she gets a jolt, for example seeing him in prison or unconscious or emaciated and then she gets flooded with feelings. 'I have hardened up a bit to protect myself.' She feels these changes have come about because of 'self-preservation'. She doesn't think he has changed. She has felt herself 'going under' and for her own survival – mentally, emotionally and financially – she has got harder.
>
> (England, mother of a drug user)

Interference with one's personal and social life was not, of course, peculiar to the English sample. The indigenous Australian culture has also been described as including a powerful emphasis on individual autonomy (see Chapter 3), and many Mexican family members, women included, spoke of restrictions on going to fiestas. What was particularly noticeable in the English interviews, however, was the expectation that one would have a life that extended beyond the household, the extended family or the local community, and that people had a right to expect to have friends who might not be connected with the family, and to pursue their own personal interests and activities. Living with excessive drinking or drug taking in the family can pose a serious threat to such expectations, and that was particularly noticeable among the English interviewees.

Uncertainty about dependence and its treatment

Of all the three socio-cultural groups, those in South-West England held most clearly to the view that problem drinking or drug taking constituted an identifiable condition of dependence or addiction for which treatment was, or should be, available. This was in contrast to the relative lack of reference to excessive drinking as a disease-like condition in the indigenous Australian sample (see Chapter 3). Family members in Mexico, while they were likely to refer to their relatives' 'alcoholism' or 'addiction', were less likely than those in England to have confidence in the availability of treatment. Thinking that a relative might be suffering from such a condition did not relieve English family members of the sense of uncertainty that was common to family members in all three groups; indeed, it may have enhanced that feeling. Thinking that a husband might have a personal drinking problem, or that a son or daughter might be a drug addict, was associated with uncertainty about the following things: confirming the existence of such a problem, gaining accurate information about its extent and seriousness, how to identify sources of treatment and to encourage the relative to accept it, and the outcome of treatment and future developments.

The language used by English family members to describe the history of the problem as they knew it was full of words and phrases such as 'think', 'realised', 'discovered', 'difficult to know', 'alarm bells', 'believe', 'secret', 'telling me lies' and 'became increasingly obvious', which indicate that the facts of a relative's drinking or drug problem are difficult for a family member to know, are often concealed and often take time to be known. Sometimes, it was a case of a son's drug use suddenly becoming known to a mother or father without prior warning. Much more often, there was a complex, worsening history of drinking or drug use and its harmful effects. Sometimes the family member had been quite well aware of what was going on, and indeed may have been an active partner in drinking or drug taking at certain stages, but there had been uncertainty about when or whether substance use constituted a problem. It was sometimes a case of things 'coming to a head' or the relative's mental state or circumstances worsening to the point at which the problem was obvious. For other family members, much of the history was unknown.

A mother and a father both expressed the uncertainty they had felt about whether their respective relatives had a problem:

> Two years ago he [the relative] was working on a building site and living with his common-law wife. He was having constant money troubles and was asking her to lend him money. She thought this was strange as he was working long hours and earning a good wage but when she asked him about this he always had some excuse such as the rates of pay had not been sorted out or the wage packets were late arriving.
>
> (England, mother of a drinker)

> He didn't really realise that his son had a real problem until this most recent bout of drinking . . . it was 'very difficult' because his son was saying that the counsellor said he didn't have a problem, that he just needed to moderate his drinking, whereas the GP was telling his son that he had got a problem. He just drinks beer. . . . As far as he [the family member] is aware alcohol in the house has never been touched. . . . He finds it very difficult to understand. At Christmas . . . his son didn't touch a drop. . . . Now he is not sure if his son has a drinking problem or not.
>
> (England, father of a drinker)

Once a family member was clear in her or his own mind that a relative's excessive drinking or use of drugs had been a major source of harm to the relative, stress for the family member, and threat to the family and home, the uncertainty was very often only just beginning. Family members then faced the uncertainty of knowing whether the relative had stopped using substances excessively; what, if anything other than total abstinence, constituted safe drinking or drug use; whether to believe what the relative said; whether treatment was needed and, if so, what kind of treatment and whether the relative was willing to undertake it; and, more generally, whether the family member could look forward to life returning to normal or whether she or he needed to be resigned to the fact that the relative would never be as had once been hoped and expected.

Once again, what has been identified are sources of variation in the universal experience of worrying about and being affected by a relative with a drinking or drug problem. Although of the three cultural groups represented, the English one was almost certainly the most unambiguously individualistic (see Chapter 9) and the one where there existed the clearest concept of dependence as an individual treatable condition, neither of those elements was unique to the English. It is not that support has been found for a hypothesis that England scores higher than Mexico or Australia on a variable that we might want to call 'threat to individual autonomy', or that English family members experience significantly greater uncertainty about whether their relatives are dependent or about how to obtain good treatment for them. It is rather that the particular sample of family members living in South-West England at the time the research was carried out, when put alongside those from the other two socio-cultural groups, has enabled these sources of variation to be identified.

Facing the threat of alcohol to Australian indigenous family life and culture

Grog as a public matter in Aboriginal Australian communities

As we had hoped they would, the Australian interviews gave fresh insights which had not been obtained from the Mexican and English data. Indeed, we had so much anticipated that the experience of living with drinking problems would be a different experience for indigenous Australians, particularly those living in small, remote, rural communities, that we were surprised that the core experience seemed much the same as it was in small town and suburban England and poor urban areas in Mexico City. There was, nevertheless, a whole element to the Australian experience, as told to the interviewers, which was relatively hidden in the material from the other two socio-cultural groups. The aspect which was hard to detect in the reports from England and Mexico, but which could not be missed in the Australian reports, was the way in which excessive drinking was seen in the latter as a public and community matter, threatening the group and its survival, and not simply as a private, family affair. There were several elements to this, including the public nature of drunkenness and associated violence, which often took extreme forms; the multitude of excessive drinkers both in the family and in the community; the phenomenon of drinking publicly in groups; statements that attributed the cause of excessive drinking to social and community difficulties and change; the threat that excessive drinking was thought to pose to the whole community, and particularly to the community's children; and the interest that participants showed in alcohol policy. So public and widespread was excessive drinking thought to be, and so prominent was it as a matter for community concern and debate, that interviews in Australia often encompassed discussion at individual, family and community levels in a way that interviews in Mexico and England did not. In the two latter groups, there appeared to be general acceptance that what was being talked about was an individual drinking or drug problem, sometimes referred to as 'alcoholism' or 'drug addiction'. That was far less often the case in the Australian interviews. The wider perspective on such problems in the Australian data was certainly related also to the wider concept of 'the family' that pertained there. Family diagrams accompanying interview reports, drawn in Australia, typically included a much larger number of individuals than those drawn in Mexico or England.

A prominent part of the picture described by Australian family members was the large number of harmful drinkers who were mentioned. It was the exception rather than the rule for 'the drinker' who was the focus of the main part of the interview to be the only harmful drinker who was mentioned. It was common for participants to talk of several members of their families with drinking problems, and family deaths attributed to drinking were very frequently mentioned. Concern was often expressed, not solely or even mainly about the focal drinker, but also about groups of drinkers, often referred to as a 'drinking mob', of which the focal drinker would frequently be a member. Furthermore, many of the incidents surrounding excessive drinking, including those involving violence, were public and hence visible to neighbouring members of the community. The extent and severity of violence described were alarming. For one thing, physical injuries resulting from violence involving attacks with spears and other objects were often extremely severe, with regular mention of the victims of violence ending up in hospital as a result of their injuries. Participants would often express concerns about the community disruption caused by excessive drinking and the threat to the future of the community that it posed:

> 'It [grog] is killing our life, our culture, our Aboriginal people. And people are getting carried away by drinking at what you might call the white man's drinking waterhole. It has taken away our life, the lives of my countrymen, most of those within the Northern Territory, Queensland, anywhere in Australia, it has taken away the life for Aboriginal people. And now it's the crying time, people crying for their land, but that grog, people have to watch or control their lives, because if we want to live for another hundred years or more, us Aboriginal people, maintain our language . . . white men came into Australia, took away our rights, but the main one is the grog, took away our lives, for Aboriginal people. That's the main one, that big waterhole where we're getting drunk and into trouble.'

> (Australia, father of a drinking son)

Worry about the effects of excessive drinking on children, mentioned in many of the interviews from all three socio-cultural groups, was very prominent in the Australian interviews. Sometimes the concern for children was for their safety; sometimes it was that drinkers would set children a bad example, or, as in one case, tell children inappropriate stories rather than fulfilling family obligations by passing on stories about Aboriginal culture and tradition; and sometimes it was concern for the long-term impact on children's schooling, stability and development generally. It was often implied that children were the future of these threatened communities, and hence the threat that excessive drinking posed for children was a threat to the very survival of a community.

When it came to trying to explain the causes of a relative's problem drinking, the Australian interviews included attributions on a social or community level, as in the following: 'families stuck in an alcohol and welfare cycle', 'disillusioned with his own culture and with the white side', 'now it takes them a long time to mature; his mother treats him like a child', 'grog is a foreign thing', 'unemployment causing young people to turn to grog'. When it came to solutions, community responses also figured large. These included responses of a religious or legal nature, involving high-profile activities on the part of the church, police, the night patrol (see Chapter 3), courts and prison. Many family members also had something to say about current measures designed to control excessive drinking in the Northern Territory. A number of participants were in favour of total prohibition, and others approved of such measures as dry areas, drinking permits, banning grog on pay days or weekends, or banning 4-litre wine casks. Most were unfavourable toward policy measures that it was thought might make alcohol more available, such as 'wet canteens'[1] and Aboriginal drinking clubs. Others favoured educational approaches.

Opportunities and difficulties in standing up to excessive drinking in Aboriginal Australia

Just as in the Mexican and English data, so with the Australian reports, certain themes found in all three socio-cultural groups took on a greater prominence. These were traced to the greater threat that excessive drinking posed to whole communities as well as to individual families, plus the more extensive structure of family obligation and the greater mobility associated with indigenous life in Northern Australia. These factors often provided family members in that socio-cultural group with greater opportunities to stand up to excessive drinking and to achieve some independence. At the same time, those same factors could create barriers to effective coping.

One theme of prominence in the Australian interviews was the emphasis on *talking* to drinkers, and the wider range of members of the extended family who might be thought to have a responsibility to do such talking. Examples were a family member getting 'sisters' and older 'brothers' and other male relatives, to speak to the drinker; references to other family members who should be telling drinkers off, such as the drinker's mother or aunts; and one family member who, as the only surviving male in the family, felt responsibility for speaking to a number of different drinkers. Reference was made to a drinker's father's brother who now felt he was the only one who could help the drinker on account of the drinker's father's chronic sickness. The overwhelming impression that the Australian interview reports gave was of a very high level of engagement on the part of the extended family. The interviews were full of references to other people, mainly family relations, who *worried* for the drinker about whom the family member was concerned, or for the family member herself or himself. At the same time, there was frustration that drinkers would listen but not really hear what concerned family members said to them. To use a commonly heard Aboriginal expression, drinkers 'have no ears'.

Another area of prominence was the frequent reference to active forms of *withdrawing* from the drinker or drinkers. The impression given was of a more active 'moving or escaping' than was present in the interviews from Mexico and England. Expressions used included 'taking off', 'running away', 'going away', 'moving away', 'getting away' and 'escaping'. Many references were made to avoiding or escaping, not from the individual drinker, but from drinkers or the drinking scene in general. For example, references were made to 'getting away from the drunks', 'getting away from drinkers', 'escaping drinkers', 'getting the drinker away from his drinking mates', 'avoiding drinkers while they are drinking', and, more generally, 'avoiding the grog' or 'removing oneself and the family from the drinking scene'. It was very noticeable in the rural interviews how many references were made specifically to moving to the capital city. One way or another, there seemed for many to be a pull toward the city, and this was often associated with escaping from the drinker, drinkers or the drinking life. It seemed to have associations of gaining freedom and independence, and of putting both physical and emotional distance between oneself and drinking-associated difficulties. In the Australian interviews as a whole, including in those carried out in the city or town, there were an equal number of references to 'moving out bush', 'back to the homeland', 'returning to a traditional life-style on a remote community', 'setting up one's own camp' or 'retreating to their outstation'.

The form of gaining independence referred to in Chapter 6 as 'getting a new and better life' was particularly strong in the Australian interviews (although once again this was not a feature confined to one group). It expressed the idea of turning one's back on a life dominated by drinkers, or by the excessive drinking of a particular family member, and achieving a better, more independent life for oneself, and, in a number of cases, for one's children. It seemed to be part of a desire to better oneself, and to improve the general standard of life for one's family. Educational opportunities played a large part in this. There were a number of references to previous lack of education for oneself or one's family, and part of the motivation for breaking away from drinkers was to gain further education for oneself or to ensure education for one's children. Getting a new and better life and breaking away from contact with harmful drinking also involved adopting a particular position on one's own drinking: several participants spoke of giving up former heavy drinking, refusing to submit to temptation to join heavy drinkers in their drinking, or to always having been an abstainer.

Among ways of trying to establish control, *protecting* actions loomed large in the Australian interview reports. For this, there appeared to be at least the following reasons. First, participants described a very great deal of alcohol-related trouble, often of a violent kind. The interviews were full of accounts of how interviewees had tried to protect themselves against the drinker's aggression and 'humbugging', trashing things inside or outside the home, or simply getting into drunken fights. Second, protecting actions were very often motivated by the desire to protect children from the effects of excessive drinking.

Ways of protecting included keeping one's eyes open for signs of trouble; defending oneself or others, or fighting back; separating drinkers who were fighting; running away from an aggressive drinker; refusing drinkers access to one's home or controlling the number and type who enter; stopping going out with the drinker; not letting children go to stay with their drinking father; and playing along with the drinker for the sake of the children's safety. A special subcategory of protecting action consisted of seeking protective help from the authorities. Sources of this kind of protection included the police, the night patrol, a court that might issue a restraining order, and housing authorities who might help, for example, by transferring a person to alternative accommodation, or, as was mentioned by a number of family members, making sure that the person's home was fitted with security measures such as window screens and fences.

When it came to family members gaining some independence, the Australian reports suggested that the subcategory we have referred to as *refusing* was of particular importance, and caused Aboriginal family members special difficulty. There appeared to be two closely related reasons for this. First, because a great deal of movement (e.g. from remote community to town, or from place to place within a town) by individual drinkers or groups of drinkers was mentioned in the interviews, and because family members often reported being on the receiving end of 'humbug' from drinkers wanting to be admitted to a person's home, refusing such admission took on great significance for a number of the participants. Second, a combination of some of the things that family members said, and comments added by some of the interviewers, suggested that refusing, which was problematic in Mexico and England too, was particularly so for indigenous Australians because of strongly held cultural obligations to share with others, particularly with others with whom one has a kinship relationship (see Chapter 3). Hence, refusing actions were often thought to be tough, even cruel, and were very often 'taken the wrong way'. For example, a wife said that when her husband ran out of money, he 'growled' her for food and beer money, but that she had always been tough about this, even though he had sometimes sworn and hit her. Such cultural expectations were shown up in stark relief in the case of a small number of families that were culturally mixed. With one couple, for example, a conflict arose about how to respond to family drinkers. The Aboriginal wife, more bound than her European husband by indigenous expectations of sharing and giving when asked, was inclined, according to her husband, to give family drinkers food, money and other things when he thought it was more appropriate to refuse.

Lifestyle is generally more public in Australian Aboriginal communities than in non-Aboriginal ones. The public, community nature of drinking in Aboriginal communities could constitute a hindrance for family members. For one thing, the large number of excessive drinkers in most people's close and extended families, and in their communities, referred to earlier, meant that family members were often surrounded by other people who, far from supporting them in their efforts, in fact seemed to be opposing them. Many family members mentioned individual relatives, other than the drinking relative about whom they were concerned, who caused them additional difficulty by drinking with that relative, encouraging the latter to drink, or simply by being a nuisance (see Chapter 7). The fact that drinking often took place in groups, and that groups when drinking were often quite mobile, thus increasing the possibilities of harassment of people who were not drinking, constituted a further hindrance to effective coping.

Attention was drawn earlier to the difficulties that family members experience in all cultures in taking a stand against excessive drinking and its harmful effects on the family. There were cultural forces operating on the Australian families that made these difficulties particularly great. Because of the emphasis on family obligation to help and support members of the extended family who might be in trouble, it was particularly difficult for many family members in the Australian group to obtain a united view from others that backed up their attempts to stand up to the drinking. Hence, hindrances in the way of consensual coping were particularly strong, as a result of traditional family member obligations, and rules about who should and who should not intervene, interfamily rivalries, the high level of cultural acceptance of drinkers' behaviour and continuing drinking, and the responsibilities of the Aboriginal family member to look after the drinker in some way.

Conclusion

In this chapter, we have tried to extract from the interview material what was particular to each of the three socio-cultural groups. We have resisted the temptation to claim that there is a simple relationship between culture and family members' experiences, or that any of the themes we have identified are unique to one culture. We have chosen, rather, to describe themes that were especially prominent in one or another group. In the Mexican data, for example, the effects of excessive drinking or drug taking on families living in poverty forced themselves on our attention, as did the importance of family gender roles and the dominance of kin in social support networks. In England, we were particularly struck by the threat that problem drinking or drug taking posed to family members' independence and self-expression, and by family members' uncertainties about alcohol or drug dependence and its treatment. In the interviews with indigenous Australians, it was the public, community nature of family members' experience of and concerns about drinking that came to the fore, as well as the strengths and difficulties of family members' coping created by an indigenous culture that could involve a complex set of obligations to members of an extended family. Throughout this chapter, we have emphasised that each of those themes is to be found in the interviews from all three groups. What has been achieved by studying family members' experiences in three contrasting socio-cultural groups is a fuller appreciation of the diversity of such experiences. We continue to believe that the core experience for family members is much the same throughout the world. But we now know much more about how that experience varies according to social context. The experience is similar in socio-cultural contexts as contrasting as the three that took part in the present research, but diversity and its sources have been more readily appreciated by carrying out interviews in three very different parts of the world.

In the following chapter, an attempt is made to integrate the findings of the present research along with the findings of previous research on the subject. We draw on our findings regarding a common core of family members' experiences as well as the conclusions of the present chapter. An integrated view of the core, universal experience is offered, plus a summary of how that experience varies depending on a number of important modifying factors. Finally, Chapter 9 will ask whether the stress of coping with excessive drinking or drug use constitutes a unique experience or whether there are close parallels with other forms of family stress.

Chapter 9

An integrated view of alcohol and drug problems in the family

Concerned and affected family members: a hidden and misunderstood group

Family members, concerned about and affected by the excessive drinking or drug taking of close relatives, have been the chief protagonists of the stories on which the previous chapters were based. They constitute a large, neglected, misunderstood and often stigmatised group. In Chapter 1, it was estimated that there might be as many as 80 million such family members worldwide. This is not a group of people who themselves suffer from a diagnosable illness, who constitute a recognised threat to public health, who cause much trouble to others, or who combine to bring pressure on politicians. They are largely unknown and uncounted, and mostly suffer in silence. Scarcely any services are dedicated to this group, even in those countries with the best-developed health and social care systems. Some agencies for people with alcohol and drug problems provide some service for family members, but it is usually secondary to their main work.

Where family members do appear in large numbers is in the ranks of those recruited to services or research dedicated to such problems as domestic violence (e.g. Brown et al., 1999; Grisso et al., 1999), mental ill health (e.g. Smith, 1971) or marital conflict (e.g. Halford and Osgarby, 1993). Although family members with close relatives with alcohol or drug problems have very often been neglected by those whose interest is in mental health more generally, there are also to be found in the mental health research literature regular hints that a relative's excessive drinking or drug taking puts family members at risk of mental ill health. One such indication, from what was to become a very large literature on stressful life-events and mental health, was a paper reported by Smith in 1971. Several hundred people, admitted to a mental health service in the USA over a period of 2 years, were compared with a local general population sample in terms of their reported experiences of 37 'critical life-events' in the prior year. 'Family member began drinking heavily' was one of the most frequent 10 such life-events reported by the patient sample (by 10%), and was one that significantly distinguished the patient and general population samples.

A number of years later, and on a worldwide scale, Fischbach and Herbert's (1997) review of the evidence confirmed a link between domestic violence (known to be associated with excessive substance use by partners) and women's depression and post-traumatic stress disorder. The latter is characterised by such symptoms as depression, sleep disturbance, trouble concentrating or memory impairment, hyperarousal alternating with psychological numbing and withdrawal, and disturbances of identity and relationship – symptoms very like those described by women partners of men with drinking problems (Wiseman, 1991; Yang, 1997; and Chapter 5 above).

In Britain, an influential series of studies on the relationship between stressful life circumstances and depression among women has regularly used examples of excessive drinking by close relatives to illustrate the kinds of stress that put family members at risk of depression (e.g. Brown and Prudo, 1981). In a later report in that series, Brown and Moran (1997) used the terms 'humiliation' and 'entrapment' life-events to refer to the types of stressful sets of life circumstances that were particularly dangerous for family members' mental health, including, as illustrations, a number of examples of relatives' excessive drinking. Despite the regularity with which excessive substance use is mentioned in the work on stress and mental health, it is noticeable how that literature never highlights the circumstances faced by family members living with serious alcohol or drug problems as deserving of special comment or attention.

The large group of people with which this book is concerned is therefore mostly a hidden one. It is well represented whenever domestic violence, psychological disorder or couple or family conflict are at issue. Even then, it is seldom recognised as an identifiable group with a special story to tell. But the problem is far worse than that. When the family members of people with drinking or drug problems have been identified, they have more often than not been written and spoken about in pejorative and stigmatising ways. In Chapter 1, we reviewed the leading perspectives from which professionals had viewed family members. The group that had received the most attention, wives of men with drinking problems, had been seen as psychopathological themselves, or, more recently, as codependent. Parents of young adults with drug problems had been viewed as inadequate in their parenting. Husbands of women with drinking problems, when they had been noticed at all, had been described in very unsympathetic terms, being stereotyped as men who left their wives at the earliest opportunity. Other family members concerned about their relatives' drinking or drug taking, such as sisters and brothers, grandparents, aunts and uncles, and cousins, had received no attention. These stereotypes are reflected, not surprisingly, in the negative or unhelpful tone of remarks often made by professional service providers about family members (Dorn et al., 1987) or directly to family members, as reported by the latter to researchers (see Chapter 7 above).

That negative view of family members is subtle and pervasive and by no means limited to the most obviously dated and extreme statements, such as those of Whalen (1953) and others writing about 'wives of alcoholics' half a century ago. The concept of codependency, for example, is ambiguous, but in most presentations it includes elements of women's assumed pathology, and its origins can be traced to the earlier, more explicit psychopathology model (e.g. Harper and Capdevila, 1990; and Chapter 1 above). Even in the writings of those who appear to be adopting a stress-coping perspective, there is often a strong judgemental element. A number of those who have researched and written about family members' ways of coping have been very explicit about the 'dysfunctional' nature of much family member coping and the need for it to change if a problem drinking or drug-taking relative is to be helped. For example, Yoshioka et al. (1992) wrote a paper entitled 'Nagging and other drinking control efforts of spouses of uncooperative alcohol abusers: assessment and modification'. They used the Spouse Sobriety Influence Inventory (SSII) to ask spouses about their drinking control (DC) behaviours, a number of which then became the targets for modification in a counselling programme. Those targeted behaviours were described as

> part of the spouse's 'old sobriety influence system' which we hope to have put aside so that other, more appropriate ways of responding can be initiated. Instances of DC are thereafter referred to as the 'old system,' a convenient short-hand concept that is readily understood.

> (pp. 312–313)

The spouse, they argued, may be reluctant to stop engaging in DC or may persist in having intense negative thoughts or feelings about the drinking, including anxiety or anger, and in such cases it may be necessary to assist the spouse further to 'back off' or 'let go', to detach and achieve greater emotional distance from the drinking and its effects. In a similar vein, but using a rather different method, Rychtarik et al. (1988) have developed programmes for family members using what they refer to as a 'skill-training' approach which very explicitly rates some coping reactions as more 'competent' than others.

Even Wiseman (1991), whose book displays one of the most serious efforts that has been made to understand, in depth, the position of wives married to men with drinking problems from their own perspective, in a few places used language that could be read as betraying a critical, impatient attitude toward wives. She devoted a special section of her book to describing family interactions at mealtimes. In view of the stigma and misunderstanding that has attached to the role of wife of an excessive drinker, what Wiseman said about wives at that point is interesting:

many women have such a strong sense of duty, or are so reluctant to give up their roles as cooks and nurturant persons to family members, that they cling to meal preparation with a tenacity that often borders on the fanatic.

(p. 133)

Wiseman drew some unflattering comparisons between wives sticking to their role as cooks in the absence of any appreciation, and fading movie stars clinging desperately to a aura of false glamour, or a colonist in an outpost of empire dressing for dinner, or a doctor or lawyer going to the office every day although the practice has dwindled to almost nothing.

The lack of understanding and negative stereotyping to which family members have been subject comes as a double blow, since they are particularly vulnerable to attack and therefore often highly sensitive to criticism. This was made clear by those who had listened to wives of men with drinking problems talking about their experiences; their conclusions were reviewed in Chapter 2. The strand of experience which Banister and Peavy (1994) called 'living in a pit' involved the erosion of a sense of self, the adoption of a victim mentality, and the taking on of blame for what was going on. The core of the experience, according to Asher (1992), was 'definitional ambivalence', which included uncertainty about, and the struggle to understand, not only the relative's behaviour and the wife's relationship with her husband, but also her own self-identity. A central element in the experience of living with a partner with a drinking problem was what she called 'personalising': believing that she was not a good enough wife, or believing the hurtful things that he said about her. Fryer (1998) also noted how wives were positioned as parties responsible for their own plight. Ussher (1998) referred to the positioning of wives as being to blame if they could not tame their husbands' drinking, and in her research in South Korea, Yang (1997) highlighted the tendency of husbands' families, and the wives themselves, to be critical of wives for not living up to the ideal of a good Korean wife.

The unsympathetic and demeaning ways in which family members have often been described by professionals therefore compounds a set of stressful life circumstances that are already undermining of family members' self-confidence. This state of affairs was put rather well by Kokin and Walker (1989) in a book entitled, *Women Married to Alcoholics: Help and Hope for Nonalcoholic Partners*, written from clinical experience:

As if the anguish of living with an alcoholic were not enough, the wife of such a person may endure further indignity because of the way in which she is so often typecast. . . . Even some of the terms that are commonly used hint in this direction. The wife or female partner of an alcoholic is referred to by such words as 'enabler', 'codependent', or 'coalcoholic'. These tags tend to suggest some complicity – the idea of an accomplice or co-conspirator who may have been responsible for the creation of her husband's drinking problem, or who, at the very least, may have cooperated with his desire not to stop drinking . . . the wife continues to be held accountable. She is a convenient scapegoat. . . . If alcoholism is a disease, how could the wife have given it to her husband? And if she is not the cause, what expertise and training is she supposed to have that would enable her to cure him of it? Our society possesses no known cure for this terrible affliction; why should the wife be expected to have some special ability in this area?

(pp. 17, 18)

The core experience: the four facets of stress and strain

How, then, are we best to conceive of the position of family members affected by and concerned about the problem drinking or drug taking of their close relatives? The remainder of this chapter is devoted to drawing together the main themes of what was told to our interviewers in Mexico City, South-West England and Northern Australia, along with the conclusions of the comparatively few previous pieces of qualitative research summarised in Chapter 2, in addition to other research on the topic and research on coping with chronic stressors more generally. We attempt here to develop a model that both does justice to what family members say about their experiences and could form a basis for a more sensitive professional approach to understanding and meeting the needs of family members. We began in Chapter 1 by outlining the stress-strain-coping-support model with which we started. Nothing that we heard in the course of this research has changed our minds about the appropriateness of that model as an overall framework, but we believe our knowledge of each of the components of that model and how they work together has been deepened as a result. Most particularly, the comparing and contrasting of accounts from three different socio-cultural groups has, we hope, helped correct what had already been seen as one of the main deficiencies of the existing model, namely, the neglect of the social and cultural context.

It was suggested in Chapter 5 that the impact of excessive drinking or drug taking on family members might usefully be described in terms of the four facets summarised in Figure 9.1. A number of these were already familiar from previous research based on interviews with women partners of men with drinking problems. Present findings suggest, however, that those elements of the experience are also described by male partners of women who drink excessively, by parents of sons or daughters with drug or alcohol problems, and by other family members affected by and concerned about relatives' drinking or drug taking, across three very different socio-cultural groups.

The first facet identified was the deteriorated nature of the relationship between family member and relative. Relationships had invariably become

THE CORE
EXPERIENCE

Sleep, eating affected

Helpless, devalued, depressed

Symptoms of ill health

Substance use

Anxious, angry, frightened

Poor general health

Signs of strain

Stressful living

Humbug

Unsure about relative

Relationship disagreeable

Threat to home and family

Worry for relative

Company

Form of substance use

Finances

Performance

Health

Self-neglect

Worry about children

Home invaded

Finances

Social life

Atmosphere

Police

Figure 9.1 Four facets of the experience of living with a close relative with an alcohol or drug problem.

disagreeable, very often aggressive, and often, but not always, physically violent. When it had occurred, violence was often of a very serious nature, even to the extent, in some instances, of the family member receiving death threats from the relative. Whether or not there was violence, family members spoke of their confusion and uncertainty about the relative's moods and what caused them, and about the relative's comings and goings, which had become erratic and unreliable. Family members spoke about the 'torture' of living with the problem, the way they were living on a 'knife edge', and the uncertainty of what was going to happen next and whether the relative could be trusted.

So much is familiar. Banister and Peavy (1994) had written of Canadian wives constantly being on guard, and Yang (1997) described the frequently very severe violence experienced by South Korean wives and the loss of posi- tive feelings toward their husbands that they often described. But it was Wiseman (1991) who had probably described the experience best. As in the present research, she highlighted the deterioration of the marital relationship as a core feature of wives' experiences. She drew out five core elements in that experience of a deteriorating relationship: abusiveness, lack of communica- tion, erosion of family mealtimes, lack of joint recreation and social activities, and deterioration of the sexual relationship.

Reports of violence and other forms of abusiveness were very common in

Wiseman's study as they were in the present research. There was much variation, however, with less than half of both Wiseman's groups of wives reporting violence directed toward them personally. But there was also a great deal of abusiveness without physical violence in the form of a general belligerence, in the course of which anything a wife or other said was 'challenged, answered with anger or argued about, its validity denied, or the veracity of the speaker questioned', and criticism of the wife involving 'sarcasm, belittling her efforts, ideas, behavior' (Wiseman, 1991, p. 96). Wives described brutality toward children, in the form not of physical attacks, but shouting, sarcasm and put-downs. Lack of communication and of joint social activities were highlighted by Wiseman as indications of the deteriorating marital relationship. Social activities had become fewer due to lack of invitations or simply because spouses took less pleasure in each other's company, wives fearing drunken scenes, husbands sensing wives' displeasure. Sexual relationships had very often, although not always, deteriorated. One way or another, wives described their relationships as no longer being what they once were, and this had been a source of sadness and self-doubt for them. Wiseman also made the point that all these aspects of a deteriorating relationship set up vicious cycles, with wives themselves being driven to avoid communication, joint social activities or sex. With all of that picture present findings concur.

There were other aspects of family life which emerged in the present research which in earlier research may have received less attention than they deserve. One is the specific component of the deteriorated family member–relative relationship that we have called 'being humbugged'. Previous research had noted the drain that heavy drinking or drug taking can cause to family finances. But no previous accounts have given the prominence that we conclude should be given to the often regular and distressing behavioural interactions during which a relative requests of a family member money or resources that the family member believes will be used, directly or indirectly, to finance excessive substance use. Such requests were rarely simple and always put family members in a quandary about how to respond. Such requests were not infrequently perceived as demanding, involving 'blackmail', putting family members on the spot, drawing other people in and so making for an even more complicated dilemma, or involving other complicating issues that made a decision about what to do even more difficult. The importance of being humbugged, in our view, lies partly in the salience of such interactions in the daily lives of family members, but also in the symbolic significance of these interactions in the total picture of life for family members struggling to cope with a relative's drinking or drug problem. An episode of humbugging brings to a head what has been going on. It brings out in acute form the disagreeable nature of the relationship between family member and relative, as well as the family member's fears and uncertainties. At the same time, it brings into sharp relief the moral and behavioural dilemmas that a family member faces in trying to cope. The focus on these acute interaction episodes which emerged so clearly in the present research complements Asher's (1992) more symbolic interactionist account of wives' 'moral careers' and their 'definitional ambivalence' (see Chapter 2).

A further facet was identified in Chapter 5: the ways in which home and family life were threatened. Others have previously noted the harmful effects on family finances, the pressure on family members to find extra work, the negative effects on family members' work and social lives (Wiseman, 1991; Casey et al., 1993; Yang, 1997), and particularly family members' concern about the effects of the problem on any children living in the family (e.g. Estes and Baker, 1982; Yang, 1997). The present research found that the greatest weight of worry about effects on the family was about possible effects on the children. The worry was of a number of different kinds: the possibility of violence or neglect, more general worry about interference with good upbringing of the children, and concern that children might repeat the relative's behaviour. One aspect of threat to home and family life, noted in Chapter 5 but not highlighted in previous research, was the way in which the very sanctity of the family home was violated and the expected boundary between home and the outside world interfered with in uncomfortable ways. Homes were 'invaded' by excessive drug use or drinking or by other excessive drinkers or drug users, and sometimes by the police or other outsiders.

There was one facet of the stressful circumstances facing family members which appears to have been largely missed by previous researchers, but which, in our understanding, is one of the central features. It is the facet that in Chapter 5 was termed 'the family member is worried about the relative'. Family members were concerned about their relatives on a number of counts. Not only did they worry about the frequency, quantity or form of the relative's substance use, but they also had complex sets of worries about his or her physical and mental health; about the way in which it was thought the relative was neglecting himself or herself; about the relative's education, work or sporting performance; about the relative's financial affairs; and about the company the relative was keeping. Although the samples of family members interviewed in the present research included some who were in varying stages of severing their commitments to their relatives, the large majority remained in committed, albeit uncomfortable, relationships with their relatives. They were in kinship relationships of obligation to their relatives or their lives were contractually and/or emotionally entwined with their relatives financially, socially and in numerous other ways. They worried for their relatives and wanted to be able to do something for them. Without appreciating that facet of family members' experience, half the picture is missing. Family members were not only personally affected in harmful ways, but they were also concerned about their relatives. It is perhaps that combination of being adversely affected and yet committed to concern about a member of one's kin whose behaviour appears to be threatening the family member, the whole family and home, and the relative himself or herself that creates such a difficult, and perhaps unique, set of coping dilemmas for partners, parents and other family members.

The last of the four facets of stress for family members, identified in Chapter 5, was 'signs of strain for family members', and here we are again on familiar ground. The mixed and ambivalent emotions experienced by family members have already been described by authors such as Dorn et al. (1987), Wiseman (1991) and Yang (1997). As was often found in the present research, such feelings include those of anger and hatred toward relatives. Murderous feelings were described in each of those previous studies and again in the present one. In all cases, such feelings were interpreted by the authors of the research reports as feelings that were understandable in the light of the multifaceted and often long-standing or worsening nature of the stressors to which family members were exposed. The frequency with which such feelings have been noted, and the interpretation put upon them, are important in view of the way in which such feelings have sometimes been interpreted in the past as indicative of family members' pathology (see Stanton, undated, for the view that parents typically harbour pathological 'death wishes' toward their drug-addicted children).

In addition to such feelings toward their problem drinking or drug-taking relatives, family members in the present research most frequently described feelings of anxiety or worry, helplessness or despair, depression or low mood, and guilt or feeling devalued. Such feelings they attributed with comparative certainty to the circumstances of living with a close relative with a drinking or drug problem. They also described a range of symptoms of poor physical and general health that were attributed less certainly to such circumstances. Such symptoms have been described by Wiseman (1991), by Yang (1997), and in a study of wives of men with drinking problems in the former Czechoslovakia (Student and Matova, 1969). The symptoms described by those various authors are shown in Table 9.1 alongside a summary of the symptoms described in the present research and listed in greater detail in Chapter 5.

Other studies from the 1960s onwards have documented the increased risk for wives of men with drinking problems of symptoms of ill health, and have demonstrated that health improves when women are no longer living with an actively drinking problem drinker, either because drinking is no longer excessive or because of separation (Haberman, 1964; Bailey, 1967; Moos et al., 1990; Brennan et al., 1994).

Coping

Affected and concerned as they are, family members search for ways of coping. Much of what the participants in Mexico, England and Australia told their interviewers about the ways they tried to cope fits with what previous researchers have found. At the same time, present findings have deepened our understanding in this area and exposed a previous tendency to oversimplify

Table 9.1 Symptoms of poor physical and general health reported by family members of relatives with drinking or drug problems

Student and Matova, 1969 Czechoslovakia	Wiseman, 1991 Finland and USA
Insomnia and tiredness	Low energy level
Headaches	Not eating and loss of weight
Uninterest in sex	Nervous diarrhoea
Loss of appetite and weight loss	Hypertension
Hypertension	Rash
Allergies	Really sick, ill
Yang, 1997 South Korea	The present research, Mexico, England, Australia
Indigestion	Poor sleep, tiredness
Migraine	Eating up or down
Hypertension	Weight loss or gain
Fatigue	Anaemia
Skin conditions	Headaches and back pain
Chest pain	Diarrhoea
Dizziness	Palpitations

the coping dilemma faced by family members by depicting it in terms of a single dimension.

Putting up with it versus withdrawing and gaining independence

The dimension about which all appear to be agreed, including the present authors, contrasts what was called in Chapter 6 'putting up with' excessive drinking or drug taking and 'withdrawing and gaining independence'. Some of the clearest examples of putting up with a relative's drinking or drug taking come from research with wives in traditional marriages. The endurance shown by Mrs Lim and other South Korean wives interviewed by Yang (1997) is a good example (see Chapter 2). A similar picture has emerged in another Ph.D. thesis (Ahuja, 2000; Ahuja et al., 2003) based on interviews with 24 Sikh wives in England, all affected by and concerned about their husbands' excessive drinking. Nearly all were first-generation immigrants to Britain, and, like many of Yang's South Korean wives, they had all had traditional arranged marriages, initially meeting their partners either on the day of their wedding or only once prior to the wedding. All had at some stage responded to their husbands' excessive drinking with varying degrees and kinds of acceptance, resignation and self-sacrifice. Ahuja referred to that way of coping as 'inactive resignation'. Wiseman (1991) also described Finnish wives as being uncertain about their right to question their husbands' drinking owing to what she saw as the less egalitarian nature of marriage relationships in Finland at that time than in the USA.

But, as was described at length in Chapter 6, putting up with a relative's problem substance use is by no means confined to traditional families, nor only to wives. In that chapter, we documented the myriad ways in which family members described being inactive, accepting, or self-sacrificing (Table 6.1). Also documented in detail were the many explanations offered by family members, either directly or indirectly, for putting up with their relatives' behaviour. They included reasons to do with keeping calm for the family's sake, believing that the relative needed the family member's support, finding it difficult to be hard with the relative, pressure from the relative, feeling helpless, and attitudes of tolerance toward drinking or drug use (Figure 6.1). Previous research has sometimes noted such factors. For example, Yang (1997) quoted the following statements by wives: 'I prefer to buy him a drink myself because if I did not he would ask the children' (p. 162) and 'I try very hard to take care of my husband's health. Every day I make a special diet and traditional remedies for him. I do not wish to be left a widow and my children fatherless' (p. 162). Yang also quoted a mother: 'I cannot face my neighbours and relatives because of my alcoholic son. . . . We do not visit anybody or entertain visitors' (p. 158). But previous research has not so clearly brought out the very difficult nature of the decisions facing family members in deciding how to cope. In the actual circumstances that family members find themselves in, usually with a complex set of strong feelings toward the relative and the relative's drinking or drug taking, and a complex set of obligations toward the relative and other family members, these are far from easy decisions. We think of them as *coping dilemmas*.

What *has* been very clearly described by a number of authors is the difficulty that family members have in withdrawing and gaining independence. Asher (1992) wrote of wives in the USA 'depersonalizing' their ambivalence about what had been going on in their families, by which she meant refocusing attention on their own rights, obligations and needs. She also wrote of the process of wives 'transforming' or redefining their ambivalence, which they were helped to do by recognising their husbands' 'alcoholism', and perhaps their own 'codependence' (although Asher was less certain about the latter concept, finding it both liberating and prescriptive at the same time). One of Banister and Peavy's (1994) three strands in the experiences of Canadian wives was 'push and pull', or conflicts that wives experienced about independence and separation. In Chapter 6, the many ways family members in Mexico, England and Australia described withdrawing and gaining more independence were listed, covering a number of elements: not worrying, doing what the family member wants to do, getting involved in other activities, escaping or getting away, sorting oneself out, and getting a new and better life for oneself and other members of the family.

Like the present authors, Wiseman identified the issue of independence for wives as a central one. She divided wives into three roughly equal groups who differed in the form of adjustment that they had made to continuing to live with their problem drinking husbands. One group had gone a considerable way in making an independent life for themselves, engaging in new activities outside the home, making new friends, and enhancing their self-image. For that group, employment and further education were crucial as means for enhancing quality of life, as they were in the present research, particularly in Australia. At the other extreme was a group, constituting about a quarter of the wives in both Finland and the USA, who were, according to Wiseman, 'stunned by all that has happened and sink[ing] further and further into inertia, lack of self-confidence, dependence, loneliness and self-pity' (Wiseman, 1991, pp. 210–211). She referred to wives in that group as 'mired in discontent' (p. 213), characterised by muddled thinking, insufficiently introspective to think of ways of getting out of the trap of marriage to an 'alcoholic', 'unable . . . to pull themselves together to do anything about their situation' (p. 215, one of the few sections of Wiseman's book where her language seems to imply impatience and criticism of wives). She suggested that this group of wives lacked the ability to think out possible steps to bring about a desire to change, and the willingness to make the effort necessary to move from one step to another; they were too emotionally exhausted to consider making plans at all, and lacked sufficient positive self-image or optimism to seek new experiences, or the ability to go ahead without support from others, or to ignore criticism from others. Present findings suggest many reasons for such apparent inaction in the face of a relative's substance misuse, and some of the quotations that Wiseman provided from interviews with women in the inactive group support that view. Some offered reasons for their apparent inertia, and others hinted at them. For example, one US wife said, 'Well, I've thought about leaving him. . . . I wouldn't have to put up with the drinking; it drives me crazy sometimes, but I need his insurance. I need a good many other things that he can give me that I wouldn't have if I left him' (p. 216). A Finnish wife said, 'I'd like to go back to work. I'm much more alert when I work, but my husband thinks I shouldn't. He thinks the State should help me with our rent' (p. 218). Others simply seemed to blame themselves for the very fact of not having done more.

The question of gaining independence from the drinking or drug problem, or putting 'distance' between oneself and the problem, widely recognised to be a principal dilemma for family members, is by no means confined to the question of separation. But the dilemma of whether to consider separation is nearly always a salient one. Wiseman (1991), along with nearly all other writers on the subject (Bannister and Peavy, 1994; Yang, 1997; Ahuja, 2000), talked of the complex set of emotional and practical barriers to separation that exist for most family members, and the acute dilemma that the thought of separation poses for a family member. Corrigan (1980) concluded that husbands of women with drinking problems faced many of the same dilemmas and barriers to separation, including consideration of the needs of their children, as did wives of men with drinking problems. Dorn et al. (1987) also described the dilemma faced by parents about whether to tell drug-misusing sons or daughters to leave home. For example, 'there was a point at which her behaviour was so intolerable to me. . . . So I said, "Well, you're not coming back." But I was absolutely sick with fear inside at having done it' (p. 37).

Although there has been recognition of the difficulties, dilemmas and barriers that family members face in moving from a position of putting up with a relative's excessive drinking or drug taking to one in which family members can achieve distance and independence (although even those dilemmas are often not fully appreciated), there has been a tendency to confine an understanding of family members' positions to the single dimension of 'putting up with it' versus 'withdrawing and gaining independence'. That has particularly been the case in reports from the USA, influenced by the 12-step movement, which have assumed that coping progresses in stages toward a 'recognition' of the relative's 'illness' and thence to resolution of the problem or to separation (Jackson, 1954; Wiseman, 1991; Asher, 1992). Another study in that tradition was reported by Richter et al. (2000), who interviewed 11 long-term Al-Anon members in the USA. With hindsight, the latter spoke of the way they had overlooked, misread or denied early signs that their relatives had drinking problems, the way in which such problems became central to their own lives, and their assumptions, now recognised to be mistaken, that they were responsible for the problem or for not being able to deal with it. At Al-Anon, these members had not only found understanding and support, but had also absorbed the message that they were not responsible for 'the illness' of alcoholism, and that they should learn to detach themselves, to stop trying to control everything around them, and to focus on their own lives.

Standing up to it

That perspective, while it identifies one of the most important forms of struggle in which family members find themselves embroiled, fails in our view to acknowledge the constraints that operate in many family members' lives and the many other forms of adjustment made by family members in the face of their relatives' substance-misusing problems. In Chapter 6, we introduced the idea that family members find a variety of ways of engaging in 'standing up to' excessive drinking or drug taking. Those ways included confronting the relative and talking to the relative in different ways, trying to control the relative's behaviour, supporting the relative while trying to control the excess, refusing to be humbugged, and protecting family interests and resources. Those were certainly not ways of withdrawing; quite the opposite in fact. They were ways of coping that required family members to invest a great deal of time and effort. Sometimes it was later concluded that such time and effort had not been well spent, but they do represent ways of surviving in the circumstances of unchanging excessive drug taking or drinking. Others have recognised the complex, multidimensional nature of family member coping. Yang (1997) noted wives' vigilance about their husbands' drinking, and both Dorn et al. (1997) and Blank (1987) described parents' efforts to control their sons' or daughters' excessive drug use. Eber (1995) wrote of indigenous women in the south of Mexico scolding their male problem drinking relatives, praying to the saints to make their relatives stop drinking, and taking on family responsibilities which should have been their husbands'. Wiseman (1991) noted the variety of direct and indirect 'home treatment' approaches used by wives. Tackling their husbands directly included confronting the latter about their drinking, complaining, attempting to limit the husband's supply of drink in one way or another, or threatening to leave.

Other ways of coping described by Wiseman were less direct. They included pretending to act normally, not as a form of resignation but rather as a form of planned behaviour intended to elicit the same of kind of behaviour in return, consisting of acting as if drinking or drunken behaviour was not occurring even when it was. Wives sometimes took over their husbands' responsibilities in the home, or tried to be 'perfect wives', hoping that this would reduce their husbands' reasons for drinking. At other times, wives worked hard to get their husbands involved in activities besides drinking. Sometimes, more often in the USA than in Finland, wives tried to withhold money from their husbands, or else spent money themselves so that less would be left for drink.

Quantitative studies using sets of standard questions about recently used ways of coping with a relative's drinking or drug-taking problem also suggest that coping under those circumstances is not unidimensional. Family members in the Mexican and English arms of the present research were asked to complete such a standard coping questionnaire. Separate factor analyses of data from Mexico and England suggested the existence of three separate factors; tolerant-inaction, engaged coping, and withdrawal, equivalent to what we are calling here, 'putting up with', 'standing up to', and 'withdrawal and independence' (Orford et al., 1998c). Holmila (1997) also reported the results of a factor analysis of 22 items of the same coping questionnaire translated into Finnish and completed by 40 family members (20 spouses, 12 children and 8 others including siblings and parents; 24 women, 16 men) who had responded to a newspaper advertisement headed: 'Does someone close to you drink too much?' She also described three components that emerged from the analysis: 'keeping out of the way of the drinker and managing one's own life' (corresponding to the withdrawal and independence factor in our analyses), 'care giving, counselling and controlling' (corresponding to our engagement factor), and 'resigning and maintaining façade' (corresponding to our tolerant-inaction).

Figure 9.2 shows in diagrammatic form one way of conceptualising the options family members have available to them for choosing how to respond to their problem drinking or drug-taking relatives. It embraces the main ways of coping described in Chapter 6 and incorporates the three dimensions identified by ourselves and others.

Within the domain of what Holmila (1997) called 'care giving, counselling and controlling'; what we have called 'engaged coping' or 'standing up to' the drinking or drug taking; and what Wiseman (1991) included as direct and indirect methods of 'home treatment', there are various options among which family members have to pick their way, without any clear advice from elsewhere, learning by trial and error as they go. Some of these ways of coping are abandoned with experience, particularly getting aggressive or otherwise emotional with their relatives or interfering in their relatives' drinking or drug taking in an effort to control it. Wiseman referred to actions such as pouring out their husband's drink, smashing bottles, hiding alcohol, or asking bars or friends not to serve him as, 'more histrionic than helpful' (p. 51), and stated that most wives, 'ruefully describe past scenes in which they poured out alcohol – a bit ashamed that they expected so simple an act to accomplish so complex a reform' (p. 51). Not only did wives in her study often recognise that these coping efforts were ineffective, but they often talked to interviewers about such efforts in self-derogating terms. As one US wife said, 'I'd be a screaming, nagging bitch, that's what I became', and

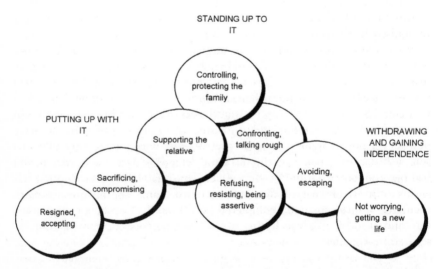

Figure 9.2 Eight ways family members cope with a close relative's problem drinking or drug taking.

another said, 'Well, he said I was nasty when he drank, so this is why [he said] he drank. Who wants to come home to a nasty woman? I admit, I did start to get nasty' (p. 45).

But, leaving aside those forms of responding, about which few family members have anything positive to say (although they are sometimes defended on the grounds that family members are expressing their true feelings, and that they may relieve feelings of anger or tension, or help family members feel that something is being done), there are many other ways which family members find to engage in trying to restore control in the family, or to fulfil their felt obligation to worry for the drinking or drug-taking relatives, or to care for or counsel them. Many of those ways were described in detail in Chapter 6. They include finding helpful ways to talk to the relative; deciding upon a strategy for responding to requests for money or other forms of humbug; setting rules or limits about drinking or use of drugs in the home; finding ways to reconcile firmness with kindness; adopting tactics for protecting children, other family members and the home, and self-protection; and looking for opportunities to support the relative in seeking treatment or in efforts to control use of drink or drugs. Sorting out how to cope among these many options involves numerous dilemmas, the making of many fine distinctions – between support for the relative and overtolerance, between being firm and cruel, between assertion and confrontation – and compromise is often involved. This is the 'grey area' of coping with a drinking or drug problem in the family, and it is probably the area in which most of the many million family members who are facing these circumstances around the world at the present time are operating. The previous literature on the subject has not done it justice.

Although it has much wider relevance, this grey area is perhaps most easily recognised in the context of traditional family organisation, where the barriers to complete independence are greatest. In her study of English Sikh wives, Ahuja (2000) found that most, having passed through a stage of inactive resignation in the face of their husbands' excessive drinking, had reached a stage of *active resignation* and *partial independence*. They no longer felt they could do anything to help their husbands overcome their drinking problems and had become resigned to the continuance of those problems, but were now trying not to allow it to have a detrimental effect on themselves or the rest of the family. They had achieved some detachment from the problem and had become somewhat more independent. But the degree of their independence was limited by their feelings of continued obligation to show loyalty to their families, to cook and clean, and otherwise give practical and emotional care and support to their husbands, and not to contemplate thoughts of separation. For example:

> In my culture you always stay with your husband regardless of the circumstances. . . . My father arranged my marriage with [husband]

and I promised to live with him always . . . I will always support my husband.

(Ahuja et al., 2003, p. 852)

To be fair to Wiseman (1991), she did recognise the possibility that wives might find ways of coping short of making an independent life for themselves, although she was lukewarm in her description of that intermediate group. That group, she wrote, 'create a partial psychic haven by increased emphasis on domesticity and its accompanying skills' (p. 219). For adult company and recreation, many of these wives turned to relatives, and this at least got wives out of the house and afforded an opportunity to socialise. A few mentioned religion. Of this group of wives, Wiseman said:

> Although these women cannot be described as having a totally independent life, they are enjoying their days more than their counterparts who, in a state of inertia, have yet to do anything about their condition. Women who have learned to enjoy whatever home and family have to offer have an outlook that is more optimistic and their thinking is less muddled. They appear to have a more positive self-concept. On the other hand, their activities can, at best, be described as a minimum plan of action. Certainly, they are avoiding any behaviour that could bring on criticism, either by their husbands or by others. Even more certainly, they cannot be called selfish about their own development.
>
> (Wiseman, 1991, p. 221)

Such damning with faint praise of family members who are struggling with the dilemma of how to cope probably reflects a limited, unidimensional view of coping, and perhaps a lack of appreciation of the realities of coping in the kinds of social and economic circumstances that countless family members find themselves in around the world.

Among the many nuances in this multifaceted and fraught domain of how family members might cope with having a close relative with a drinking or drug problem, mention should finally be made of the role of religion. The latter recurs as a theme in discussions about coping, sometimes as a factor that encourages family members to put up with such problems and discourages independence (praying, for example, is sometimes portrayed as a passive form of coping, and priests are sometimes said to encourage endurance and sacrifice in the face of hardship), sometimes as an institution that offers coping tactics which give family members hope (as in taking a pledge or oath: see Ahuja et al., 2003, and Chapter 8 here), and sometimes as an active form of coping support (e.g. a church group praying together and providing mutual support).

Social support

The whole of Chapter 7 was devoted to the topic of social support because we concluded that it was so important in the lives of family members, and particularly that it was so problematic. The present research is not alone in concluding that family members in these circumstances, who it might be thought are in particular need of support from others, experience special difficulty in finding good support. The picture is not entirely bleak, however, since family members in the present and earlier research (e.g. Dorn et al., 1997) often spoke of receiving very good support of several different kinds, emotional, informational and material, from any one of a variety of different sources (Tables 7.1 and 7.2).

Nevertheless, what was striking was the existence of so many barriers to receiving good support, falling under the headings of family members not involving others, others not getting involved, family members finding others to be unhelpful, and others being critical of family members. Other research has found the same thing. Wiseman described social support for wives as 'fragile'. As we did in Chapter 7, Wiseman provided a considerable number of reasons why the list of possible sources of family help gets severely trimmed when individual others are considered. Wiseman wrote that help often 'dwindles' to the offer of a room to enable a wife to escape from her husband's violence, and that this indicated helplessness or reluctance to do more. Our interpretation of this would be different, since the offer of accommodation was a form of material support that we found family members were often appreciative of. Furthermore, almost all of Wiseman's discussion of help from significant others referred to the family, and all she said about friends is that they had largely been lost, and were not considered as sources of help. Those who remained as friends could only listen to the wives' woes and offer sympathy. Again, our interpretation would be different since, particularly in England, family members often referred to friends, and being listened to was one of the most frequently mentioned sources of real support. Wiseman said much the same of ministers or priests who were approached by a few US wives. They gave spiritual comfort, but the help wives would have liked was beyond them.

Dorn et al. (1997) recognised the sensitivity of parents to other people's comments about their sons' or daughters' drug problems. For example, one parent said, 'It hurts me so much when people assume that by rejecting what your son's doing, you're rejecting him. Because that isn't so' (p. 38), and another said, 'People are apt to say things that have no sort of relevance at all. My friends were saying, "can't you get her off of it, can't you get her interested in a hobby or something like that?" – but it's not like that at all' (p. 23). Yang (1997) also had much to say about the criticism and lack of support that South Korean wives experienced from family and neighbours. For example, 'When I asked for help from my neighbours, they said, "How can a man survive without drink in our society? You should change your attitude towards your husband's drinking." After this incident I never asked for help again' (p. 160). Wives often experienced pressure from other people to endure the problems they were facing, to be patient, to preserve family honour, and not to think of independence. As we also found, others have not always found professionals to be helpful:

> Our doctor kept saying, keep calm and cool. Eventually I said, 'It's all very well for you to say this, but it's impossible.'
>
> (Dorn et al., 1997, p. 10)

> I went to see the psychiatrist but he said I was too sensitive about my husband's drinking problem. He also said any man can drink like my husband. It's natural and he advised me to accept his drinking.
>
> (Yang, 1997, p. 204)

Although we found examples of positive things that family members said about contacts with professionals, it comes as no surprise that the latter are not always found to be helpful, schooled as many of them must have been in the largely uninformed and unsympathetic professional perspectives summarised in Chapter 1.

Present findings on social support for family members, as well as confirming much of what others have said, have also extended understanding in a number of directions. It has been pointed out by a number of writers on the subject of social support generally (e.g. Cohen and Wills, 1985; Wethington and Kessler, 1986) that what counts as good social support may much depend upon the exact nature of the stress that a person is facing. Accordingly, they called for more specific research to be carried out into the links between specific stressors and sources and types of useful support. The present research can claim to have done exactly that, in the process deepening our understanding of social support for people coping with drinking and drug problems in their families, and at the same time extending knowledge about social support generally. Two aspects were highlighted in Chapter 7.

The first aspect was the particular value that family members, affected by and concerned about a close relative with a drinking or drug problem, put upon support from others, which backed up the ways they as family members were trying to cope. What counts as good support under those circumstances includes someone else sharing the work of worrying about the relative, uniting with the family member in coping efforts, helping the family member in the latter's search for a way of understanding what is going on, and even defending the family member's position in the face of criticism from others. In Chapter 7, we called that type of support 'coping support'. It is, we argue, a special kind of support that arises under the special circumstances of a family member trying to cope with a relative's substance problem. It appears to be of much importance to family members themselves, and, conceptually, it helps us link the domains of coping and social support. It might be thought of as a special variety of 'emotional support', but we believe it deserves to be identified as an important source of support in its own right.

The second special feature of social support in coping with excessive drinking or drug taking in the family is the sensitive nature of the triangular relationship between family member, relative and other person or group who may or may not be perceived as giving the family member good support. The conclusion in Chapter 7 was that other people were frequently perceived as unsupportive if they took a negative position (which might be critical or avoiding, for example) toward the relative. Although circumstances were described in which family members might appreciate other people helping to restrain or control the relative, and other circumstances in which friends or associates of the relative were perceived as very unhelpful owing to their support or encouragement for the relative's excessive substance use, it was mostly the case that others were seen as supportive if they took a positive stance toward the relative. On the whole, family members did not find it supportive for other people to adopt a critical stance toward the relative, or to avoid the relative altogether, or to counsel the family member to separate from the relative if that was not what the family member had decided to do.

An integrated view of the core experience

Identifying those features of effective and ineffective social support in the specific context of coping with having a close relative with a drinking or drug problem helps us to integrate what we have learned about stress, strain, coping and social support for family members into a more integrated and detailed picture than was previously available. That picture is summarised in Figure 9.3. Family members face a form of chronic stress that affects them at a number of different levels. It includes daily hassles of an unpleasant kind as well as relationships that deteriorate over what may be a very lengthy time span. The situation contains a number of threats, to oneself, the home and the family; particularly to children; and perhaps to the whole community. There is much uncertainty for family members. Part of that uncertainty is how to understand and account for what is happening, which appears to be caused by the excessive behaviour of a loved one, who seems to be threatening his or her own health and well-being as much as that of the family. A family member under those circumstances is appropriately seen both as someone negatively affected by the excessive drinking or drug taking and as someone who worries about the problem substance-using relative. How to respond to the relative and his or her drinking or drug taking, in ways that reconcile the needs of the family, the relative and the family member her/himself, poses a number of agonising dilemmas. Should a family member put up with it, stand up to it, or withdraw and seek a degree of independence? Those are perhaps the

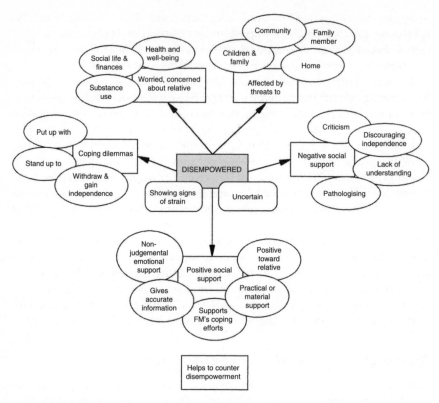

Figure 9.3 An integrated view of the impact of a close relative's excessive drinking or drug taking.

main options, but those apparently simple questions only begin to reflect the complexity of a family member's struggles for meaning and action.

Hence, family members find themselves in a very disempowered position. The erosion of control that they feel over their own lives and that of their families is often compounded by the lack of understanding and often outright criticism that they receive from other kin, neighbours and other people, and the pathologising and scapegoating that they have often experienced at the hands of professional service providers, researchers and writers. Forms of social support which are empowering for family members are therefore those that recognise the multilayered nature of the stress that a family member is likely to be under, the mixed feelings that she or he is likely to have toward the relative, the competing needs and obligations that a family member needs to bear in mind, the ways in which a family member may be deprived of useful knowledge or information, the criticism and blame which may have been directed toward the family member, and the complexity of the coping dilemmas that the family member faces. It can therefore be understood why family members might find it so important that others who wish to be supportive adopt a non-judgemental stance toward family members, that they do not condemn the drinking or drug-taking relative or take sides, and that they support family members (with emotional, informational or material support as appropriate) in standing up to the excessive drinking or drug taking or, if that is what a family member wants, in accommodating to it or achieving a measure of independence from it.

How the core experience is modified by socio-cultural differences

The neglect of the socio-cultural context in models of alcohol, drugs and the family was drawn attention to in Chapter 1. That neglect extended to stress-coping models such as the stress-strain-coping-support model that formed the basis for the present work. A number of authors had begun to outline ecological, community or feminist perspectives (Harwin, 1982; Fryer, 1998; Ussher, 1998), but there was no single, widely accepted model. The review of previous qualitative studies in Chapter 2 was able to point to Wiseman's (1991) major study, in which wives from Finland and the USA were compared, and also to a number of studies of women in traditional families in a single country or group that led authors to speculate about socio-cultural differences (Eber, 1995; Yang, 1997). It was a principal aim of the present work to incorporate the socio-cultural dimension, and that was the major motivation for seeking to interview family members in three contrasting groups in different parts of the world. To what extent are we now in a position to remedy the previous state of neglect of the socio-cultural context in our understanding of the experiences of family members coping with excessive drinking or drug taking?

Wiseman (1991) expressed some disappointment that the differences between the experiences of Finnish and US wives were not stronger than they in fact turned out to be. It was the similarities that Wiseman found to be more compelling, and she concluded that the experience of having an 'alcoholic' husband overrode cultural differences. It may be, of course, that Finnish and US cultures did not provide very much of a contrast, although Wiseman was able to draw attention to a number of differences in wives' experiences in the two countries which make sense in the light of the present findings. Despite the evident contrasts between the cultures of Mexico City, South-West England and indigenous Australia, our initial impression was similar to Wiseman's. It was the similarities, documented in detail in Chapters 5–7, that impressed us. It has been striking in fact how those who observe a single cultural group believe that what is being observed is unique to that culture and can be explained in terms of local cultural history, even when it turns out that the same experiences are described by people in quite different cultures. That was the case, for example, with the conflictual relationship between family members and in-laws noted by Yang (1997) in South Korea and attributed by her to the influence of Confucianism, although it was found again in the present study. It applies also to the difficulty that indigenous Australians are said to experience in resisting 'humbug' from relatives, and to the supposed cultural tendency of Mexican mothers to fear that their husbands will be too severe with their drug-taking offspring. Both those features are thought to be specific to those cultures, but in fact were described in all three socio-cultural groups in the present research.

On closer analysis, important differences do start to emerge. Although the conclusion is that there seems to be a core experience shared by family members throughout the world who worry for close relatives who are drinking or taking drugs excessively, there are variations in that experience according to how family members are situated. Part of that situation is the culture that family members share with others in their group. There is no simple, fixed and unchanging relationship between culture and family members' experiences, but culture does constitute one set of factors that mould that experience and give it its detail. Another way of looking at the question of cultural influence is in terms of themes that may remain relatively hidden in one socio-cultural group but force themselves upon researchers' attention in another group. That was the case, for example, for the confounding effect of excessive drinking or drug taking on family poverty, which was a theme much more prominent in Mexican interviews than in those from the other groups. The Mexican interviews allowed us to identify that theme and to accommodate it in a fuller picture of family members' experiences, acknowledging that it was more or less a feature of the experience of family members in all three groups but particularly among family members in Mexico City.

A number of authors explicitly or implicitly attribute differences to *traditional versus modern* marital or family norms and expectations. Wiseman (1991) concluded that, despite the many similarities between accounts given by Finnish and US wives, the more polarised drinking habits of men and women in Finland and their less egalitarian marriages meant that coping with their husbands' problem drinking was on the whole less assertive in style in Finland than in the USA. Finnish wives were thought by Wiseman to be more reticent about telling other people about the problem, and their husbands were very strongly against others being involved. Finnish wives' threats to leave home were less realistic because they often had no savings of their own, property was often in their husbands' names, and affordable accommodation was scarce.

In her study of English Sikh wives, Ahuja (2000) concluded that it was the traditional nature of their marriages (most were first-generation immigrants to Britain; all had had arranged marriages; and eating, clothing, language and socialising practices were mostly traditional) that was responsible for their predominant 'active resignation' style of coping, characterised by only partial independence and continued commitment to wifely duties. Wives themselves often drew on a cultural explanation for the positions they were taking. For example:

> It is my duty to look after my husband, not to start seeking help for myself. . . . In our community this sort of behaviour brings disgrace to your family . . . in our community it is best to keep the problem in the family.
>
> (Ahuja et al., 2003, p. 851)

> A marriage is for life, for better or for worse this is the person that you have to care for and spend the rest of your life with. . . . I am not like the English where you can just leave your husband and marry someone else, in my culture you always have to stay with your husband and look after him.
>
> (Ahuja et al., 2003, p. 852)

Their daughters also had recourse to cultural explanations, usually drawing a contrast between their mothers' positions and their own. For example:

> My mother is less concerned about her own happiness and more concerned about what people will say if she left him. Occasionally she agrees to leave him but she never goes through with it. . . . My mother believes that English people divorce their partners after an argument but Asian people always try and work things out. . . . I went out with a boy who had a drinking problem and I was left with no alternative but to end our relationship. I want a proper relationship and I want to marry for love. . . . My mother does not envisage my marriage being successful because she believes that I cannot tolerate any unbearable behaviour.
>
> (Ahuja et al., 2003, p. 858)

Yang (1997) believed there was evidence in her own material to support the view that South Korean wives in more traditional marriages were more accepting and less challenging of their husbands' problem drinking. The Confucian legacy, traditional family organisation emphasising patrilineal descent and male dominance, and the premium placed on family honour were responsible in Yang's view. As one wife put it:

> Everybody praised me saying that I was a typical 'good Korean woman' because I am quiet and patient. They said I looked after my husband very well and I was very patient with his drinking behaviour.
>
> (Yang, 1997, p. 202)

Although the traditional–modern family dimension may go a long way in helping explain cultural variations, it cannot provide a complete account, as

Eber's (1995) research among indigenous Mexican women suggests. Their family lives corresponded to what others have referred to as 'traditional' in certain respects, as for example, in terms of the relatively strict sexual division of labour in households. Eber's description of how indigenous women coped with their menfolk's drinking, however, suggested a way of coping quite unlike that of Yang's more traditional South Korean wives, Wiseman's more traditional Finnish wives or Ahuja's traditional Sikh wives. For example:

> Despite Victorio's compulsive drinking, Angélika never seemed power-less to me. When Victorio did not fulfil his duties I saw her draw on her personal strengths, her work selling chicha [a regional fermented fruit drink], her children's support, and service to saints. Selling chicha beside her daughters she joked and laughed, while continually exploring ways to improve their lives. . . . While Angélika may have been upset at times by her husband's actions, I did not see Victorio as pivotal for her or her children's lives. I also did not see the shame, secrecy, and denial reported for enabling family members [in the USA]. . . . Even though these women live in daily contact with an alcoholic, they seem in touch with their own lives. Angélika continues to evaluate her life and look for direction through the collective awareness of her people, expressed in dreams, prayer, and service to the gods and saints. Mónica turns to more household-centered strategies, like raising her children and keeping her store running smoothly to balance her own and others' needs.
>
> (Eber, 1995, pp. 141–142)

The present research, which for the first time has allowed data on the experiences of family members coping with excessive drinking or drug taking to be compared across three socio-cultural groups, also makes it clear that no single dimension such as traditional–modern can account for the predominance of different themes in different groups as spelt out in Chapter 8. At one time, we thought that a dimension related to traditional–modern, namely, *individualism–collectivism*, might go a long way toward helping understand the predominance of different themes in interviews from Mexico and England. The concept of individualism–collectivism has become a leading one in the field of cross-cultural psychology, since the influential study of Hofstede (1994). He collected data on work-related values among employees in 40 different countries between the late 1960s and early 1970s, later adding data from a further 10 countries. He discovered that much of the variance between countries could be accounted for by the dimension of individualism–collectivism. Other studies of cultural values and the world of work, across multiple countries, have also identified that dimension (e.g. Trompenaars, 1993, cited by Goodwin, 1999; Merritt, 2000). Some of the main components of the contrast between relatively individualist and relatively collectivist cultures are shown in Table 9.2. Western nations tend to rate highly

Table 9.2 Some of the main distinctions between individualistic and collectivist cultures (adapted from Triandis, 1994)

Individualistic	Collectivist
Self is defined as an independent entity	Self is defined in terms of in-groups, relationships
Change the situation to fit the self	Change the self to fit the situation
Emotions tend to be self-focused (e.g. anger)	Emotions tend to be other-focused (e.g. empathy)
Focus on own needs, rights, capacity (contracts)	Focus on the needs of the in-group (obligations)
Favour beliefs reflecting independence, emotional detachment	Favour beliefs reflecting interdependence
Value pleasure, achievement, competition, freedom, autonomy, fair exchange	Value security, obedience, duty, in-group harmony, personalised relationships
Less willingness to sacrifice self for the group	Self-sacrifice for the group is natural

on individualism (Hofstede found the USA, Australia and the UK to be the three highest scoring nations), and Asian, African and Latin American countries tend to score highest on collectivism. Religion may be a factor: Confucianism, and possibly Roman Catholicism as opposed to Protestantism, may promote greater collectivism (Goodwin, 1999).

The unidimensional concept of individualism versus collectivism has been criticised on a number of grounds. For one thing, it is compounded with personal wealth, since there is a high correlation between individualistic cultures and indices of wealth such as GNP (Schwartz, 1994). It has also been suggested that it is in fact a multidimensional construct with collectivism embracing components such as family integrity, interdependence, belief in hierarchy and conservatism, which are only loosely correlated and might be considered separately (Kim et al., 1994; Schwartz, 1994). Goodwin (1999) has pointed out that cultures, as well as individuals within cultures, are often relatively individualistic in some respects but more collectivist in others. Measures of individualism–collectivism tend to be low in internal reliability. Much of the data in the large-scale studies has been collected from middle-class, professional employees or students and teachers. Furthermore, there have been important cultural changes since the collection of Hofstede's data. For example, Goodwin suggested that Mexico had become more individually oriented during that time.

In fact, the contrast between individualism and collectivism, particularly the familial component of that dimension, may go some way toward helping understand why in England it was threats to personal autonomy, including resentment felt by family members about the impact on their well-being, recreational activities and social lives, that were predominant, and more diverse networks of non-kin support that were available to family members, while in Mexico City it was self-blame and self-sacrificing actions that predominated, and finding social support outside the family was difficult. Even so, differences in level of material resources available to families in those two socio-cultural groups may offer a more parsimonious explanation of such differences. Mentions of excessive drinking or drug taking as a threat to family financial stability were more prominent in the Mexican than other interviews.

Analysis of the indigenous Australian interviews reinforced two conclusions. One is the point, made earlier, that features found to be particularly noticeable in interviews with members of one socio-cultural group in fact are also present, albeit relatively hidden, in other socio-cultural groups. The second conclusion is that a single dimension, such as traditional–modern or individualistic–collectivistic, is very unlikely to provide more than a partial explanation of the variations that analysts believe they are seeing. What Aboriginal Australian family members said about the ways they attempted to cope with relatives' excessive drinking was in some ways reminiscent of descriptions of collectivist cultures – for example, the strength of obligations to share with others with whom one had particular kinship relations. But in other ways what they said was more like descriptions of more individualistic cultures – for example, a belief that individuals were responsible for their own behaviour without interference from others. In some ways, family lives sounded very traditional, particularly in remote rural communities, but in other ways they sounded quite modern, as in the desire to gain distance from family difficulties and to create a better life for oneself that drew on the best of indigenous and non-indigenous traditions.

The theme that was most apparent in the Australian interviews, and in contrast to those from the other two groups, was the public nature of much excessive drinking, and the way the latter was discussed as a community issue, and not just a personal or family one. The fact that grog was a public matter and a community issue for many indigenous Australians offered family members both strengths and weaknesses in their efforts to cope. On the one hand, there were potentially many other people who could assist family members in the work of worrying for relatives, which is very different from the emphasis on family privacy and secrecy to be found in many Mexican and English families, or in the Finnish families described by Wiseman (1991). On the other hand, the pressure of excessive drinking by a multitude of people in the family or community, combined with complex sets of often competing obligations to different family members, and interfamily rivalries, often made it difficult to achieve consensus in ways of coping. Those are problems for family members trying to cope with excessive drinking or drug problems everywhere, whether in Finland, England, South Korea, the USA, or indigenous Australia or Mexico, but they were particularly to the fore in what was said to interviewers by Australian Aboriginal participants.

Gender, relationship, substance and other factors that modify the core experience

Gender roles

As already pointed out in Chapter 1, gender roles figure large in what little work there has been that tries to place the experience of family members in social context. Authors have sometimes commented on the active role of women as producers and sellers of alcoholic beverages in traditional cultures (e.g. Hagaman, 1980), but women have more often been described as witnesses to their husbands' excessive drinking and the loss of family resources caused by it. They have been seen as the ones who must live up to an image of the respectable and self-sacrificing wife, the submissive partner in an unequal relationship, charged with the responsibility for taming and controlling their men's drinking, and even held to blame if they do not succeed in that task (e.g. Holmila, 1988; Wiseman, 1991; Banister and Peavy, 1994; Yang, 1997; Ussher, 1998). The emphasis on gender roles, and particularly the influence of role expectations on wives of husbands with drinking problems, reflects the relative weight of previous research and writing that has been devoted to female partners of men with drinking problems. Indeed, the controversy about how best to construe the circumstances facing family members of relatives with drinking or drug problems, discussed in Chapter 1, has in effect been a debate about how best to understand the special position of women who are partners of excessive drinkers:

> Much of the literature on alcoholic spouses of the past three decades is now properly construed as sexist. It was subtly suggested that the wife somehow was responsible for her husband's problem drinking, or if she was not, she certainly had an investment in keeping him drunk.
>
> (Burnett, 1984, p. 51)

The present research certainly provided further evidence of the disempowerment experienced by wives of excessive drinkers. Wives, or female partners, constituted one of the largest groups in each of the three socio-cultural groups. Among the experiences they spoke of were those of continuing to provide for their relatives, supplying food and cooking, cleaning up and generally looking after relatives, providing sexual services, protecting children, feeling the effects of family poverty and being required to work outside the home as well as within it. Women waited on their partners, and often found themselves literally waiting *for* them. Wives' accounts were full of evidence of struggles for independence, often in the face of some opposition from their mothers-in-law and other older women. Interviews with wives were full of stories of domestic violence, sometimes of an extremely brutal nature, and there were a number of wives and their children who had been appreciative of the possibility of alternative accommodation, when others had offered it.

The samples of family members included in the present research are almost unique, however, in including men as well as women. Husbands of women with drinking problems have been the objects of unsympathetic professional descriptions, as was shown in Chapter 2, in much the same way as have wives of men with drinking problems. Of the very few studies of male partners that do exist, a few have taken a more sympathetic view, describing many of the same experiences as those described by wives in other research (Corrigan, 1980; Estes and Baker, 1982). The detailed presentation of results in Chapters 5–8 included a number of examples of male partners of women with drinking or drug problems, illustrating the way in which male partners may also feel undermined by their relatives' behaviour, and may feel isolated in their attempts to cope, in much the same way as is described by female partners of male relatives. Men were also represented in the present research as fathers, and less often as brothers or uncles. Present findings support Dorn et al.'s (1987) observations about the stress of being the father of a son or daughter with a drug problem, and illustrate the thesis that gender modifies the expression of the core experience but does not alter its essential nature.

The inclusion of men enables us to raise a question that has not been directly addressed in previous research. Is it the case, as proposed here, that the experience of family members facing drug and alcohol problems is powerful enough to override differences in gender roles? Or is it the case, as many will suppose, that gender role remains the more powerful determinant of action, and that what we have construed as excessive substance use on the part of a relative and coping by a family member are best understood as reflections of the operation of family gender norms and expectations? More analysis of data from the present study and perhaps the collection of further material are necessary in order to be at all confident in attempting to answer that question. What we can claim the present findings have done is to raise the question and to propose the hypothesis that there exists a core to family members' experience whatever their socio-cultural group and sex. According to that hypothesis, being female or male, wife or husband, mother or father, sister or brother, colours that experience but does not alter its essence.

Parents, partners, siblings and others

Apart from gender, whether a family member is a mother, father, wife, husband, sister, brother, uncle, aunt or some other relation to a relative who is drinking or taking drugs excessively is itself bound to colour the experience and give it a particular quality. For one thing, different kinds of relationship are vulnerable in different ways to the threat posed by excessive drinking or drug taking. To take one obvious example, partners have, or at least have had, a sexual relationship, which is very often adversely affected (Nirenberg et al., 1990; O'Farrell et al., 1997).

Partners, and particularly female partners, were numerous as participants in the present study, and had been most often the participants in previous research. Because of the partnership relationship with a man or woman who was drinking or taking drugs excessively, family members who were partners were perhaps as hard pressed and faced coping dilemmas as difficult as any group of family members. The questionnaire study that accompanied the present qualitative research showed that partners reported more coping efforts than parents. Wives or female partners were most likely to show a pattern of coping that was high on tolerant-inactive (putting up with the drinking or drug taking) and engaged (standing up to it), both of which were found to be positively correlated with family members' symptom levels. That pattern was particularly the case for wives of men with alcohol problems in Mexico City and wives of men with drug problems in South-West England (Orford et al., 2001).

There are likely to be numerous other variables that between them define the unique position of a particular partner. Age and the duration of the partnership are just two such variables that seem likely to be important. Both Ahuja et al. (2003) and Orford (1998) have noted a 'honeymoon effect' whereby partners who have not long been in a relationship with their problem drinking or drug-taking relatives may show a relatively high level of support for their partners, including putting up with the latter's excessive substance use. At the other end of the scale, Brennan et al. (1994) reported a study that was unusual because the participants were spouses of older problem drinkers (55–65 years of age), married on average for 30 years. Their findings suggested that these spouses did not have the explosive, anger-ridden relationships with their partners that were characteristic of many young couples, but did describe their relationships as lacking in intimacy, empathy and provision of moral support. They also concluded that spouses of older problem drinkers, unlike their younger counterparts, were no more likely than spouses of non-problem drinkers to make active, behavioural efforts to change the stressors they were under, but might have 'retreated into cognitive modes of coping' (p. 454).

Among the particular experiences of *parents* were feelings of responsibility for the upbringing and development of sons and daughters with drinking or other drug problems, and it was common for parents to blame themselves for what had happened. Unlike partners, who often had comparatively good knowledge of the relative's current patterns of alcohol or drug use, parents were often in the dark about the relative's current consumption pattern, but were able to give a lot of details about stages in a son's or daughter's earlier alcohol or drug use. Where there were two parents living together, a mother and father might give each other valued support, but the mother–father relationship was also vulnerable to tension and disagreement about how to cope. Some mothers tried to deal with the problem without much support from their partners. In other families, fathers were involved but sometimes took a harder, more disciplinary line, sometimes resorting to beating or calling the police. The positions adopted by parents varied greatly, but mothers were sometimes inclined to be softer on and more caring toward the problem drinking or drug-taking daughter or son. Mothers might refer to the difficulty of putting aside maternal feelings.

The options for *other members* of relatives' families were wider. For example, comparatively few adult daughters and sons, and brothers and sisters, volunteered to take part in the research. When they did take part, they generally had special reasons for being worried about their relatives and feeling some responsibility for what happened to them. Other senior members of families, if involved at all, might take on particular roles. There was talk, for example, of aunts or grandmothers adopting a protective position toward a problem drinking or drug-taking nephew or niece, granddaughter or grandson. In Australian Aboriginal families, in accordance with custom, fathers' older brothers and mothers' older sisters might effectively take on the role of fathers and mothers.

In her study of English Sikh families where the husbands/fathers had drinking problems, Ahuja (2000) interviewed a number of daughters and compared the latter's position with that of their mothers. Most daughters, like their mothers, had gone through a stage of actively standing up to their fathers' drinking, and in all cases they had reached a position of active resignation, detachment and partial independence. Differences in emphasis between daughters and wives lay in the greater speed with which daughters had reached that position, the greater degree of detachment and independence that they had achieved (although that was still limited), and the explanation that daughters gave for their continued limited independence and continued sense of practical obligation to the family. The latter was in terms of their concern for and obligation toward their mothers, not, as was the case for wives, a continued sense of responsibility for the problem drinking husbands/fathers.

Alcohol and other drugs

In the reports of interviews carried out in Mexico and England, there were suggestions that family members' experiences might differ in at least two different ways, depending upon whether the concern was with a relative's alcohol consumption or with the taking of other drugs (alcohol was always the main problem substance in the Australian interviews). One possible difference concerned the experience of discovering a relative's drinking or drug use. The shock of discovering that a son or daughter is misusing drugs has been described by Blank (1987) and Dorn et al. (1987). It seemed from present findings that the intensity of the experience reported by a number of family members at the time of discovering the drug use, which was particularly great if it involved injecting or use associated with clear signs of physical damage, was not so evident when the concern was excessive drinking. The words used in the sentences and paragraphs where discoveries of drug use were described are indicative of a strong emotional experience: e.g. 'knocked me for six', 'shocked'. In the alcohol interviews, the absence of such comments suggested that the process leading to realisation of a problem with drinking was usually more gradual.

The apparently greater role of criminal involvement and interactions with police in families where the relative was misusing illicit drugs stood out in the English data, but the distinction was less clear-cut in the Mexican interviews, and prominence of family–police contact in Australia, especially in the remoter rural areas, provided another example of how difficult it is to arrive at generalisations that hold up across different cultures.

Other likely sources of variation

The present work has enlarged upon previous studies of family members coping with excessive drinking or drug taking by close relatives. Nearly all that research, with the occasional exception (e.g. Raine, 1994) had concentrated either on the impact of excessive drinking or the impact of drug misuse, but not both, and virtually all had focused on family members bearing one type of kin relationship to their relatives. The large bulk of research had concentrated on wives of men with drinking problems, a focus in research sampling that has remained virtually unchanged since Jackson's (1954) pioneering study of 50 years ago. Of equal if not greater significance, previous research had been confined, with one notable exception (Wiseman, 1991), to one socio-cultural group, usually white family members living in one of the rich, Western countries. Broadening the scope of this type of enquiry, as has been done in the present work, has enabled us to suggest the existence of what may be a common core to family members' experience irrespective of substance, relationship or socio-cultural group, while at the same time illustrating the many ways in which the unique positions occupied by family members modify and shape that experience.

At the same time, there are without doubt further sources of variation that have not been touched on here. Some represent possible limitations in our sampling. Or rather, since the present research is qualitative in kind and does not therefore pretend to be representative in its sampling, it may be more correct to say that ways can now be seen of extending the sampling of family members to make the group yet more diverse. Extending the sample after the analysis of existing data would correspond to what, in the terms of the grounded theory approach to qualitative research, would be called 'theoretical sampling' (Strauss and Corbin, 1998; Willig, 2001).

One such source of variation, to which perhaps insufficient attention has been given in work on families affected by problem drinking and drug taking, including the present research, is the *pattern of substance use* engaged in by the relative. For present purposes, a particularly interesting finding, arising in the work of Jacob and his colleagues (e.g. Jacob and Leonard, 1988), concerns the possible relationship between couple interaction and a problem drinker's place and pattern of drinking. To be specific, Jacob and his group distinguished between problem drinking that was 'steady' (drinking more or less the same amount on a day-to-day basis) or in 'binges' (drinking large amounts occasionally with little or nothing on other days), and between those who mostly drank 'at home' and those who mostly drank 'out-of-home'. Combining results of laboratory observational studies with those from questionnaires and reports of daily drinking and marital satisfaction, Jacob and Seilhamer (1987) suggested a typology in which different styles of drinking were associated with very different family experiences. At one extreme were binge-out-of-home drinkers (BO). Problem drinkers in that group had more problems, such as quitting jobs, missing meals, fights, traffic offences and wife abuse, and couple marital satisfaction was lower. Wives' marital satisfaction was lower on days on which their husbands drank, and interactions under laboratory conditions tended to be negative and got worse as a session progressed or if drinking was allowed. At the other extreme were steady-in-home drinkers (SI). Although problem drinkers in the latter group reported consuming a larger volume of alcohol, they also reported fewer social problems, and couple marital satisfaction was higher. Wives' marital satisfaction was not worse on drinking days, and there was little effect of drinking in the laboratory setting on negative interactions (Jacob et al., 2001). It is interesting to note that Wiseman's (1991) observation about differences between the drinking patterns of Finnish and US husbands was that the former involved more binge drinking away from home and the latter more steady drinking at home.

One limitation of present sampling may be attributed in part to the stress-coping model underlying the work. That model is predicated on the notion of there being one member of the family (termed 'the relative' throughout this book) who is drinking or taking drugs in a way that is excessive and problematic for at least one other member of the family (the 'family member') who bears the impact of that problematic excess. We continue to believe that this is a powerful model, superior to others that have been employed in the field, and it is one that serves us well most of the time. It should be noted that it does not assume that the family member, the research participant, is necessarily the only member of the family who is concerned and affected. Although we have not drawn on these additional data here, second and even occasionally third family members were also interviewed in a proportion of families who took part in the present research.

There were hints in the present findings of the limitations that we might have imposed on sampling by requiring that the relative have a drinking or drug problem that had been active at some time in the previous 6 months, and that the interviewed family member should *not* have such a problem (or, as in a few families, should have a less severe problem). One such hint arose in the analysis of the reasons family members gave for putting up with a relative's excessive drinking or drug taking (Chapter 6, Figure 6.1). Those reasons included a family member's tolerance of drinking or drug use, one element of which was the family member and relative using drugs together. This begins to blur the distinction between the roles of relative and family member. Another hint came from the Australian interviews, during which a number of family members spoke about their own former drinking problems. Jacob's work on different drinking patterns, referred to earlier, also suggests that the distinction between 'the relative' and 'family member' may become blurred in the case of steady-in-home drinking patterns. His research and other studies from the USA on dual drug-misusing couples (Fals-Stewart et al., 1999) and on discrepant and non-discrepant drinking patterns in newly-wed couples (Leonard and Roberts, 1998), do suggest a limitation of family work, such as our own, which is confined to families where the focus is on the excessive drinking or drug taking of just one person in the family. It remains a task for the future to extend the present research to include family members who themselves are experiencing substance problems while at the same time living with relatives who share such problems. Many family members who took part in the present research could nominate more than one close relative with such a problem.

Coping with a drinking or drug problem in the family as a variform universal

It is not only in alcohol and drug studies that culture has been neglected. Summarising the growth of cross-cultural psychology as a discipline, Segall et al. (1998) agreed that psychology had long ignored 'culture' as a source of influence on self and behaviour, but that it was now possible to say, 'Cross-cultural psychology has grown from a whisper and a hope circa 1960 into a large and thriving intellectual enterprise circa 2000' (p. 1108). In that enterprise, the search has been either for differences across cultural groups, or for similarities, or, as is increasingly the case, for both. In the early days, cross-cultural psychology was hampered by an excess of studies that compared only two cultural groups, providing results that were difficult to interpret. It is generally agreed, as Segall et al. wrote, that a minimum of three cultures should be involved if meaningful comparisons are to be made. Berry et al., (1992; cited by Segall et al., 1998) described three theoretical orientations in cross-cultural psychology. The first, 'absolutism', assumed that human phenomena are basically the same in all cultures, culture playing little or no role in the meaning or display of human characteristics. The second, 'relativism', at the opposite extreme, took the view that psychological processes and structures differed so fundamentally in different contexts that comparison was pointless. Few students of culture are now to be found at either of those poles, according to Segall et al., most now adopting some variant of the third position, 'universalism'. It assumes that basic human characteristics are common to all members of the species but that culture influences the development and display of them. They are what Lonner (1980; cited by Segall et al., 1998) termed 'variform universals'.

Living with excessive drinking or drug taking in a close relative can be seen as a good example of a variform universal. The essential core of that experience remains invariant. Individuals, families and communities are positioned differently in relation to substance use and misuse, however, and their varying positions significantly modify the core experience. Some of the factors that we now know to act as modifiers are shown in Figure 9.4. Among them are a family's material circumstances, the traditional versus modern arrangement of marital and family roles, the public versus private nature of excessive substance use, the individualistic versus familial collectivistic versus community collectivistic nature of the culture, the gender of the concerned and affected family member, her or his relationship to the problem drinking or drug-taking relative, the substance being misused and the position of that kind of substance use in the local culture, and the pattern of the relative's excessive use. No doubt, there are other sources of variation on the common themes which have not yet been identified. We suspect, for example, that the family member's own extent of involvement in drinking or drug taking may be one such variable.

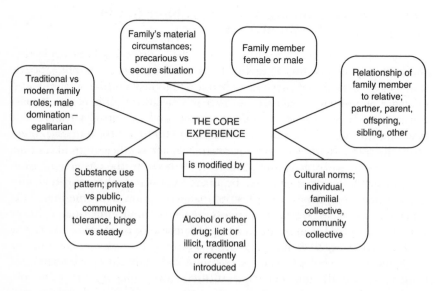

Figure 9.4 A summary of some of the main factors that modify the core, universal experience of being affected by and concerned about a close relative's excessive drinking or drug taking.

The experience of an Aboriginal man living in a remote community near the centre of the Australian continent, worrying for his deceased elder brother's daughter who is drinking excessively, is therefore not the same as that of a man living on the edge of Mexico City, alarmed at the discovery of his son's drug use. Neither of those experiences is the same as that of a South Korean wife enduring her husband's problem drinking in the context of a traditional, patriarchal marriage. The experiences of the wife of an excessive drinker in a more egalitarian marriage in the USA, or of a sister concerned about her brother's drug use in South-West England, or of a Sikh daughter of a problem drinking father in the English Midlands, are each different again. The stories that could be told by wives and mothers in Finland are not identical to those told by indigenous women in Chiapas. Yet each of those experiences and stories is likely to contain common, recognisable elements that constitute the common core. If they could speak directly to each other, we believe they would identify readily with each other's accounts and would have common cause together.

Does having to cope with excessive drinking or drug taking in the family constitute a unique set of stressors?

One last question remains to be addressed in this chapter: is there much about the experience of facing the drinking or drug problem of a close relative that is specific to that experience, or have we in this book been dealing with experiences that are, in all important respects, common to a large number of different types of stressful life circumstances? There exists a large literature on ways of coping with stress (Zeidner and Endler, 1996), and in much of that literature the assumption is made that the precise nature of the stress is immaterial. In fact, in many reports of research in that tradition, the stressful events or circumstances being faced are not described at all or are mentioned only in a footnote. On the other hand, there have been calls for greater study of coping in specific contexts (e.g. Dewe and Guest, 1990), and the present research is one that has answered that call. Numerous other pieces of research have studied the experiences of people who have faced stressors varying from taking a medical school entrance examination (Bolger, 1990) to receiving a spinal cord injury (McColl et al., 1995) to persecution, as in the Holocaust (Levav, 1998). Perhaps closest in kind to the stressful circumstances dealt with in the present book are examples of circumstances faced by family members who are concerned about and affected by the illness, disability or behaviour of a close relative or some aspect of joint family circumstances (Orford, 1987). Examples of such work are listed in Table 9.3.

That body of work on family member coping makes it evident that many of the elements of the variform universal experience of facing a substance problem in the family are common to a number of types of family

Table 9.3 Examples of research on other forms of stressful life circumstances for family members

Family members coping with	References to examples of published work
Domestic violence	Dobash and Dobash, 1987; Surtees and Miller, 1994; Hoffman et al., 1994; Yoshihama, 2002
A relative's chronic physical illness, e.g. cancer, heart disease, diabetes, renal failure, kidney transplantation, rheumatic disorder, multiple sclerosis, Parkinson's disease	Nichols, 1987; Gallagher et al., 1994; Tix and Frazier, 1998; Fang and Manne, 2001; Bigatti and Cronan, 2002; Pakenham, 2002
Hospitalisation of partner, death of partner	Bar-Tal and Spitzer, 1993; Surtees and Miller, 1994
A relative's HIV positive status and AIDS-related illness	Folkman et al., 1994; Siegl and Morse, 1994; Folkman, 1997; Castro et al., 1998; Billings et al., 2000
A child's chronic illness	Eiser, 1987; Kupst and Schulman, 1988
Traumatic injury to children	Wade et al., 2001
Children with autistic, learning or biological disabilities	Pahl and Quine, 1987; Sloman and Konstantareas, 1990; Huws et al., 2001
Children with disruptive behaviour disorder	Herbert, 1995
Couples entering an *in vitro* fertilisation programme	Edelmann et al., 1994
Dual career couples with role overload and work/home conflict	Wiersma, 1994; Paden and Buehler, 1995
A relative's severe, persisting mental illness	Birchwood and Smith, 1987; Winefield and Burnett, 1996; Magliano et al., 1998; Barrowclough and Parle, 1997; St-Onge and Lavoie, 1997; Scazufca and Kuipers, 1998
A partner's involuntary unemployment	Liem and Liem, 1988
A husband's combat stress reaction	Rosenheck and Thomson, 1986; Soloman et al., 1992
Brain damage to a relative	Moffat, 1987
Dementia in an older relative	Gilhooly, 1987; Gallagher et al., 1994

circumstance. To pick out just a few prominent examples of such elements, we can note the following: appraisal processes, the importance of the relative's distress and disturbed behaviour, and the family member's self-confidence. Each of those elements will now be considered in turn.

The appraisal of a set of circumstances as potentially threatening was central to one of the most influential theories of coping with stress (Lazarus and Folkman, 1984) and has figured large in the research in the stress-coping field. Primary appraisal of the threats involved has been distinguished from secondary appraisal of one's ability to cope (e.g. Barraclough and Parle, 1997). At the level of primary appraisal, different kinds of threat can be distinguished; for example, threats to one's own self-esteem and threats to a loved one's well-being (Folkman et al., 1986). Both kinds of threat exist for family members trying to cope with a relative's alcohol or drug problem, and we would add threat to the whole family and to the home, and perceived threat to the local community. Different kinds of threats were more prominent in different socio-cultural groups in the present research: threat to the family in Mexico City, threat to personal self-esteem in South-West England, and threat to the local community in indigenous Australia.

One of the aspects of secondary appraisal that has received most attention is the degree to which a person believes the stressful circumstances to be amenable to that person's own change efforts (e.g. Terry, 1994). When that is believed to be the case, active, problem-solving forms of coping are more likely. The question of whether a family member has any power to influence a close relative's excessive alcohol or drug consumption is a moot one. Many family members engage in trying to stand up to the excess, while others engage in forms of coping to protect themselves and their families; there are many examples of forms of active resignation or partial independence, while others actively withdraw or seek a greater degree of independence (Wiseman, 1991; Ahuja, 2000). As we shall see in Chapter 10, forms of professional help for family members that are now being developed are based on the assumption that family members of relatives with alcohol or drug problems do have the power to influence their relatives' excessive consumption.

Much of the work listed in Table 9.3 points to the conclusion that it is disturbances of behaviour, apparent changes in personality or extreme distress, on the part of a close relative, that are most disturbing and difficult for family members to handle. That has been said to be the case, for example, with rudeness, aggression or suspicion on the part of relatives diagnosed with schizophrenia (Birchwood and Smith, 1987); temper tantrums, destructiveness and aggression on the part of children with learning difficulties (Pahl and Quine, 1987); demanding behaviour by relatives with dementia (Gilhooly, 1987); disturbances of mood or behaviour in a brain-damaged relative (Moffat, 1987); the degree of distress shown by relatives with cancer (Fang and Manne, 2001); abuse and withdrawal from the family by war veterans with combat stress reaction (Solomon et al., 1992); and the extent of distress shown by husbands recently made unemployed (Liem and Liem, 1988). Results from the present research suggest that such disturbances of interpersonal behaviour are highly salient components of the stress experienced by family members of relatives with drinking or drug problems (Chapter 5). It is therefore safe to conclude that while the latter experience may share many elements with other forms of stress for family members, facing a serious drinking or drug problem is likely to be as threatening and difficult to handle as other forms of family stressors which involve disturbances of interpersonal behaviour.

A recurring theme in the literature on family coping has to do with the family member's own feelings of self-confidence. This sometimes takes the form of pointing out the importance for active coping of a sense of mastery or confidence (e.g. Holahan and Moos, 1990; Hobfoll et al., 1994). Elsewhere it appears in the form of the threat to feelings of self that the stressful circumstances bring with them. References to feelings of guilt, shame and self-blame are very common. For example, in the case of chronic physical illness in a relative, there may be shame because a formerly active relative has changed dramatically, or feelings of guilt because one family member is fit while the relative is ill (Nichols, 1987). When a relative is unable to go out by reason of illness or handicap, there may be guilt feelings because the family member may be able sometimes to go out and enjoy herself instead of continually caring for the relative (Birchwood and Smith, 1987; Gilhooly, 1987). Parents of HIV-positive sons may experience a feeling of 'emotional exile' characterised by feelings of stigma and reticence to disclose to others (Siegl and Morse, 1994). Parents of children with disruptive behaviour disorders, who often feel themselves to be criticised and scapegoated, can suffer from low self-confidence (Herbert, 1995). Once again, we see that the undermining effect on a family member's self-confidence, described by the present research participants and by others who have written about the impact of alcohol problems on family members (Wiseman, 1991; Asher, 1992; Banister and Peavy, 1994; Yang, 1997), is not an experience unique to that set of circumstances.

Ways of coping

When it comes to ways of coping there is no shortage of typologies and suggestions about ways that are more or less effective. Very popular has been a three-way division based upon the aim of the coping effort: coping may be problem-focused, aiming to change or deal with the stressful events or circumstances; perception-focused, aiming not to change the stressor itself, but to change the way it is perceived or appraised; or emotion-focused, targeted, not at the stressor, but at controlling the distress that it arouses in the stressed individual (Pearlin and Schooler, 1978; Endler and Parker, 1990). Some of the most important ways of coping may combine the different types. In fact, some researchers have found that coping efforts are more often than not combinations of problem-, perception-, and emotion-focused coping (Lazarus, 1993). Moos and his colleagues have preferred a simple division of coping strategies into those that might be termed approach strategies and those characterised by avoidance, each taking behavioural or cognitive forms, thus creating four types (Holahan and Moos, 1990; Valentiner et al., 1994; Moos, 2002).

Then there are other ways of coping identified in this kind of research which do not fit easily into these categories. One that is regularly found is 'seeking social support' from other people (e.g. Folkman et al., 1986; Hobfoll et al., 1994). Another is reliance on religious faith. The latter is difficult to classify – for example, it can be emotion-focused or active – and it has been neglected in this line of research. When it has been included, it has generally been found to be very important (McCrae and Costa, 1986; Tix and Frazier, 1998). Folkman et al. (1986) found it necessary to add the item, 'I prayed', in a revision of their Ways of Coping Checklist.

Some prominent coping researchers have been reluctant to commit themselves on the question of whether there is evidence that some ways of coping work better than others. Lazarus (1993), for example, was firmly of the view that coping is a process – a 'fluid, contextually sensitive struggle', he called it at one point (p. 238) – and that what is effective at one moment (waiting for an operation, for example) may not be effective at another (for example, after the operation). He went so far as to say, 'There may be no universally good or bad coping processes' (p. 235). Concurring with the views of many family members in the present research, however, and with most of the literature on coping with relatives' drinking or drug problems, is the general conclusion of the stress-coping literature that ways of coping that are hostile, confrontational, coercive, critical or emotionally negative in some way are not effective, either for family members themselves or for the relatives about whom they may be concerned (e.g. Folkman et al., 1986; McCrae and Costa, 1986; Bentelspacher et al., 1994; Folkman and Lazarus, 1998; Scazufca and Kuipers, 1998).

It is also the case that when attempts have been made to assess the effectiveness of coping – usually by means of standard questionnaire measures of anxiety and depression – active coping methods generally come out well and certain kinds of avoidance coping come out badly. Lazarus admitted that the 'wishful thinking' subset of avoidance strategies has never been found to have positive adaptational value in their research. On the other hand, considering specifically how women cope with stressful circumstances, Banyard and Graham-Bermann (1993) cited examples of women coping in ways that might be labelled as passive and helpless, but which under the circumstances might be seen as purposeful and sensible. As examples they cited women choosing to deal with a chronic stressor such as racial discrimination, which was not immediately amenable to direct behavioural coping actions, by choosing not to deal directly with the problem but rather to focus on something else; and a victim of rape who elected not to press charges or to take advantage of counselling services that were offered, realising that others would not testify on her behalf and that prosecuting might further endanger her family, and preferring to leave hospital as quickly as possible and return to care for her young child. Similarly, Yoshihama (2002) drew attention to the likely importance of cultural differences in a study comparing Japan-born and US-born women of Japanese descent who had been the subjects of domestic violence in the USA. The Japan-born women were significantly less likely to use active coping strategies such as confronting their partners, asserting their rights, seeking outside assistance or leaving the relationship, and perceived such strategies to be less effective than did US-born women. Moos (2002) has referred to a distinction between assimilative coping, in which individuals try to adjust the context to match their own agendas, and accommodative coping in which individuals adjust themselves to fit the context. Lazarus (1993), too, acknowledged that there might be situations in which no ways of active coping were possible, where even wishful thinking could be useful.

As in research on family members concerned about and affected by relatives' excessive substance use, gender has been largely invisible as a variable in research on coping; according to Banyard and Graham-Bermann (1993), when gender has been addressed, there has often been a value judgement that ascribes to women more passive and ineffective ways of coping. Others have noted, for example, the greater tendency of husbands to withdraw as a form of coping in dual-income couples experiencing role overload and conflict (Paden and Buehler, 1995), women using more prosocial and 'cautious action' ways of coping with interpersonal or work stressors, while men used more anti-social and aggressive strategies (Hobfoll et al., 1994), fathers more than mothers relying on 'carry on' and 'brave front' ways of coping as parents of HIV-positive sons (Siegl and Morse, 1994), and male graduate teaching students using more 'suppression' coping (an emotion-focused form of coping characterised by restraint, withdrawal, and ignoring the problem) than women in coping with work-related stress (Parkes, 1990).

In view of the strong emergence of the public-level, community threat and coping theme in the present Australian data, it is interesting to note that the general psychological literature on coping, almost all of which comes from Western countries, the large bulk from the USA, treats stress and coping only at an individual level. Stress is experienced by individuals, and it is individual people who find their own ways of coping with it. Only a very few coping researchers and theorists mention the possibility of collective coping, which may be more relevant to non-Western cultures, or may be required when it is beyond an individual to be able to cope (e.g. Parkes, 1990; Banyard and Graham-Bermann, 1993).

We may conclude, therefore, that a consideration of the ways in which family members cope with relatives' problem drinking or drug taking should not be divorced from wider consideration of how family members cope with sets of stressors of related kinds. The wider literature on coping offers many points of contact and raises a number of potentially fruitful questions. Can 'putting up with' a relative's excessive drinking or drug taking be equated with 'avoidance' or 'accommodative' coping? How does coping of the 'withdrawal and gaining independence' type fit into the general coping typologies that appear in the wider literature? Has the present work added to general knowledge about coping with family stresses; for example, by describing particular instances of active, problem-solving coping (including ways of 'standing up to' problem drinking or drug taking) or of the way in which religion may be used to support very different ways of coping. The biggest contribution that the present research might make to the general body of knowledge on coping, however, is in terms of viewing coping in socio-cultural context. The latter is a dimension that remains largely ignored in the wider psychological literature.

Social support

The topic of social support, so important in the understanding of the lives of family members of excessively drinking or drug-taking relatives, has also been a strong theme in the wider literature on stress and coping. Two features of the way social support has been dealt with in that body of work are particularly relevant here. The first is the recognition, mirroring present findings (Chapter 7), that people in family members' social networks very often fail to provide positive social support (Banyard and Graham-Bermann, 1993; Oakland and Ostell, 1996). Some researchers have gone on to develop scales of the negative aspects of social support (Rauktis et al., 1995; Holahan et al., 1997), which have been ignored in much of the work on social support in the social sciences, and which have been referred to by various terms such as 'social conflict', 'social network stressors', 'interpersonal obstacles', 'negative social interactions', 'negative social support', 'negativity' and 'social network upset' (Rauktis et al., 1995).

The second point of interest here concerns the ways in which the concepts of social support and coping have been integrated. One way, already mentioned, is to view the seeking of social support as one of the methods of coping. One of the most popular ways of integrating the two concepts, and the one we subscribed to at the outset of the present research (see Chapter 1) is to view social support as a resource or form of assistance in coping (e.g. Thoits, 1986; Holahan et al., 1997). Schreurs and de Ridder (1997) identified two other ways in which the link between social support and coping has been conceptualised. One considers social support as being dependent on coping rather than the other way around. According to that line of reasoning, the way people cope may serve to encourage or discourage helpful social support from others. Alternatively, coping and social support are occasionally viewed as inseparable parts of a social system, resulting in concepts such as family coping, family coordination or consensus, relationship coping or joint problem-solving coping (Reiss and Oliveri, 1980; Lewis et al., 1993; cited by Schreurs and de Ridder, 1997).

Nor is it the case that family members worried about their relatives' alcohol or other drug problems are alone in feeling stigmatised and neglected by professionals. Many of the writers and researchers who have addressed the circumstances faced by family members coping with chronic illness, disability or a behavioural problem in relatives have had something to say which is critical of the approach taken by professionals. Family members have looked in that direction for understanding, information and support, but have often been disappointed. When a relative is mentally ill, treatment staff may appear to family members to be inaccessible to them, information may be viewed as unhelpful to coping efforts, staff may not feel it is their job or concern to look after family members' needs, may fail to provide information because of confidentiality rules, and may even be seen to blame family members and to feel that it is their job to protect their patients from the family members (Birchwood and Smith, 1987; Kuipers, 1987; Winefield and Burnett, 1996). In cases of chronic childhood or adult illness or disability, family members may feel that there is a lack of communication, that they are abandoned to care at home, that information is withheld from them, or even that the professionals are condescending or rude to them (Eiser, 1987; Nichols, 1987; Pahl and Quine, 1987).

These failures of professional response are often attributed to an absence of appropriate professional understanding of family experiences, and in many cases to the positively harmful influence of existing professional theories. For example, Birchwood and Smith (1987) and Kuipers (1987) referred to the once-held theories, for which there is no conclusive evidence, that families might be 'depressogenic' or 'schizophrenogenic'. A popular concept in social psychiatry has been that of family members' 'expressed emotion', implying that some family members contribute to their relatives' relapse by their criticism of and hostility to their relatives or their overinvolvement with them. Most of that work has been carried out with family members whose relatives are diagnosed as mentally ill, but that line of research was extended for the first time to family members of relatives with drinking problems by O'Farrell et al. (1998). Scazufca and Kuipers (1998) have shown how family members' expressed emotion varies with their relatives' role performance and the amount of stress family members are under, and have recommended a more integrative, interactive model of expressed emotion and functioning of the whole family in a way that is less blaming of family members. Sloman and Konstantareas (1990) were as critical, as we have been (Chapter 2), of the family systems approach and associated professional views that implied a parental contribution to the etiology of, in their case, childhood autism. Pahl and Quine (1987) referred to pathological models of the family which stressed the way in which parents might 'overprotect' their disabled children, or alternatively might 'fail to accept' the fact of handicap. Their own approach, by contrast, emphasised the essential normality of families. Similarly, Herbert (1995) was critical of professional approaches that pathologised parents of children with disruptive behaviour disorders.

Returning to the question that was raised at the beginning of this section, are we therefore to conclude that the stress of trying to deal with life with a relative who is drinking or taking drugs excessively is, in all important respects, just like many other forms of coping with chronic disorder in the family? There are a number of close comparisons. In some respects, it shares many features with the circumstances faced by family members of close relatives with HIV-positive status and AIDS, who may be required to cope with the multiple stressors involved in caring for a chronically ill and perhaps dying partner, son or daughter in circumstances that may involve the initial shock of discovery, the search for explanations, ambivalence about support or rejection from others, attempts at concealment, feelings of stigma, increasing threat to the family's material circumstances, and dilemmas about how to cope (Siegl and Morse, 1994; Folkman, 1997; Castro et al., 1998; Billings et al., 2000).

A core feature of living with a relative with a drinking or drug problem, however, is the excessive and out-of-control behaviour of the relative, and the deteriorated and often abusive relationship that develops between relative and family member. A close parallel, in that sense, lies with the experiences of parents of children with conduct or disruptive behaviour disorders described by Herbert (1995). Such problems, like drinking and drug problems, are highly prevalent. Parents, especially mothers, feel undermined and attacked by their children's behaviour, and, instead of being supported by others, are often criticised and scapegoated.

Another close comparison, involving adult relatives, is with the circumstances that wives are faced with when their husbands return from active military service in a state of continuing severe psychological distress – variously described as combat trauma, combat stress reaction, or post-traumatic war stress disorder (Rosenheck and Thomson, 1986; Solomon et al., 1992). Like wives of men with drinking problems, they often say that their spouses and their relationships with them have changed, that their husbands are preoccupied with their memories and have withdrawn from their families. Such husbands offer no explanation of these changes, and are often physically or emotionally abusive toward their wives, who are increasingly lonely, without social support, sometimes overfunctioning in order to compensate for their husbands' unavailability, uncertain how to understand what is going on, caught in a 'compassion trap', and at risk of displaying their own signs of psychological strain.

Despite the many points of similarity with other forms of chronic family stress, we believe the circumstances described by our research participants represent a unique combination of elements. For one thing, the many-faceted, threatening nature of substance misuse in the family, potentially attacking the family on many levels – emotional, behavioural, social and financial – can place it among the most threatening and difficult to manage family stressors. Peculiarly, the threat comes from the damaging behaviour of an adult relative who would normally be expected to behave responsibly. Furthermore, the consumption of alcohol or other drugs is part of social and cultural life, and hence family members find themselves caught in a web of supportive and unsupportive influences, with no clear direction of how to cope. These, and

Table 9.4 The particular qualities of having to cope with excessive drinking or drug taking in the family which, in combination, make it unique and highly stressful

- Has the nature of severe stress, threat and abuse
- Involves multiple sources of threat to self and family, including emotional, social, financial, health and safety
- Caused by the irresponsible behaviour of an adult family member who is expected to behave responsibly
- Worry for that family member is a prominent feature
- There are influences in the form of individual people and societal attitudes that encourage the troubling behaviour
- Attempting to cope creates difficult dilemmas, and there is no guidance on the subject
- Social support for the family is needed but tends to fail
- Professionals who might help are often at best badly informed and at worst critical

some other features that lend to coping with excessive drinking and drug use its particular qualities, are summarised in Table 9.4.

The present chapter has provided a theoretical integration based on the findings of the present research, the results of earlier research by others, and some of the conclusions of the larger body of knowledge on coping with family stressors. In Chapter 10, we turn to a consideration of practice, drawing out implications of the present work in developing ways of helping family members. Writing about help for parents of children displaying disruptive behaviour, Herbert (1995) called for a much more collaborative approach between professionals and family members, one that empowered rather than disempowered them. Our call in Chapter 10 is for very much the same kind of collaborative and empowering approach to helping family members of relatives with substance problems.

Chapter 10

Ways of empowering family members

In the light of the foregoing chapters, summarised in Chapter 9, we turn in the present chapter to review the ways in which we and others have tried to help family members. We have drawn attention to the ways in the past that family members of relatives with substance misuse problems have often been alienated and disempowered by the approaches that professionals have taken toward them. They have usually either been excluded entirely from any interventions oriented toward the substance misusers, or viewed explicitly or implicitly in stereotyped and unsympathetic ways, even to the point of being demonised as the cause or maintainer of the substance misuse problems. Family members themselves have often expressed the view that professionals who could have been supportive were seen not to have been so. Dorn et al. (1987) cited several examples, including a parent who said, 'I went to my doctor and I might as well have talked to the wall really, he really did not want to know . . . made me feel that small' (p. 27). In Chapter 7, we gave some similar examples from the present study: as an English father put it, 'no one seems to be able to advise you'. Although in all three socio-cultural groups there were examples of family members reporting positively about their contacts with professionals and those in authority, the picture was very mixed. We conclude that this is a consequence of the lack of a family orientation in professional training and practice, in addition to the existence of a number of models of family functioning that cast family members in a negative light. Those who might be in a position to help have therefore frequently lacked the kind of understanding of the position of family members that is gained only by listening closely and patiently to what family members have to say about their experiences.

The work reported in this book so far corresponds to phase one of a programme of research which was from the outset conceived as having two phases. The first aimed to deepen our understanding of the lives of family members affected by substance problems and develop theory based on that understanding. That aim, we believe, has been achieved. The results were presented in full in earlier chapters. The second aimed to build on the first phase by developing and evaluating forms of help for family members. In this chapter, we will first look at each of the three countries where this work has been undertaken, and examine what has been done by our group in terms of developing relevant interventions. That work continues and hence what we report here is in the nature of work in progress. Next, we will look at relevant interventions in the published literature, and draw some conclusions about the potential gains for family members, for family health, and for the person who is misusing alcohol or drugs that can be achieved by involving and helping family members facing alcohol and drug problems.

Using our model to empower families in Mexico, England and Australia

In each of the three countries where we have been working and where we have explored the impact of family substance misuse problems, we have also developed interventions based on that work, and on the stress-strain-coping-support model. Those developments are summarised in Table 10.1 There are several general features of those programmes that should be highlighted.

First, it needs to be emphasised that the lead in developing the interventions summarised in Table 10.1 has been taken locally by those of us working in the area of health services development and research in one of the three countries that took part in the research described in earlier chapters. No attempt was made to import, wholesale, programmes from one country to another. Thus, the work took different forms in the different countries. In Mexico, the workplace was the chosen site for a family intervention because, in a country with uneven health service coverage, the workplace is a prominent arena for the provision of health-promoting activities. In England, with its comprehensive primary health-care coverage, primary health-care centres were an obvious location for project work, and specialist nurses (health visitors and practice nurses), as well as general medical practitioners, were obvious candidates as personnel to deliver family interventions. In the Northern Territory, Australia, the interventions were delivered in remote Aboriginal communities, and extreme care was taken to ensure maximum community ownership of a project. In one sense, therefore, the strategy that is guiding the intervention phase of this work is an opportunistic one. In our different countries, we are searching for the best opportunities to overcome the neglect that has surrounded understanding and responding to the experiences of concerned and affected family members.

That neglect has been apparent in all three countries. In Mexico, it was noted that family members would often present to doctors with physical stress-related symptoms, and that the health and social security system allowed insufficient time for underlying causes to be explored. In England, services are strongly oriented toward helping the problem drug- or alcohol-using relative, and family members are rarely seen as more than an adjunct to treatment. Specialist services for families and children are scarce. In the

Table 10.1 Attempting to empower family members in Mexico, England and Australia

Details of project	Description of project	Results of evaluation
Mexico		
A manual-based intervention to be used by community workers with family members (Natera and Casco, 1993; Natera et al. 1998; Natera and Tiburcio, 1998; Tiburcio, 2002)	This approach has been piloted and tested in a variety of settings over the last decade with various generic community workers.	Two early pilots of the manual showed that it was possible to train family workers, but that few of those trained went on to recruit family members. Nonetheless, the intervention has proved very popular, with more than 3000 copies of the manual printed and sold at low cost (50 pesos or US$4). A short version of the manual has also been printed and made available for family members themselves. Further evaluations have also demonstrated that the information contained within the manual is helpful, but further work is needed to assess the impact of the intervention with families themselves.
Family work as part of workplace drug- and alcohol-misuse prevention programmes (Natera and Tiburcio, 1998)	To integrate family work within more general drug- and alcohol-misuse prevention programmes within the workplace. The same manual as used in the previous work was adapted. Other materials have been developed to go alongside the manual, including materials for family members themselves.	An initial survey and focus groups found positive attitudes to the idea of developing a family component to work-based drug- and alcohol-misuse prevention programmes. The whole programme has been evaluated with 120 employees, 97% of whom completed baseline data and 78% contributed follow-up data. Impact reported to be positive; 82% had read the leaflet, 67% said a relative had read the leaflet, 83% had found the information useful for themselves or others, 91% said that the leaflet gave good advice on responding to the problem. Employees also showed that they had a good understanding of the different ways of responding to the problem, and which coping strategies were believed to be associated with more positive outcomes.
Working directly with family members in the community (Tiburcio and Natera, 2003)	Development of an intervention aimed at family members recruited through the community, psychology and other treatment agencies.	A preliminary evaluation of this way of working collected data from 28 family members at baseline and follow-up (3 months). Results showed a decrease in physical and psychological symptoms and a change in coping. There was a high level of satisfaction with the intervention.

Table 10.1 (Contd.)

Details of project	Description of project	Results of evaluation
England		
Primary care feasibility study (Copello et al., 2000a,b)	To assess the feasibility of a brief intervention for use by primary health-care professionals with family members.	Thirty-six primary health-care professionals tested the brief intervention with 37 family members, with data collected at baseline and 3 months. There was a significant decrease in family members' physical and psychological symptoms as well as a reduction in engaged and tolerant forms of coping. Furthermore, there was a significant increase in positive attitudes toward working with family members among the primary health-care professionals who tested the intervention compared with those who did not.
Primary care cluster randomised controlled trial (Copello et al., 2005; Orford et al., 2005)	To compare two levels of a brief intervention for use by primary health-care professionals with family members – self-help manual or manual plus up to five extra face-to-face sessions.	Primary health-care professionals tested the brief intervention with 143 family members with data collected at baseline, 3 months and 12 months. There was a significant decrease in family members' physical and psychological symptoms as well as a reduction in engaged and tolerant forms of coping in both groups. There were no differences between the groups, although qualitative data suggested that some level of face-to-face input is a preferred option for both family members and professionals. Furthermore, there was a significant increase in positive attitudes of the primary health-care professionals who tested the intervention, compared with those who did not, toward working with family members.
Australia		
Families Coping with Drug (including Alcohol) Use in Remote Communities Program (FCP)	A process of delivering workshops aimed at providing indigenous families, individuals and communities with information and skill development to assist positive coping with excessive drinking and other drug use. Step 1: a Northern Territory-wide workshop with frontline alcohol and other drug workers. Step 2: regional workshops	Workshop process and content, with supporting resources, have been positively received within Aboriginal communities across the NT. They are reported to be culturally appropriate, interactive, using narrative techniques, many visual components, and have been successfully delivered with indigenous people. In locations closer to the capital city, the process has developed well with connections built with local communities, networking with other service providers, professional development workshops held, and a number of family-coping workshops conducted. The process has

for workers. Step 3: coping workshops for family members, community organisations and workers in five locations across the NT (in some locations problem drinking relatives also attend). Key personnel are drug and alcohol community support officers (CSOs), working on the Family Coping Project (FCP) part-time, located at five sites across the Territory. A family-coping workshop is held over three days and sessions include: alcohol, petrol sniffing and gunja (cannabis); stress and how to cope with it; impact of stress and substances on the families and the community; developing coping strategies for family members; nutrition for family members and relatives; and anger management. This phase is to be followed by the establishment of a small grants programme to aid the development of practical interventions for family members in remote indigenous communities adapted to local circumstances and need.

been less successful in the more remote areas where it has been difficult to provide more than limited support to CSOs. An independent impact evaluation of 63 participants of family-coping workshops that have been held reported very positively about the immediate impact on knowledge and skills. Level of perceived benefit was high and other families, unable to attend, have requested further workshops. Wider benefits were reported in terms of improved relationships between agencies and the building of community capacity. The second phase is still to be planned and implemented.

Northern Territory, it was noted that the treatment programmes that were available to indigenous people tended to adopt an individual approach, and the view taken by the Australian group was that there was a need for alcohol and drug use to be viewed more within the context of the well-being of the community rather than being seen as a matter of individual 'pathology'.

Although we concluded (Chapter 9) that many of the experiences for affected family members were universal, we also concluded that the experience was in the nature of a 'variform universal' in which the core experience, likely to be common to all socio-cultural groups, was modified by a variety of factors that included the socio-cultural setting. We highlighted, for example, the poverty and the high level of tolerance of heavy male alcohol consumption among disadvantaged groups in Mexico City, the threat to individual autonomy in England, and the mix of opportunities and obstacles to coping presented by indigenous reciprocity norms in the Northern Territory (Chapters 8 and 9). These and other cultural variations constituted further, and perhaps the most important, reasons for adopting a strategy that did not involve imposing an identical form of intervention in three very different socio-cultural settings.

What is common in the work being carried out in the three countries, however, is the way interventions are all based upon the stress-strain-coping-support model. As described in earlier chapters (Chapters 1 and 9), that model views family members of relatives with substance problems as being subject to multiple stressors and vulnerable to signs of strain in the form of mental and physical ill health, with the stress–strain relationship being buffered by finding ways of coping that work for the individual family member or network of family members and others and by the availability of appropriate support from others. Unlike some other models of alcohol, drugs and the family, it does not view family members or a family as a whole as possessing any particular form of dysfunction or psychopathology that has contributed to the substance problem. As indicated throughout the present book, we subscribe to the view that the latter type of perspective stigmatises family members, while the stress-strain-coping-support model is of a kind that is potentially empowering of family members. Although the specific programmes for family members vary in their details, most or all of the following five components, based on the stress-strain-coping-support model, are to be found in each of them:

- allowing family members to talk about their experiences and listening non-judgementally to what they have to say
- providing information about substances and substance use and misuse where that is thought to be helpful
- exploring family members' ways of coping with the problem and discussing the advantages and disadvantages of different ways of coping in a family member's particular circumstances

- discussing how support for family members can be strengthening
- exploring whether family members have need of additional help or support in the light of particular stressors experienced or forms of resulting strain that a family member may be suffering.

A further general principle that guided work in each of the countries was the requirement that work be carried out in primary care settings, rather than in specialist treatment services, using primary care workers as the agents for delivering the intervention. That principle was based upon the premises that alcohol and other substance problems are highly prevalent in all three countries, that primary care services are more easily accessible to family members, and that family members are likely to be known in larger numbers to primary care workers than to specialist workers, even though the nature of their circumstances may be very imperfectly known.

In practice, what constitutes primary care, who qualifies as a primary care worker, and what forms of primary care are most accessible, varies from country to country. Indeed, the term 'primary health-care worker', used widely in England, was not readily understood in Mexico. The term 'counsellor' was preferred for the Mexican pilot study, and a group who were trained included a schoolteacher, a priest and a university professor as well as a doctor, a nurse and social workers. In England, the group of primary health-care professionals who have delivered the interventions have been core staff of primary care health centres, including general medical practitioners, health visitors and practice nurses. Their service is comparatively easily accessible since almost the whole UK population is registered with a primary health-care practice, and the majority of people visit their general medical practitioner at least once a year. Possibilities for intervention with members of the indigenous Australian population are very different. Treatment services which indigenous people can access are few and far between. Indigenous people comprise about 27% of the Northern Territory population, but some 63% of this group live in remote communities, outstations and cattle stations. On the other hand, alcohol and drug intervention and treatment programmes within the Northern Territory are concentrated in the urban and semi-urban locations far from where most of the indigenous people live. The family workshops that took place in remote communities involved individual family members, sometimes two or more members from the same family, members of community organisations, and 'frontline workers'.

From all that was learnt in the research reported in earlier chapters about the difficult circumstances experienced by family members in the face of relatives' drinking or drug problems, it is not surprising to find that the work in all three countries has been challenging and has met with barriers and difficulties that we are continuing to struggle with in each location. For example, it has been the experience both in Mexico and England that even when primary care workers or counsellors are trained to deliver a family intervention, and are keen to do so, by no means all go on to deliver an intervention with a family member. There are many reasons for that, including factors attributable to the family member and her or his circumstances (e.g. concern about talking of family matters to an outsider), and some attributable to factors associated with a worker's perception of the nature of the problem (e.g. that the problem is too complicated, or not confined to excessive substance use). In the Mexican workplace project, understandable barriers needed to be overcome in the form of reluctance on the part of some employees to involve the family (sometimes an employee was an affected and concerned family member, while other employees were themselves excessively drinking or drug-using relatives). In the Northern Territory, the challenges of this work are complicated further by the need to recruit and support community support officers in remote locations, and to obtain funding to take the work forward to a stage beyond the workshop stage.

A useful start has been made in subjecting these lines of work to careful evaluation, although much remains to be done. The three strands of work in Mexico, particularly the workplace family programme, have all been the subject of what might be termed 'impact evaluation', in the sense that participants were systematically asked what the immediate impact had been for them. For example, 82% reported having read the leaflet *Guidance for Families*, and 67% reported that the leaflet had also been read by a relative; 83% reported that it had been useful either for themselves or for relatives who were heavy drinkers, and others had handed the leaflet to fellow workers who did have the problem. Similarly, high levels of satisfaction with the intervention were recorded by participants in the third Mexican programme that was aimed at family members recruited through community, psychology and treatment agencies. A similar form of impact evaluation was used in Australia. For example, 100% of those taking part in family coping workshops responded 'Yes' when asked whether they had gained more knowledge about alcohol, cannabis and petrol sniffing as a result of the workshops, and 98% said that they had benefited from the workshop.

Although that style of impact evaluation is encouraging, suggesting that programmes are well received and therefore promising, they leave open the all-important question of whether they are effective in achieving programme goals. In both Mexico and England, some progress has been made in using an evaluation design, with standard measures and controls, that goes some way in addressing that question. In the third Mexican programme, for affected family members, and in the two English primary care studies, a before–after design was employed with standard measures of ways of coping (the Coping Questionnaire (CQ)) and of common psychological and physical symptoms (the Symptom Rating Test (SRT)). Both the CQ and the SRT were completed by participants before and after the intervention. In that way, participants served as their own controls. In all of those studies, significant changes, in hoped-for directions, were found: participants reported reduced tolerant and engaged forms of coping and lower levels of symptoms after the intervention. In the two English studies, before-to-after changes were also recorded in the attitudes of primary care health professionals (the Attitudes to Addiction-Related Family Problems Questionnaire (AAFPQ)) who had become more positive toward working with concerned and affected family members. In the second English primary care project, an additional feature was added to the research design in the form of randomisation of primary care practices, half of whom gave family members the self-help manual based on the stress-strain-coping-support model with the addition of up to five additional face-to-face sessions, the other half giving the manual at a single session. Before-to-after changes on the CQ and the SRT were positive for both groups, with no differences in outcome being apparent between the two forms of intervention.

In Australia, reflecting the way in which excessive substance use is seen as a threat to whole indigenous communities (see Chapter 8), the family coping workshops, as well as including components such as 'anger management' and identifying the connection between substance problems and nutrition as a priority health issue, have had wider objectives. The latter include providing comprehensive information about substance use and misuse to Aboriginal families, individuals and community agencies; the building of better relationships between government and non-government organisations; and general community capacity building. Furthermore, the Australian programme involved an ambitious target of providing workshops in several regions across the Northern Territory. At the time of writing, that objective had been achieved in some regions, but not in all.

Evaluation of intervention projects that are based upon the model and research results described earlier in this book presents a considerable challenge. Ideally, we need to evaluate the effectiveness of such work on a number of different levels, including the following:

■ Is success achieved in setting up programmes such as workplace pro-grammes in Mexico, primary health-care-based projects in England, or family and community workshop programmes in remote Northern Territory, Australia? In other words, are such programmes feasible at all?

■ Can suitable personnel be recruited and trained to deliver such inter-ventions? For example, can community 'counsellors' be recruited and trained in Mexico, primary care nurses in England, or community support officers in regions across the Northern Territory?

■ Can concerned and affected family members be identified and recruited to participate in such projects?

■ What do participants report as the immediate impact of taking part? Do they read written material provided? Do they participate actively? Do they find project content to be relevant? Do they feel better informed or empowered as a result?

■   Is it possible to carry out outcome or 'summative evaluation' to determine whether desired outcomes are achieved?

Each of those questions is important and not easy to answer. The last, concerning outcome evaluation, often considered to be the most important, is particularly challenging. The before–after design, using participants as their own control, has a number of weaknesses in comparison with other experimental and quasi-experimental designs (Cook and Campbell, 1979; Shadish et al., 2002). The most powerful such design that we have employed to date is the cluster randomisation design used in the second English primary care project. In that study, primary care health practices were randomly assigned to the manual-single session or manual-plus-five extra sessions conditions, and results were analysed at the level of individual participating family members, controlling statistically for within-practice homogeneity.

Other interventions that aim to empower family members

The work of our group is not, of course, the only work that has been undertaken to engage and help family members affected by the excessive drinking or drug taking of close relatives. Table 10.2 summarises the types of family intervention that have been developed and reported in the English-language literature. Most of that work has been carried out in the USA, with some contributions from the UK, Australia, Canada and the former Yugoslavia. It is possible that some important lines of work are missing from Table 10.2, particularly, perhaps, work published in other languages, but we believe the table is a fairly comprehensive summary of the various ways in which serious attempts have been made to involve family members.

The studies shown in Table 10.2 have been grouped into three categories. Group A consists of those forms of intervention, such as couple, family or network approaches, that involve working with family members and the relatives about whom they are concerned, together. Group B includes those forms of intervention, sometimes referred to as 'unilateral' family methods, that involve working with family members with the aim of encouraging their problem drinking or drug-taking relatives to enter treatment or to continue to engage in treatment. The third category, C, includes approaches that are most similar to those we have been developing (described earlier in this chapter; see Table 10.1) because they focus more directly on helping family members in their own right. It is noticeable that most work falls into groups A or B. Furthermore, the key outcomes assessed in the various studies have mostly focused on the problem drinking or drug-taking relatives, particularly level of alcohol or drug consumption (especially in group A studies) or relatives' take-up of or engagement in treatment (especially group B). Some have made assessments at the level of the dyadic relationship between family

Table 10.2 Other projects for empowering family members reported in the literature[a,b]

Details of project	Description of the project	Results of evaluation
(A) Joint involvement of family members and their relatives in the treatment of the latter's problem alcohol/drug use		
Family/home rehabilitation (Pattison, 1965; Davies and Hagood, 1979)	Intensive work by public-health nurses in the home for multiproblem families with an excessive drinker/ intensive 6-week treatment by family rehabilitation coordinators for all household members in families with a mother who drank excessively.	No control groups, case series only. Reports of positive changes for some families in alcohol consumption, family harmony and communication and household management.
Conjoint family group therapy (Corder et al., 1972; Cadogan, 1973; Steinglass, 1979)	Varying from once-weekly, open outpatient groups, to intensive 4-day conjoint treatment at the end of treatment for the problem drinker, to an intensive research and treatment programme involving conjoint hospital admission.	The better evaluated of these studies found less drinking, unemployment and divorce or separation 6 months after intensive 4-day conjoint treatment compared to no family member involvement.
Behavioural couples therapy (Hedburg and Campbell, 1974; O'Farrell et al., 1985, 1992, 1993, 1998; O'Farrell and Murphy, 1995; Fals-Stewart et al., 1996; Kelley and Fals-Stewart, 2002; Winters et al., 2002)	Combinations of couples treatment in individual couple and group formats, sometimes with booster sessions spread over 12 months. Has been applied to both men and women and to both alcohol and other substance problems.	A series of randomised, controlled trials has shown positive changes in alcohol/drug use, relationship quality, domestic violence and psychological functioning of children in the family, compared to no-couple or no-treatment control groups. Sometimes, gains have dissipated over the follow-up interval; sometimes, gains maintained for up to 3 years.
Joint advice with follow-up (Orford and Edwards, 1977 (UK); Zweben et al., 1988 (Canada))	A single session of advice counselling for an alcohol problem, in the presence of spouse, plus follow-up.	Two controlled trials found advice counselling and follow-up as effective as conjoint treatment or treatment as usual, in terms of drinking and marital outcomes.

Table 10.2 (Contd.)

Details of project	Description of the project	Results of evaluation
Family therapy for drug abuse (Gacic et al., 1980; Stanton et al., 1982; Szapocznik et al., 1988; McLellan et al., 1993; Bernal et al., 1997)	Family therapy described as structural-strategic, Bowen type or contextual. Sometimes very intensive.	Controlled trials showing family therapy more effective in engaging the drug misusers and superior at post-treatment or follow-up in terms of drug use or family functioning.
Network therapy (Galanter, 1993, 1999; Galanter et al., 2004)	Used alongside individual therapy for the problem substance user, NT uses an active approach to engage members of the substance user's social network in the treatment process.	One study of a series suggests that family members and friends can be engaged. A controlled trial found less concurrent use of opioids and better outcome at end of treatment for a network therapy group compared to medication management only for problem drug users on medication maintenance.
Social behaviour and network therapy (SBNT) (UK) (Copello et al., 2002; UKATT Research Team, 2005)	Aims to help a substance misuser identify potentially supportive family members or friends and to enlist them in providing support for change, where possible engaging them in treatment sessions.	An initial study confirmed the feasibility of engaging family members and friends of those with alcohol problems and gave evidence of positive impact. A subsequent multicentre control-led trial showed SBNT to be as effective and cost-effective as a briefer motivational treatment (motivational enhancement therapy) that did not involve family members or friends. A later study suggested the feasibility and impact of SBNT in the treatment of people with problems of illicit drug misuse.
Mutual-help organisations (Humphreys, 2004)	Danshukai (Japan), Croix Bleue (France and other countries), Vie Libre (France and Belgium), Jewish Alcoholics, Chemically Dependent Persons, and Significant Others (USA and other countries), the Links (Sweden and other Scandinavian countries). All examples of organisations that actively involve family members in meetings and activities.	None (but see Humphreys, 2004, for a discussion of the appropriateness of evaluation for mutual-help organisations).

(B) Working with family members to encourage their relatives' engagement in treatment for the latter's alcohol or drug problem

'Intervention' (or 'benevolent confrontation') (Johnson, 1986; Liepman, 1995; Miller et al., 1999)	Social networks of concerned family members and friends are trained to stage a confrontation, during which attempts are made to reduce 'denial' about 'alcoholism' and engage the relative in treatment.	Limited evaluations which suggest that preparatory work with the network frequently does not lead to a confrontation, and that fewer relatives engage in treatment compared to CRAFT.
Community reinforcement and family training (CRAFT) (Sisson and Azrin, 1986; Miller et al., 1999; Meyers et al., 1999)	Uses the principles of the community reinforcement approach (Hunt and Azrin, 1973) that focus on the influence of the family, social and vocational aspects in reinforcing abstinence and assisting substance-related behaviour change.	In a randomised, controlled trial for concerned significant others (CSOs), CRAFT led to significantly more engagement of relatives in treatment than 'benevolent confrontation' (Liepman, 1993) and Al-Anon controls. All three conditions led to improvements for CSOs for anger, depression, family conflict and family cohesion, irrespective of whether the relative entered treatment. In a second study, without a control group, applying CRAFT to parents and partners of treatment-resistant drug users led to the majority of the latter beginning treatment.
Unilateral family therapy (UFT) (Thomas et al., 1987; Thomas and Ager, 1993)	Partners of relatives with alcohol problems are trained to act as a 'rehabilitative influence'. In three parts: preparation, intervention to reduce drinking or help the drinker enter treatment, and maintenance of gains.	In two studies, more relatives reduced drinking and/ or entered treatment than in a no-family treatment control group.
Cooperative counselling (Yates, 1988 (UK))	Aims to develop a coordinated strategy for change, working with anyone concerned enough to take positive action in response to another's alcohol problem.	In half of a case series, treatment-resistant problem drinkers agreed to approach treatment services. Concerned others reported positive impacts, including support in the belief that a significant drinking problem existed.

Table 10.2 (Contd.)

Details of project	Description of the project	Results of evaluation
Pressures to change (PTC) (Australia) (Barber and Crisp, 1995; Barber and Gilbertson, 1996)	Designed for spouses of relatives with alcohol problems. Aims to create change in the behaviour of those concerned in order to achieve treatment entry for the relative. By focusing on education; discussion of family member's response to drinking situations; setting up activities incompatible with drinking; and preparing the family member to confront the relative and request that the latter approaches services to seek help.	Two studies found more PTC relatives sought treatment and/or reduced alcohol consumption compared to no-treatment or Al-Anon controls (no difference between individual and group PTC). No improvements were found in one study for the family members' well-being, self-esteem, depression or marital discord.
A relational intervention sequence for engagement (ARISE) (Garrett et al., 1998, 1999)	A development of 'intervention' that places less emphasis on confrontation and more on support for family member and relatives prior to, during and after treatment entry. A series of strategies are used to respond to calls from concerned others aiming to mobilise family members and social networks to assist the problem substance user's treatment engagement.	Two-thirds of calls from parents, partners, siblings and some from co-workers and employers, concerning alcohol and other drugs, were followed by the problem substance user entering treatment or mutual-help.
(C) Responding to the needs of family members affected by and concerned about a relative's problem alcohol/drug use		
Concurrent group treatment (Ewing et al., 1961; Smith, 1969)	Group therapy for wives of men with drinking problems, running concurrently with treatment for their problem drinking husbands.	Uncontrolled studies, positive results reported, but sometimes only a small proportion of partners agreed to participate.
Family casework (Cohen and Krause, 1971)	Two types of family social work, one based on a view of alcohol abuse as the primary family disorder, the other on the traditional casework view that excessive drinking was a symptom of other problems in the alcoholic and members of his family.	A randomised, controlled trial, but high attrition and other method problems. Report of greater reduced drinking in the alcohol as primary disorder group. No improvements in either group in terms of wives' self-appraisal, satisfaction with family relationships, etc. A high rate of divorce in the alcohol as primary disorder group.

Approach	Description	Evidence
Al-Anon family groups/Families Anonymous (Gorman and Rooney, 1979; Miller et al., 1999; Humphreys, 2004)	Mutual-help groups for family members, meeting separately from, but affiliated to, mutual-help organisations for problem drinking or drug-taking relatives.	Evidence that problem drinking husbands have relatively good drinking outcomes when their wives attend Al-Anon. Research showing that members of Al-Anon reduce controlling ways of coping. A controlled trial showed as good outcomes for wives, in terms of depression, anger, family conflict and relationship satisfaction, as for two non-Al-Anon family treatment conditions.
A psycho-educational approach (Dittrich and Trapold, 1984; Dittrich, 1993)	Based on understanding of 'alcoholism' as a 'family disease'; attempts to increase understanding of alcoholism and family interaction; identify and decrease 'enabling' behaviours; increase self-esteem; decrease depression and anxiety. Organised in three phases: educational, experiential (in which assertive responses are practised), and goal setting and planning.	In a small, randomised trial women married to men with alcohol problems who received the intervention, compared to waiting list control, showed greater change in self-concept, depression and anxiety, and enabling behaviours. The delayed treatment group subsequently showed the same changes. At 12-month follow-up, half the women were still meeting informally or attending Al-Anon, over a third were divorced or separated, and half the husbands had entered treatment or mutual help.
Counselling for partners in their own right (UK) (Howells, 1996; Howells and Orford, 2005)	Counselling, mostly delivered by trained volunteers, for partners (mostly wives) of relatives with drinking problems, as part of specialised, secondary care services. Emphasises stress experienced by partners and discussion of ways of coping.	Before–after comparison showed significant reductions in self-sacrificing and engaged coping and in level of common symptoms. Detailed case studies, comparison with a small, delayed-treatment control group, and partial follow-up to 12 months provided supportive evidence of positive outcome and detail of process.

Table 10.2 (Contd.)

Details of project	Description of the project	Results of evaluation
Behavioural exchange systems training (BEST) (Australia) (Toumbourou et al., 1997, 2001)	An 8-week group programme for parents of drug-using adolescents: first 4 weeks focus on improving parents' well-being; later weeks aim to increase assertive parenting responses.	A quasi-experimental design showed that BEST was associated with greater reductions in mental health symptoms, increased parental satisfaction and use of assertive parenting behaviours compared to a waiting list comparison. The latter group showed the same pattern of changes once they received the intervention.
Supported counselling versus stress management versus alcohol-focused couples therapy (Halford et al., 2001)	A randomised, controlled trial of three forms of help for women partners of men with alcohol problems. Each 15 sessions of 1 hour aiming to reduce risk of violence; assist the family member to choose whether to remain in the relationship; and to help her enact a decision to leave or, alternatively, to improve coping and empower her to influence the partner's drinking. Based, respectively, on education and non-directive counselling; reducing the stressful impact of the problem for the family member and helping to influence the partner's drinking (Sisson and Azrin, 1986); and behavioural couple therapy based on contingency reinforcement of efforts to control drinking and communication and problem-solving training for the couple (O'Farrell and Rotunda, 1997).	The trial found reductions in psychological symptoms for family members, post-treatment and at 6-month follow-up, irrespective of type of treatment. None of the treatments produced significant reductions in relatives' drinking or level of relationship stress. Only a minority of problem drinkers agreed to pursue couple treatment.
Parent coping skills training (McGillicuddy et al., 2001)	Based on a behavioural-analytic model of skill training (Goldfried and D'Zurilla, 1969). Consists of eight, weekly, 2-hour sessions to teach 'more effective' coping skills in responding to their adolescents' substance use. Uses group discussion and role play around a standard set of frequently encountered situations.	A small, randomised trial showed greater improvement in parental coping skills, parents' own functioning, family communication and the relative's marijuana use than waiting list control.

a. In a number of cases, only a sample of available references has been supplied.
b. Work has taken place in the USA unless otherwise stated.

member and relative, and only a few have focused on the family members. This of course reflects the all too familiar positioning of family members at the edge of most practitioners' and researchers' interests.

In fact, the divisions between those three categories are quite fuzzy. For example, some studies in group A (e.g. behavioural couples therapy (e.g. Winters et al., 2002)) and in group B (e.g. the comparison of CRAFT with two other interventions (Miller et al., 1999)) have reported interpersonal outcomes, such as relationship satisfaction or family conflict or cohesion, and family member outcomes, such as depression, as well as the much more commonly used relative-focused outcomes, such as level of drinking or drug taking, or proportion of relatives who became engaged in treatment. Similarly, studies in group C have sometimes reported on the latter type of outcomes as well as those relating to family members in their own right. An illustration of the fuzziness of these categories is our placement of such approaches as Al-Anon and counselling for partners in group C on the grounds that they are principally aimed at the needs of affected family members. At the same time, those approaches may well be effective in also helping a drinking relative stop drinking.

That reflects the view of most authors who have written about involving family members, namely, that the twin aims of this work – to engage and support problem substance users in their change efforts, and to empower concerned and affected family members – are not incompatible. Indeed, most would consider progress toward those two aims as mutually reinforcing. It is also consistent with the findings of the research reported earlier in this book, particularly that reported in Chapter 7. A conclusion there was that most family members put a priority on finding ways to help their relatives change. They found other people to be most supportive when those others, whether family, friends or professionals, maintained a positive stance toward the family members' problem substance-using relatives. Most of the family members we interviewed saw helping their relatives and helping themselves as one and the same thing, although it is important to recognise that some women partners, for example, who may have been on the receiving end of domestic violence, may have a very different view of the kind of support they need (see Howells, 1996; Halford et al., 2001).

Nevertheless, the predominance of studies in groups A or B in Table 10.2 helps draw attention to one of the main features of this body of work. Most studies have not assessed outcomes that pertain directly to family member health or ways of coping, or to the quality of family relationships. The primary focus has been on outcomes for the problem substance user, with family members being thought of as agents who can play an adjunctive role in treatment by influencing relatives' behaviour. Some of the studies in group C are comparatively recent and provide a hopeful indication that the needs of family members are beginning to be recognised.

It is apparent from Table 10.2 that there is no shortage of ideas about ways of involving family members in treatment. Although some approaches, such as conjoint family group therapy, have gone out of fashion, and others, such as the network therapies that aim to involve supportive people whether they be family members, friends, work colleagues or others (Galanter, 1999; Copello et al., 2002), are relative newcomers, it is the variety of approaches that stands out. Methods vary from family therapy with a structural-strategic orientation (see the review by Stanton and Shadish, 1997), to the behavioural approach of behavioural marital therapy and community reinforcement and family training (CRAFT), to the social support orientation of social behaviour and network therapy (SBNT), and the 12-step philosophy of Al-Anon.

In terms of evaluation, the picture is a mixed one. By and large, the numbers of participants in the studies shown in Table 10.2 have been small, control groups have been weak or absent, and follow-up rates have been disappointing. It has therefore been difficult to draw confident conclusions. Certain approaches stand out. The behavioural marital or couples therapy approach of O'Farrell and Fals-Stewart and their colleagues in the USA has been the subject of a whole programme of well-designed studies. The emphasis has been upon engagement in treatment of the problem substance-using relative and subsequent reductions in alcohol or drug use, but there have also been reports from that programme of improvements in marital adjustment and reductions in levels of domestic violence (e.g. O'Farrell et al., 1992; O'Farrell and Murphy, 1995). In the UK, a large multicentre trial found SBNT to be as effective as motivational enhancement therapy in the treatment of alcohol problems, but family member outcomes were not systematically evaluated (UKATT Research Team, 2005). A review of a number of controlled trials of family therapy in the treatment of problem drug use concluded that treatments involving partners or other family members (i.e. couples or family therapy) were more effective than methods that did not, although outcomes were confined to assessments of drug use (Stanton and Shadish, 1977). The CRAFT approach has been the subject of two well-designed trials which found the method to be more effective than others in engaging problem using relatives in treatment (Miller et al., 1999; Meyers et al., 2002). In the Miller et al. (1999) study, improvements for family members, in terms of anger, depression, family conflict and family cohesion, were reported irrespective of whether the problem drinking relative entered treatment.

We would agree with Miller et al.'s (1999) suggestion that an improvement to this area of research will involve, not only the better use of good trial methodology, but also the collection of qualitative data. The latter would help explore and understand in more detail important issues, such as what aspects of an approach such as CRAFT family members find to be of benefit, and by what processes changes occur in family ways of coping, family cohesion and family members' health and well-being.

The greatest limitation of this treatment literature, however, lies in its very specialist nature. The work has been 'specialist' in a number of senses. Some of the best of it has been carried out in a very small number of specialist research centres in the Western world using approaches which may be less applicable elsewhere and research designs, usually some variety of the randomised, controlled trial, which are difficult to apply in most settings. Furthermore, in terms of treatment delivery systems, virtually all this work has been specialist in the sense that the providers of the interventions were specialists in the treatment of alcohol or drug problems. The emphasis of our own work in Mexico, England and Australia has been on the attempt to provide help for family members in the context of primary care, however that is defined and arranged in different countries. The evidence is incontrovertible that the very large majority of the tens of millions of affected family members around the world have no access to specialist services, or do not choose to use those that are available to them. Hence, although the studies summarised in Table 10.2 provide many creative ideas about ways in which family members might be involved, and sometimes helped in their own right, and much useful information about what may be most effective for achieving which ends, they are not so helpful in dealing with the pragmatics of delivering help to family members on a larger scale and in a variety of socio-cultural settings.

In the earlier part of this chapter we wrote about the attempts, often frustrating, of trying to deliver a service in a Mexican workplace, a general primary care health practice in England, and remote indigenous communities in Northern Australia. They are examples of complex community interventions, all of which are required to grapple with issues of negotiating access to sites where help can be delivered, difficulties of identifying and recruiting family members to take part, adapting methods and procedures to local circumstances, and such problems as maintaining contact with, and support and supervision for, those responsible for delivering interventions in remote settings. These programmes are in fact rather less like circumscribed 'treatments' that can be subjected to controlled trial evaluation methods, and rather more like community-based, often multicomponent projects, such as some that have involved family members, typically parents, in programmes designed to prevent future drug misuse (e.g. the Strengthening Families Programme; Spoth et al., 2002; the Logan Square project; Godley and Velasquez, 1998; or the NE Choices Programme; MacKintosh et al. 2001). These programmes were excluded from Table 10.2 because they were designed for families in which a young person was thought to be at risk of future drug misuse, rather than for family members already affected by and concerned about problematic drug use. Those complex community prevention programmes have needed to find the best combination of delivery, impact, process and outcome evaluation, sometimes involving the creative use of quasi-experimental designs in which randomisation is impossible or unethical.

What can we now conclude about ways of empowering family members?

In the early 1980s, Harwin (1982), writing about the excessive drinker and the family, said:

> It is still unusual for families to participate in all phases of the drinker's treatment. Frequently, relatives are regarded as useful adjuncts to the initial assessment, thereafter to be ignored. . . . The variability in the provision of family-focused help is surprising since experimentation in this area first began over 25 years ago.
>
> (p. 201)

The work discussed in this chapter, both our own and that of others, suggests that a great deal of progress has been made since the time that Harwin was writing. In a number of countries, methods have been developed – in total, an impressive range of methods – for engaging affected and concerned family members, and in a number of instances they have been subject to some degree of controlled evaluation. In other respects, however, the position might be said to be little better than it was in the early 1980s. The field is still a very patchy and fragmented one. No one method has emerged as a leader in the field, and with few exceptions standards of evaluation have not been high. More seriously, from the perspective adopted in this book, family members have sometimes been included in ways that pay little attention to their experiences or needs in comparison with the imperative to engage their problem drinking or drug-taking relatives in treatment. Of most concern is the worry that the promising methods discussed in the present chapter are not being disseminated much beyond the few specialist research and treatment centres where they have been developed and tested in preliminary fashion. We know that to be true in the UK (Robinson and Hassell, 2000; Copello and Orford, 2002), and we can only presume that in many parts of the world help for family members that recognises the special experiences of those concerned about and affected by their relatives' excessive substance use is completely lacking. Does the body of work reviewed in this chapter offer us a way forward?

For example, can joint treatment of family members and their relatives (group A in Table 10.2) be recommended as the model? Our tentative conclusion is that the various joint treatments that have been tried are all promising, and that none should be excluded from consideration. Behavioural couples therapy must be counted as a strong contender because of the series of sound evaluations that have been carried out, suggesting a range of positive outcomes, including those focusing on family members, both adults and children. But family therapy approaches, often derived from a very different philosophical background, have also met with good outcomes, not all confined to relatives' alcohol or drug consumption. Conjoint, professionally led treatments, which looked promising in the 1970s, have not been followed up, although mutual-help organisations in several countries have used a similar conjoint format and have survived and grown. Network methods (network therapy and SBNT) are comparatively new and look promising. They have the advantage of extending joint treatment to people who are concerned about another person's drinking or drug use, but who are not family members. Unlike other conjoint methods, they do not require the attendance of family members or friends, although that is encouraged. The focus remains principally on the problem substance-using person, and it remains to be seen whether such approaches can develop greater focus on family members or can be integrated with other methods that have such a focus.

Each of the group A approaches may fit with local contexts in different parts of the world, depending upon cultural norms and the extent and type of existing service provision for families. The problem with each of those methods is likely to be the feasibility of applying them on a large scale. We note, for example, Halford et al.'s (2001) finding that only a minority of relatives agreed to enter couples treatment. A large part of the failure to develop good, accessible services for family members is likely to be due to the overelaborate nature of specialist theories and treatment methods and the overdemanding requirement of specialist treatment procedures.

What can be learnt from the 'unilateral' approaches (group B in Table 10.2)? The conclusion here is that a further range of very promising approaches exists, with evidence that working with family members in those ways facilitates the entry of their relatives into treatment. In some cases, if procedures become too elaborate, as in the demanding 'intervention' method, procedures may not be followed through, and there may not always be positive outcomes for family members. But with due attention paid to the needs of family members, as in the ARISE, cooperative counselling and CRAFT approaches, there can be such positive outcomes and those are not necessarily dependent on relatives entering treatment.

It is our view that, if family members are to get the help they need, and if that help is to reach more than a tiny proportion of those who might benefit from it, then the way ahead lies in adapting those among the conjoint and unilateral approaches that are most locally relevant, and combining them with approaches that aim to respond to family members in their own right (summarised in Table 10.1 and group C in Table 10.2). Our own work in Mexico, England and Australia has deliberately taken the approach of developing procedures that are applicable to family members concerned about the problematic use of alcohol *and/or* of other drugs. One of the conclusions of the research reported earlier was that the particular substance of concern, although it was one of the factors that made for variation in the precise experiences of family members, did not alter the core family experience. We also know that for many people a problem of substance use combines the excessive consumption of alcohol and other drugs. In many settings, indigenous communities in the Northern Territory being one such, it makes little sense to divorce family and community concern about one substance, such as alcohol, from their concern about another, such as petrol sniffing. In the rest of the small published literature on responding to the needs of family members, alcohol and other substances have tended to be treated separately, as in mutual-help groups such as Al-Anon and professionally led methods that have tended to focus on the women partners of men with drinking problems or on helping parents of drug-misusing adolescents. Whatever their focus, however, the approaches that aim to respond to family members in their own right look promising in terms of helping family members find ways of coping that they find to be more effective, and in improving family members' health and well-being. A number of studies in the literature (in each of the categories in Table 10.2) suggest that, when it comes to outcomes for family members, the specific procedure adopted (Al-Anon, benevolent confrontation or CRAFT; non-directive counselling, stress counselling, and behavioural couple therapy; or self-help manual with or without extra face-to-face contact) may be less important than engaging with family members in ways that acknowledge their concern and appreciate how they may have been affected.

In closing, we return to the three countries that took part in the research on which this book has been based and where we are continuing to develop ways that will help services involve family members, rather than, as has sadly often been the case in the past, excluding or criticising them. Although much remains to be done in terms of both programme development and evaluation, we believe the results obtained so far are very encouraging. Reports from all three, very different, parts of the world are that the stress-strain-coping-support perspective is a relevant, understandable and potentially empowering model. Experience has shown that it is possible, albeit with difficulty, to recruit workplaces, primary care practices and remote communities to take part in work based upon that way of viewing the problem, and that agents who deliver such interventions and family members who receive them report positive impact.

Work continues in all three countries. In Mexico, one measure of success is the large number of manuals for counsellors that have been requested and distributed, and another is the considerable number of training events that we have been asked to undertake in different States of the republic. The model and Castilian-language materials that have been developed as a result are now finding application in both primary care and specialist health-care settings. One such innovation is being applied with parents of patients attending the hospital attached to the premier Institute of Psychiatry in Mexico City. A contrasting application is a current adaptation of the manual for bilingual, Castilian-speaking, indigenous groups in Mexico.

In England, we are now moving to a stage in which we try to disseminate the model and associated ways of working by targeting primary and specialist health-care service units. The principal aim is now to change ways of working at the organisational level, aiming to alter the whole staff group toward adopting a stress-strain-coping-support model and the five-step and network approaches that go with it. Following the two primary care projects, we shall now focus on two whole primary care practices, aiming to develop them as 'demonstration sites'. Two pilot studies have also been undertaken, in two separate areas of the country, adapting the five-step method of work to specialist addiction treatment settings. Preliminary results suggest that the pattern of change in terms of family members' ways of coping and symptoms is equivalent to that observed in primary care. We aim to follow those pilot studies by working with two specialist treatment organisations as demonstration sites at the specialist level. Plans also include the development of Internet-based materials, based on those already developed, which can be accessed by those giving or receiving help at primary or secondary level, or by those who are not in touch with services.

We are also very aware that the present book has had little to say about children and adolescents who are concerned about and affected by parental excessive substance use. Possible effects on children are high on the list of concerns of adult family members (see Chapter 5), and one of the most important, hoped-for outcomes of effectively empowering adult family members is the strengthening effect that may have on any children living in the family. Alongside the English work described earlier, the English group is part of a new European network of care for children affected by risky environments within the family, including excessive parental substance use (ENCARE), and a further project will develop a tool kit to support a range of alcohol and drug specialist and generic professionals in developing or establishing work with children and families affected by the substance misuse of someone else in the family.

In the Northern Territory, Australia, where excessive drinking has been identified by indigenous people as a problem of such great magnitude (see Chapter 3), the model and methods associated with it have been well received. Their significance has lain particularly in their capacity to challenge current individualistic approaches to substance problems that focus on the substance 'user', ignoring the contribution of the family or pathologising family members. It is also the case that families have often been delighted to know that their concerns and problems were not unique, but are in fact shared with people in two other countries, albeit often presenting in different circumstances. The other very important outcome has been the development of culturally sensitive resources. The workshop process was about taking research findings back to the communities from whence the information had come so that they could be discussed and assessed for relevance and appropriateness. A substantial amount of work was involved in presenting the information (telling the story), much of which was quite new to communities and programme staff, and putting it into a format relevant to indigenous people across the Northern Territory. That involved tailoring workshops to meet the specific needs of each community, attempting to overcome problems of very heterogeneous cultural groups across the territory, as well as the significant barriers created by the distances involved and climatic factors. There has been a definite feeling of greater control being exercised by communities to deal with the disruption and harm that can come from alcohol. In the process, more control has been given back to communities.

What appears to have particularly found favour among family members and practitioners in our three countries, and is referred to often in the manuals and workshops, is the emphasis in the model on which the work is based that family members can, however stressful and intractable their circumstances may appear to be, find positive ways of coping and thereby regain some control over their lives. There is a long way to go before we can be truly confident about that. If such an empowerment goal was achieved, it would be a just and fitting reward for the efforts of family members, researchers and practitioners that have gone in to the production of this book, and some testimony to the sufferings of family members and the relatives about whom they are so concerned.

Notes

Preface

1. The focus of the present work is on *adult* family members. It does not include, therefore, consideration of the experiences of children and adolescents below the age of 16 years, who constitute one of the largest, and arguably the most important, group of family members affected by relatives' (mostly parents in that case) excessive drinking or drug taking. There are a number of reasons for not including children under 16 in the present work. First, there has been a comparatively great amount of research attention given to the children of problem drinking parents (although much less attention to the children of problem drug-using parents) (Velleman and Orford, 1999). Second, understanding the experiences of affected adult family members, such as wives, husbands and partners, may be of great importance in understanding the experiences of children, since adult family members who themselves do not drink or take drugs excessively but are affected by the drinking or drug taking of another adult in the family, may have a crucial role to play in protecting children. Third, and most obviously, the research that forms the core of the present book was confined to interviews with family members aged 16 years or over. Although it can itself, therefore, say little directly about the experiences of children, it does complement the earlier work on the children of problem drinking parents carried out by two of the present authors (Velleman and Orford, 1990, 1993, 1999).

Chapter 1

1. The word 'Aboriginal' has often been used to refer to Australians who were living in Australia prior to European conquest, and to their descendants. The term is not confined to reference to Australians, however, often being used, for example, to refer to indigenous Canadians. Although the term 'Aboriginal' will often be used in the present book, the more generic term 'indigenous' will more generally be used. It will be used to refer to preconquest Australians and their descendants, who form one of the main participant groups in the research to be reported in this book, but it will also be used with reference to other preconquest groups such as indigenous Mexicans.

Chapter 2

1. The term 'drug abuse' is used here because it was the term used in the source to which we are referring, in this case from the USA. The term 'drug misuse' is more

commonly used in some other countries. We have mostly used the terms 'drug problem', 'problem drug use' or 'excessive drug use'.

Chapter 3

1. During the 1990s, the Northern Territory (NT) was the site of a unique health programme, the Living with Alcohol (LWA) Program, directed at reducing alcohol-related harm in the territory. The NT government committed itself to a 10-year programme funded by an extra levy on the sale of any alcoholic beverages containing more than 3% alcohol. It was a multicomponent programme covering additional treatment services, more high-profile prevention and a range of controls, including price increases, lowered legal blood alcohol level for driving, and restrictions on hours of trading for licensed premises (d'Abbs, 2001; Stockwell et al., 2001). Part of the overall work was the Aboriginal LWA programme.
2. The term *colonias populares* is difficult to translate into English, combining as it does the idea of areas that are poor and marginal with the idea of popularity among members of the large lower socio-economic status section of Mexico City's population.
3. Figure provided by Alcoholics Anonymous General Services Coordination in Mexico.
4. Refractyl is the brand name for cyclopentolate, an ophthalmic solution to dilate pupils before eye examination. Flunitrazepam, also known as Rohypnol, is a benzodiazepine used to treat insomnia.
5. In UK terms, a 'unit' of alcohol contains 8 g of absolute alcohol.

Chapter 4

1. The terms 'etic' and 'emic', derived from linguistics, refer, respectively, to comparative, cross-cultural studies, and careful, internal exploration of psychological phenomena within an individual culture. The former needs to use some common procedures in the different cultures, with all the dangers of imposing methods derived in and appropriate for one of the cultures (often referred to as an 'imposed etic'), while the latter would study the culture in its own, local terms. The distinction is similar to that between nomothetic and idiographic procedures in the psychological study of individual people. The distinction between emic and etic research is not so clear-cut in the case of qualitative research. The latter, and particularly the analytic technique of continually comparing aspects of the data both within and across socio-cultural groups, makes it possible simultaneously to examine the experiences within a socio-cultural group in depth (corresponding to the emic approach) while at the same time comparing and contrasting across groups (a form of etic approach).

Chapter 5

1. *Humbug*, as a noun, is said by Arthur (1996, p. 99) to have a wide range of senses in Australian Aboriginal English, including 'nuisance, trouble, difficulty, nonsense, rubbish, dishonesty, flirting, playing up'.

Chapter 8

1. 'Wet canteens' are licensed clubs in remote Aboriginal communities that would otherwise be declared restricted areas under the Northern Territory (NT) Liquor Act. The term is more commonly used in Queensland. In the NT, they are usually known as 'social clubs'.

References

Ablon, J. (1979). Research frontiers for anthropologists in family studies. A case in point: alcoholism and the family, *Human Organisation*, 38: 196–200.

Ablon, J., Ames, G. and Cunningham, W. (1982). To all appearances: the ideal American family. In: E. Kaufman (ed.) *Power to Change: Family Case Studies in the Treatment of Alcoholism*, New York: Gardner Press, pp. 199–235.

Ablon, J. and Cunningham, W. (1981). Implications of cultural patterning for the delivery of alcoholism services: case studies, *Journal of Studies on Alcohol*, Suppl No. 9: 185–206.

Aboriginal Health Council (1994). Reclaiming our stories, reclaiming our lives. Report of the Aboriginal Deaths in Custody Counselling Project.

Acuda, W. (1983). Alcohol and rapid socio-economic change. In: A. Arif and J. Jaffe (eds) *Drug Use and Misuse*, London: Croom Helm, pp. 77–83.

Adams, D.W. and Deveau, E.J. (1987). When a brother or sister is dying of cancer: the vulnerability of the adolescent sibling, *Death Studies*, 11: 279–295.

Adonis, A. and Pollard, S. (1998). *A Class Act: The Myth of Britain's Classless Society*, London: Penguin.

Ahuja, A. (2000). Understanding family coping with alcohol problems in the Sikh community. Unpublished Ph.D. thesis, University of Birmingham.

Ahuja, A., Orford, J. and Copello, A. (2003). Understanding how families cope with alcohol problems in the UK West Midlands Sikh community. *Contemporary Drug Problems*, 30: 839–873.

Alati, R. (1996). *The Role of Alcohol and Drug Rehabilitation and Treatment Amongst Aboriginal People*, Canberra: National Drug Strategy, Commonwealth Department of Human Services and Health.

Alexander, K. (ed.) (1990). *Aboriginal Alcohol Use and Related Problems: Report and Recommendations Prepared by the Expert Working Group for the Royal Commission in Aboriginal Deaths in Custody*, Canberra, Australia: Australian Council on Alcohol and Other Drugs.

Alford, K. (1999). Washed away on a tide of white history, *Guardian Weekly*, 21 March.

Amery, R. and Bourke, C. (1998). Australian languages: our heritage. In: C. Bourke, E. Bourke and B. Edwards (eds) *Aboriginal Australia*, Queensland: University of Queensland Press, pp. 122–146.

Arthur, J.M. (1996). *Aboriginal English: A Cultural Study*, Melbourne: Oxford University Press.

Asher, R.M. (1992). *Women with Alcoholic Husbands: Ambivalence and the Trap of Codependency*, London: University of North Carolina Press.

Australian Bureau of Statistics (2000). *1996 Census of Population and Housing Basic Community Profile: Australia*, Canberra: Commonwealth of Australia.

Bailey, M.B. (1961). Alcoholism and marriage: a review of research and professional literature, *Quarterly Journal of Studies on Alcohol*, 22: 81–97.

Bailey, M.B. (1967). Psychophysiological impairment in wives of alcoholics as related to their husbands' drinking and sobriety. In: R. Fox (ed.) *Alcoholism: Behavioral Research, Therapeutic Approaches*, New York: Springer, pp. 134–144.

Ballard, R.G. (1959). The interrelatedness of alcoholism and marital conflict. Symposium, 1958, 3. The interaction between marital conflict and alcoholism as seen through MMPI's of marriage partners, *American Journal of Orthopsychiatry*, 29: 528–546.

Banister. E.M. and Peavy, R.V. (1994). The erosion of self: an ethnographic study of women's experience of marriage to alcoholic husbands, *Canadian Journal of Counselling*, 28: 206–221.

Banyard, V.L. and Graham-Bermann, S.A. (1993). Can women cope? A gender analysis of theories of coping with stress, *Psychology of Women Quarterly*, 17: 303–318.

Barber, J.G. and Crisp, B.R. (1995). The 'pressures to change' approach to working with the partners of heavy drinkers, *Addiction*, 90: 269–276.

Barber, J.G. and Gilberston, R. (1996). An experimental study of brief unilateral intervention for the partners of heavy drinkers, *Research Social Work Practice*, 6: 325–336.

Barrowclough, C. and Parle, M. (1997). Appraisal, psychological adjustment and expressed emotion in relatives of patients suffering from schizophrenia, *British Journal of Psychiatry*, 171: 26–30.

Bar-Tal, Y. and Spitzer, A. (1993). Coping use versus effectiveness as moderating the stress-strain relationship, *Journal of Community and Applied Social Psychology*, 3: 1–10.

Barton, J.A. (1991). Parental adaptation to adolescent drug abuse: an ethnographic study of role formulation in response to courtesy stigma, *Public Health Nursing*, 8, 39–45.

Beattie, M. (1987). *Co-dependent No More*, New York: Harper/Hazelden.

Bell, D. (1983). *Daughters of the Dreaming*, London: George Allen and Unwin.

Bentelspacher, C.E., Chitran, S. and Rahman, A. (1994). Coping and adaptation patterns among Chinese, Indian, and Malay families caring for a mentally ill relative, *Families in Society, The Journal of Contemporary Human Services*, 5: 287–294.

Bernal, G., Flores-Ortiz, Y., Sorenson, J.L., Miranda, J., Diamond, G. and Bonilla, J. (1997). Intergenerational family therapy with methadone maintenance patients and family members: findings of a clinical outcome study. Manuscript submitted for publication (cited by Stanton and Shadish, 1997).

Berridge, V. (1979). Morality and medical science: concepts of narcotic addiction in Britain, 1820–1926, *Annals of Science*, 36: 67–85.

Berry, J.W., Poortinga, Y.H., Segall, M.H. and Dasen, P.R. (1992). *Cross-Cultural Psychology: Research and Applications*, New York: Cambridge University Press.

Bevia, F.J.O. (1976). La familia de la mujer alcoholica, *Actas Luso-Espanolas de Neurologia y Psiquiatría y Ciencias Afines*, 4: 227–238.

Bigatti, S.M. and Cronan, T.A. (2002). An examination of the physical health, health care use, and psychological well-being of spouses of people with fibromyalgia syndrome, *Health Psychology*, 21: 157–166.

Billings, D.W., Folkman, S., Acree, M. and Moskowitz, J.T. (2000). Coping and physical health during caregiving: the roles of positive and negative affect, *Journal of Personality and Social Psychology*, 79: 131–142.

Birchwood, M. and Smith, J. (1987). Schizophrenia and the family. In: J. Orford (ed.) *Coping with Disorder in the Family*, London: Croom Helm, pp. 7–38.

Blake, B.J. (1991). *Australian Aboriginal Languages: A General Introduction* (2nd edition), St Lucia, Brisbane: University of Queensland Press (first published 1981).

Blank, M. (1987). Hannah's family, *Nursing Times*, 83: 6–62.

Bolger, N. (1991). *Aboriginal Women and Violence: A Report for the Criminology Research Council and the Northern Territory Commissioner of Police*. Darwin: Australian National University, North Australian Research Unit.

Bolger, N. (1990). Coping as a personality process: a prospective study, *Journal of Personality and Social Psychology*, 59: 525–537.

Bourke, E. (1998). Australia's first peoples: identity and population. In: C. Bourke, E. Bourke and B. Edwards (eds) *Aboriginal Australia*, Queensland: University of Queensland Press, pp. 38–55.

Bourke, C. and Cox, H. (1998). Two laws: one land. In: C. Bourke, E. Bourke and B. Edwards (eds) *Aboriginal Australia*, Queensland: University of Queensland Press, pp. 56–76.

Bourke, C. and Edwards, B. (1998). Family and kinship. In: C. Bourke, E. Bourke and B. Edwards (eds) *Aboriginal Australia*, Queensland: University of Queensland Press, pp. 100–121.

Brady, M. (1988). *Where the Beer Truck Stopped: Drinking in a Northern Australian Town*, Darwin: Australian National University, North Australia Research Unit.

Brady, M. (1992). *Heavy Metal: The Social Meaning of Petrol Sniffing in Australia*, Canberra: Aboriginal Studies Press.

Brady, M. (1994). Petrol sniffing among Aborigines: differing social meanings, *International Journal on Drug Policy*, 2: 28–31.

Brady, M. and Palmer, K. (1984). *Alcohol in the Outback: Two Studies of Drinking*, Darwin: Monograph of the Australian National University, North Australia Research Unit.

Brennan, P.L. Moos, R.H. and Kelly, K.M. (1994). Spouses of late-life problem drinkers: functioning, coping responses, and family contexts, *Journal of Family Psychology*, 8: 447–457.

Brown, G. and Moran, P. (1997). Single mothers, poverty and depression, *Psychological Medicine*, 27: 21–33.

Brown, G. and Prudo, R. (1981). Psychiatric disorder in a rural and an urban population. I. Etiology of depression, *Psychological Medicine*, 11: 581–599.

Brown, T.G., Wek, A., Caplan, T. and Seraganian, P. (1999). Violent substance abusers in domestic violence treatment, *Violence and Victims*, 14: 179–190.

Bullock, S.C. and Mudd, E.H. (1959). The inter-relatedness of alcoholism and marital conflict. Symposium, 1958, 2. The interaction of alcoholic husbands and their non-alcoholic wives during counselling, *American Journal of Orthopsychiatry*, 29: 519–527.

Burden, J. (1998). Health: an holistic approach. In: C. Bourke, E. Bourke and B. Edwards (eds) *Aboriginal Australia*, Queensland: University of Queensland Press, pp. 189–218.

Burnett, M.M. (1984). Toward a model for counselling the wives of alcoholics: a feminist approach, *Alcoholism Treatment Quarterly*, 1: 51–60.

Cadogan, D.A. (1973). Marital group therapy in the treatment of alcoholism, *Quarterly Journal of Studies on Alcohol*, 34: 1187–1194.

Casey, J.C., Griffin, M.L. and Googins, B.K. (1993). The role of work for wives of alcoholics, *American Journal of Drug and Alcohol Abuse*, 19: 119–131.

Castro, R., Orozco, E., Aggleton, P., Eroza, E. and Herenandez, J.J. (1998). Family responses to HIV/AIDS in Mexico, *Social Science and Medicine*, 47: 1473–1484.

Champion, T., Wong, C., Rooke, A., Dorling, D., Crombes, M. and Brunsdon, C. (1996). *The Population of Britain in the 1990s*, New York: Oxford University Press.

Clark, D.B., Neighbors, B.D., Lesnick, L.A., Lynch, K.G. and Donovan, J.E. (1998). Family functioning and adolescent alcohol use disorders, *Journal of Family Psychology*, 12: 81–92.

Cobb, S. (1976). Social support as a moderator of life stress, *Psychosomatic Medicine*, 38: 300–314.

Cohen, P.C. and Krause, M.D. (1971). *Casework with the Wives of Alcoholics*, New York: Family Service Association of America.

Cohen, S. and Wills, S. (1985). Stress, social support and the buffering hypothesis, *Psychological Bulletin*, 98: 310–357.

Consultores Internacionales (1999). Prospectiva del mercado Mexicano de bebidas alcohólicas destiladas al año 2025. Informe preparado para la Fundación de Investigaciones Sociales A.C. México.

Cook, T. and Campbell, D. (1979). *Quasi-Experimentation: Design and Analysis Issues for Field Settings*, Chicago: Rand McNally.

Cook, B., Cook, E. and San Roque, C. (1994). *Story about Intjartnama, a Healing Place: An Account of Work in Progress at Intjartnama Outstation, Ntaria-Hermannsburg, Alice Springs*, Canberra: National Drug Strategy, Commonwealth Department of Human Services and Health.

Copello, A. (2002). Responding to addiction in the family: natural and assisted change in coping behaviour. Unpublished Ph.D. thesis, University of Birmingham.

Copello, A. and Orford, J. (2002). Addiction and the family: is it time for services to take notice of the evidence? *Addiction*, 97: 1361–1363.

Copello, A., Orford, J., Hodgson, R., Tober, G. and Barrett, C. on behalf of the UKATT Research Team (2002). Social Behaviour and Network Therapy: basic principles and early experiences, *Addictive Behaviors*, 27: 345–366.

Copello, A., Orford, J., Velleman, R., Templeton, L. and Krishnan, M. (2000a). Methods for reducing alcohol and drug related harm in non-specialist settings, *Journal of Mental Health*, 9: 319–343.

Copello, A., Templeton, L., Krishnan, M., Orford, J. and Velleman, R. (2000b). A treatment package to improve primary care services for relatives of people with alcohol and drug problems, *Addiction Research*, 8: 471–484.

Copello, A., Templeton, L., Patel, A., Velleman, R., Orford, J. and Moore, L. (2005). The relative efficacy of two primary care brief interventions for family members affected by the addiction problems of a close relative: a randomised trial (submitted).

Corbett, K., Mora, J. and Ames, G. (1991). Drinking patterns and drinking-related problems of Mexican-American husbands and wives, *Journal of Studies on Alcohol*, 52: 215–223.

Corder, B.F., Corder, R.F. and Laidlaw, N.D. (1972). An intensive treatment program for alcoholics and their wives, *Quarterly Journal of Studies on Alcohol*, 33: 1144–1146.

Corrigan, E.M. (1980). *Alcoholic Women in Treatment*, Oxford: Oxford University Press.

Crisp, B.R. and Barber, J.G. (1995). The drinker's partner distress scale: an instrument for measuring the distress caused by drinkers to their partners, *International Journal of the Addictions*, 30: 1009–1017.

Crundall, I. (1995). The NT Living with Alcohol Program: climbing through a window of opportunity. In: *Dealing with Drugs: Ethics, Economics and Efficiency*, Queensland: Alcohol and Drug Foundation, pp. 98–105.

Curry, R.L. (1993). Beverage alcohol as a constraint to development in the Third World, *International Journal of the Addictions*, 28: 1227–1242.

Cutland, L. (1998). A codependency perspective. In: R. Velleman, A. Copello and J. Maslin (eds) *Living with Drink: Women Who Live with Problem Drinkers*, London: Longman, pp. 89–98.

D'Abbs, P. (1990). *Responding to Aboriginal Substance Misuse: A Review of Programs Conducted by the Council for Aboriginal Alcohol Program Services (CAAPS), Northern Territory*, Darwin, Northern Territory: Northern Territory Government, Department of Health and Community Services.

D'Abbs, P. (2001). Living with alcohol: learning from the Northern Territory experience, *Drug and Alcohol Review*, 20: 253–255.

D'Abbs, P., Hunter, E., Reser, J. and Martin, D. (1994). *Alcohol-Related Violence in Aboriginal and Torres Strait Islander Communities: A Literature Review*. Report 8 in a series of reports prepared for the National Symposium on Alcohol Misuse and Violence. Canberra: Australian Government Publishing Service.

Davis, T.S. and Hagood, L. (1979). In-home support for recovering alcoholic mothers and their families: the Family Rehabilitation Coordination Project, *Journal of Studies on Alcohol*, 40: 313–317.

De la Cancela, V. (1991). Working affirmatively with Puerto Rican men: professional and personal reflections. In: M. Bograd (ed.) *Feminist Approaches for Men in Family Therapy*, New York: Hawthorn Press, pp. 195–211.

De Silva, P. (1983). The Buddhist attitude to alcoholism. In: G. Edwards, A. Arif and J. Jaffe (eds) *Drug Use and Misuse*, London: Croom Helm, 33–41.

Dewe, P.J. and Guest, D.E. (1990). Methods of coping with stress at work: a conceptual analysis and empirical study of measurement issues, *Journal of Organizational Behavior*, 11: 135–150.

Díaz Guerrero, R. (1994). Psicología del Mexicano. Descubrimiento de la etnopsicología, 6th edition, México: Ed. Trillas.

Ditton, J. and Hammersley, R. (1996). *A Very Greedy Drug: Cocaine in Context*, Reading, UK: Harwood Academic Press.

Dittrich, J. (1993). Group programs for wives of alcoholics. In: T.J. O'Farrell (ed.) *Treating Alcohol Problems: Marital and Family Interventions*, New York: Guilford Press, pp. 78–114.

Dittrich, J. and Trapold, M.A. (1984). A treatment program for wives of alcoholics: an evaluation, *Bulletin of the Society of Psychologists in Addictive Behaviors*, 3: 91–102.

Djerrkura, G. (1999). ATSIC: achievements and prospects, *Canberra Bulletin of Public Administration*, 94: 24–27.

Dobash, R.E. and Dobash, R.P. (1987). Violence towards wives. In: J. Orford (ed.) *Coping with Disorder in the Family*, London: Croom Helm, pp. 169–193.

Dorn, N., Ribbens, J. and South, N. (1987). *Coping with a Nightmare: Family Feelings About Long-term Drug Use*, London: Institute for the Study of Drug Dependence.

Dorschner, J. (1983). Rajput alcohol use in India, *Journal of Studies on Alcohol*, 44: 538–544.

Drewery, J. and Rae, J.B. (1969). A group comparison of alcoholic and non-alcoholic marriages using the interpersonal perception technique, *British Journal of Psychiatry*, 115: 287–300.

Eber, C. (1995). *Women and Alcohol in a Highland Maya Town: Water of Hope, Water of Sorrow*, Austin, TX: University of Texas Press.

Eber, C. (2001). 'Take my water': liberation through prohibition in San Pedro Chenalho, Chiapas, Mexico, *Social Science and Medicine*, 53: 251–262.

Edelmann, R.J., Connolly, K.J. and Bartlett, H. (1994). Coping strategies and psychological adjustment of couples presenting for IVF, *Journal of Psychosomatic Research*, 38: 355–364.

Edwards, B. (1998). Living the dreaming. In: C. Bourke, E. Bourke and B. Edwards (eds) *Aboriginal Australia*, Queensland: University of Queensland Press, pp. 77–99.

Egginton, R. and Parker, H. (2002). From one-off triers to regular users: measuring the regularity of drug taking in a cohort of English adolescents (1996–1999), *Addiction Research and Theory*, 10: 97–114.

Eiser, C. (1987). Chronic disease in childhood. In: J. Orford (ed.) *Coping with Disorder in the Family*, London: Croom Helm, pp. 217–237.

ENA (Encuesta Nacional de Adicciones) (1998). Tercera Encuesta, 1999. Secretaría de Salud, Instituto Mexicano de Psiquiatría, Dirección General de Epidemiología: México.

Endler, N.S. and Parker, J.D.A. (1990). Multidimensional assessment of coping: a critical evaluation, *Journal of Personality and Social Psychology*, 58: 844–854.

Enriquez, V.G. (1993). Developing a Filipino psychology. In: U. Kim and J. W. Berry (eds) *Indigenous Psychologies: Research and Experience in Cultural Context*, Newbury Park, CA: Sage, pp. 152–169.

Estes, N.J. and Baker, J.M. (1982). Spouses of alcoholic women. In: N.J. Estes and M.E. Heinemann (eds) *Alcoholism: Development, Consequences and Interventions*, St Louis, MD: Mosby, pp. 231–238.

Ewing, J.A., Long, V. and Wenzel, G.G. (1961). Concurrent group psychotherapy of alcoholic patients and their wives, *International Journal of Group Psychotherapy*, 11: 329–338.

Fals-Stewart, W., Birchler, G.R. and O'Farrell, T.J. (1996). Behavioral couples therapy for male substance-abusing patients: effects on relationship adjustment and drug-using behavior, *Journal of Consulting and Clinical Psychology*, 64, 959–972.

Fals-Stewart, W., Birchler, G.R. and O'Farrell, T.J. (1999). Drug-abusing patients and their intimate partners: dyadic adjustment, relationship stability and substance use, *Journal of Abnormal Psychology*, 108: 11–23.

Fang, C.Y. and Manne, S.L. (2001). Functional impairment, marital quality, and patient psychological distress as predictors of psychological distress among cancer patients' spouses, *Health Psychology*, 20: 452–457.

Figueroa-Rosales, R. (1971). Alcoholism and its relation to aspects of social and community development, *Revista Medicana de Psicología*, 6: 244–250.

Fischbach, R.L. and Herbert, B. (1997). Domestic violence and mental health: correlates and conundrums within and across cultures, *Social Science and Medicine*, 45: 1161–1176.

Fleming, J., Watson, C., McDonald, D. and Alexander, K. (1991). Drug use patterns in Northern Territory Aboriginal communities, *Drug and Alcohol Review*, 10: 367–380.

Folkman, S. (1997). Positive psychological states and coping with severe stress, *Social Science and Medicine*, 45: 1207–1221.

Folkman, S., Chesney, M.A., Cooke, M., Boccellari, A. and Collette, L. (1994). Caregiver burden in HIV-positive and HIV-negative partners of men with AIDS, *Journal of Consulting and Clinical Psychology*, 62: 746–756.

Folkman, S., Lazarus, R.S., Schetter, C., DeLongis, A. and Gruen, R.J. (1986). Dynamics of a stressful encounter: cognitive appraisal, coping, and encounter outcomes, *Journal of Personality and Social Psychology*, 50: 992–1003.

Folkman, S. and Lazarus, R.S. (1988). Coping as a mediator of emotion, *Journal of Personality and Social Psychology*, 54: 466–475.

Foulkes, E.F. (1987). Social stratification and alcohol use in north Alaska, *Journal of Community Psychology*, 15: 349–356.

Frischer, M., Hickman, M., Kraus, L., Mariani, F. and Wiessing, L. (2001). A comparison of different methods for estimating the prevalence of problematic drug issue in Great Britain, *Addiction*, 96: 1465–1476.

Fryer, D. (1998). A community psychological perspective. In: R. Velleman, A. Copello and J. Maslin (eds) *Living with Drink: Women Who Live with Problem Drinkers*, London: Longman, pp. 162–180.

Fuentes, C. (2000). Prólogo en El Alma de México. Compilador Héctor Tajonar. Coedición. Grupo Océano. Fondo de Cultura de México, CCONACULTA, Televisa, UNAM. Editado en España.

Fundación Mexicana para la Salud (FUNSALUD) (1994). Economía y Salud. Propuestas para el avance del sistema de salud en México. Visión de Conjunto.

Futterman, S. (1953). Personality trends in wives of alcoholics, *Journal of Psychiatry and Social Work*, 23: 37–41.

Gacic, B. (1978). General system theory and alcoholism, *Psihijatrija Danas*, 10: 309–316 (Abst. No. 79156443 *Excerpta Medicine*).

Gacic, B., Sedmak, T., Ivanovic, M., Gardinovacki, I. and Gacic, R. (1980). Familial treatment of alcoholism as a modality of psychiatry in the community, *Toxicomanies*, 13: 217–224 (Abst. No. 1169418 Social Science Research).

Galanter, M. (1993). Network therapy for substance abuse: a clinical trial, *Psychotherapy*, 30: 251–258.

Galanter, M. (1999). *Network Therapy for Alcohol and Drug Abuse* (Expanded edition), New York: Guilford Press.

Galanter, M., Dermatis, H., Glickman, L., Maslansky, R., Brealyn Sellers, M.,

Neumann, E. and Rahman-Dujarric, C. (2004). Network therapy: decreased secondary opioid use during buprenorphine maintenance, *Journal of Substance Abuse Treatment*, 26: 313–318.

Gallagher, T.J., Wagenfeld, M.O., Baro, F. and Haepers, K. (1994). Sense of coherence, coping and caregiver role overload, *Social Science and Medicine*, 39: 1615–1622.

García Canclini, N. (1996). Culturas híbridas. Estrategias para entrar y salir de la modernidad. Ed. Grijalbo, Consejo Nacional para la Cultura y las Artes.

Garrett, J., Landau, J., Shea, R., Stanton, D., Baciewicz, G. and Brinkman-Sull, D. (1998). The ARISE intervention: using family and network links to engage addicted persons in treatment, *Journal of Substance Abuse Treatment*, 15: 333–343.

Garrett, J., Stanton, D., Landau, J., Baciewicz, G., Brinkman-Sull, D. and Shea, R. (1999). The 'concerned other' call: using family links and networks to overcome resistance to addiction treatment, *Substance Use and Misuse*, 34: 363–382.

Gil, E.F. and Bob, S. (1999). Culturally competent research: an ethical perspective, *Clinical Psychology Review*, 19: 45–55.

Gilhooly, M.L.M. (1987). Senile dementia and the family. In: J. Orford (ed.) *Coping with Disorder in the Family*. London: Croom Helm, pp. 138–168.

Glaser, B.G. (1992). *Emergence vs Forcing: Basics of Grounded Theory Analysis*, Mill Valley, CA: Sociology Press.

Glaser, B.G. and Strauss, A.L. (1967). *The Discovery of Grounded Theory: Strategies for Qualitative Research*, New York: Aldine.

Glatt, M.M. (1973). Jewish alcoholics and addicts in the London area, *Toxicomanies*, 6: 33–39.

Godley, M.D. and Velasquez, R. (1998). Effectiveness of the Logan Square Prevention Project: interim results, *Drugs and Society*, 12: 87–103.

Goldfried, M. and D'Zurilla, T. (1969). A behaviour-analytic model for assessing competence. In: C. Spielberger (ed.) *Current Topics in Clinical and Community Psychology*, New York: Academic Press, pp. 151–196.

Goodwin, R. (1999). *Personal Relationships Across Cultures*, London: Routledge.

Gorman, J.M. and Rooney, J.F. (1979). The influence of Al-Anon on the coping behaviour of wives of alcoholics, *Journal of Studies on Alcohol*, 40: 1030–1038.

Gorski, T. and Miller, M. (1984). The family's involvement, *Focus on the Family and Chemical Dependency*, 7: 3–14 (cited by Harper and Capdevilla, 1990).

Gossop, M. (1993). Volatile substances and the law, *Addiction*, 88: 311–313.

Gostin, O. and Chong, A. (1998). Living wisdom: Aborigines and the environment. In: C. Bourke, E. Bourke and B. Edwards (eds) *Aboriginal Australia*, Queensland: University of Queensland Press, pp. 147–167.

Gracey, M. (1998). Substance misuse in Aboriginal Australians, *Addiction Biology*, 3: 29–46.

Grant, B.F. (2000). Estimates of U.S. children exposed to alcohol abuse and dependence in the family, *American Journal of Public Health*, 90: 112–115.

Grant, M. (1992). International perspectives on alcoholism and the family: an overview of WHO activities. In: S. Saitoh, P. Steinglass and M.A. Schuckit (eds) *Alcoholism and the Family: The 4th International Symposium of the Psychiatric Research Institute of Tokyo*, Tokyo: Seiwa Shoten/New York: Brunner-Mazel, pp. 97–116.

Greenaway, J.R. (1998). The 'improved' public house, 1870–1950: the key to civilised drinking or the primrose path to drunkenness?, *Addiction*, 93: 173–181.

Grisso, J.A., Schwarz, D.F., Hirschinger, N., Sammel, M., Brensinger, C., Santanna,

J., Lowe, R.A., Anderson, E., Shaw, L.M., Bethel, C.A. and Teeple, L. (1999). Violent injuries among women in an urban area, *New England Journal of Medicine*, 341: 1899–1905.

Groome, H. (1998). Education: the search for relevance. In: C. Bourke, E. Bourke and B. Edwards (eds) *Aboriginal Australia*, Queensland: University of Queensland Press, pp. 168–188.

Haberman, P.W. (1964). Psychological test score changes for wives of alcoholics during periods of drinking and sobriety, *Journal of Clinical Psychology*, 20: 230–232.

Hagaman, B.L. (1980). Food for thought: beer in a social and ritual context in a West African society, *Journal of Drug Issues*, 10: 203–214.

Halford, W., Price, J., Kelly, A., Bouma, R. and Young, R. (2001). Helping the female partners of men abusing alcohol: a comparison of three treatments, *Addiction*, 96: 1497–1508.

Halford, W.K. and Osgarby, S.M. (1993). Alcohol abuse in clients presenting with marital problems, *Journal of Family Psychology*, 6: 245–254.

Hall, W., Hunter, E. and Spargo, R. (1993). Alcohol-related problems among Aboriginal drinkers in the Kimberley region of Western Australia, *Addiction*, 88: 1091–1100.

Harding, R.W., Broadhurst, R., Ferrante, A. and Loh, N. (1995). *Aboriginal Contact with the Criminal Justice System and the Impact of the Royal Commission into Aboriginal Deaths in Custody*, Annandale, New South Wales: Hawkins Press (cited by Saggers and Gray, 1998).

Harper, J. and Capdevila, C. (1990). Codependency: a critique, *Journal of Psychoactive Drugs*, 3: 285–292.

Harris, J. (1993). Losing and gaining a language: the story of Kriol in the Northern Territory. In: M. Walsh and C. Yallop (eds) *Language and Culture in Aboriginal Australia*, Canberra: Aboriginal Studies Press, pp. 145–154.

Harris, J. (1994). *Private Lives, Public Spirit: Britain 1870–1914*, London: Penguin.

Harwin, J. (1982). The excessive drinker and the family: approaches to treatment. In: J. Orford and J. Harwin (eds) *Alcohol and the Family*, London: Croom-Helm, pp. 201–240.

Hazlehurst, K.M. (1994). *A Healing Place: Indigenous Visions for Personal Empowerment and Community Recovery*, Rockhampton, Queensland: Central Queensland University Press.

Heath, D.B. (1987). Anthropology and alcohol studies: current issues, *Annual Review of Anthropology*, 16: 99–120.

Hedberg, A.G. and Campbell, L. (1974). A comparison of four behavioural treatments of alcoholism, *Journal of Behaviour Therapy and Experimental Psychiatry*, 5: 251–256.

Hedlund, H. and Lundahl, M. (1984). The economic role of beer in rural Zambia, *Human Organisation*, 32: 61–65.

Hemmer, C. (1979). The problem of alcoholism from the viewpoint of a communication theory approach, *Soziologenkorrespondenz*, 6: 71–91.

Henwood, K. and Pidgeon, N. (1994). Beyond the qualitative paradigm: a framework for introducing diversity within qualitative psychology, *Journal of Community and Applied Social Psychology*, 4: 225–238.

Herbert, M. (1995). A collaborative model of training for parents of children with disruptive behaviour disorders, *British Journal of Clinical Psychology*, 34: 325–342.

Hobfoll, S.E., Dunahoo, C.L., Ben-Porath, Y. and Monnier, J. (1994). Gender and coping: the dual-axis model of coping, *American Journal of Community Psychology*, 22: 49–82.

Hoffman, K.L., Demo, D.H. and Edwards, J.N. (1994). Physical wife abuse in a non-western society: an integrated theoretical approach, *Journal of Marriage and the Family*, 56: 131–146.

Hofstede, G.H. (1994). *Uncommon Sense About Organizations: Cases, Studies and Field Observations*. Thousand Oaks, CA: Sage.

Holahan, C.J. and Moos, R.H. (1990). Life stressors, resistance factors, and improved psychological functioning: an extension of the stress resistance paradigm, *Journal of Personality and Social Psychology*, 58: 909–917.

Holahan, C.J., Moos, R.H., Holahan, C.K. and Brennan, P.L. (1997). Social context, coping strategies, and depressive symptoms: an expanded model with cardiac patients, *Journal of Personality and Social Psychology*, 72: 918–928.

Holmes, T.H. and Rahe, R.H. (1967). The social readjustment rating scale, *Journal of Psychosomatic Research*, 11: 213–218.

Holmes, W., Stewart, P., Garrow, A., Anderson, I. and Thorpe, L. (2002). Researching Aboriginal health: experience from a study of urban young people's health and well-being, *Social Science and Medicine*, 54: 1267–1279.

Holmila, M. (1988). *Wives, Husbands and Alcohol: A Study of Informal Drinking Control Within the Family*, Finnish Foundation for Alcohol Studies, Vol. 36.

Holmila, M. (1997). Family roles and being a problem drinker's intimate other, *European Addiction Research*, 3: 37–42.

Howells, E. (1996). Coping with a problem drinker: the development and evaluation of a therapeutic intervention for the partners of problem drinkers, in their own right. Unpublished Ph.D. thesis, University of Birmingham, UK.

Howells, E. and Orford, J. (2005). Coping with a problem drinker: a therapeutic intervention for the partners of problem drinkers, in their own right, *Journal of Substance Use* (in press).

Humphreys, K. (2004). *Circles of Recovery: Self-Help Organizations for Addictions*, Cambridge: Cambridge University Press.

Hunt, G.M. and Azrin, N.H. (1973). A community-reinforcement approach to alcoholism, *Behaviour Research and Therapy*, 11: 91–104.

Hunt, G. and Satterlee, S. (1985). The pub, the village and the people, *New Directions in the Study of Alcohol Group Journal*, 8: 18–54.

Hunter, E.M. (1991). The intercultural and socio-historical context of Aboriginal personal violence in remote Australia, *Australian Psychologist*, 26: 89–98.

Hunter, E.M. (1993). *Aboriginal Health and History: Power and Prejudice in Remote Australia*. Cambridge: Cambridge University Press.

Huws, J.C., Jones, R.S.P. and Ingledew, D.K. (2001). Parents of children with autism using an email group: a grounded theory study, *Journal of Health Psychology*, 6: 569–584.

Igersheimer, W.W. (1959). Group psychotherapy for non-alcoholic wives of alcoholics, *Quarterly Journal of Studies on Alcohol*, 20: 77–85.

Instituto Nacional de Estadística, Geografía e Informática (INEGI) (1996). Estados

Unidos Mexicanos. Conteo de Población y Vivienda 1995. Resultados definitivos. Tabulados básicos. INEGI, México.

Instituto Nacional de Estadística, Geografía e Informática (INEGI) (2002). Estados Unidos Mexicanos. Perfil Sociodemográfico. XII Censo General de Población y Vivienda 2000. INEGI, México.

Jackson, J.K. (1954). The adjustment of the family to the crisis of alcoholism, *Quarterly Journal of Studies on Alcohol*, 15: 562–586.

Jacob, T. and Leonard, K.E. (1988). Alcoholic-spouse interaction as a function of alcoholism subtype and alcohol consumption interaction, *Journal of Abnormal Psychology*, 97: 231–237.

Jacob, T., Leonard, K. and Haber, J.R. (2001). Family interactions of alcoholics related to alcoholism type and drinking condition, *Alcoholism: Clinical and Experimental Research*, 25: 835–843.

Jacob, T. and Seilhamer, R. (1987). Alcoholism and family interaction. In: T. Jacob (ed.) *Family Interaction and Psychopathology: Theories, Methods and Findings*, New York: Plenum Press, pp. 535–580.

Jilek, W.G. (1981). Anomic depression, alcoholism and a culture-congenial Indian response, *Journal of Studies on Alcohol*, 42 (Suppl 9): 159–170.

Johnson, V.E. (1986). *Intervention: How to Help Those Who Don't Want Help*, Minneapolis, MN: Author.

Jurich, A.P., Polson, C.J., Jurich, J.A. and Bates, R.A. (1985). Family factors in the lives of drug users and abusers, *Adolescence*, 77: 143–159.

Kahn, M.W., Hunter, E., Heather, N. and Tebbutt, J. (1990). Australian Aborigines and alcohol: a review, *Drug and Alcohol Review*, 10: 351–366.

Kaufman, E. (1981). Family structure of narcotic addicts, *International Journal of the Addictions*, 16: 273–282.

Keen, I. (ed.) (1991). *Being Black: Aboriginal Cultures in Settled Australia*, Canberra: Aboriginal Studies Press.

Kelley, M.L. and Fals-Stewart, W. (2002). Couples- versus individual-based therapy for alcohol and drug abuse: effects on children's psychosocial functioning, *Journal of Consulting and Clinical Psychology*, 70, 417–427.

Kellner, R. and Sheffield, B.F. (1973). A self-rating scale of distress, *Psychological Medicine*, 3: 88–100.

Kim, U., Park, Y. and Park. D. (2000). The challenge of cross-cultural psychology: the role of the indigenous psychologies, *Journal of Cross-Cultural Psychology*, 31: 63–75.

Kim, U., Triandis, H.C., Kagitcibasi, C., Choi, S. and Yoon, G. (1994). Introduction. In: U. Kim, H.C. Triandis, C. Kagitcibasi, S. Choi and G. Yoon (eds) *Individualism and Collectivism*, London: Sage, pp. 1–16.

Klee, H.H. (1992). A new target for behaviour research – amphetamine misuse, *British Journal of Addiction*, 87: 439–446.

Kokin, M. and Walker, I. (1989). *Women Married to Alcoholics: Help and Hope for Nonalcoholic Partners*, New York: William Morrow.

Kooyman, M. (1993). *The Therapeutic Community for Addicts*, Amsterdam: Swets and Zeitlinger.

Korkia, P. and Stimson, G.V. (1993). *Anabolic Steroid use in Great Britain: An Exploratory Investigation*, Centre for Research on Drugs and Health Behaviour, Imperial College of Medicine, London.

Kozakiewicz, M. (1982). The rural woman and social change, *Wies Wspolczesna*, 26: 73–82 (Abst. No. 1711105 CAB Absts).

Krestan, J. and Bepko, C. (1991). Codependency: the social reconstruction of female experience. In: C. Bepko (ed.) *Feminism and Addiction*, New York: Haworth, pp. 49–66.

Kuipers, L. (1987). Depression and the family. In: J. Orford (ed.) *Coping with Disorder in the Family*, London: Croom Helm, pp. 194–216.

Kupst, M.J. and Schulman, J.L. (1988). Long-term coping with pediatric leukaemia: a six-year follow-up study, *Journal of Pediatric Psychology*, 13: 7–22.

Langton, M. (1992). Too much sorry business, *Aboriginal and Islander Health Worker Journal*, March/April 10–23 (cited by Saggers and Gray, 1998).

Lara, C.A. and Salgado, S.N. (1994). Mujer, pobreza y salud mental. En: Las Mujeres en la Pobreza. Grupo Interdisciplinario sobre Mujer, Trabajo y Pobreza (GIMTP). El Colegio De México.

Lazarus, R.S. (1993). Coping theory and research: past, present, and future, *Psychosomatic Medicine*, 55: 234–247.

Lazarus, R. and Folkman, S. (1984). *Stress, Appraisal and Coping*, New York: Springer.

Lazic, N. (1977). A systematic approach to solving the problem of an 'unending struggle' between marital partners, *Psihijatrija Danas*, 9: 449–457.

Lemert, E.M. (1960). The occurrence and sequence of events in the adjustment of families to alcoholism, *Quarterly Journal of Studies on Alcohol*, 21: 679–697.

Leñero, L. (1992). Los varones ante sí mismos: una interpretación de la perspectiva de género masculino aplicada a la reproducción familiar. En L. Leñero, *De Carne y Hueso: Estudios Sociales sobre Género y Reproducción*. IMES.

Leonard, K.E. and Roberts, L.J. (1998). Marital aggression, quality, and stability in the first year of marriage: findings from the Buffalo Newlywed Study. In: T.N. Bradbury (ed.) New York: Cambridge University Press, pp. 44–73.

Levav, I. (1998). Individuals under conditions of maximum adversity: the Holocaust. In: B.P. Dohrenwend (ed.) *Adversity, Stress, and Psychopathology*, Oxford: Oxford University Press, 13–33.

Lewis, F.M., Hammond, M.A. and Woods, N.F. (1993). The family's functioning with newly diagnosed breast cancer in the mother: the development of an explanatory model, *Journal of Behavioural Medicine*, 16: 351–370 (cited by Schreurs and de Ridder, 1997).

Lewis, O. (1961). *The Children of Sánchez: Autobiography of a Mexican Family*, London: Secker and Warburg.

Liem, R. and Liem, J.H. (1988). Psychological effects of unemployment on workers and their families, *Journal of Social Issues*, 44: 87–105.

Liepman, M. (1993). Using family influence to motivate resistant alcoholics to enter treatment: the Johnson Institute approach. In: T.J. O'Farrell (ed.) *Treating Alcohol Problems: Marital and Family Interventions*, New York: Guilford Press, pp. 54–77.

Lisansky Gomberg, E.S. (1989). On terms used and abused: the concept of 'codependency', *Drugs and Society*, 113–132.

Lonner, W.J. (1980). The search for psychological universals. In: H.C. Triandis and W.W. Lambert (eds) *Handbook of Cross-Cultural Psychology: Perspectives*, Vol 1, Boston, MA: Allyn and Bacon, pp. 143–204.

MacAndrew, C. and Edgerton, R. (1970). *Drunken Comportment: A Social Explanation*, London: Nelson.

McColl, M.A., Lei, H. and Skinner, H. (1995). Structural relationships between social support and coping, *Social Science and Medicine*, 41: 395–407.

McCorquodale, J. (1987). *Aborigines and the Law: A Digest*, Canberra: Australian Studies Press (cited by Bourke, 1998).

McCrae, R.R. and Costa, P.T. (1986). Personality, coping, and coping effectiveness in an adult sample, *Journal of Personality*, 54: 386–405.

McDermott, P. (1993). Ecstasy and the rave scene: new drug, new sub-culture, old problems? Executive Summary, the Centre for Research on Drugs and Health Behaviour, 25 May.

Macdonald, D.E. (1956). Mental disorders in wives of alcoholics, *Quarterly Journal of Studies on Alcohol*, 17: 282–287.

Macdonald, D.E. (1958). Group psychotherapy with wives of alcoholics, *Quarterly Journal of Studies on Alcohol*, 19: 125–132.

McGillicuddy, N.B., Rychtarik, R.G., Duquette, J.A. and Morsheimer, E.T. (2001). Development of a skill training program for parents of substance-abusing adolescents, *Journal of Substance Abuse Treatment*, 20: 59–68.

MacKintosh, A.M., Stead, M., Eadie, D. and Hastings, G. (2001). *NE Choices: The Results of a Multi-Component Drug Prevention Programme for Adolescents*. DPAS paper 14. London: Home Office/Drugs Prevention Advisory Service.

McLellan, A., Arndt, I., Metzger, D., Woody, G. and O'Brien, C. (1993). The effects of psychosocial services in substance abuse treatment, *Journal of the American Medical Association*, 269: 1953–1959 (cited by Stanton and Shadish, 1977).

Magliano, L., Fadden, G., Economou, M., Xavier, M., Held, T., Guarneri, M., Marasco, C., Tosini, P. and Maj, M. (1998). Social and clinical factors influencing the choice of coping strategies in relatives of patients with schizophrenia: results of the Biomed 1 Study, *Social Psychiatry and Epidemiology*, 33: 413–419.

Mass Observation (1943). *The Pub and the People: a Worktown Study*, London: Victor Gollancz.

Mayo, Y. (1993). The utilization of mental health services, acculturation and machismo among Puerto Rican men. Unpublished doctoral dissertation, School of Social Work, Adelphi University, Garden City, New York. Cited in B. Torres (ed.) (1998) Masculinity and gender roles among Puerto Rican men: Machismo on the US mainland, *American Journal of Orthopsychiatry*, 68: 16–26.

Measham, F., Aldrige, J. and Parker, H. (2000). *Dancing on Drugs: Risk, Health and Hedonism in the British Club Scene*, London: Free Association Books.

Medina-Mora, M.E. (1994). Consumo y opresión de la mujer: la experiencia en México: Comments on Ikuesan's 'Drinking Problems and the Position of Women in Nigeria', and Mphi's 'Females' Alcoholism Problems in Lesotho', *Addiction*, 89: 951–960.

Medina-Mora, M.E. (2001). Women and alcohol in developing countries, *Salud Mental*, 24: 3–10.

Medina-Mora, M.E., Rascon, M.L., Otero, B.R. and Gutierrez, E. (1988). Patrones de consumo de alcohol en Mexico. In: J. Gilbert (ed.) *Alcohol Consumption Among Mexican Americans. A Binational Perspective*, UCLA: Spanish Speaking Mental Health Research Center, pp. 27–50.

Meltzer, H., Gill, B. and Petticrew, M. (1994). *The Prevalence of Psychiatric Morbidity Among Adults Aged 16–61, Living in Private Households, in Great Britain*, OPCS Surveys of Psychiatric Morbidity in Great Britain, London: HMSO.

Meltzer, H., Gill, B., Petticrew, M. and Hinds, K. (1995). *Economic Activity and Social Functioning of Adults with Psychiatric Disorders*, OPCS Surveys of Psychiatric Morbidity in Great Britain, London: HMSO.

Merritt, A. (2000). Culture in the cockpit: do Hofstede's dimensions replicate?, *Journal of Cross-Cultural Psychology*, 31: 283–301.

Meyers, R., Miller, W., Hill, D. and Tonigan, J. (1999). Community reinforcement and family training (CRAFT): engaging unmotivated drug users in treatment, *Journal of Substance Abuse*, 10: 291–308.

Meyers, R.J., Miller, W.R., Smith, J.E. and Tonigan, J.S. (2002). A randomised trial of two methods for engaging treatment-refusing drug users through concerned significant others, *Journal of Consulting and Clinical Psychology*, 70: 1182–1185.

Miller, A., Velleman, R., Bennett, G., Orford, J., Rigby, K. and Tod, A. (1997). The use of vignettes in the analysis of interview data: relatives of people with drug problems. In: N. Hayes (ed.) *Doing Qualitative Analysis in Psychology*, Hove: Psychology Press, pp. 201–225.

Miller, K. (1994). The co-dependency concept: does it offer a solution to the spouses of alcoholics?, *Journal of Substance Abuse Treatment*, 11: 339–345.

Miller, M. (1987). Co-dependent contradictions? *The US Journal of Drug and Alcohol Dependence*, 11 May 1987 (cited by Lisanksy Gomberg, 1989).

Miller, W., Meyers, R. and Tonigan, J. (1999). Engaging the unmotivated in treatment for alcohol problems: a comparison of three strategies for intervention through family members, *Journal of Consulting and Clinical Psychology*, 67: 688–697.

Ministry of Aboriginal Affairs (1992). *Social Justice for Indigenous Australians*, Budget paper No. 7, Canberra: Australian Government Publishing Service (cited by Roberts, 1998).

Minuchin, S. (1975). *Families and Family Therapy*, Cambridge: MA: Harvard University Press (cited by Kaufman, 1981).

Moffat, N. (1987). Brain damage and the family. In: J. Orford (ed.) *Coping with Disorder in the Family*, London: Croom Helm, pp. 238–265.

Mohan, D., Prabhakar, A.K., Mohun, M. and Chitkara (1978). Factors associated with the prevalence of drug abuse among Delhi university students, *Indian Journal of Psychiatry*, 20: 332–338.

Moos, R.H. (2002). The mystery of human context and coping: an unravelling of clues, *American Journal of Community Psychology*, 30: 67–88.

Moos, R.H., Finney, J.W. and Cronkite, R. (1990). *Alcoholism Treatment: Context, Process and Outcome*, New York: Oxford University Press.

Moos, R.H. and Moos, R. (1981). *Family Environment Scale Manual*, Palo Alto, CA: Consulting Psychologist Press.

Morgan, D.L., Slade, M.D. and Morgan, C.M.A. (1997). Aboriginal philosophy and its impact on health care outcomes, *Australian and New Zealand Journal of Public Health*, 21: 597–600.

Natera, G. and Casco, M. (1993). Informe de evalución de la prueba piloto del 'Manual de capacitación destinado a los orientadores de prevención de alcohol y drogas en los países Latinoamericanos, para su trabajo de intervención y apoyo a las familias que se enfrentan a problemas de consumo excesivo de sustancias en sus hogares'. Reporte Interno, Instituto Mexicano de Psiquiatría, Mexico.

Natera, G. and Holmila, M. (1990). El papel de los roles sexuales en la familia y el consumo de alcohol. Una comparación entre México y Finlandia, *Salud Mental*, 13: 20–26.

Natera, G., Orford, J., Tiburcio. M. and Mora, J. (1998). Prevención del Consumo de Alcohol y Drogas en el Trabajador y sus Familiares. Manual para el Orientador. OIT-OMS-SSA-IMP, Mexico, 90.

Natera, G. and Orozco, C. (1981). Opiniones sobre el consumo de alcohol en una comunidad semirural, *Salud Pública de México*, 29: 473–482.

Natera, G., Tenorio, R., Figueroa, E. and Ruíz, G. (2002). Espacio urbano, la vida cotidiana y las adicciones: un studio etnográfico sobre el alcoholismo en el Centro Histórico de la Ciudad de México, *Salud Mental*, 25: 17–31.

Natera, G. and Tiburcio, M. (1998). Results from the family component. Mexico. Work presented at Final Review Meeting of the ILO/UNDCP/WHO Project on Model Programmes of Drug and Alcohol Abuse Prevention Among Workers and Their Families. Geneva, Switzerland, 3–5 February.

National Aboriginal Health Strategy Working Party (1989). *A National Aboriginal Health Strategy*, Canberra: Australian Government Publishing Service (cited by Burden, 1998).

Nichols, K.A. (1987). Chronic physical disorder in adults. In: J. Orford (ed.) *Coping with Disorder in the Family*, London: Croom Helm, pp. 62–85.

Nirenberg, T.D., Liepman, M.R., Begin, A.M., Doolittle, R.H. and Broffman, T.E. (1990). The sexual relationship of male alcoholics and their female partners during periods of drinking and abstinence, *Journal of Studies on Alcohol*, 51: 565–568.

Noel, N.E., McCrady, B.S., Stout, R.L. and Fisher-Nelson, H. (1991). Gender differences in marital functioning of male and female alcoholics, *Family Dynamics Addiction*, 1: 31–38.

Norwood, R. (1986). *Women Who Love Too Much*, Los Angeles, CA: Tarcker.

Oakland, S. and Ostell, A. (1996). Measuring coping: a review and critique, *Human Relations*, 49: 133–153.

Obot, I.S. (2001). The role of the family in promoting drug free communities in Nigeria, *Journal of Family Social Work*, 6: 53–67.

Obot, I.S. and Anthony, J.C. (2004). Mental health problems in adolescent children of alcohol dependent parents: epidemiologic research with a nationally representative sample, *Journal of Child and Adolescent Substance Abuse*, 13: 83–96.

O'Connor, J. (1978). *The Young Drinkers: A Cross-National Study of Social and Cultural Influences*, London: Tavistock.

O'Donoghue, L. (1997). In indigenous affairs nothing is new, just forgotten, *Australian Journal of Public Administration*, 56: 5–10.

O'Farrell, T.J., Choquette, K.A., Cutter, H.S.G. and Birchler, G.R. (1997). Sexual satisfaction and dysfunction in marriages of male alcoholics: comparison with non-alcoholic maritally conflicted and nonconflicted couples, *Journal of Studies on Alcohol*, 58: 91–99.

O'Farrell, T.J., Choquette, K.A., Cutter, H.S.G., Brown, E.D. and McCourt, W.F. (1993). Behavioral marital therapy with and without additional couples relapse prevention sessions for alcoholics and their wives, *Journal of Studies on Alcohol*, 54: 652–666.

O'Farrell, T.J., Cutter, H.S.G., Choquette, K.A., Floyd, F.J. and Bayog, R.D. (1992).

Behavioral marital therapy for male alcoholics: marital and drinking adjustment during the two years after treatment, *Behavior Therapy*, 23: 529–549.

O'Farrell, T.J., Cutter, H.S.G. and Floyd, F.J. (1985). Evaluating behavioral marital therapy for male alcoholics: effects on marital adjustment and communication from before to after treatment, *Behavior Therapy*, 16: 147–167.

O'Farrell, T.J., Hooley, J., Fals-Stewart, W. and Cutter, H.S.G. (1998). Expressed emotion and relapse in alcoholic patients, *Journal of Consulting and Clinical Psychology*, 66: 744–752.

O'Farrell, T.J. and Murphy, C.M. (1995). Marital violence before and after alcoholism treatment, *Journal of Consulting and Clinical Psychology*, 63: 256–262.

O'Farrell, T.J. and Rotunda, R.J. (1997). Couples intervention and alcohol abuse. In: W.K. Halford and H.J. Markman (eds) *Clinical Handbook of Marriage and Couple Interventions*, Chichester: Wiley, pp. 555–558.

Office for National Statistics (1997). *Health Inequalities* Decennial Supplement No. 15, London: Stationery Office.

Office for National Statistics (1998). *Living in Britain: Results of the 1996 General Household Survey*, London: Stationery Office.

Orford, J. (ed.) (1987). *Coping with Disorder in the Family*, London: Croom Helm.

Orford, J. (1990). *Risks to Family Health from Alcohol and other Drugs That Can be Abused: Understanding and Strengthening Natural Family Coping Methods in Primary Health Care Settings: A Proposal*, Geneva: World Health Organisation.

Orford, J. (1994). Empowering family and friends: a new approach to the secondary prevention of addiction, *Drug and Alcohol Review*, 13: 417–429.

Orford, J. (1998). The coping perspective. In: R. Velleman, A. Copello, and J. Maslin (eds) *Living with Drink: Women Who Live with Problem Drinkers*, London: Longman, pp. 128–149.

Orford, J. and Edwards, G. (1977). *Alcoholism: A Comparison of Treatment and Advice, with a Study of the Influence of Marriage*, Oxford: Oxford University Press.

Orford, J., Guthrie, S., Nicholls, P., Oppenheimer, E., Egert, S. and Hensman, C. (1975). Self-reported coping behaviour of wives of alcoholics and its association with drinking outcome, *Journal of Studies on Alcohol*, 36: 1254–1267.

Orford, J., Oppenheimer, E., Egert, S., Hensman, C. and Guthrie, S. (1976). The cohesiveness of alcoholism-complicated marriages and its influence on treatment outcome, *British Journal of Psychiatry*, 128: 318–339.

Orford, J., Natera, G., Casco, M., Nava, A. and Ollinger, E. (1990). Coping with alcohol and drug use in the family. Report of a Mexican feasibility study. Report prepared for the WHO Division of Mental Health, Geneva.

Orford, J., Natera, G., Davies, J., Nava, A., Mora, J., Rigby, K., Bradbury, C., Copello, A. and Velleman, R. (1998a). Stresses and strains for family members living with drinking or drug problems in England and Mexico, *Salud Mental* (Mexico), 21: 1–13.

Orford, J., Natera, G., Davies, J., Nava, A., Mora, J., Rigby, K., Bradbury, C., Copello, A. and Velleman, R. (1998b). Social support in coping with alcohol and drug problems at home: findings from Mexican and English families, *Addiction Research*, 6: 395–420.

Orford, J., Natera, G., Davies, J., Nava, A., Mora, J., Rigby, K., Bradbury, C., Bowie, N., Copello, A. and Velleman, R. (1998c). Tolerate, engage or withdraw: a study of the structure of family coping in England and Mexico, *Addiction*, 93: 1799–1813.

Orford, J., Natera, G., Velleman, R., Copello, A., Bowie, N., Bradbury, C., Davies, J. Mora, J., Nava, A., Rigby, K. and Tiburcio, M. (2001). Ways of coping and the health of relatives facing drug and alcohol problems in Mexico and England, *Addiction*, 96: 761–774.

Orford, J., Rigby, K., Tod, A., Miller, T., Bennett, G. and Velleman, R. (1992). How close relatives cope with drug problems in the family: a study of 50 close relatives, *Journal of Community and Applied Social Psychology*, 2: 163–183.

Orford, J., Templeton, L., Patel, A., Copello, A. and Velleman, R. (2005). Qualitative study of a controlled family intervention trial in primary care. I. The views of family members (submitted).

Paden, S.L. and Buehler, C. (1995). Coping with the dual-income lifestyle, *Journal of Marriage and the Family*, 57: 101–110.

Pahl, J. and Quine, L. (1987). Families with mentally handicapped children. In: J. Orford (ed.) *Coping with Disorder in the Family*, London: Croom Helm, pp. 39–61.

Pakenham, K.I. (2002). Development of a measure of coping with multiple sclerosis caregiving, *Psychology and Health*, 17: 97–118.

Paolino, T. and McCrady, B. (1977). *The Alcoholic Marriage*, New York: Grune and Stratton (cited by Harper and Capdevilla, 1990).

Parker, H., Aldridge, J. and Measham, F. (1998). *Illegal Leisure: The Normalization of Adolescent Recreational Drug Use*, London: Routledge.

Parkes, K.R. (1990). Coping, negative affectivity, and the work environment: additive and interactive predictors of mental health, *Journal of Applied Psychology*, 75: 399–409.

Pattison, E.M. (1965). Treatment of alcoholic families with nurse home visits, *Family Process*, 4: 75–94.

Pattison, E.M., Courlas, P.G., Patti, R., Mann, B. and Mullen, D. (1965). Diagnostic-therapeutic intake groups for wives of alcoholics, *Quarterly Journal of Studies on Alcohol*, 26: 605–616.

Paxman, J. (1999). *The English: A Portrait of a People*, London: Penguin.

Pearlin, L.J. and Schooler, C. (1978). The structure of coping, *Journal of Health and Social Behaviour*, 19: 2–21.

Perkins, J.J., Sanson-Fisher, R.W., Blunden, S., Lunnay, D., Redman, S. and Hensley, M.J. (1994). The prevalence of drug use in urban Aboriginal communities, *Addiction*, 89: 1319–1331.

Peterson, N. (1993). Demand sharing: reciprocity and the pressure for generosity among foragers, *American Anthropologist*, 95: 860–874.

Price, G.M. (1945). A study of the wives of 20 alcoholics, *Quarterly Journal of Studies on Alcohol*, 5: 620–627.

Race Discrimination Commissioner (1995). *Alcohol Report*, Canberra: Australian Government Publishing Service.

Rae, J.B. and Forbes, A.R. (1966). Clinical and psychometric characteristics of wives of alcoholics, *British Journal of Psychiatry*, 112: 197–200.

Raine, P. (1994). Families and substance dependency, *Social Action*, 2: 11–17.

Rauktis, M.E., Koeske, G.F. and Tereshko, O. (1995). Negative social interactions, distress, and depression among those caring for a seriously and persistently mentally ill relative, *American Journal of Community Psychology*, 23: 279–299.

Reid, J. and Trompf, P. (eds) (1991). *The Health of Aboriginal Australia*, Sydney: Harcourt Brace Jovanovich.

Reiss, D. and Oliveri, M.E. (1980). Family paradigm and family coping: a proposal for linking the family's intrinsic adaptive capacities to its responses to stress, *Family Relations*, 29: 431–444.

Richter, L., Chatterji, P. and Pierce, J. (2000). Perspectives on family substance abuse: the voices of longer-term Al-Anon members, *Journal of Family Social Work*, 4: 61–78.

Riddett, L.A. (1990). *Kine, Kin and Country: The Victoria River District of the Northern Territory 1911–1966*, Darwin, Northern Territory; Australian National University, North Australia Research Unit Monograph.

Rizzola, N. and Rosadini, I. (1974). Family and social determinants of female alcoholism, *Neuropsichiatria*, 30: 71–78.

Roberts, D. (1998). Self-determination and the struggle for Aboriginal equality. In: C. Bourke, E. Bourke and B. Edwards (eds) *Aboriginal Australia*, Queensland: University of Queensland Press, pp. 259–288.

Robinson, W. and Hassell, J. (2000). Alcohol problems and the family: from stigma to solution, London: Alcohol Recovery Project and National Society for the Prevention of Cruelty to Children.

Rogler, L.H. (1999). Methodological sources of cultural insensitivity in mental health research, *American Psychologist*, 54: 424–433.

Rose, D.B. (1991). *Hidden Histories: Black Stories from Victoria River Downs, Humbert River and Wave Hill Stations*, Canberra: Aboriginal Studies Press.

Rosenheck, R. and Thomson, J. (1986). 'Detoxification' of Vietnam war trauma: a combined family-individual approach, *Family Process*, 25: 559–569.

Rosovsky, H. (2001). Salud pública, disponibilidad y consumo de alcohol: implicaciones y controversias. En: C.R. Tapia (ed.) *Las Adicciones: Dimensión, Impacto y Perspectivas*. México: Manual Modern, 2nd edition, pp. 169–185.

Rowse, T. (1993). *After Mabo: Interpreting Indigenous Traditions*, Melbourne: Melbourne University Press.

Rychtarik, R.G., Carstensen, L., Alford, G., Schlundt, D. and Scott, W. (1988). Situational assessment of alcohol-related coping skills in wives of alcoholics, *Psychology of Addictive Behaviours*, 2: 66–73.

Saggers, S. and Gray, D. (1991). *Aboriginal Health and Society: The Traditional and Contemporary Aboriginal Struggle for Better Health*, St Leonards, New South Wales: Allen and Unwin.

Saggers, S. and Gray, D. (1998). *Dealing with Alcohol: Indigenous Usage in Australia, New Zealand and Canada*, Cambridge: Cambridge University Press.

Sansom, B. (1980). *The Camp at Wallaby Cross: Aboriginal Fringe Dwellers in Darwin*. Canberra: Australian Institute of Aboriginal Studies.

Santamaria, J.M. (1983). Australia: alcohol and the aboriginals. In: G. Edwards, A. Arif and J. Jaffe (eds) *Drug Use and Misuse*, London: Croom Helm, pp. 93–100.

Scazufca, M. and Kuipers, E. (1998). Stability of expressed emotion in relatives of those with schizophrenia and its relationship with burden of care and perception of patients' social functioning, *Psychological Medicine*, 28: 453–461.

Schreurs, K.M.G. and de Ridder, D.T.D. (1997). Integration of coping and social support perspectives: implications for the study of adaptation to chronic disease, *Clinical Psychology Review*, 17: 89–112.

Schwartz, S.H. (1994). Beyond individualism/collectivism: new cultural dimensions of values. In: U. Kim, H. Triandis, C. Kagitcibasi, S. Choi and G. Yoon (eds) *Individualism and Collectivism*, Thousand Oaks, CA: Sage, pp. 85–119.

Secretaría de Salud (SSA) (1997). Principales causas de mortalidad, México. Dirección General de Epidemiología: México.

Secretaría de Salud (SSA) (1999). Tercera Encuesta Nacional de Adicciones (ENA) 1998. Instituto Mexicano de Psiquiatría, Dirección General de Epidemiología, México.

Segall, M.H., Lonner, W.J. and Berry, J.W. (1998). Cross-cultural psychology as a scholarly discipline, *American Psychologist*, 53: 1101–1110.

Shadish, W.R., Cook, T. and Campbell, D. (2002). *Experimental and Quasi-Experimental Designs for Generalised Causal Inference*, Boston: Houghton Mifflin.

Shiman, L.L. (1988). *Crusade Against Drink in Victorian England*, Macmillan Press, London.

Siegl, D. and Morse, J.M. (1994). Tolerating reality: the experience of parents of HIV positive sons, *Social Science and Medicine*, 38: 959–971.

Sisson, R.W. and Azrin, N.H. (1986). Family-member involvement to initiate and promote treatment of problem drinkers, *Journal of Behavioral Therapy and Experimental Psychiatry*, 17: 15–21.

Sloman, L. and Konstantareas, M.M. (1990). Why families of children with biological deficits require a systems approach, *Family Process*, 29: 415–427.

Smith, C.G. (1969). Alcoholics: their treatment and their wives, *British Journal of Psychiatry*, 115: 1039–1042.

Smith, W.G. (1971). Critical life-events and prevention strategies in mental health, *Archives of General Psychiatry*, 25: 103–109.

Solomon, Z., Waysman, M., Levy, G., Fried, B., Mikulincer, M., Benbenishty, R., Florian, V. and Bleich, A. (1992). From front line to home front: a study of secondary traumatization, *Family Process*, 31: 289–302.

Spoth, R.L., Redmond, C., Trudeau, L. and Shin, C. (2002). Longitudinal substance initiation outcomes for a universal preventive intervention combining family and school programs, *Psychology of Addictive Behaviors*, 16: 129–134

Stanner, W.H. (1987). The dreaming. In: W.H. Edwards (ed.) *Traditional Aboriginal Religion: A Reader*, South Melbourne: Macmillan (cited by Edwards, 1998).

Stanton, M.D. (1971). Some outcome results and aspects of structural family therapy with drug addicts. Paper presented at the National Drug Abuse Conference, San Francisco, California, 5–9 May (cited by Kaufman, 1981).

Stanton, M.D. (undated). The addict as savior: heroin, death, and the family, *Family Process*, 16: 191–197.

Stanton, M.D. and Shadish, W.R. (1997). Outcome, attrition, and family – couples treatment for drug abuse: a meta-analysis and review of the controlled, comparative studies, *Psychological Bulletin*, 122: 170–191.

Stanton, M.D., Todd, T.C. and Associates (1982). *The Family Therapy of Drug Abuse and Addiction*, New York: Guilford Press.

Stanton, M.D. and Todd, T.C. (1992). Structural-strategic family therapy with drug addicts. In: E. Kaufman and P. Kaufman (eds) *Family Therapy of Drug and Alcohol Abuse* (2nd edn). Needham Heights, MA: Allyn and Bacon, pp. 46–62.

Staples, R. (1990). Substance abuse and the black family crisis: an overview, *Western Journal of Black Studies*, 14: 196–204.

Steinglass, P. (1979). An experimental treatment program for alcoholic couples, *Journal of Studies on Alcohol*, 40: 149–182.

Steinglass, P. (1982). The roles of alcohol in family systems. In: J. Orford and J. Harwin (eds) *Alcohol and the Family*, London: Croom Helm, pp. 127–150.

Steinglass, P., Bennett, L.A., Wolin, S.J. and Reiss, D. (1988). *The Alcoholic Family: Drinking Problems in a Family Context*, London: Hutchinson.

Stockwell, T., Chikritzhs, T., Hendrie, D., Fordham, R., Ying, F., Phillips, M., Cronin, J. and O'Reilly, B. (2001). The public health and safety benefits of the Northern Territory's Living with Alcohol programme, *Drug and Alcohol Review*, 20: 167–180.

St-Onge, M. and Lavoie, F. (1997). The experience of caregiving among mothers of adults suffering from psychotic disorders: factors associated with their psychological distress, *American Journal of Community Psychology*, 25: 73–94.

Strauss, A. and Corbin, J. (1990). *Basics of Qualitative Research: Grounded Theory Procedures and Techniques*. Newbury Park, CA: Sage.

Strauss, A. and Corbin, J. (1998). *Basics of Qualitative Research: Grounded Theory Procedures and Techniques*, 2nd edition, Newbury Park, CA: Sage.

Student, V. and Matova, A. (1969). Development of mental disorders in the wives of alcoholics, *Ceskoslovanoka Psychiatrie*, 65: 23–29.

Subby, R. (1987). *Lost in the Shuffle*, Deerfield Beech, FL: Health Communications.

Surtees, P.G. and Miller, P.M. (1994). Partners in adversity: coping and mood, *European Archives of Psychiatry*, 243: 319–327.

Szapocznik, J., Perez-Vidal, A., Brickman, A.L., Foote, F.H., Santisteban, D., Hervis, O. and Kurtines, W.M. (1988). Engaging adolescent drug abusers and their families in treatment: a strategic structural systems approach, *Journal of Consulting and Clinical Psychology*, 56: 552–557.

Terry, D.J. (1994). Determinants of coping: the role of stable and situational factors, *Journal of Personality and Social Psychology*, 66: 895–910.

Tesch, R. (1990). *Qualitative Research: Analysis Types and Software Tools*, New York: Falmer.

Thoits, P.A. (1986). Social support as coping assistance, *Journal of Consulting and Clinical Psychology*, 54: 416–423.

Thomas, E. and Ager, R.D. (1993). Unilateral family therapy with spouses of uncooperative alcohol abusers. In: T. O'Farrell (ed.) *Treating Alcohol Problems: Marital and Family Interventions*, New York: Guilford Press, pp. 3–33.

Thomas, E., Santa, C., Bronson, D. and Oyserman, D. (1987). Unilateral family therapy with the spouses of alcoholics, *Journal of Social Service Research*, 10: 145–162.

Tiburcio, M. (2002). Reporte de experiencia professional. Tesis de Maestría, Facultad de Psicología, Universidad Nacional Autónoma de México, Mexico.

Tiburcio, M. and Natera, G. (2003). Evaluación de un modelo de intervención breve para familiares de usuarios de alcohol y drogas: un studio piloto, *Salud Mental*, 26: 33–42.

Tix, A.P. and Frazier, P.A. (1998). The use of religious coping during stressful life-events: main effects, moderation, and mediation, *Journal of Consulting and Clinical Psychology*, 66: 411–422.

Tolsdorf, C. (1976). Social networks, support, and coping: an exploratory study, *Family Process*, 15: 407–417.

Torres, B. (1998). Masculinity and gender roles among Puerto Rican men: machismo on the US mainland, *American Journal of Orthopsychiatry*, 68: 16–26.

Toumbourou, J., Blyth, A., Bamberg, J., Bowes, G. and Douvos, T. (1997). Behaviour exchange systems training: the BEST approach for parents stressed by adolescent drug problems, *Australian and New Zealand Journal of Family Therapy*, 18: 92–98.

Toumbourou, J., Blyth, A., Bamberg, J. and Forer, D. (2001). Early impact of the BEST intervention for parents stressed by adolescent substance abuse, *Journal of Community and Applied Social Psychology*, 11: 291–304.

Triandis, H.C. (1994). Theoretical and methodological approaches to the study of collectivism and individualism. In: U. Kim, H.C. Triandis, C. Kagitcibasi, S. Choi and G. Yoon (eds) *Individualism and Collectivism: Theory, Method, and Applications*, Thousand Oaks, CA: Sage, pp. 41–51.

Troise, F.P. (1995). An examination of Cermak's conceptualization of codependency as personality disorder, *Alcoholism Treatment Quarterly*, 12: 1–15.

Trompenaars, F. (1993). *Riding the Waves of Culture: Understanding Cultural Diversity in Business*, London: Nicholas Brealey (cited by Goodwin, 1999).

Tuhiwai-Smith, L. (1999). *Decolonizing Methodologies: Research and Indigenous Peoples*, London: University of Otago Press.

UKATT Research Team (2005). Effectiveness of treatment for alcohol problems: Findings of the randomised United Kingdom Alcohol Treatment Trial (UKATT), *British Medical Journal* (in press).

UNODC (United Nations Office on Drugs and Crime) (2004). *2004 World Drug Report*, Vienna: UNODC.

Ussher, J. (1998). A feminist perspective. In: R. Velleman, A. Copello and J. Maslin (eds) *Living with Drink: Women Who Live with Problem Drinkers*, London: Longman, pp. 150–161.

Vaillant, G.A. (1966). A 12-year follow-up of New York narcotic addicts, *Archives of General Psychiatry*, 15: 599–609 (cited by Kaufman, 1981).

Valentiner, D.P., Holahan, C.J. and Moos, R.H. (1994). Social support, appraisals of event controllability, and coping: an integrative model, *Journal of Personality and Social Psychology*, 66: 1094–1102.

Van de Vijver, F.J.R. and Leung, K. (2000). Methodological issues in psychological research on culture, *Journal of Cross-Cultural Psychology*, 31: 33–51.

Van Hemert, D.A., Baerveldt, C. and Vermande, M. (2001). Assessing cross-cultural item bias in questionnaires: acculturation and the measurement of social support and family cohesion for adolescents, *Journal of Cross-Cultural Psychology*, 32: 381–396.

Velleman, R., Bennett, G., Miller, T., Orford, J., Rigby, K. and Tod, A. (1993). The families of problem drug users: a study of 50 close relatives, *Addiction*, 88: 1281–1289.

Velleman, R., Copello, A., and Maslin, J. (eds) (1998). *Living with Drink: Women Who Live with Problem Drinkers*, London: Longman.

Velleman, R. and Orford, J. (1990). Young adult offspring of parents with drinking problems: recollections of parents' drinking and its immediate effects, *British Journal of Clinical Psychology*, 29: 297–317.

Velleman, R. and Orford, J. (1993). The importance of family discord in explaining childhood problems in the children of problem drinkers, *Addiction Research*, 1: 39–57.

Velleman, R. and Orford, J. (1999). *Risk and Resilience: Adults Who Were the Children of Problem Drinkers*. Reading: Harwood.

Vetere, A. (1998). A family systems perspective. In: R. Velleman, A. Copello and J. Maslin (eds) *Living with Drink: Women Who Live with Problem Drinkers*, London: Longman, pp. 113–127.

Vetere, A. and Henley, M. (2001). Integrating couples and family therapy into a community alcohol service: a pantheoretical approach, *Association for Family Therapy and Systemic Practice*, 23: 85–101.

Wade, S., Yeates, K.O., Borawski, E.A., Taylor, G., Drotar, D. and Stancin, T. (2001). The relationship of caregiver coping to family outcomes during the initial year following pediatric traumatic injury, *Journal of Consulting and Clinical Psychology*, 69: 406–415.

Walsh, M. (1993). Languages and their status in Aboriginal Australia. In: M. Walsh and C. Yallop (eds) *Language and Culture in Aboriginal Australia*, Canberra: Aboriginal Studies Press, pp. 1–13.

Wethington, E. and Kessler, R. (1986). Perceived support, received support, and adjustment to stressful life-events, *Journal of Health and Social Behaviour*, 27: 78–89.

Whalen, T. (1953). Wives of alcoholics; four types observed in a family service agency, *Quarterly Journal of Studies on Alcohol*, 14: 632–641.

Whittaker, J.O. (1982). Alcohol and the Standing Rock Sioux tribe: a twenty-year follow-up study, *Journal of Studies on Alcohol*, 43: 191–200.

Whittaker, J.O. and Whittaker, S.J. (1992). Alcoholism and the native American family. In: S. Saitoh, P. Steinglass and M.A. Schuckit (eds) *Alcoholism and the Family: The 4th International Symposium of the Psychiatric Research Institute of Tokyo*, Tokyo: Seiwa Shoten/New York: Brunner-Mazel, pp. 127–139.

Wiersma, U.J. (1994). A taxonomy of behavioural strategies for coping with work–home role conflict, *Human Relations*, 47: 211–221.

Willig, C. (2001). *Introducing Qualitative Research in Psychology: Adventures in Theory and Method*, Buckingham, UK: Open University Press.

Winefield, H.R. and Burnett, P.L. (1996). Barriers to an alliance between family and professional caregivers in chronic schizophrenia, *Journal of Mental Health*, 5: 223–232.

Winters, J., Fals-Stewart, W., O'Farrell, T.J., Birchler, G.R. and Kelley, M.L. (2002). Behavioral couples therapy for female substance-abusing patients: effects on substance use and relationship adjustment, *Journal of Consulting and Clinical Psychology*, 70: 344–355.

Wiseman, J.P. (1991). *The Other Half: Wives of Alcoholics and Their Social-Psychological Situation*, New York: Aldine de Gruyter.

Wolcott, H. (1974). *The African Beer Gardens of Bulawayo: Integrated Drinking in a Segregated Society*, New Brunswick, NJ: Rutgers Centre of Alcohol Studies.

World Health Organisation (2002). *The World Health Report 2002*, Geneva: WHO.

World Health Organisation (2004a). *Global Status Report: Alcohol Policy*, Geneva: WHO.

World Health Organisation (2004b). *The World Health Report 2004*, Geneva: WHO.

Yang, J. (1997). *Culture, Family and Alcoholism in South Korea*. Unpublished Ph.D. thesis, Goldsmiths College, University of London.

Yates, F.E. (1988). The evaluation of a 'co-operative counselling' alcohol service which uses family and affected others to reach and influence problem drinkers, *British Journal of Addiction*, 83: 1309–1319.

Yoshihama, M. (2002). Battered women's coping strategies and psychological distress: differences by immigration status, *American Journal of Community Psychology*, 30: 429–452.

Yoshioka, M.R. Thomas, E.J. and Ager, R.D. (1992). Nagging and other drinking control efforts of spouses of uncooperative alcohol abusers: assessment and modification, *Journal of Substance Abuse*, 4: 309–318.

Zeidner, M. and Endler, N.S. (eds) (1996). *Handbook of Coping: Theory, Research, Applications*, London: Wiley.

Zweben, A., Pearlman, S. and Li, S. (1988). A comparison of brief advice and conjoint therapy in the treatment of alcohol abuse: the results of the marital systems study, *British Journal of Addiction*, 83: 899–916.

Author index

Subject index

a relational intervention sequence for engagement (ARISE) 244, 251
AA *see* Alcoholics Anonymous
AAFPQ *see* Attitudes to Addiction-Related Family Problems Questionnaire
Aboriginal Australians 16, 42–3, 57–68, 221, 255n; characteristics of family members 77–9; cultural context 168–70, 177, 179–84, 185, 208, 212–13, 236; 'humbug' 99, 208, 256n; individual autonomy 63, 64, 176; individualism 169, 212; interventions 232, 234–6, 237, 238, 239, 253–4; interviews and interviewers 70–1, 72, 73–4, 75, 94; kinship system 63, 79, 216; material and social environment 87–91; recruitment of family members 70–2; research sensitivity 92; social support 163, 167; talking and listening 141, 181; threats 223; worry concept 105
absolutism 219
abuse 18, 97, 102, 191–2; *see also* domestic violence; violence
accommodative coping 226
addiction 4, 47, 177, 179
ADF *see* Alcohol, Drugs and the Family Group
adoption research model 92
age 215
aggressiveness 97–8, 102, 103, 139, 162, 183; *see also* violence
Al-Anon 143, 247, 252; research studies 21, 22, 198, 243, 244, 245; 12-step philosophy 248
Alcohol, Drugs and the Family (ADF) Group 42

alcohol use: Aboriginal Australians 43, 61, 64–8, 71–2, 179–84, 212; binge-drinking 12, 218; codependency models 8–9, 10; contrast with drug use 216–17; coping with 118–44, 181–4, 195–202, 228–30; disease/disability xi, 48; England 42, 54–6, 70, 175–9; family pathology models 5–7; family systems theory 11–12, 14; financial instability in Mexico 170–1; impact on family members 95–117; integrated view of core experience 205–7; interventions 232–54; male partners of women with drinking problems 31–3, 40, 187, 198, 214; mental health issues 186–7; Mexico 41–2, 45, 47–9, 70, 79–80, 170–5; overlap with drug use xiii; patterns of drinking 218, 219; prevalence xii, xiv, 55–6; sampling limitations 219; social contextual models 14–17; spouse drinking control behaviours 188; strain upon family members 96, 110–17, 194; stress caused by 95–103, 190–4, 221, 223, 228–9; stress-strain-coping-support model 2, 4, 236; support for family members 39, 145–67, 203–5; threat to family life 95–6, 106–10, 193; variform universals 220; wives of men with drinking problems 5–7, 21–31, 40, 187–90, 194–202, 207–10, 213–15, 245; worries of family members 95, 103–5, 193–4
Alcoholics Anonymous (AA) 21, 33, 47, 138, 141, 151, 173
alcoholism 4, 68, 177, 179, 189–90;